Civil War Taxes

ALSO BY JOHN MARTIN DAVIS, JR.

Texas Land Grants, 1750–1900: A Documentary History
(McFarland, 2016)

BY JOHN MARTIN DAVIS, JR., AND GEORGE B. TREMMEL

Parole, Pardon, Pass and Amnesty Documents of the Civil War: An Illustrated History
(McFarland, 2014)

Civil War Taxes

A Documentary History, 1861–1900

JOHN MARTIN DAVIS, JR.

Foreword by Mary L. Volcansek

McFarland & Company, Inc., Publishers
Jefferson, North Carolina

All photographs are from the author's collection

Library of Congress Cataloguing-in-Publication Data

Library of Congress Cataloging-in-Publication Data
Names: Davis, John Martin, Jr., 1944– author.
Title: Civil war taxes : a documentary history, 1861–1900 /
John Martin Davis, Jr. ; foreword by Mary L. Volcansek.
Description: Jefferson, North Carolina : McFarland & Company, Inc.,
Publishers, 2019 | Includes bibliographical references and index.
Identifiers: LCCN 2019026993 | ISBN 9781476677941 (paperback : acid free paper ∞)
Subjects: LCSH: Taxation—United States—History—19th century. |
Taxation—Confederate States of America. | United States—History—
Civil War, 1861–1865—Finance.
Classification: LCC HJ2371 .D38 2019 | DDC 332.600973/09034—dc23
LC record available at https://lccn.loc.gov/2019026993

British Library cataloguing data are available

ISBN (print) 978-1-4766-7794-1
ISBN (ebook) 978-1-4766-3671-9

Front cover images *top* "The More You Work, The More Taxes You Must Pay," *Harper's Weekly*, March 2, 1878. *Bottom clockwise from left*, 25¢ Fractional Currency Act of March 3, 1863 / "Receivable for all Stamps" / Washington Assistant Treasurers and Designated Depositories • $10.00 "War Scrip" County Judge / La Grange, Fayette County, Texas / March 31, 1862 • Receipt for Tax Withheld on Salary Withheld for Quarter, November 1864, Paymaster / New Orleans / December 17, 1864 • War Tax Receipt, Collector, No. 64 / Lavaca, Washington, Brazos, Karnes and Guadalupe Counties, Texas / April 10, 1862 • Military $2.00 Poll Tax, State Controller / Butte County, California / May 12, 1865 (author collection)

Printed in the United States of America

McFarland & Company, Inc., Publishers
Box 611, Jefferson, North Carolina 28640
www.mcfarlandpub.com

Table of Contents

Foreword
by Mary Volcansek

Politics and economics are intrinsically intertwined, as fiscal and monetary policies drive the choices of political actors and motivate voters at the ballot box. Regardless of the school of economic thought to which one subscribes, all concur that governments raise taxes at their peril. Marty Davis's treatment of how both the Union and Confederacy raised revenue during the Civil War captures how governments cope or fail to do so when faced with the twin ills of raising revenue and pursuing a war. Only death is more loathsome to citizens than taxes and war, and, of course, death frequently accompanies the prosecution of a war. A political death-spiral trifecta!

Too many political scientists and historians choose to ignore the economic side of politics, but more than one political party or incumbent politician has met political doom by trying to juggle accumulating sufficient revenue to run a government through some combination of taxes, fees, tariffs, and debt without alienating the public. As Davis notes, both sides in the American Civil War implemented quite similar policies to generate revenue, but with quite distinct results. The key differences, as he notes, resided in the starting point for each side when the Civil War commenced. The Union was an established nation, with good credit both with domestic and foreign creditors, along with gold reserves and export products sought by foreign countries. The South had, on the other hand, no credit and an economy based on a single product that did not translate well for foreign markets. Those divergent starting points drove the options available to office-holders in their attempts to finance a war and the basic functions of government.

The most common form of taxation known to twenty-first century American citizens, the income tax, did not arrive in the form that we know it until a half-century after the Civil War was fought. Instead, both sides had to rely on direct and indirect taxation and extend taxation to foreigners through tariffs and customs duties. Direct taxation, such as property and poll taxes, rendered policy makers most vulnerable to public ire. Indirect taxes, those placed on, for example, manufacturers or service providers, were less risky and less visible, even though they were ultimately passed on to consumers.

Though both sides in the war employed similar fiscal policies, the South was hampered by its reliance on cotton as its main export, and that was effectively eliminated by the imposition of a blockade. Even the victorious Union also learned a great deal about the limits of various sources for revenue. Every form of possible duty or excise tax was tapped in the Civil War, and the ineffectiveness of those forms of taxation, coupled with the political hazards that they carried became obvious. Such was not attempted subsequently.

History does not repeat itself, contrary to the old adage. History is, however, instructive. Politicians, policy makers, and political scientists would do well to understand the intricacies and pitfalls of revenue-raising schemes used in emergency times like the Civil War. The lessons in Davis's *Civil War Taxes* potentially reach beyond the shores of the United States. In both the post-colonial era and the post–Soviet era, new nations were designed or created, mostly without a defined fiscal policy, credit rating, or sufficient resources. The message of this book rings even more true for new political entities resulting from civil wars, as in Sudan and South Sudan and the nations created out of the former Yugoslavia. One of the latter, Montenegro, was sufficiently cognizant of the pitfalls that rather than attempting to create its own currency, it simply adopted the euro, a currency under the auspices of the European Union in which Montenegro has no say, no membership. Perhaps most importantly, policy makers in all democracies would benefit from the lessons of *Civil War Taxes* about the political delicacy of balancing revenue with votes.

Mary L. Volcansek, Ph.D., is a professor of political science emerita at Texas Christian University.

Preface

Borrowing from Daniel Defoe, Benjamin Franklin wrote "in the world nothing can be said to be certain, except death and taxes." To that adage "war" could be joined. Revolutions, insurrections and wars are inextricably conjoined with death and taxes if the survival of a nation is at risk. Tariffs and excises that might be adequate in peacetime require supplemented funds in times of war. War taxes are as crucial to survival as conscription and the conversion of industry to military production.

Americans have experienced war in cycles ever since the Revolution. War taxes are part of the national defense strategy. American taxpayers have little patience for war taxes during peacetime, even if threats are looming. A clear danger like Fort Sumter or Pearl Harbor prompts mobilization and defense funding. The Boston Tea Party, Whiskey Rebellion and Nullification Crisis evidence an American "tax phobia." "Taxation" for purposes herein is defined as a sovereign's lawful taking of private property for public purposes without compensation. This includes admiralty prizes, contraband seizures, impressments and confiscations. Failure to pay war taxes can be deemed "disloyal." Americans during war time accept that "The More You Work, The More Taxes You Must Pay" (Fig. 1).

In prehistory, communal hunting and gathering supported the tribe. After forming homesteads, chieftains demanded tribute of foodstuffs and articles to sustain the tribe. In early Greece, citizens were assessed fees to support the government. The "taxo" was based on an estimate of the taxpayers' holdings. In ancient Rome the process expanded to include the citizen's worth. Roman "taxatio" assessed empire taxes in the name of Caesar. By the sixteenth century, European crowns directed tax collectors to use cadastral survey maps that identified owners of timbers, crops and tenements. Under that system, vassals, tradesmen and merchants were charged in-kind and license fees. The district sheriff was normally the district collector who remitted to his nobleman. The nobility apportioned dues for the Crown through the Office of the Exchequer. To evade or withhold taxes was a high crime.

Early taxation had the elements of assessment, collection and penalties still used today. I became familiar with that system a half century ago as a tax clerk while in high school. Summers working in a family accounting practice, cleaning the office, cutting the lawn and making entries in ledgers and tax returns filled my vacation. Third year at SMU, after passing the CPA exam, I discovered the economics of taxation, banking and fiscal policy. The Supreme Court decision in *Corn Products*, 350 U.S. 46 (1955), taught me the importance of intent in the characterization of "capital" or "ordinary" asset and the resultant tax difference. A taxpayer's purpose for holding an asset was consequential to higher or lower taxes. Metaphysical distinctions for taxable transactions were intriguing.

My professional career was interrupted by years in the U.S. Navy Judge Advocate Generals Corps. Afterwards, I joined a national accounting firm in Savannah, Georgia, where the "Late War" was a part of daily life. The archives of the Georgia Historical Society were blocks from my home. My interest in Civil War economic history became an avocation. I next returned to Dallas for thirty years to manage a local firm, but I returned to the Carolina Low Country annually. The Savannah, Charleston and Columbia archives became the basis of articles on the economic history of Beaufort, South Carolina. Personal collections led to exhibitions, books and articles on Civil War paroles, the Confederate Treasury and Texas Land Grants.

This work is a continuation of those prior studies of the Civil War Treasuries. The approach is a comparison of the United States and Confederate States tax systems along a timeline. Post–Civil War economics were examined by Professor Joseph A. Schumpeter in his cycle theory of "creative destruction." Postwar taxes rekindled broken economies with new production methods and markets if capital was allowed to invest. Such was the case after the Civil War.

War tax collectors, along with tax-evading profiteers, are not mustered out with the troops. Rebuilding required capitalists, eager to supply the needs of consumers and willing to risk the capital. Be they innovators, rebuilders or profiteers, all share "loyalty" to the victor. Even during the Civil War, speculators, merchants and investors were among the first to occupy captured cities. Martial law restrictions always create shortages, leading to higher prices even with controls.

Set prices are the profiteers' key, especially if free of competition. This Civil War tax history begins with antebellum taxes, through the War and Reconstruction, and concludes with passage of the Sixteenth Amendment to the Constitution.

A couple of early studies were used for background, statistics and taxes in general. For the earliest history, Edwin R.A. Seligman's classic work *Income Tax: A Study of the History, Theory and Practice of Income Taxation at Home and Abroad* (1911) was fundamental. His discussions of revenue devices during the Napoleonic Wars showed experimentation that carried over to America during the first half of the nineteenth century. Consumptive, luxury and income taxation were born during this period. Harry Edwin Smith's statistics-laden *The United States Federal Internal Tax History from 1861 to 1871* had an appendix of twenty-nine tables, making possible this study. Dale W. Forsythe's *Taxation and Politics of Change on the Young Nation, 1781–1833* (1979) connects the nation's taxes with the "Whiskey Tax Rebellion" and "Tariff Nullification Crisis," forerunners of the Civil War.

Two early Brookings Institution monographs detailed national revenue sources during the nineteenth century. *The Bureau of Internal Revenue* (No. 25) traced excise and internal taxes through passage of the Sixteenth Amendment. *The Customs Service* (No. 33) explained custom duties that provided the bulk of taxes before the Civil War. In Richard Cecil Todd's *Confederate Finance* (1954), the Confederate Treasury is explained. Initially the Confederate Treasury matched, tit-for-tat, all U.S. tax acts. Both sides of the conflict soon realized custom duties were insufficient to fund a war.

The public policy of taxes was the subject of Robert Stanley's *Demission of Law in the Sense of Order: Origins of the Federal of Income Tax, 1861–1913*. Stanley follows the shift from the reliance on customs to internal taxes. He emphasized that westerners disfavored protective tariffs which benefited manufacturers and financers. Consumers realized that excise taxes caused higher retail prices. The income tax with progressive rates was responsive to such complaints. A sense of egalitarian fairness favored progressive rates, along with estate and luxury taxes. Wage earners and farmers wanted the wealthy to be assessed on their prosperity. Such wealth levies were less important to the nation's finances than was the *perception* that the privileged were also taxed. American Democratic capitalism depended upon tax fairness.

The single most distinguishing feature contrasting the performance of the United States and Confederate Treasuries was fiscal and monetary policy. The National Bank Acts converted most state-chartered banks to federal institutions. "Greenback" currency declared legal tender was essential to the credit worthiness of the United States. Both helped to control inflation and improve market acceptances of bond issues. Bray Hammond's *Sovereignty and an Empty Purse: Banks and Politics in the Civil War* (1970) chronicles this process. Taxation was the incentive that prompted a fast-paced adoption of the federal banking system.

My methodology, termed "forensic history," uses primary documents to construct a historical framework. Field practices have proven more indicative of policies than acts and regulations. For example: a tax receipt discloses purpose, officials, dates and penalties, and on the reverse, actions. The more distant a collector from the capital, the more lax an official was regarding late payments, mistakes or failures to file. Local collectors accepted excuses more often from their neighbors.

The targeted reader is any taxpayer dreading that "the taxman cometh." Financial and political histories of the past have concentrated on tables and statutes. Collectors and archivists may find useful a classification of documents, mindful of the need for precise definitions while exploring a technically complex and factually convoluted subject; terms such as levy, duty, excise and tariff are not as exacting as would be expected. Such was the relaxed use in newspapers at that time. Precision was secondary to persuasion, and more people read editorials than government statistics.

The chapter composition of an annual timeline was apparent after other organizational attempts. Although initially awkward, the approach highlights the different practices of the two Treasuries faced with similar challenges. To lessen confusion, a generous use of "United States" and "Confederate" descriptions is made. The subtleties of their different approaches caused different results.

Over a decade of research and collecting preceded the writing of the Civil War tax story. Fellow author and collector George B. Trammel again joined in the effort with his standard high-quality reproductions of the documents that are the primary source of much of the information within. This is the third collaboration we have shared. Our shared passion for previously overlooked Civil War ephemera is our bond.

Two long-time Civil War historians nurtured my study. Their direction encouraged me to seek out more than the mere catalog of documents. We all resided in Beaufort, South Carolina, birthplace of the New South. They co-authored Beaufort's history. Lawrence S. Rowland, Ph.D., distinguished professor emeritus of history at the University of South Carolina, Beaufort, taught me to appreciate the stories of history as much as the facts and dates. Dr. Stephen R. Wise, director of the Marine Corps Recruit Depot, Parris Island, Museum, encouraged research with exactness. For years both Drs. Rowland and Wise listened to my discussion of my research into the civil administration of Union-occupied Beaufort and Port Royal. Much of the analysis of the United States Direct Tax is also a history of Beaufort, both during and after the Civil War.

Two former officials in the U.S. Office of the Comptroller

of Currency added insight into the National Banking system enacted during the War. Emory Wayne Rushton, retired Deputy of Comptroller and Chief National Bank Examiner, added insight into the practical aspects of regulation and administrative complexity within a political setting.

Retired Chief Historian of the Office of the United States Comptroller of Currency, Jesse Stiller, Ph.D., perused my summation of that Office history in the nineteenth century. His familiarity with the topic produced much-needed corrections.

Suggestions from forewordist Mary Volcansek prompted references to the Federalist and Anti-Federalist Papers published in newspapers during the U.S. Constitutional debates. Her direction revealed an underlying framework for most tax policy debates that continue until today.

Mary Bones, director of the Museum of the Big Bend, again managed to produce a typed manuscript from my sometimes undecipherable scribblings. She is a master "code breaker."

Last, and foremost, I dedicate this book to my wife of thirty years, Yana. Attendance at auctions, travels to archives around the world and a myriad trips to state and university libraries substituted for vacations. Yana was always there during my quest for just one more footnote.

Chapter I

Antebellum United States Taxes, 1789–1860

Since recorded history, sovereign takings of property from loyal subjects have been deemed taxation. From enemies, spoils, contraband and admiralty prizes were seized under international law for civilized nations. English Philosopher John Locke, in his 1689 work *Second Treatise of Civil Government,* stated that taxes were what people relinquished from their personal estates in return for security and defense by their sovereign. Almost a century later, Frenchman Jean-Jacques Rousseau extended the bargain to include general welfare for the taxes submitted voluntarily. The American colonists appreciated these political philosophies at the time of their revolution. The Article of Confederation and Perpetual Union, ratified in 1781, established an association of the thirteen breakaway states. Article VIII of the Constitution provided that confederation defense could only be requested from the states, and only after acceptance could taxes be "laid or levied" by the states. Taxes were apportioned.

Only two-thirds of the American confederation tax requests were fulfilled. Unable to provide funds to sustain an effective army and navy, the Continental Congress called for a convention in Philadelphia February 21, 1787, to consider a new Constitution for the United States. Taxation was a deficiency most concerning.

Most published after the Convention were articles circulated in the New York press. Those favoring limited central government, known as Anti-Federalists, published a series of essays under the pseudonym "Brutus," and feared federal power over the "purse and sword." Brutus editorially argued tax should be limited to custom dues on imported goods rather than direct taxes such as property or poll taxes, which were costly to administer and discretionary. Export taxes were deemed counterproductive because they were harmful to domestic producers and manufacturers. In an editorial October 10, 1787, a distinction was made between external taxes, like customs, and internal taxes such as polls (capitation), property and excises (on domestic goods and services). Since Congress would have the power to "suppress insurrection" and tax accordingly, no limit would exist for internal taxes. At the time, the annual cost of state governments was four times that of the expected national budget.

New Yorker Melancton Smith, an Anti-Federalist writer, under the pseudonym "Brutus," on December 13, 1787, editorialized that a central government's tax power could become absolute and possibly "extend to every possible way of raising money." Article I, Section 8, the power to lay and collect, he reasoned, allowed federal tax collectors to preempt state collectors, because no two tax powers could occupy the same space. He feared Old World–style assessments on everything from windows and fireplaces to stamps and spirits. Smith suggested adding other tax exclusions in addition to export duties. He feared that during times of national emergency or war, swarms of revenue officers would target industry. In a speech on June 27, 1788, Smith warned that government officials would "find use for as much money as they can raise."

The other side wanted a stronger central government. The Federalists, led by Alexander Hamilton, James Madison and John Jay, published over eighty essays in New York newspapers in 1788. Under their assumed name, "Publicus," Alexander Hamilton in Federalist Paper Number 31 of January 1, 1788, argued that in the new republic, the power to cover contingencies should be "unconfined." In Number 32, two days later, he explained that custom duties had to be exclusively federal, free of state involvement, except for "inspection" for health and safety. Both state and federal sovereigns could concurrently assess excises and licenses. To quell any anxiety that federal custom duties might become excessive, he reminded readers that history had shown that high duties increased smuggling and was limiting on custom rates charged for imported goods. To debunk the double taxation argument for license and excise fees, Hamilton, in Number 36 of January 8, 1788, reminded voters that "the wants of the Union are to be supplied in one way or another." The government during time of war could seize or tax what it needed in order to survive.

One of the first acts of the constituted United States Congress was creation of a Treasury Department. The Treasury's first Secretary, Alexander Hamilton, pressed for strong fiscal policy. Federal revenue was from "customary tolls," or custom dues, collected from importers at ports of entry. Most European countries had already discontinued export duties on their domestically produced goods to improve balance of payments. Most local taxes were on property, assessed annually, termed "ad valorem." Local taxes were supplemented with polls, licenses, and fees for things such as bridges or canals. In the South, head taxes were assessed for each adult male and slaves. Excise taxes on spirits were enforced when government revenues proved inadequate. Before the Constitution, state governments could only be requested to contribute tax revenue to the federal government. Under the new Constitution, federal taxes required only passage by Congress and execution by the President, bypassing state legislatures.

The first United States tariff act, July 4, 1790, provided for the collection of funds "necessary for the support of government, for the discharge of the debts of the United States, and the encouragement and protection of manufacturers." On March 3, 1791, an excise tax on distilled spirits was enacted. The targets were farmers accustomed to distilling surplus grain into alcohol. The "moonshine" was convertible into hard money that was scarce during the winter. The farmer distillers rebelled against the federal whiskey tax. President George Washington in 1794 called national troops to subdue the so-called "Whiskey Rebellion." After the ruckus subsided, the spirits tax was repealed. To make up for lost revenue, a series of internal taxes, such as revenue stamps, carriage taxes and licenses replaced the liquor tax. By 1802, after the military crisis passed, these taxes were also repealed. For a decade import duties of about ten million dollars annually, combined with sales of the public domain, provided the nation's revenue.[1]

The new excise taxes included a levy "on carriages for the conveyance of persons, kept for the use of the owner." The tax was assessed and paid by only a few wealthy Americans. Carriage owner David Hylton of Virginia possessed over one hundred "chariots for the conveyance of persons." He was penalized for failing to render and pay his carriage tax on his fleet of hacks. He argued the tax was unconstitutional. The case was heard by the U.S. Supreme Court and reported in *Hylton v. United States* 3 U.S. 171 (1796). This was the first judicial review by the High Court of a federal tax's constitutionality. The carriage owner claimed that the carriage excise was a "direct tax" under Article I, section 9 and as such had to be apportioned among the states based on the census. The majority ruled in favor of the government holding that the carriage tax was a permissible "excise" under Section 8, not subject to an allocation among states. The impracticality of such a process for insignificant levies affecting so few probably favored the outcome.

Great Britain had experimented with multiple internal taxes during the Napoleonic Wars. Excise taxes on consumption collected at the producer level was popular because it was almost invisible to consumers. After the War of 1812, the United States adopted similar excises while protecting domestic industry. Indirect duties subsidized local industry at the expense of foreign manufacturers. This policy was crucial if the domestic goods were strategically important to the nation's security. John Quincy Adams always supported assistance to vital domestic industries as a component of national security. Imported goods not taxed by custom collectors were deemed "duty free." Duties were identified, measured and assessed at ports of entry prior to unloading. Complex and ever-changing tariff schedules were usually updated each session of Congress. Lobbyists were active when tariffs were debated.

A second tax rebellion erupted in northeastern Pennsylvania after passage of the U.S. Direct Tax of 1798, in preparation for an expected war with France. The ringleader, John Fries, and two others were pardoned from execution by President John Adams in 1799 after being sentenced to be hanged for treason. The clemency angered the leaders of the Federalist Party and affected the next year's national election. Fries's Rebellion was the second armed tax revolt after passage of the Constitution.

British goods such as textiles, iron, paper, and glassware were less costly than American goods. United States protective tariffs increased between 1816 and 1832. During the third decade, tariffs were relaxed, but re-imposed after the Panic of 1837. Custom dues from foreign imports fell during panics. Technological innovations by American industry, such as the use of anthracite coal in iron foundries, improved domestic competitiveness. Consumption of imported goods as a percentage declined as American industry matured. The advantage was offset by the rise in foreign luxury goods such as silk, wine and instruments. Federal port of entry staffs expanded. The ranking customs officials, like collectors, surveyors and naval officers, were presidential appointees. Skilled employees included measurers, gaugers and warehousemen. Clerks completed the payrolls.[2]

Cargos at ports of entry were inspected, and if subject to duty, counted, weighed and graded. "Duty free" cargos were examined for contraband, such as smuggled or banned goods. Cargo numbers were reported to the surveyor for assessment. Philadelphia Measurer Robert McCulloch weighed 123,400 bushels of salt, stored in seventy-four bags, that totaled one million seven hundred pounds at the Port of Philadelphia in 1848. Former U.S. Congressman and General of the Pennsylvania State Troops, John Davis, receipted the cargo as Surveyor. He was appointed by James K. Polk. (Fig. 2). The vessel's master was "burdened" with the computed duty before transferring the cargo to a bonded warehouse. If any of the assessed salt in the warehouse was later shipped out of the country, that portion of the duty could be redeemed by the shipmaster or his bondsman. Such a refunded duty or "Drawback" was documented in 1798 by Baltimore's first custom collector, Robert Purviance. The collector returned $514 (Fig. 3).

The law also allowed refunds of import duties for articles destroyed if in bonded warehouses. If the goods were bonded, rebate credits were allowed only upon proof of loss. If the article was consumed in the manufacturing process of another product, resulting into two or more final products, the drawback was computed on the value of the imported merchandise as a percentage of the total cost. Most articles were assessed according to a specific rate schedule. Over time, more were taxed by a general "ad valorem" duty based in the value of the goods at point of purchase overseas. Between 1802 and 1804, custom duties increased from $14 million to over $20 million. Drawbacks ranged between $4 million to almost $7 million in 1804 according to Joseph Nourse, Register of the Treasury Department, in his June 14, 1806, report to Congress. The two most drawback items were coffee and sugar processed by domestic manufacturers. By 1804, drawbacks amounted to a third of all customs collected. The almost seven million dollar tax refund was costly to the Treasury. As American manufacturing increased, drawbacks continued to grow. The industrialization of the young nation was counterproductive to customs collections from imported foreign goods.[3]

Ship captains maintained credit relations with local bankers, factors and sureties at ports they visited. If not, the master would need gold or local currency to pay dockage and duties. Local bailsmen, for a fee, would guarantee payment of custom dues before any goods were removed from a bonded warehouse. Individuals jointly and severally often assured the collector. The guarantee survived a surety's death. The promise was strictly enforced because unpaid duties were charged personally to the port collector, who was also bonded. The Master of the Brig, Arathuse King, of LaMatanza, Buenos Aires, had such a third-party surety arrangement at the District of Mississippi custom house. The guarantee was payable to the United States, not the port collector. The New Orleans Collector assessed $3,720 on the ship's cargo and required bond for half or $1,860 on April 29, 1836 (Fig. 4).

Under tariff rules, duties were assessed at the port of origin. Imported goods were valued according to the local market. To lessen collusion and fraud, affidavits were required verifying local prices, exchange rates and physical presence of cargo bound for the United States. Dr. Franklin Littlefield of Massachusetts, the mid-century consul for the State Department at Puerto Cabello, Venezuela, on May 10, 1838, certified the price of coffee in an invoice as the "actual cost" in stated currency of that country. He allowed a 20 percent exchange discount between the "Mocoquina" and United States dollars (Fig. 5).

Each U.S. port collector was also responsible for collecting the "tonnage tax" based on cargo capacity of vessels entering his port. Enacted in the same year as the Customs Act, the "tonnage tax" was also charged to American vessels. The tax collected was dedicated to the care and maintenance of navigational aids such as buoys. The collector deposited collections with a U.S. Treasury depository and maintained records. The port naval officer was responsible for making calculations of capacity to determine "tonnage." A bulk cargo ton is a thousand cubic feet. Standard cargo loads were forty cubic feet. Sailing ships had larger cargo capacity than steam vessels because of engines. The more costly steam ships were less taxed than sailing vessels of comparable displacement.

Similar to tonnage tax, "Light Money" was collected for maintaining the network of lighthouses along the American sea frontier. The coastline was divided into "Light Districts," supervised by the "Light Board," a bureau of the Treasury Department. When enacted in 1790, the nation had only eleven beacons. "Light Money" was assessed at fifty cents per ship tonnage and was due upon arrival at the port. Custom houses also provided ship registration papers as well as sailor's proof of citizenship affidavits. During malaria or yellow fever outbreaks, quarantine stations became more active. Ships were not cleared for entry unless declared disease free. In 1791, all services were available in the fourteen revenue districts with fifty-nine custom districts. Custom officials and army surgeons supervised most public health concerns. Citizenship certificates were necessary to reduce the number of American sailors being shanghaied for foreign vessels.[4]

Another provision of the 1790 Customs Act concerned sailor clinics and Marine Hospitals. This was the country's first public health program. Twenty cents per month was collected from every able-bodied seaman to provide for the care of sick or disabled sailors. The port collectors supervised the hospitals in their regions. Medical doctors at the Marine Hospitals worked alongside the collector, as both were presidential appointments. Quarantine became federal responsibility in 1796, and the President directed collectors to "aid in the execution of quarantine" laws and assist state health officers. By 1837 hospitals existed inland, such as the one at Louisville, Kentucky, "benefiting sick seamen, boatmen and other navigators on the Western rivers and lakes, such as the Great Lakes and the Ohio Canal and Mississippi River." After 1799, officers, seaman and marines of the United States Navy became eligible for treatment at Marine Hospitals. If a ship captain did not believe the Marine Hospital tax was due, such as for barge traffic along the Erie Canal, he could protest payment and seek an exemption.[5]

As explained in the Federalist Papers, national taxes were

limited. Direct taxes had to be apportioned. Before the Civil War, Congress twice passed a Direct Tax, apportioned among the states as required by the Constitution, to raise revenue during a national emergency. After assaults upon American merchant vessels, Congress, in July of 1798, passed a two-million-dollar Direct Tax to build up the Navy. Sixteen states and territories were assessed their federally allocated portion of the tax. The division was based on population. The property tax was based on values with several classifications. The progressive rate excluded small cabins and shanties. Rates began at 2⁄10 of 1 percent of value and rose to 1 percent for expensive townhouses and mansions. Slave property was assessed for workers between the ages of twelve and fifty. A fifty-cent poll tax was also due for white males. The balance of taxable property was tenements, commercial and agricultural property. Each state had discretion in both method of assessment and time of collection. State Boards of Tax Commissioners were responsible to the U.S. Treasury. Collections continued until the law was repealed April 6, 1806.[6]

The second Direct Tax was caused by the War of 1812. The Direct Tax Act of July 22 and August 2, 1813, assessed ad valorem tax according to the census enumeration. By the time the Secretary of the Treasury filed his report October 20, 1814, all but Louisiana had collected some Direct Tax. The Louisiana Tax Collector had not even been appointed due to enemy occupation. Additional assessments were approved for the subsequent two years. These taxes were augmented with excise taxes. By 1817, the U.S. Commissioner of Revenue reported almost ten million dollars from excise and Direct Tax collections. The Direct Tax was revoked the following year and the Office of the Commissioner of Revenue dismantled. State Boards of Tax Commissioners afterwards closed their ledgers and remitted balances. Some excise continued.[7]

Incomplete assessment, poor collections, minimal supervision and lax enforcement hampered the effectiveness of the Direct Tax. Unpaid assessments plagued the system. Most State Tax Boards were elected. The Direct Tax Act of April 2, 1814, permitted state governments to assume their apportioned share on behalf of their citizens. New Jersey, Pennsylvania, Virginia, South Carolina, Georgia, Ohio and Kentucky paid and received a prepayment discount. Early remittance with discounts by seven states came at a heavy cost. The Commissioner's Report to Congress in 1817 listed nine states that had paid another $700,000 to the Treasury. No tax collections were remitted by Louisiana or Tennessee according to that report. By 1818, the two-million-dollar tax was deemed cleared or written off (Fig. 6).

At the time, tariff rates averaged 25 percent for specialty imported goods. Protective tariffs increased and by 1828 some were at 50 percent. The tariffs were lessened after some states strongly protested. During the Mexican War, war taxes reappeared but only for a brief period. Peacetime prosperity soon returned allowing war debts to be retired and a budgetary surplus appeared. Custom duties were providing 85 percent of the federal revenue.[8]

The experience of the American military imposing martial rule while occupying Mexico would prove invaluable. The General in Command, Winfield Scott, at Vera Cruz in March 1847, by General Order, proclaimed that a "temporary and moderate tariff of duties" be established to cover the costs and providing for the population. In his Message to the U.S. Senate, February 10, 1848, President James K. Polk said that any nation at war had the right "to shift cost" to the enemy and exact contributions from their citizens. President Polk stated that such was preferable to the ancient custom of "pillaging." The manner, method and level of any martial levy was at the discretion of the senior officer present. On January 2, 1849, President Polk reported that he had permitted his Commander of Army and Naval Forces in Mexico to levy and collect a tariff on all vessels and merchandise entering occupied Mexican ports under the "right of conquest" as provided by the law of war. Also, all taxes, internal and external, due the Mexican government were seized. The funds were to be used in Mexico.

With the addition of more Western territories after the Mexican War, the public domain doubled. For the first half of the nineteenth century, federal land sales, although varying from year to year, contributed about a tenth of the federal budget. Economic panics depressed sales from a high of $2.50 per acre down to $1.25 per acre. The Panic of 1837 virtually halted sales. The General Land Office was competing with Texas land sales, which had retained all its public domain. The Texas offering price was less than half the United States minimum. By 1856, U.S. land sales had fallen to only seven million dollars, a tenth of that year's customs, which in 1836 had been equal.

Few politicians or businessmen appreciated the cause and nature of financial panics. Congress and States only reacted after markets collapsed. One example was the return of a federal surplus to the states only one year before the Panic of 1837. The cost efficiency of one tax, such as tariffs over another, was underappreciated. More intensive collection, wider coverage and higher rates were the normal tools used to enhanced revenue. Secretary of the Treasury Alexander J. Dallas, in his 1815 "Statement of the Emoluments of the Officers In the Collection of the Customs," detailed a roll of revenue collectors and assistants. This list would soon be dwarfed (Fig. 7).

With an accumulated surplus of $40 million in 1836 in the U.S. Treasury, the majority in Congress voted to return excess funds to the States. To tax one citizen and refund to another was unfair. It was proposed that the Treasury return to the States all funds in excess of five million dollars, which would be reserved as a contingency fund. Available was about $30 million for refund. Two distribution methods were debated. The first was based on a census apportionment like the Direct Tax, which favored older states by $1.5 million. The other, similar to the Electoral College head count, benefited newer states. The census-based apportionment prevailed. New York, Philadelphia, Charleston and Boston benefited most.

After the Mexican War, the National economy recovered to prosperity within a decade. When Secretary of the Treasury James Guthrie, from Kentucky, was appointed by President Franklin Pierce in 1853, he had already served as a U.S. Senator. He was a "hard money" state banker and supported publicly financed internal improvements like roads and canals. Guthrie gained respect and influence in the Pierce Cabinet. He was assisted by the discovery of gold in California. As an efficient administrator, he improved reporting and enlarged the National Treasury building. After office, Guthrie became President of the Louisville & Nashville Railroad. Opposed to secession, Guthrie, a slave owner, was a member of the Peace Congress of 1861, which worked to avert a Civil War. Guthrie always disfavored import taxes. In his Report to the U.S. Senate in December 1, 1856, he wrote "a tariff on imports is a tax, and that tax is paid by the consumer on the imports, and that it is undeniable that no tax should be imposed or continued [if] not sequestered for the economical administration of the government." Excess taxes, in his opinion, created extravagance and waste. Secretary Guthrie served to 1857 and was followed by Georgian Howell Cobb. These two Secretaries were followed by Phillip F. Thomas of Maryland and John A. Dix of New York, an Ohio bank lawyer. Abolitionist Salmon P. Chase became President Lincoln's Secretary of the Treasury on March 5, 1861. Secretary Chase was assisted by a treasurer, auditor, solicitor, and commissioner of customs, along with assistants. The Bureau of Customs at the time had a hundred presidentially appointed collectors, along with a dozen naval officers, eighty surveyors and many gaugers, measurers, clerks and laborers. Ports of delivery extended to the inland stations of Frontera at El Paso out to San Francisco. Customs Collector Hiram Barney of the Port of New York City earned a salary of twenty-five thousand dollars, including fees, fines and commissions. As the highest paid federal official, his power and influence, along with his four hundred employees, could not be ignored.[9]

Local taxes were more innovative than federal. Some, like federal direct and poll taxes, had to be apportioned by population. A particularly unique levy, the "pew tax" traces its history back to medieval Europe. Courts allowed churches to "tax" parishioners for reserved church pews. The Natchez Presbyterian Church, in 1850, collected $75.00 from the Executor of the Estate of John Kerr of Good Hope Plantation to continue his family's use of two pews after the patriarch's death. This practice had all but disappeared in America except in very traditional congregations, mostly in the South (Fig. 8).

Since the fifteenth century, sovereigns have relied upon head or "poll" taxes, ad valorem taxes and produce taxes to fund public projects like roads, bridges and public halls. Essential to that system were surveys of land owned. In America, ad valorem taxes were normally computed in mills, a tenth of a cent. The millage tax rate was applied annually against the value of the property such as a residence, commercial building or farmland. Most states set a fixed value per acre for agricultural land since the majority of voters were farmers. A ten-mills tax rate on a thousand-dollar home would cause a $1.00 tax. The Republic of Texas received a quarter of its income from such real estate taxes. In 1840 the Texas Commissioner of Revenue acknowledged payment of $4.60 for a half section of land owned by M.C. Hamilton. The past due tax for 1839 was included with his 1840 payment (Fig. 9).[10]

Local governments by mid-century had a menu of taxes to select from. The tax collector and sheriff of Wetzel County, Virginia, in 1857 assessed poll taxes against white and slave adult males. Local ferries and toll bridges were taxed. Both a "poor" and income tax was assessed. The Virginia municipality simply tacked on a 30 percent surcharge to cover the county budget (Fig. 10). The sheriff and tax collector of Jackson, Hinds County, Mississippi, in the subsequent year collected taxes from auctioneers, peddlers, and on liquor, carriages, watches, clocks, ten pin alleys, theaters, race tracks, dirk and Bowie knives, sword canes, silver plate, pianos and some livestock (Fig. 11). Many of those taxes would become part of later tax codes.

Chapter II

United States Taxes, 1861

Prior to the election of 1860, the Treasury was preparing more debt. From the first loan of August 4, 1790, private lenders usually required the government to pledge duties to secure debt. The Bank of the United States, the nation's fiscal agent, chartered by Congress, provided two million dollars under the Act of July 16, 1798, to build a navy. This hypothecated debt was partially liquidated by the first Direct Tax. Periodically the Bank arranged public loans. The Bank's Charter, authorized up to $35 million in capital. Private bankers became the nation's primary lenders.[11]

To successfully float debt, creditors had to believe that revenue was sufficient to cover annual principal and interest. After a $250 million loan in 1861, higher tariffs, under the Morrill Tariff Act of March 2, 1861, projected needed revenue. Customs had risen to $80 million. Railroad, bridge and canal improvement projects were suspended. Pennsylvania had borrowed $3 million and Connecticut, New York, New Jersey and Ohio also borrowed in lesser amounts. U.S. bonds were market priced at a 6 percent discount to yield 12 percent to attract cautious lenders. That spring, Fort Sumter began the rebellion.[12]

Several loyal states made direct loans to the U.S. Treasury, after President Abraham Lincoln's first military call-up. Some Border States withheld money and troops, and denied passage by U.S. Army soldiers, wagons and trains. The San Francisco *Daily Alta Californian* on August 6, 1861, gave editorial support and stated its readers were willing to be "taxed from the crown of their heads to the sole of their feet" for victory over the rebels. The editor suggested that the air they breathed might be taxed. An Eastern newspaper, although "inimical to taxation," was open to more taxes if the cause was just and "human rights and popular rule assured." As months rolled by, the moral cause became justification for more spending, debt and taxes.[13]

The increased tariff schedule under the March 2, 1861, Morrill Act was passed just before President Lincoln's inauguration. The Morrill Act was popular with Northern industrialists, financers and factory workers as a protection to domestic industry and commerce. The rates made domestic goods more competitive with imports. Protective duties were part of the platform of the Republican Party. Midwestern farmers were not pleased with tariffs. The divide between East and Central States as well as manufacturers and farmers added political complexity. In a propaganda article published by "The Loyal Publication Society of New York Union League" styled "Facts for the People," the writer cautioned that "soon we will see a small army of tax gatherers in our midst." The tax collectors were coming, but few appreciated the number.[14]

The new tariffs increased duties for imported wool, iron, textiles and other goods. Objectives were simple: to raise more revenue. Naturally, manufacturers welcomed the new import tariffs on foreign competition. A 5 percent surcharge was applied to almost everything, from rifles and watches to toys. Low-cost goods were surcharged an additional 10 percent if the exporting city was east of the Cape of Good Hope. Collectors received pamphlets such as one dated July 17, 1862, explaining "Tariffs of Merchandise" under the July 14, 1862, Act. Private rulings, published in Boston newspapers in January 1863, announced that the "Tonnage Tax" would apply to all fishing vessels even if not ported in Boston Harbor.

Treasury instructions for new tariffs did not reach the field until 1862. Complex enforcement provisions required training for custom officers. Southern ports were closed. Only after a rebel port was captured, secured and occupied were U.S. custom houses reopened by Presidential order. Such was the case in Brownsville, Texas. This last occupied custom house admitted duty-free Mexican imports in 1865. The war procedures continued after the war. On January 11, 1868, a cargo of Manila rope was withdrawn from a Philadelphia public warehouse for reshipment. The "Drawback Certificate" credited customs of $35.87 as provided by the Act of August 5, 1861, on forms still used (Fig. 12). War taxes and procedures continued for years.

Secretary Chase updated his budget annually. He estimated that tariffs would produce another $30 million annually. He proposed a Direct Tax for another $20 million. Some in Congress demanded that the secessionists bear the cost of the war. Michigan Representative F. C. Beaman on May 24, 1862, proposed rebel property be confiscated for the benefit of the Treasury. He argued that the U.S. Constitution was ratified "to secure, the blessing of liberty, not to encourage rebellion, treason and despotism." Beaman favored exempting Border States, except for slave holdings, to discourage more seccessions.[15]

President Lincoln appointed custom officials to collect revenue in occupied ports when secure. This added duties. The appointments made, under the Act of July 14, 1862, were slow to evolve:

Official	*Port*	*Position*
George S. Denison	New Orleans, LA	Acting Collector
George H. Carleton	Memphis, TN	Acting Surveyor
J. E. Dillon	Nashville, TN	Acting Surveyor
T.C Severence	Port Royal, SC	Acting Collector
Charles J. West	Eastfield, VA	Acting Collector
Charles Worthington	Brownsville, TX	Acting Collector

As acting officials all reported to New York Collector Hiram Barney. Collector Severence at Port Royal was a staunch Boston abolitionist, taking office in 1862. The last was Collector Worthington, who did not arrive until 1864. New Orleans Collector Denison was the highest paid, earning $6,000 in salary alone. He was from Vermont but lived in San Antonio at the time of secession. Denison was a relative of Secretary Chase. Acting Surveyors earned $2,000 annually, plus commissions.[16]

Treasury officers within rebel territory took custody, accounted and transported abandoned rebel property. Abandoned property included real estate, stores, livestock and slaves. If an owner later proved loyalty to the United States and disavowed allegiance to the rebel cause, property would be released, except slaves. Abandoned is distinguishable from confiscable property or contraband because no legal action is necessary. Contraband, such as rebel arms and military supplies, were illegal, seizable or destructible upon capture. Property subject to legal confiscation required legal notice, under several acts, with judicial supervision. If the owner was disloyal, the property was not recoverable. Congressmen Lyman Trumbull and Benjamin F. Wade long advocated that the Confiscation Act of August 6, 1861, be expanded and strictly enforced. The Confiscation Acts had some protection for private property rights. Eventually, Union traitors, draft dodgers and deserters were subject to confiscations.[17]

Slave property at first was not confiscable. In Virginia, slaves were deemed "contraband" by General Benjamin Butler and seized. In Port Royal, freed slaves were housed, fed and employed as "abandoned property" under the supervision of General Rufus Saxton at Port Royal, South Carolina. International law allowed taking enemy property used in support of a rebellion. No statutory authority under the Rules of War was needed to treat slave property as contraband. Federal and international laws controlled captured property of enemies. Upon occupation of a rebel city, army collection agents gathered livestock, produce and "freed" slaves if "abandoned." Title was in limbo until a court determined it not contraband. After the Act of July 13, 1861, Army collectors of abandoned property worked with Special Agents of the Treasury in the transfer, sale and disposition of rebel property.[18]

After the Union Expeditionary Forces commanded by General Thomas Sherman and Commodore Samuel F. Du Pont landed at Port Royal, South Carolina, November 7, 1861, area planters realized their property was at risk. The editor of the *Charleston Daily Courier* predicted the worst was ahead after the loss of Forts Walker and Beauregard just south of Charleston. He advised Sea Island planters to remove stores and slaves inland beyond the "plundering barbarians, now threatening our coast." Almost all cotton, rice, turpentine and cows in the barn were in harm's way. By the end of the year, Union quartermaster Colonel H. Nobles was collecting cotton around Beaufort with the assistance of paid abandoned slaves. The island enclave was occupied by 12,000 Union soldiers and sailors. All but a few locals and slaves had escaped to the mainland across the Port Royal crossing. Colonel Nobles, in addition to his army salary, earned a 6 percent commission on cotton collected, shipped and auctioned in New York. About seven thousand bags of Army cotton were forwarded, realizing almost a hundred thousand dollars.[19]

Colonel Nobles was soon joined by William H. Reynolds from the New York Custom House. His father-in-law, Governor William Sprague of Rhode Island, had arranged the appointment. Captured rebel property personally benefited each with commissions. Next to enter the fray was Special Treasury Agent Edward L. Pierce of Massachusetts, a Bostonian abolitionist, who had served as General Benjamin Butler's "Chief of Contrabands" at Fortress Monroe. Pierce owed his appointment to Massachusetts Congressman Henry L. Pierce, his brother. Edward Pierce later became acting Collector of Internal Revenues for the Third District. Nobles, Reynolds and Pierce battled over jurisdiction. Cotton shipments continued. The steamer *Atlantic* delivered 25,000 pounds for auction in New York mid-year. Due to poor baling, auction results were only eighteen to sixty-three cents a pound. Even at only twenty cents a pound, almost $200,000 was realized, of which the Port Royal agents earned 6 percent, or $12,000.[20]

The Beaufort District of South Carolina was responsible for thousands of bales of cotton sold in New York. With more care in storing and shipping, prices rose to seventy-two cents a pound. Sailors financially benefited from admiralty prizes shared with crews. Soldiers earned nothing more than a private's pay for captured enemy property. In occupied Savannah, Treasury agents were known as sharks and rascals that hang around like birds of prey. Officials lived in rebel mansions. Prized horses were taken by officers. The Beaufort College library was sent to Washington for auction. Sadly, the volumes burned before sale. Several Port Royal lumber contractors were expelled for bribes and operating without permits. Few profited from the property losses of the rebels.[21]

Unlike the Carolina occupations, New Orleans had many rebel residents remaining within Union lines. General Benjamin Butler declared martial law and his Provost Marshal, under General Orders No. 76, required all unwilling to make a written oath of loyalty to the United States to be placed beyond the lines as an "Enemy of the United States" (Fig. 13). Such designation subjected disloyal persons to confiscations. William Moore of Shadows Plantation was declared an "enemy" by Provost Captain C.W. Kilborn October 2, 1862. Moore's property was auctioned June 3, 1863. The *Montgomery Weekly Advertiser* reported that thousands had arrived from New Orleans before the May 15, 1863, deadline.

New Orleans Special Treasury Agent Benjamin Flanders took charge of "Enemy Alien" property in the summer of 1863. The confiscation of disloyal real estate was completed by the end of that year. Agents prepared descriptions, inventories and appraisals for all sites. Retail establishments, tenements and commercial properties were transferred to the official in charge of leases. Title was to be determined by a court. J.G. Parnharm, a rebel soldier absent from the occupied city, lost his property, which was turned over to Supervisory Special Agent Benjamin F. Flanders September 1, 1863. This was the one hundred and thirteenth "disloyal" to suffer loss of real estate. Parnharm owned three furnished properties, comprising two tenements plus a townhouse. The total value was estimated to be $9,000. The seized structures were placed in the Treasury's pool of rental properties (Fig. 14).

Owners suffering confiscation could later apply for property redemption. Pleas could be made to the local adjutant general. After federal courts opened, recoveries were judicially available. Simultaneously, claims could be filed with the Treasury. New Orleans property owner John H. Stevenson lost his home on August 3, 1863. The building was leased by the Board of Education for the Department of the Gulf to a Refugees and Freedmen school operating through 1866. During that time, former owner Stevenson paid local taxes. On August 10, 1866, Stevenson filed a recovery claim supported by tax receipts paid to the First District of New Orleans. Assistant Quartermaster of the Bureau of Refugees, Freedmen and Abandoned Lands, Louisiana supported his statement of facts and forwarded the request for relief. The property was eventually recovered (Fig. 15).

President Lincoln on July 25, 1862, threatened secessionists that if they did not return to the Union and affirm their loyalty they would soon suffer the "pain of forfeiture and seizure of estates." Such power was granted to him by Congress in the Confiscation Acts.

Military Governors were appointed by the President. General Rufus Saxton was assigned South Carolina and Florida. George F. Shapley oversaw New Orleans, and U.S. Senator Andrew Johnson became Military Governor of Tennessee at Nashville. In Tennessee, Governor Johnson imposed taxes to offset the costs of the city's homeless.

Cairo, Illinois, was homeport for the United States Mississippi River Gunboats. Secretary of the Navy Gideon Wells, on February 18, 1862, informed Special Agent Allen A. Hill to receive enemy cotton, tobacco and property from Tennessee. Personal property remained under the jurisdiction of Special Treasury Agents. General Saxton set up municipal government for civil affairs. Included were plantation courts, schools, mediation boards and precinct patrols. Property seizures were regulated by Attorney General Edward Bates after his pronouncement of January 8, 1863. Seizures, in the future, were to be made by a military officer or U.S. Marshal. Custody was transferred to federal court. All seizures were reported to the U.S. Attorney. Only federal judges heard confiscation cases.[22]

Federal confiscation cases resembled admiralty hearings and were brought against property rather than owners. No personal service of the owner or his presence was required. Federal judges heard the facts and applied law. Loyalty of ship, cargo and owners were a primary issue. Confederates, in retaliation, issued "Letter of Marque and Reprisal" that allowed rebel privateers to attack, board and seize U.S. ships. Neutral ships could not be boarded. Under international law, a "Letter of Marque" was protection against the crew being charged with piracy. The United States never recognized this Confederate tactic and considered such acts piracy. The question lingered.[23]

President Lincoln in the spring of 1861 warned that any person seizing shipping under a "Letter of Marque" or molesting the crew would be charged with American piracy. Congress in support of that Presidential threat on August 5, 1861, declared that "Letters of Marque" issued by the so-called Confederate government were null and void. That act declared ten Southern states to be in rebellion and were not an "Enemy" under international law. Federal courts mostly followed this interpretation. To the United States Navy, rebel or foreign vessels breaking the port closures were subject to boarding, inspection and seizure if caught in possession of contraband. If taken as an admiralty "prize" the vessel and crew were escorted to the nearest district court for adjudication. Before a federal judge, the U.S. Naval officer presented an affidavit stating that "the ship was seized by this vessel under my command on the [________] day of [__________], 186[__], off the port of [__________] or violating blockade."[24]

Atlantic privateers were taken to Philadelphia or New York. Gulf-captured vessels were escorted to Key West. Union captains complained they neither had the ships or crews for such duty. The New Orleans judge eventually heard admiralty cases. Provisional Court Judge Charles A. Peabody was reluctant to decide admiralty or confiscation cases. Military Governor George F. Shepley assured Judge Peabody that he had jurisdiction under his Presidential Instructions. Peabody complained it was still impossible because New Orleans was under Martial Law. After the relaxation of martial rule, June 14, 1863, Judge Peabody heard prize cases unless involving cotton or sugar that were directed to New York. Admiralty cases captured off Western Florida, Alabama, Mississippi and Louisiana were also held in New Orleans.[25]

The first year of the South Atlantic Blockading Squadron credited eleven prizes. The Squadron, at Port Royal, saw that number quadruple. Admiral David D. Porter's Mississippi Blockading Squadron shared $60,000 in prizes. Half the proceeds went to the officers and crew, allocated according to their rank. The balance was deposited to the U.S. Treasury. Soldiers were precluded by the Articles of War from financially benefiting from captured enemy property. A thousand admiralty prizes were taken in 1863 and that increased 40 percent the following year. Prize cases were great propaganda for the Union, and were well reported.[26]

Crewmembers welcomed blockading duty that may result in a prize. Each crew member individually filed a prize claim for his share of the proceeds. New York was the most common admiralty court involved. The prize claim had to be signed and sworn to before two witnesses and a notary. Coal heaver Thomas McKenna, aboard the USS *Quaker City* in 1863, participated in the capture of forty bales of cotton. Irishman McKenna enlisted at Boston, April 22, 1863, and served aboard the ship from November 1863 to his discharge in August 1864. Claims Agent Charles H. Swan of New York submitted his claim. It was approved for payment and forwarded to the Fourth Auditor of the Treasury Department. The prize claim, affidavit, discharge and copy of paymaster records plus a nickel revenue stamp made up the package (Fig. 16). The *Quaker City* was a heavy sidewheel steamship. The forty bales of cotton were recovered floating at sea.

It was not uncommon for a sailor's share of prize money to exceed his annual pay. Later, crews were shocked to learn they owed income taxes on their bounty. Internal Revenue Commissioner E. A. Rollins on December 30, 1867, in response to Georgetown Attorney A. H. Mechlen's request for an opinion on the applicability of Section 123 of the Income Tax Act of June 30, 1864, to prize money, ruled upon the question, "If a prize was taken prior to passage of the income tax, was it still taxable?" The Commissioner recognized the law was silent, but ruled that Section 116 imposed income tax upon gains, profits and income derived from any kind of property. Not only were the prizes taxed retroactively, paymaster and treasury disbursing agents were instructed in the future to withhold at a 5 percent rate without regard to the time when the captures were made (Fig. 17).

The 1861 Direct Tax contributed some to the Treasury, but at a slow pace. This was the third time a constitutionally restricted Direct Tax passed Congress. Direct Tax collections were delayed until states created collection procedures and made appointments. The North held three-quarters of the nation's wealth, or about $15 billion. Congress elected to tax all states and territories, loyal or in rebellion. Dwellings valued in excess of $500 were assessed as of April 1, 1862. No Southern state paid any of its share. Loyal states received a 15 percent prepayment discount. All but Delaware and Colorado paid early and took the credit.[27]

Chapter III

Confederate States Taxes, 1861

Both Confederate and United States Congressmen delayed increased taxation the first year. Until homes and families were at risk, citizens considered the war a short disruption. The Confederate Provisional Constitution mirrored the United States except for slavery and a few other differences. Fortunate for the Confederates, they inherited a trained military of former Union officers and civil bureaucrats along with procedures necessary to form a republic. Laws were enacted similar to those in the United States. Article I, Section 8 of its Provisional Constitution permitted the national government to collect taxes, duties, import and excises as necessary to meet debts, provide for defense and carry on the business of government. Direct Taxes under the same constraint of enumeration as in the U.S. Constitution were provided. Tax laws required a two-third legislative majority. Except for navigational aids, no national expenditures for internal improvements or protection of domestic industries were possible. Such were left to state and local governments.

Few economists lived in the South. Fiscal discussions mostly concerned statistical data. The most authoritative business journal was *DeBow's Review*, published in New Orleans. Most articles covered agricultural and transportation issues. Insurance, banks and industry were sometimes mentioned. The editor supported a slave based economy for his agriculturist readership. Seed selection, crop rotation and fertilizers had greater coverage than monetary concerns. Another economist noted that at the time the Southern "reading public was small, probably the thinking public also!" The agriculture boom and bust cycles caused most planters to be debtors. Historically agriculture was less taxed than commerce, finance and railroads. In rural communities, internal improvements such as bridges, canals and turnpikes were negligible.[28]

Charleston and New Orleans were the most prosperous towns in the South. New Orleans was a banking center. By mid-century, Charleston had trollies, telegraphs and gas lighting. In an April 1857 report styled "The Disabilities of Charleston for Complete and Equal Taxation and the Influence of State Taxation in Her Property," the City Council moved for a five million dollar, forty-five year bond issue. To extend through 1892, the bonds ranged from $45,000 to $320,000 annually. Church glebe lands, plantations, banks, teachers and preachers were tax favored. Three-fourths of tax was from urban taxpayers. In Charleston, a third of its tax revenue came from town lots and two-thirds from commercial real estate. In 1784, the state property tax was replaced by a stationary sixty cents per $100 valuation. Slaves were taxed at a seventy cents poll tax and freed blacks owed two dollars.

States had long resorted to head or "poll" taxes for municipal government. Bridge, ferry or railroad projects required special assessments. By mid-century, Mississippi and Virginia had passed sales, income and inheritance taxation. The Carolinas, Alabama, Louisiana and Texas licensed professionals and occupations. After the financial Panic of 1837, banks struggled financially in the South. Mississippi, Alabama and Texas had no chartered banking at secession. Commercial houses, private bankers and factors provided agricultural credits.[29]

The permanent Confederate Constitution carried over most taxes in the provisional document. Lawmakers expected customs to fund the government. Added was an export duty prohibited under the U.S. Constitution. The Confederate Customs Act, except for export duties, was almost verbatim a copy of the U.S. Code. In fact, the new law stated it meant to give effect to all U.S. duties and tariffs in effect November 1, 1860, unless "inconsistent with the provisional Constitution." By that backdate, the U.S. Morrill Tariffs enacted in 1861 were not included. Confederate Tariffs were amended February 10, 1861, with a "duty free" list of strategic materials. The unique "export duty" of 8 percent on baled cotton was aspirational, but little practical effect. The blockade reduced exports. The Confederate Congress enacted tit-for-tat almost every form of federal tax passed by the U.S. Congress.[30]

The organization of the Confederate Treasury postponed assessments as passed by the provisional Congress. To expedite the process, existing U.S. regulations were adjusted and reissued as Confederate. Oaths were taken from all carryover officials such as collectors, surveyors, naval officers and light board members. Few refused to serve the new government. Assuming office February 21, 1861, Secretary of the Treasury Christopher Memminger appointed C. C. Walker, formerly of the New York Customs House, to inspect all ports of entry and recommend possible closures and staff reductions. The government roll of four hundred employees was more than the budget could afford. Most delivery stations were closed by the end of the year. The customs receipts estimated to be $25 million was overly optimistic. After the Union ports closure, customs receipts seldom reached 10 percent of estimates and failed even to cover expenses at some ports.[31]

Half the U.S. Custom officials in New Orleans became Confederate. Included were Collectors F. H. Hatch at New Orleans and Robert N. McMillen at Franklin, on Teche Bayou, plus surveyors in New Orleans and Shreveport. Eleven Texas collectors in Galveston, Point Isabel, LaSalle and Eagle Pass stayed. Surveyors at Sabine City, Aransas, Copano, Corpus Christi, Lavaca, Matagorda and Brownsville also remained. Inspectors at the inland port of Laredo on the Rio Grande continued to man the entry to Mexico. After closures and staff reductions, import duties for 1862 and 1863, amounting to only a million dollars a year, did not cover collection costs. Congress's grand plan for more revenue under the Acts of February 18, March 15 and May 21, 1861, did not materialize. Import duties were paid in Treasury notes, bond coupons or gold. Duties from the beginning were disappointing.[32]

In the interim between the Provisional and Permanent Confederate Congress, inland revenue stations were active along borders and the Mississippi. River traffic was cleared into the Confederacy at Nelson's Landing, Mississippi. Inland stations at rail terminals near the border were manned by railroad and express agents. Adams Express Company agents notified shippers that through March 15, 1861, cargo would pass "duty free" into the Confederacy. The Company's Augusta agent, H.B. Plant, arranged for the ports of Savannah and Charleston to accept cargos duty free if loaded before the deadline. The Mississippi River "duty free" period ended April 10, 1861. By summer, the Texas Commanding General questioned the wisdom of closing ports of delivery at El Paso, Eagle Pass, Rio Grande City, Point Isabel and Brownsville because of the heavy traffic. A few were later reopened.[33]

The inland revenue stations were short-lived. Offices at Hernando, Holly Springs, Corinth, Stevenson, Atlanta, Augusta, Athens, Chester, Florence and Norfolk were shuttered. Stations for Tennessee and North Carolina were no longer necessary after each joined the alliance. On May 17, 1861, Secretary Memminger ordered all remaining inland stations to wind down, forward collections to depositaries and close out their ledgers. Collector F. R. Shackelford of Atlanta forwarded $100.95 to the Assistant Treasurer at Charleston, B. C. Pressley, July 27, 1861 (Fig. 18). On March 15, 1861, the collector at the port of Charleston, South Carolina, transferred $700 to Assistant Treasurer Pressley (Fig. 19). Although some small custom stations remained operational, most efforts were for naught.[34]

Cotton exports were sharply reduced after the Union blockade. Only vessels willing to run the risk of becoming a prize made the potentially lucrative trip. By 1862, exported cotton destined for Great Britain had dropped to only thirty thousand bales for the year. Most blockade runners avoided Confederate export duty by stealth and smuggling. Pre-war, about 20 percent of Southern cotton was shipped North. This commodity dependence gave false confidence to the Confederate Congress, believing that their products were essential to "Hundreds of thousands" laboring in the factories. Vice President Alexander Stevens, while in Augusta, early in the war, spoke of this false premise. Such bluster diverted needed economic debate. Beyond the half million acres dedicated to cotton and the billion dollars invested in slaves, the Confederacy had little of value to foreign markets other than military purchases.[35]

After revenue stations and ports of delivery were closed, import and export duties were no longer a budgetary consideration. Custom House collectors were reassigned or given additional duties. Confederate Depositaries, responsible for paying, receiving and issuing bonds and notes, were often trained accountants or bank cashiers. All were bonded for faithful performance of their duties. Despite reductions, customs operations continued at major ports such as Richmond, Wilmington, Savannah, Charleston, Mobile and Galveston throughout the war. Richmond collector R. H. Lorton, appointed April 5, 1862, issued a custom receipt in April 1863 after forwarding $6,122.55 to the Confederate Treasurer Edward C. Elmore at Richmond, only a smidgen of that originally expected (Fig. 20).

The Confederate Collectors were responsible for Light Houses and Marine Hospitals. Benevolent groups assumed supervision of most hospitals after secession. U.S. Light Districts in Virginia (Number 5) to Texas (Number Nine) were under the Confederate Light Board. Foreign and domestic vessels after May 1, 1861, had to pay "light money" prior to docking at Southern ports. The "Light Certificate" was a verbatim copy of the federal form. "Light Boards" were suspended in July 1861. Expensive lenses, lights and oil were moved inland. Navigational aids were darkened along the coastline to create hazards to enemy vessels. The unmarked ports were navigational risks for both Confederate blockade runners and Union Blockading Squadrons. Local pilots were essential to both sides. These were well-paid private contractors.[36]

President Lincoln vacillated between characterizing the rebellion being a civil insurrection or state of war. Propaganda and politics clouded the issue. An enemy belligerent had certain rights under international rules of war agreed to by civilized nations. Although at first his Proclamation was deemed a port closure, the U.S. Navy imposed a blockade patterned after actions to ports in Mexico during that war. The ships were termed Blockade Squadrons, not "Port Closure" squadrons. The nation was at war and enemy ports were under blockade. On May 21, 1861, Southern lawmakers passed a "Sequestration Act" in retaliation to threats of seizure. Property held or owed to an "enemy alien" was ordered turned over to Confederate Receivers to be held by a Court during the war. Income, such as rent, interest and dividends owed to "enemy aliens" could be used to indemnify citizens suffering losses from enemy action. Draft dodgers and deserters were treated as "enemy aliens."[37]

Parties indebted to Northern creditors received notice under the Sequestration Act in the fall of 1861. Newspapers encouraged neighbors to report persons ignoring the sequestration order. Suspects included factors, shippers and importers who were known to do business with Northern merchants. Both sides used the term "enemy aliens." A Sequestration Receiver was assigned to each District Court and was charged with receiving and investigating those holding enemy property. Failure to turn over such property was punishable by up to six months in jail and a $5,000 fine. The Eastern District Court of Texas ordered all persons having "in their possession or control, any property, notes, bills or credits, belonging to an enemy aliens" to relinquish to the Court no later June 23, 1862. Newspapers periodically ran such court orders. The law applied to agents and managers of "enemy alien" rental property. This real estate provision was seldom used because most rents were just not paid. Few complained.[38]

Under Sequestration, "enemy alien" property was not subject to judicial hearings on confiscation. Northern creditors retained title and only income was seized. The Columbia, Mississippi, Sequestration Receiver, C. R. Crusoe, published notice to those owing debts to "enemy aliens" as of December 24, 1861. He quoted language from Treasury Regulations. The Little Rock Receiver filed a writ of sequestration with Judge David Ringo detailing debts owed to Dean & Hale of Cincinnati, Ohio. After review in February 1862, Judge Ringo issued a warrant for the seizure of items and placed them in the court repository (Fig. 21). The Sequestration Law applied to all persons within the Confederacy, including resident aliens, doing business with enemy persons. Failure to comply could result in garnishment of property.

Annual accountings made by Sequestration Receivers were given to persons releasing property. All interest, dividends and other payments due the "enemy alien" were held in trust. The Attorney General issued an advisory opinion stating this in no way affected the terms, conditions, or enforceability of the contracts. Foreclosure actions were available for breach of contract or default. The Attorney General early reported to Congress that two million dollars were held in court repository. Not mentioned were the costs devoted to enforcement. Confederate judges, clerks, marshals, receivers and military officers were all involved. The true benefit to the government was propaganda rather than revenue. Sequestration was an act of a sovereign nation. Commissions paid to the receivers were small and few wanted the job.[39]

The Sequestration Act was the Confederate version of the U.S. Confiscation Acts. To justify seizures of enemy alien property, the lawmakers kept the holding temporary. During debates of the Sequestration bill, the act was considered necessary by the North's "departing from the usage of civilized warfare." The Act excluded Sequestration within Border States. The Congress hoped for their support and did not want to anger friendly neighbors. Receivers appointed by judges were officers of the court. A Court of Claims was planned to adjudicate validity of war claims but for budgetary reasons never materialized. Instead, a Board of Commissioners decided damage claims. Judge George P. Scarbrough, formerly of the U.S. Court of Claims, Walker Brooke, Mississippi Congressman, and Lieutenant Governor of Missouri, Thomas C. Reynolds, formed that Board.[40]

Five hundred sequestration cases, concerning a half million dollars in property, were heard in Georgia alone. Almost the same was tried in Nashville. Of the four thousand claims for losses submitted by loyal Southerners, only a third was ruled valid. For a short period, John D. Morris reviewed claims for Kentucky. Income held from the sequestered property approached a quarter million dollars which was supposedly available to the Board of Commissioners to disburse for losses. Identified Texas Sequestration Receivers include[41]:

Receiver	*City*
James H. Starr	Tyler
W.P. Ballinger	Galveston
T. A. Patillo	Marshall
J. Giddings	Brenham
N. Maxen	Brownsville
James A. Ware	Corpus Christi
John A. Green	Austin
J. B. Murphy	San Patricio
W. A. Glass	Victoria
F. Fauntleroy	Goliad
William Milbourn	Wharton
John Ireland	Sequin
N. O. Green	San Antonio
J. L. L. McCall	Waco
J. M. Smith	Fort Worth
J. C. Rushing	Weatherford
Thomas Moore	Burnet

Texas Sequestration Receiver James H. Starr held notes owed to Robert W. Field considered an "enemy alien." Starr filed the accounting for interest due from May 21, 1861, to May 21, 1862, computed between 5 and 7 percent. The notes ranged from a low of $185.65 to a high of $1,034.20 for a total debt of about four thousand dollars. The interest paid June 5, 1862, was $256.44. The court rendering was remitted to Deputy Marshal James H. Johnson (Fig. 22). Such accountings continued through the war. Charleston Receiver G. W. Simon on October 31, 1863, filed his interest computation due August 30, 1862. A Charleston pharmacist on King Street deposited interest owed to Northern creditors on October 31, 1863. Dr. G. W. Aimar's was the primary drug store in Charleston. He deposited $38.30 with the receiver and was given an Evans & Coswell printed paid-in-full receipt (Fig. 23).

The second retributional act imposed by the Confederate Congress granted authority to President Davis the issuance of "Letter of Marque and Reprisals" to privateers. This followed President Lincoln's port closures proclamation of April 19, 1861. President Davis threatened to arm private vessels under the seal of the government with orders to harass, attack and take prizes of enemy shipping as long as the blockade lasted. Privateers were to be awarded bonuses for the capture of enemy sailors and merchant marines, dead or alive. On August 5, 1861, the U.S. lawmakers declared seizures of U.S. vessels and any harm to sailors would be piracy subject to the death penalty. Notice was given to European shipmasters, by both sides, if captured with contraband, their vessels and cargo could be considered prizes.[42]

After May 6, 1861, a State of War existed and the Confederates considered themselves foreign belligerents, not insurrectionist, and subject to the rules of War. Confederate privateers with "Letters," under the rules of War, held $5,000 surety bonds for crews less than fifty. Larger vessels posted a $10,000 bond for losses inflicted upon innocent parties. The Confederate port collector received 5 percent of the proceeds for the relief of widows and orphans of privateer crews. Contraband seized included arms, naval stores and copper. After the Confederate privateer *Savannah* was captured and the crew charged with piracy in a New York federal court, the two State Departments began negotiations. Capital punishment was averted through a prisoner exchange in July 1862.[43]

The Confederate Congress also duplicated the United States Direct Tax. New Orleans' banker, James D. Denegre, urged Secretary Memminger to recommend a Direct Tax early in 1861. Assessable Southern property was four billion dollars, a third of that in the North. Land and slaves were the bulk of Southern wealth. With a theoretical Tax rate of two mills, Denegre estimated three million dollars in Direct Taxes. He assumed a realization rate of half the assessments, which was the standard slippage to cover fraud and corruption. Secretary Memminger recommended a Direct Tax of five mills assessed against realty, slaves and securities. His gross tax estimate was $20 million, exactly the same as the federal expectation. The act passed August 19, 1861, but was amended for procedural reasons December 10, 1861. Collections for a variety of reasons were delayed for a year.[44]

Taxes alone could not support the Southern war budget. The first Confederate loan of $15 million on February 28, 1861, was commonly referred to as the "Bankers Loan" because that was the targeted creditor. A New York printer provided the "gold" bonds yielding 8 percent interest. Purchasers subscribed to the issue by depositing 5 percent with bond commissioners. By mid-summer half the issue was subscribed. The plan was to dedicate the gold from export duties to the semi-annual bond interest requirement. Sales efforts were most successful in the banking houses of Savannah, Charleston, New Orleans and Mobile. Subscription slowed the second half of the year, after opening April 17, 1861. This was the most successful of all Confederate bond issues.[45]

Debts always overwhelmed the Confederacy. Delinquent contracts and military back pay threatened the very existence of their infant government. Again, Southern lawmakers copied their federal counterparts and issued treasury notes to pay debts. Gold and silver reserves, slim from the start in the South, disappeared completely. The Confederacy did not have the benefit of the California gold fields to replenish reserves. On March 9, 1861, the Treasury issued a million dollars in interest-paying treasury notes. The notes printed by the American Banknote Company of New York were issued in $50, $100, $500 and $1,000 denominations. It was expected that the 3.65 percent (penny a day) interest provision would be a valuable investment. Debts continued and bills were partially paid. On May 16, twenty million dollars more in treasury notes were emitted but this time they were non-interest bearing. More notes and bonds followed at an accelerating rate.[46]

Chapter IV

United States Taxes, 1862

Emergency issues of U.S. Treasury notes covered shortfalls in federal revenue regularly. Morrill Act tariff revenues initially, less than expected, slowly increased. The Direct Tax passed by Congress in August of 1861 languished as offices were organized and staffed. Apportionment of the Direct Tax among states and territories was simpler because the 1860 U.S. Census preliminary numbers were available. More complicated was the multitude of credits claimed by states. Almost all but a couple assumed the tax burden for the benefit of their citizens in return for the prepayment discount. The next added was more internal taxes. Secretary Chase approached Congress for an additional $50 million in excise and other internal taxes. The New York Chamber of Commerce had proposed up to $250 million in such taxes, claiming that amount could be absorbed annually without damaging the economy. Congress passed several internal taxes hoping to add another $100 million annually. The five million dollar income tax provision of that year passed with little debate.[47]

With optimistic Treasury, Chamber and Congressional support, the $320 million 1862 budget was initially encouraging. The $80 million shortfall, partially due to delays in Direct Taxes and organizational difficulties was revenue-challenging. Tariff receipts fell short by $22 million. Government land sales virtually ceased. Vital contractors such as printers, telegraph and railroads demanded payment in advance. Military pay, civil expenses and suppliers were in arrears. Several states, sensitive to the Treasury's predicament, remitted funds early. This relief was offset by states, such as Missouri, that offset their direct tax apportionment with moneys claimed due them. With a quarter of the Direct Tax of $20 million assigned to the seceding states, payment was never expected. In fact, that allocation reduced by a fourth the burden that should have been allotted to loyal states.

Direct Taxes apportioned by population under the 1860 Preliminary Census, was questioned because the center of population had shifted westward, giving relief to wealthier older states. The Direct Tax had to be amended, extending the assessment and collection deadlines. The August 5, 1861, Act was modified on July 1, 1862, and again on June 30, 1864. The change in census demographics showed increased population in disloyal states. Twenty percent population growth over the prior decade occurred mostly in four Southern states. New York grew only 13 percent and Pennsylvania 10 percent. These two along, with Massachusetts and Ohio, accounted for the bulk of the twenty-two loyal states' and territories' allocation. The gross tax was $19,637,126, rather than $20 million as authorized by Congress, due to recalculations.[48]

The United States Direct Tax, an emergency measure for quick revenue, was doomed from inception. Frugal state governments reduced by 15 percent their share of the tax by early payment. This "haircut" was in addition to the quarter share assigned to nonpaying disloyal states. The third "haircut" were offsets by loyal states and territories for military expenses, appropriations and disputes. Territories received gratuitous appropriations increases to cover their Direct Taxes. Connecticut redeemed U.S. bonds held in their Treasury to pay the tax. Maryland issued state bonds, sold at deep discounts, to satisfy their tax bill. Because of enemy incursions, Kansas was allowed an extension. Delaware and Colorado failed to take advantage of the prepayment discounts, and took years to remit. Direct taxes were symbolic but not effective as a fiscal policy.[49]

With the rapid depletion of monetary reserves, the nation's credit worthiness was threatened. Secretary Chase, fully aware of the consequences of defaults, saw discounts and inflation worsen. Internal Revenue increases were crucial. The Tax Office was headed by a former governor of Massachusetts, long experienced in financial matters. George S. Boutwell of Boston took office July 17, 1862, for only eight months. He left for the House of Representatives. By his departure, the Bureau had four thousand employees. Commissioner Boutwell prescribed rules and regulations necessary for the administration and enforcement of the Internal Revenue agency. Soon thousands of tax assessors, collectors and revenue agents scoured the country in search of taxes.[50]

Forms and the creation of instructions was time-consuming and expensive to produce. Commercial center collectors used local job printers. Standard forms were in short supply. Local collectors and assistants in rural communities had to make do. At Chillicothe, Ohio, Collector Nathan Denny of the 12th District and his deputy of the Second Sub Division adopted generic bank checks to receipt income and excise tax payments. Taxpayer Mrs. L. Sopman paid and was receipted for her "Class C" luxury carriage tax along with her 1862 "Income Tax" on December 19, 1863. Her payment was evidenced by a form with a pastoral scene (Fig 24).

Newspapers announced the "Tax Man was coming!" A popular fable described layers of taxes, incomprehensible instructions, and conflicting rules. As one story told, a farmer sold his only cow to a cattle broker who in turn took it to the local slaughterhouse. The animal was rendered and the meat sold to the butcher, hide to a tanner and bones to a fertilizer company. Afterwards the hide was tanned, the leather went to a bootmaker. A month later, the farmer bought a pair of shoes from that cobbler. At every stage, internal taxes were added. Permits, licenses, sales, income and special excises totaled more than the price of the shoes. Although extreme, if import tariffs, legacy and excess profit taxes were added to the fabled bill, the total could exceed the price of the cow and boots. Tax protestors held fast to this popular hyperbole.

As overreaching as the farmer's cow story may seem, the Treasury took seriously its duty to exact every penny of tax. Necessary to that collection process were instructional guides and forms. Due to the assortment of ever-changing taxes requiring specialized reports, Commissioner Boutwell allowed wide discretion to local districts. An example, similar to the fictional farmer's transaction, was an "Excise Tax on Slaughtered Cattle" form created by Collector Dillon Luther of the 8th District of Pennsylvania. The monthly return was to be filed and paid within ten days of demand. If not, the excise tax increased by a penalty. The October 1865 tax return was paid by the butcher December 4, 1865, causing a 1 percent late payment penalty (Fig. 25).

Issues other than tax intrusiveness also caught the attention of editors. Few fully appreciated the lucrative position of being appointed a tax collector. Although custom officials in general were well compensated, the nature of that appointment involved more political patronage. Commissioner Boutwell's salary was $4,000 annually. His second earned $2,500, and deputies received a thousand dollars. The most prized field position was to be appointed tax collector in a commercial center like New York City. Compensation was capped at $10,000. Collectors paid assistants from their earned commissions. A collector could elect to receive a flat $5,000 a year and the Treasury would pay assistants. Revenue officers earned $2,000 annually. Collectors appointed spirit and tobacco inspectors who were paid by manufacturers, stores and smoke shops inspected.

Frank Leslie's *Illustrated News* ran a full-page cover story styled "Scenes of the Tax Collector's Officers, New York City" (Fig. 26). The November 1, 1862, article depicted citizens in line at the tax assessor's window with another long line before the cashiers' cage. Also shown was a clerk stamping occupational licenses. The office, located at 83 Cedar Street at Broadway. was headquarters for the 32nd New York Collection District, in the heart of the financial district. District Collector Sheridan Shook shared space with revenue officers, spirit and tobacco inspectors and detectives. District Assessor S. P. Gilbert had several assistants. Revenue Agent A. N. Lewis headed the Treasury Detective Agency. Fraud and evasion were pervasive. By war's end, the 32nd Collection District had sold over two million dollars in occupational taxes alone. Monthly that office accounted for three quarters of million dollars in tax assessments.

Lawmakers long remained tepid to imposing more taxes. The Secretary's projections were bold because he realized the size of future budget deficits. Tobacco and spirit taxes were promising and above estimates. Projected at $62 million, the "sin taxes" were followed with $40 million from stamps. Occupational, cotton, luxury and income taxes were expected to be $90 million, evenly divided. Legacy and inheritance taxes were budgeted at $50 million. The Commissioner's Office was issuing more rulings in response to public inquiries. By 1863, the Tax Bureau had grown to four hundred offices scattered among 185 tax districts. Almost 2,500 assistant assessors met regularly with taxpayers.[51]

Collection of U.S. taxes improved in 1863. The tax receipts for sales, revenue, luxury and income taxes were given daily. A cottage industry of Master Tax Guides publishers appeared. *Harpers Weekly* on July 26, 1862, carried four separate advertisements for such guides. The promoted pamphlets included "The New National Tax Law" by Beedle and Company priced at only a dime (Fig. 27). The guide "embodying the organic sections" was complete with alphabetized schedules of articles and rates. Competitor R. C. Richards and Company assured readers his booklet was "more easily understood." Wholesaler P. Haskins priced his paperback instructions at only three cents if purchased in bulk. Penalties were negligible. Barter, cash trades and creative bookkeeping were invisible and left no trace of unreported income.

A sense of egalitarian fairness prompted the passage of excise taxes on gold, silver, luxury carriages, yachts and inheritances. Symbolism did little to ease the Treasury's financial predicament. The Treasury was initially unable to identify untaxed persons and businesses. On-the-job trained officials were unfamiliar with deceptions. Congress, on June 30, 1864, added more luxury taxes, even dividing yachts into classes. Fancy carriages were taxed by number of horses. Gold watches and pianos had two classes. By the time of repeal on July 14, 1870, the tax had produced less than nine million dollars. The perception of fairness was needed but not revenue-measurable. A 20 percent expected fraud loss was built into the Treasury's projection of internal taxes.[52]

Revenue stamps, "Schedule B" assessments as identified on excise tax returns, were passed under the Act of July 1, 1862. Stamped tax paper dated back to the eighteenth century and was familiar to both English and Spanish colonists. All land grants from Mexico were executed on prepaid tax-stamped documents. Failure to comply brought the validity of titles into question. The U.S. Revenue Tax, Section 95, declared any document without a stamp would have "no effect." Additionally, there was a fifty dollar fine. Loyalty oaths, death certificates and marriage licenses all required stamps. The image of George Washington in various colors and sizes was embossed on the new revenue stamps. The value of the transaction or article determined the stamps required. Proprietary items like playing cards and perfume were taxed at fixed rates. Stamp values eventually would go up to $5,000[53] (Fig. 28).

Playing cards, cosmetics and patent medicines, all "Schedule C" articles, were taxed at retail for revenue stamp purposes. A bottle of perfume required a two cent stamp, the same for a deck of cards. Stationery and tobacco stores sold stamps. The retailers were commissioned at 2 percent on fifty dollars or less on their sales of revenue stamps. The compensation increased to 5 percent if exceeding a thousand dollars. Later post offices carried revenue stamps and postmasters also received commissions. The Postmaster at Mount Holly, Pennsylvania, announced on December 1, 1865, that in the future he would carry an assortment of revenue stamps priced at prevailing Pennsylvania rates (Fig. 29). The complex matrix of stamp categories and denominations created shortages of particular stamps. By the end of the war, stamps became generic and were acceptable if values were correct. Stamps were often unavailable in the West. "Unstamped" paper could be validated if stamps were later affixed, but only if the failure was due to lack of stamps and was not an attempt to defraud the United States. Such was the case in Marshall, Texas, shortly after the war[54] (Fig. 30).

The "Occupational Tax" under the July 1, 1862, Act covered businesses. The Treasury estimated licenses could produce three million dollars annually. If a tradesman or professional did business without a current license, he was fined three times the fee. Exempted were small businesses, defined as one doing less than a thousand dollars annually, but not dealing in tobacco or liquor. Even if a single-day auction, a license was required. Most complex were liquor and beer taxes and permits. If convicted of fraud a dealer could lose inventory, land and personal assets, but actual prosecutions were rare. To control inventory before the excises were paid, merchandise was to be secured in bonded warehouses (Fig. 31). Monthly inspections were conducted to reduce fraud.[55]

Breweries and distilleries prior to the war produced yearly revenue of about ninety million dollars. The industry averaged between two and four million tax dollars annually. Depending upon the scale, brewers and distillers also paid special occupational taxes. The permit for a Business Retail Liquor Dealer was $25.00 (Fig. 32). Brewers manufacturing less than 500 barrels annually paid a $50.00 license fee. High quality forms from the Bureau of Printing and Engraving evidenced payment (Fig. 33). A barrel of beer was thirty-one gallons. For distillers the license under the July 1, 1862, Act was twenty cents a gallon but rose to sixty cents under the March 7, 1864, Act. The Deputy Commissioner of Internal Revenue ruled that inspection fees were set by District Collectors since no standard was provided and were absorbed by manufacturers.[56]

The second "sin tax" was tobacco, as provided in the Acts of July 4, 1862, and June 30, 1864. Tobacco manufacturers displayed current special occupation license to remain open. If a tobacco manufacturer's annual sales were less than $1,000 the license was a mere $5.00. However, if the business produced other products, such as cigars or snuff, a second permit was required. Failure to publicly display a current license was penalized five dollars a day (Fig. 34). In addition to the licenses, the manufacturer was subject to an Internal Revenue excise tax depending on the type of products manufactured. Raw tobacco was assessed at fifteen cents a pound. Smoking tobacco was a nickel and snuff twenty cents. Cheaper cigars were taxed at five dollars a hundred while the best were taxed at $350 per hundred count. The facility was subject to monthly inspections, and filed reports on Form 62 along with the remittance of the monthly excise. During the war, tobacco provided between three and eleven million dollars annually. Petroleum products, in comparison, only provided about a tenth of that sum.[57]

The excise tax as amended March 3, 1863 (Section 68), required manufacturers to also pay a monthly gross sales tax. Failure to file returns or remit the tax could result in the loss of the business and property. Rates depended upon industry. Candle makers were charged 3 percent. Coffee grinders were taxed three mills per pound and confectioners a penny a pound. Originally about a half dozen industries were covered. Auction sales, including real estate, insurance and securities brokers, paid ten mills. These taxes were due ten days from the sale. Railroads, shippers and ferries, included under Section 80 of the Act, paid excises on ticket sales and freight revenue. Banks, insurers and trust companies were taxed 10 percent on dividends paid and other distributions. Excise taxes raised about ten million dollars annually during the war.[58]

The revised excise identified sixty other articles assessable at special rates. In 1863 about $400,000 in excises were collected for luxury carriages, watches and silver plate. Collections for fancy carriages had increased 20 percent. Added were excises on billiard tables and yachts, but only raised $13,000. The Wheeling, Ohio, Tax Collector, D. Howell, District 14, evidenced such luxury tax for $2.00 on December 2, 1863 (Fig. 35). This early excise tax was the exception. Most collecting offices were not organized until the next year. Congress expanded the definition of "luxuries" and added musical instruments, imported spirits and wines. Few voiced concern over such taxes, because these levies provided less than 1 percent of the excise revenue.

Tax experimentation was widespread. Not all was productive. In some instances, the tax was a secondary motive. Such was the case for death and legacy taxes. Several states, Pennsylvania, Maryland, North Carolina and Alabama, had death taxes before the war. Widow legacies and small estates were exempted from the federal death tax. Gifts and transfers to kinfolk were taxed upon the death of the donor. Rates varied according to the degree of heirship if estates were more than $1,000. Direct descendants were taxed ¾ of a percent while nieces and nephews paid 1¼ percent Next in line were aunts and uncles at 3 percent and cousins at 4 percent. Unrelated heirs paid 5 percent. When real property was added on June 30, 1864, widowers were taxed at 6 percent but widows remained tax free. The District Tax Collector of Wayne County, Ohio, issued his first legacy tax receipt to the Executor of the Estate of R.R. Donlly on October 12, 1863, for $54.00. The 3 percent rate indicated that the heirs were aunts and uncles. The taxable estate was $1,800[59] (Fig. 36).

The U.S. tax act of 1862 was slow to evolve. Few realized the scope and complexity of the bureau created. Tax receipts almost always fell short of projections. The National Debt soon passed a billion dollars. Internal revenue at first was only $36 million. From New England came $8 million while the Middle States contributed $16 million and the Western States $7 million. Border States provided $4 million. The Pacific Coast only collected a million dollars. First year occupational taxes provided $154,000, but rose quickly. The territories provided $89,000 in total. The Bureau of Internal Revenue was more productive each year.[60]

Chapter V

Confederate States Taxes, 1862

To make clear the intention of the United States Ports Closure Act of July 13, 1861, President Lincoln proclaimed a blockade of all Southern ports to both foreign and domestic traffic. In retaliation, lawmakers in Texas made illegal all commercial intercourse with "enemy aliens." If such aliens remained within Texas, they had to swear allegiance to the Confederate States of America. If not, they had to leave within twenty days. Any sale, exchange or donation of property to an enemy was treason triable by military commission without the benefit of a jury. The U.S. Navy Gulf Blockading Squadron enforced the blockade out of New Orleans beginning in August 1862. New Orleans had been occupied by General Benjamin Butler's task force from the spring. New Orleans banks were closed to Texans. Although the State began the war debt-free, it had no banks. "Enemy alien" property discovered in Texas was subject to Sequestration, and deposited with receivers.[61]

The loss of New Orleans aggravated the financial problems of the Confederate Treasury in Richmond. Before occupation, the seizure of a million dollars held in gold from the U.S. Mints and Custom Houses in New Orleans helped the Confederates. Eighty percent of expenditures were paid with Treasury notes. Unpaid balances were satisfied with deeply discounted bonds and certificates. Private donations helped support the government's plan. Gold was reserved for foreign purchases.

State tax collections declined across the South. The Texas Comptroller reported a third of the half million ad valorem assessment was delinquent and scheduled for foreclosure. This was similar to the foreclosure rate during the Panic of 1837. The Texas legislature added a four cent specie tax surcharge to fund interest on its one-million-dollar frontier defense loan authorized April 18, 1861. The Tax Commissioner noted that over thirty-four million acres of land had not been rendered for assessment. Texas did collect $128,000 in poll taxes and $43,000 in occupational licenses that year. Governor Francis R. Lubbock on November 15, 1861, advised lawmakers that the treasury had "no gold or silver in its vaults" and strongly recommended that the ad valorem rate increase and the minimum price for public land drop to fifty cents an acre, as first set by the Republic. The consequences of a "cashless" economy bewildered officials.[62]

The "Special Loan Tax" was collected. On October 11, 1862, the Newton County Tax Collector transferred $378 in specie to the Texas Comptroller, to be used to pay the frontier bond interest (Fig. 37). The Arkansas Legislature also adopted emergency measures such as on May 28, 1861, "An Ordinance to Provide Revenue for the State of Arkansas." The state auditor instructed tax collectors "to collect a supplemental tax" of ⅙ of 1 percent on all property assessed that year (Fig. 38). The Pulaski Sheriff on March 4, 1862, acknowledged payment of that "Especial County War Tax for the year 1861" by Christian Deihl on his forty acres, four horses, seven cows and a poll of $5.91 (Fig. 39). In Mississippi, the Jefferson County Sheriff received $1.10 from the guardian of minor Mary E. Montgomery on April 15, 1862. This represented a surtax of 50 percent for the Military Fund (Fig. 40). Counties also issued "scrip" to pay expenses. In Texas, Fayette County issued a $10.00 War Scrip that carried 12 percent interest. The scrip was good for county taxes (Fig. 41). Ersatz taxes substituted for cash in county business.

The Confederate Produce Loan of August 19, 1861, included a "War Tax" provision. Southern assets totaled about $5 billion, half in slaves, 40 percent in land and the balance in cash and securities. The Direct Tax rate of half of 1 percent, with exemptions for families, seemed encouraging. State Tax Collectors were responsible for assessments with payments due by May 1, 1862. Like the federal law, all was delayed. Also, similar to the U.S. Direct Tax, the Confederates offered a prepayment credit to states assuming the obligation for their citizens if paid by April 1, 1862. All, except Texas and Mississippi, took the 10 percent credit for early payment. After the banks in New Orleans suspended specie payments in September 1861, the Treasury forgot about gold or silver payments. Direct Tax receipts did not begin to reach Richmond until the latter half of 1862.[63]

Texas Governor Edward Clark assumed office when Sam Houston resigned after secession. Governor Clark, on November 7, 1861, summarized his war mission. He insisted that the Texas frontier needed to be guarded against "ruthless Indian foes: the lives of our men, women and children, preserved from the tomahawk and scalping knife." Taxes were necessary to that defense. He urged Texans to "cheerfully meet such taxation as may be necessary to carry on our State Government with efficiency." Richmond taxes were only secondary. Alabama Governor A. B. Moore was also not convinced national taxes were the solution. On October 28, 1861, in a letter to President Davis, he described the "War Tax" as "onerous and complicated," but agreed to enforce because of patriotism. He noted the tax was twelve times the peacetime assessments. Chief Tax Collectors for the Confederate States appointed to oversee Direct Tax were: Wm. H. Haliburton (AK), El Blockman (FL), E. Stormes (GA), Robert Lashe (LA), John Hardy (MS), Wm. Lane (NC), Joseph Pope (SC), J. Ramsey (TN), George Durham (TX), and Henry Garnett (VA). The annual administrative cost was about $25,000. In all but Mississippi and Texas, the tax burden was lessened after States paid the Direct Tax apportionments directly.[64]

Confederates were more frugal in pay to their tax collectors and assessors. The October 11, 1862, regulations established precincts for each Congressional district. District collectors earned $400 annually. Assessors earned less and only worked several months. There was difficulty in filling the low-paying jobs. Many did realize that tax positions were safe from conscription. President Davis was not pleased with this loophole. He wrote Governor John Milton of Florida reminding him that such positions were to be reserved for the old and infirm and under no conditions to be filled with "persons qualified for field service." President Davis warned others he would remedy the oversight if improper appointments persisted.[65]

The War Tax due date had a three-week grace period. Late payment penalties were imposed if payment was not made by March 1, 1862. Collectors imposed a 100 percent late penalty. Exempt from assessment were schools, churches and agencies. Delinquent taxpayers could redeem property before the tax auction if penalties and taxes were paid before the redemption deadline expired. If unpaid, public auctions were held in the county where the property was located. Active members of the armed services were spared foreclosure until released from service. If no bids were received, the real estate could be bid on by the government. If purchased by a third party, delinquent taxpayers still had two years to clear tax, penalties and interest outstanding. Direct Tax land foreclosures took place in Texas and Mississippi.[66]

Some Southern lawmakers had argued that Direct Tax assessments should be suspended until a new census was conducted as required by the Constitution. The War Tax was launched with the best information available. President Davis on April 24, 1863, supported that approach, but Congressional debate continued. The Senate Committee overseeing an "Enumeration of Farmers and Planters," did not abandon the new census issue until January 1865. The corresponding House Committee did the same March 13, 1865. Only then was the census debate closed. Pragmatism trumped legalism during war.[67]

The Confederate Treasury eventually gave credit for $16 million of the budgeted $20 million War Tax. The accounting was soft, full of offsets and estimates. Most had made early payments, reduced by discounts. Texas instead collected from its tax payers and sent Treasury notes. Texas Collector for District No. 64 receipted $90.22 on April 10, 1862, for acreage in Lavaca, Washington, Brazos, Karnes and Guadalupe counties (Fig. 42). The Chief Tax Collector of Mississippi, James Hardy, at Canton, on May 17, 1862, accepted $3.60 from the fiduciary of the Estate of C. C. Coleman for land in Yazoo County (Fig. 43). Both those states paid fully their share of War Taxes. Some states, like Georgia and South Carolina, paid the direct tax prior to assessing their citizens. Despite missing discount deadline, full credit was usually allowed. Each year, rules relaxed more.[68]

South Carolina assumed the tax, paid early and took the discount. To fund the transfer, the State floated bonds. Palmetto State taxpayers were given tax bills for their apportioned share. If the taxpayer paid in timely fashion, a 5 percent discount, half the credit previously taken, was allowed. The Estate of General S. Cruikshank received its 5 percent discount from a $120 tax bill by paying before July 31, 1862 (Fig. 44). Georgia had a similar process but retained the 10 percent discount. The Georgia collector at Schley County received the direct tax payment from the Administrator of the Estate of R. W. Stemart in full (Fig. 45).

The southern tax moratorium in Border States was lifted, but few collections were made. The occupation of Louisiana disrupted that State's War Tax efforts. Chief Collector Robert M. Lusher barely escaped capture by Union forces, salvaging papers and tax rolls. Collector Lusher completed his assignment and remitted the Louisiana taxes to Richmond. Amazingly he made an overpayment of $74,000. In Tennessee, after Memphis and Nashville were occupied, collections virtually ceased. State Collector Dr. J. G. M. Ramsey of Tennessee informed the Treasury he expected no more than half the tax assigned. In Huntsville, Alabama, the State Collector exited the city as Union troops approached. His papers were lost. Alabama was given full payment credit. Some Districts were behind enemy lines. South Carolina, Virginia and Florida had entire Collection Districts occupied. The Indian Territory by treaty was exempt from Confederate and Union taxes.[69]

In Arkansas, Chief Collector William H. Haliburton faced different obstacles. Major General Thomas C. Hindman, Commander, Department of the Trans-Mississippi (TMD), headquartered at Little Rock, ordered his officers to "impress" war tax collections and not forward them to Richmond. General Hindman, exhausted of funds, needed to make payroll. Arkansas Senator Charles B. Mitchell apologized for tax delinquencies because of General Hindman's unauthorized action. Senator Mitchell requested credit for the taxes collected, but was denied. Arkansas only forwarded 60 percent of its share of War Tax. Tax records west of Mississippi were few. Similarly valued properties in different states paid different direct tax rates. Equality was only among state tax payers. Each state taxed differently. The allocation anomaly escaped editorial comment.[70]

Even before the tax accounting was available, the Confederate tax office was reorganized. Chief Clerk Thomas Allan became Commissioner of Taxes May 1, 1863. Next, five Chief Collectors were replaced with new appointments: T. C. Green (VA), E. G. Caboniss (GA), G. F. Neill (MS), A. Greenwood (AR) and D. N. Kennedy (TN). Assistant collectors and assessors were hired. Virginia Chief Collector T. C. Green selected Greenbrier resident James C. Spotte to be the assessor for District No. 71 as informed July 28, 1863. The nominated assessor was to forward his loyalty oath, sworn before a justice of the peace, prior to his commission becoming effective. The assessor was to be provided papers, ledgers and forms (Fig. 46). Tax assessors earned three dollars a day plus travel. After passage of the April 1863 act, collection officials in the field increased to almost five hundred persons. The Tax Bureau's Chief Clerk, after the reorganization, oversaw field operations and personnel.

On May 15, 1863, the Confederate Secretary of the Treasury forwarded "Instructions for Collectors of Taxes." Each official was required to execute an oath and forward with a surety bond for faithful performance of duties. Bond amounts depended on expected tax collections. The commercial centers required sureties up to $100,000. Georgia, Louisiana, Mississippi, Virginia and the Carolinas had such limits. The others were between $35,000 and $60,000. Sureties were in $5,000 increments if joint and several bondsmen. District collectors had to be over forty years old or exempt or discharged from military service. Collectors were promised all necessary forms, but seldom received.

After 1863 came to a close, the Confederate States War Tax Office reported 80 percent of the Direct Taxes had been cleared. Discounts, lost collections and waivers were used to satisfy a portion of the allotments. Before the passage of the April 1863 tax act, Secretary Memminger urged Congress to impose more levies against businesses and citizens. If not, he doubted the success of bond issues. Creditors, in his opinion, had little evidence that lawmakers were capable of collecting "permanent taxes." Because most funding was through loans, foreign and domestic, lenders wanted "good faith" efforts to secure repayment. Southerners held three hundred million dollars in cash, notes and securities, available for bond purchases, but timely interest was crucial. The Secretary projected that a new 10 percent sales tax could raise another $28 million annually. North Carolina Governor Z. B. Vance remained skeptical as expressed in his letter of September 7, 1863, to the President, because his voters would simply fail to report sales. Tax resistance was growing.[71]

Past-due real estate taxes in Texas had serious consequences for owners. Postings for Direct Tax delinquencies occurred in the populated counties. Most un-rendered rural land was ignored after the government price was lowered to fifty cents an acre. Collector D. Bragg of Freestone County certified that landowner E. Bolton had rendered and paid his War Tax for 1861 on a quarter section of land in Wise County, thereby avoiding a tax auction sale. Tax payment for property in more than one county was always a problem (Fig. 47). Collector Ben E. Rope of Harris County, held an auction on August 9, 1862, and issued a "Certificate for Purchase of Real Estate at Tax Sale." The auction bidder for the ten auction lots in Block 172, paid $38.00, which included the 20 percent interest charge and costs (Fig. 48). The tax-foreclosed owner had two years to redeem the property. If not redeemed, a "Deed for Unrendered Land Sold for Tax of 1861" was to be issued by the District Collector. Buyer B. F. Weeks held a tax certificate deed for a half section in Bosque County tax foreclosed on W. S. Rather. The 320 acres cost $5.40, or two cents an acre. The tax deed referenced survey and field notes as recorded in Abstract No. 458 of the General Land Office[72] (Fig. 49).

In addition to state and Confederate War Taxes, citizens were assessed municipal, military relief and defense levies locally. Located below the Indian Territory, Grayson County had a "Special War Tax." The assessor accepted payment from an estate on May 12, 1864, for $130.00 (Fig. 50). On March 25, 1863, the Sheriff of Jefferson County, Mississippi, issued a receipt to the Estate of Isaac Garrett for $19.41 in payment of its 1862 County Military and Relief Tax. The military portion was $2.29 and relief was $3.18 on 242 acres of land valued at $968. The Sheriff also collected polls on eight slaves and a five dollar luxury tax. Isaac Garrett was a deceased cotton planter (Fig. 51).

Chapter VI

United States Taxes, 1863

The Union Army securely occupied the civilian populations of Hampton Roads, VA, Port Royal, SC, Beaufort, NC, and New Orleans, LA. Property abandoned by enemies as defined by Article 79 of the Rules of War was collected. If contraband, the goods were either transferred for reuse or destroyed. Perishable goods were consumed as rations by soldiers, refugees and freedmen. If the quantity was large, the goods could be auctioned. No person, loyal or rebel, could file claims for seized contraband. In fact, a person charged under the Articles of War with dealing in contraband was triable before a U.S. Military Commission without benefit of an attorney or jury. On July 13, 1861, Congress had authorized the President to issue a commercial license for dealers to purchase and sell cotton and other valuable commodities acquired from the enemy. This privilege was reserved for political patrons. Licensed cotton dealers could sell cotton at 75 percent of the New York market price. Profits were potentially enormous.[73]

Union enclaves became commercially active. Hilton Head, headquarters of the Department of the South and the South Atlantic Blockading Squadron, was a prime example of profitable occupation. The President realized that freedmen consumed the occupying forces time and effort. No quartermaster could meet such expenditures simply through military appropriations. Self-funding for freedmen and refugees was preferable. E. L. Pierce, head of Contraband Labor at Fort Monroe, was familiar with sustaining former slaves, was requested to devise a plan for cultivating cotton with free labor at Port Royal. Pierce's proposed plan used Treasury cotton superintendents. The solution met with the approval of both President Lincoln and Secretary Chase. This became the Port Royal Experiment. It was only one of several approaches the administration considered without Congressional approval.[74]

West Point graduate Rufus Saxton, Quartermaster of the Port Royal Expedition, was appointed to oversee the free labor cotton experiment. He was promoted to Brigadier General and became Military Governor. By end of the war, he was serving as Assistant Superintendent of the Bureau of Abandoned Lands, Freedmen and Refugees for Georgia and South Carolina. Despite good planning and enthusiasm, the first year's cotton yield was a quarter of Pierce's projections. A late planting, scarcity of tools, seeds and money coupled with an early freeze, reduced the harvest. The second year, superintendents allowed plantation "drivers" to use the old "task" system of work that rewarded industry with less hours. This work schedule had positive results which approached Antebellum yields. Production soon met Pierce's estimates. Cotton funds from auction sales were held by the New York Port Collector. These were the principal funds for freedmen housing and food. Home gardens, a dairy cow, pig pens and chicken coops, kept freedmen villages fed. Shotguns and fishing hooks added protein.[75]

Rebel property continued to be collected by military and Treasury agents. After the port was opened to commercial traffic, abolitionist Theodoric C. Severance, from Cleveland, was appointed the acting Port Royal Revenue Collector. He reported directly to Collector Hiram Barney in New York. Under the Act of March 12, 1863, Treasury Supervisory Special Agents were "to provide for the collection of abandoned property." Edward L. Pierce temporarily held the position from June through August of 1863. He was followed by Albert G. Browne and assistant John H. Pillsbury. Agents earned six dollars a day plus a dime a mile for travel. Acting port inspector, C. Morris and clerks Otis T. Simmonds and Orlando Lead joined Collector Severance at the Hilton Head custom house located across from the long dock at Hilton Head.[76]

U.S. Treasury regulations explained the mechanics of licensing within rebel territory as announced March 12, 1863. The Treasury encouraged Agents collecting captured and abandoned property. Seizures were making planters pay for the war. "Supervising Special Agents" in Saint Louis, Norfolk, Beaufort, Port Royal and New Orleans were active:

Agency	*Region*	*Special Agent*	*Assistants*
1	North Central	Saint Louis William P. Mellen	14
2	Virginia	Norfolk Hansen A. Risley	2
3	North Carolina	Beaufort David Heaton	2
4	South Carolina	Port Royal Albert G. Browne	2
5	South Central	New Orleans Benjamin Flanders	2

Special Agents were lucrative positions with commissions of 5 percent from auction, after expenses were paid. Albert G. Browne at Port Royal had been an attorney from Salem, Massachusetts, and served as Governor John J. Andrew's Military Secretary. Although abolitionists received most Port Royal appointments, some were merely profiteers.[77]

To complete the transfer of seized property from military to U.S. Treasury, the Army's Adjutant General on March 24, 1863, instructed that abandoned and captured property except for contraband, prizes and confiscations be released to Treasury agents who gave receipts after describing condition, quality and location. Treasury Circular, July 3, 1863, described four property categories with separate procedures for each. Abandoned and captured property initially was the most plentiful. Commercial property required inventorying, repairing and renting. The final, confiscated property, was subject to judicial oversight. Owners of confiscated property, loyal and rebel, could file claims for recovery or damage as decided by the Court of Claims. Requests were to be filed within two years of the seizure. Unless the owner was unquestionably loyal, the claim was denied. Slaves were never returned. The fugitive slave act was no longer the "Law of the Land," after the people were deemed abandoned "contraband" property."[78]

Federally licensed cotton dealers in rebel territory were permitted under the Acts of July 13, 1861, and July 1, 1862. Licenses, sales, income and cotton taxes along with revenue stamps were required. Licensed buyers could purchase rebel sugar, tobacco and rice for resale. Except for tobacco and cotton, articles could be auctioned in Saint Louis. Treasury Agents familiar with local markets were responsible for auctions. Structures such as seized warehouses, hospitals or homes were added to the rental pool. Agents were well compensated. The most active Treasury real estate agent was O. N. Cutler of New Orleans. He collected millions of dollars before closing his books in July 1865. In Memphis, Agent George H. Elberg had similar success. Leasing was subject to minimal control and no audits.[79]

Union victories at Vicksburg and Gettysburg during the summer of 1863, divided the Confederacy. Smuggling and blockade running increased afterwards. Luxury goods such as imported brandy, silk and perfume became scarce. Rebel transports unloaded in international waters at the mouth of the Rio Grande, and the foreign ports of Halifax, Havana and Bermuda. George Washington Brackenridge of Texas, a profitable blockade runner, abandoned that enterprise after Vicksburg, moved to New Orleans and took the loyalty oath. Because of his familiarity with the cotton in Texas, he became a New Orleans Special Treasury Agent. He returned to East Texas after occupation to recover Confederate cotton. He earned hefty commissions when the contraband was auctioned.

Applying for a license in rebel territory, required completing an "Application and Affidavit for Special License to Purchase in Insurrectionary States and Ship Northwardly." New Orleans cotton brokers, E. L. Shipp & Company, through its agent R. Clague, made its application to New Orleans Special Agent G. S. Denison July 9, 1864. Loyalty oaths were sworn and fees paid before the permit could be issued. The broker had contracted for five bales of cotton, valued at $2,310.00, in Accession. The permit fee of $92.60 was based on the value of that purchase. Federal revenue stamps were attached to the license. The dealer promised no one would "give aid, comfort, information or encouragement to persons in arms against the United States." This pledge of good behavior followed the shippers promise that he was "in all respects, loyal and true to the government of the United States" (Fig. 52).

Anomalies occasionally occurred during occupied tax administration. Commerce continued regardless of which Army's martial law was enforced. For instance, as the Confederate Direct Tax was being assessed in Beaufort, South Carolina, the Union Expeditionary Force took control of the district. Beaufort property owners were in process of paying their Direct Tax. The Confederate Collector relocated to the mainland at Pocataligo. Within a year, the United States Direct Tax Office was operational for the Beaufort District. It is conceivable that a few taxpayers would pay both taxes. In order to sell land after the war, the Estate of S. Hargrove had to prove all his property taxes, including the 1862 Confederate tax of $57.50, were paid. That rebel tax receipt was affixed with a United States two cent revenue stamp before his land sale could close. Tax officials had few politics other than collections (Fig. 53).

When territory came under federal control, boundaries for Special Treasury Agencies were redrawn on September 11, 1863, and again July 29, 1864. William P. Mellen, of the Saint Louis agency, was promoted to General Agent with two Supervisory Agencies at Nashville and Knoxville reporting to him. That office was re-designated the "Second" after Helena, Natchez and Vicksburg were added. Parts of Arkansas and Mississippi were grouped with New Orleans, which was renumbered the Third Agency. Texas was split from the Fifth and became part of the Fourth. The Port Royal Agency absorbed Eastern Florida. North Carolina joined the Eighth while Virginia and Maryland remained in the Seventh. After capture, Savannah and Charleston became the Eighth. After the war, the Gulf Coast, except New Orleans and Texas, formed the Ninth Agency. This series of re-designations precluded meaningful comparative reports of personnel, receipts and expenses. Those financially benefiting appreciated confusion.[80]

The rules for a licensed trader were detailed in an Executive Order of September 24, 1864, covering storage, documentation, transportation and auction procedures. Traders were independent contractors, assuming risk of loss and entitled to profits, limited to three quarters of the New York market price. Property other than cotton and sugar, were also sold in Cincinnati, Charleston, Savannah and Mobile. Over two million dollars in auction sales were subject to commissions benefiting the Special Agents. New Orleans Special Agent Simon Draper was credited with moving one hundred thousand cotton bales. Ignoring commissions, patronage and fraud, the press reported favorably.[81]

The U.S. Treasury did not disclose sales and commissions paid under the rebel territory license program during the war. On February 20, 1867, Treasury Secretary H. McCulloch provided a tabulation of cotton and other goods sold under the Purchasing Act of July 2, 1864. This report was in addition to an accounting for proceeds from captured and abandoned property. Fifty thousand bales of cotton were auctioned under that program. The average price realized under the cotton program was $143 a bale with costs of about $65 per bale, or a quarter a pound. Gross proceeds exceeded three and a half million dollars. Other than commissions, expenses were about 5 percent. Individual commissions were never revealed. It is estimated in Charleston $100,000 commissions were paid. The St. Louis Special Agency probably received the greatest. New Orleans Special Agents G. W. Dent and G. S. Denison shared commissions on 100,000 bales.[82]

The 1867 Treasury report to Congress detailed captured, collected and abandoned property from April 1, 1861, through the end of the war. Abandoned cotton was about 11,000 bales at Port Royal. This was followed by 156,000 bales found in warehouses and barns. About 20 percent of the seizures later proved to be property of loyal owners. Loyal owners could reclaim property, unless auctioned, then only monetary damages in lieu of cotton could be claimed. About 12 percent of the purchased cotton by Special Purchasing Agents had to be refunded due to fraudulent titles. Abandoned cotton proceeds were two million dollars and captured cotton netted fifteen million. A million dollars from household goods and livestock were noted. No accounting was made for the leasing of seized buildings and dwellings.[83]

The Memphis Bulletin printed a broadside titled "Regulations and Executive and Official Orders, Governing the Purchase of Products in Insurrectionary States." The rules promulgated by Secretary W. P. Fessenden and approved by President Lincoln became effective September 24, 1864. Approved offices for rebel products were Memphis, New Orleans, Nashville, Pensacola, Port Royal, Beaufort and Norfolk. Certified Purchasing Agents were governed by regulations for passes, permits, certificates and safe conduct. Navy Secretary Gideon Welles on December 1, 1864, in General Order No. 42 directed naval vessels on the Mississippi River to adopt measures "to ensure the strict observance" of commercial intercourse in insurrectionary states. Standard surety bonds were required. All auction proceeds, net of expenses, were to be deposited at the most convenient U.S. depository and credited as "purchasing funds" to the benefit of the New York Collector. Revenue stamps were to be added prior to auction. Any unpermitted trader could be charged as an enemy spy.

Dealers normally established friendly relations with Treasury officials. Cotton was often bought from questionable persons. Although reputed owners had necessary paperwork, the actual owners often came forward with proof of fraud. Treasury officials considered such claims. Proof of loyalty was the first prerequisite before any complaint could be processed. All taxes had to be paid before the claim was resolved. Any refund of taxes were made by filing Internal Revenue Form No. 47 "Claim for Remission of Taxes" (Fig. 54). Defrauded owners certified ownership, loyalty and amount of loss. Supporting documents, affidavits, depositions and witness statements completed the package. If a claim was approved by the District Collector, the file was forwarded to the Washington Court of Claims. If approved, the actual refund awaited Congressional appropriation for payment.

If an unlicensed dealer was caught smuggling, he could be referred to a Military Commission as provided under War Department General Order No. 257 of September 15, 1864. Illegal cotton dealers from both sides of the Mason-Dixon Line, were active in the Mississippi Delta. Treasury officials often were bribed to facilitate shipments and paperwork. The "Red River" cotton rings received wide coverage in the Northern press. As a result, in May 1862 Collector Benjamin P. Flanders replaced Charles L. Latrop as the Third Special Agent of the "Gulf District." In June 1863, Secretary Chase appointed his nephew, George S. Denison, to coordinate the purchasing program. Secretary of the Navy Gideon Welles questioned the integrity of Denison due to a bad reputation. Denison afterwards became a "Cotton Surveyor" at New Orleans. His replacement was Special Agent Cuthbert Bullitt. Collector Bullitt gave notice May 3, 1863, that he would abolish the "Blackmail and Monopoly" by sutlers doing business in his district. The region's Commanding General had favorably endorsed Collector Bullitt's appointment. By summer, requests required truthful affidavits and command approval.[84]

Career officers were often outraged by such clandestine operations. General U.S. Grant, after reports of corruption in New Orleans, detailed Lieutenant Colonel James Hughes Stoker to investigate the situation and report back. Colonel Stoker, from Maryland, although a West Point graduate, had few friends among line officers because he was an "auditor" from a Border State. After performing a cursory review, he recognized the fraud, bribery and corruption. A hundred thousand dollars was missing from the "Corps dé Afrique" hospital fund. Most wrongdoers purged their records. He forwarded his report to Washington, but the accused officers closed ranks. Files necessary to his report vanished. Little resulted from the Stoker Audit Report besides the end of his career.[85]

Few illicit trades made it to trial. If convicted, the standard penalty was a cease and desist order along with a minimal fine. Such was the case in Vicksburg. Two relatives of the District Commanding Officer, Major General Napoleon V. T. Dana, were caught with unlicensed cotton loaded on their boat, the *Golden Gate*. Such craft were called a "Cotton Thief." Elisha Tracy and George Moore, agents of the cotton firm G. W. Graham and Conway of New Orleans, had obtained fraudulent papers from the Provost Office. The two were put in irons, placed below deck and transported for a trial before a Military Commission. The referring officer did not wish to disguise "his opinion the two were among the traitors and enemies of the country" who come with "lots of money to buy cotton" behind enemy lines. Tracy and Moore, in the referring officer's opinion, were only "a sample of a multitude which have long infested this valley, to the great injury of the nation and of the cause for which our troops are shedding their blood." Small fines were imposed (Fig. 55).

The "cotton rings" in New York City became legendary. Collector Hiram Barney was arrested by the U.S. Marshal for illegal dealings by order of the Secretary of War. The charge was communicating with the enemy. The prior year, New York Deputy Collector Henry B. Stanton and his son were accused of providing fraudulent papers for shipments from Brownsville and Mobile to New York. Although Collector Barney was subpoenaed to testify before Congress, he was never charged. After the November 1864 election, President Lincoln replaced Collector Barney with the New York "whimsical bagman" Simon Draper, who was part of "Boss" Tweed's gang. Draper's appointment was given in return for his Republican Club's support for President Lincoln's re-election.[86]

Accusations and subpoenas did not deter the New York "cotton rings." Special Treasury Agent Hanson A. Risley, whose office was in the Astor House Hotel, conspired with George S. Denison of New Orleans. Naval officers had long complained that smuggled shipments of cotton from Mobile, Brownsville and New Orleans had falsified papers. Secretary of the Navy Gideon Welles long accused Draper and Denison as "swindlers" and predicted they would benefit "regardless of public or private rights."[87]

Seized property, tariffs and excises, little reduced the Treasury's debt issues. The currency used to purchase cotton was "Greenback Dollars." Regardless of Confederate laws making it a felony to accept Union money, the "greenbacks" were preferred if offered. A revealing entry in the ledger book of the Camden, Arkansas, Confederate Depository reveals how collectors, postmasters and agents exchanged Confederate notes, at face value, for captured "greenbacks." At the Camden Depositary, Brown, closing out his accounts in 1864, paid his back salary with "greenbacks" he had exchanged for old currency. Despite the enormous flow of greenbacks, values were closer to gold than Confederate money. Legal tender was more valuable than the rebel shinplasters. "Greenbacks" were circulating notes bearing no interest. This massive interest-free loan was consumer welcomed.

Congress declared circulating notes, "greenbacks," as "legal tender," and merchants and soldiers accepted the currency as payment at face value. No rejection or discounting was allowed. Another monetary innovation to the benefit of the war effort was the National Banking system. Inspired by Alexander Hamilton's Bank of the United States, enacted February 25, 1791, central banks provided government funds "in sudden emergencies." The original loan limit was $400,000 and only $50,000 could assist any state, and only twice that amount was available to the central government. The Second United States Bank of 1816 was capitalized for $35 million and managed by twenty-five directors of which most were appointed by the President. Interest was limited to 12 percent and specie redemption of circulating notes required. The Act of June 23, 1836, dispersed that capital among state-chartered banks. The charter expired. United States circulating notes, beginning March 3, 1837, were withdrawn from circulation.[88]

The 1860 Census counted over 1,600 state-chartered banks with capital totaling $430 million with $200 million in deposits. Three-quarters were located in loyal states. New Orleans was home to the most solvent Southern banks. Western "wildcat" banks were known for bankruptcies and unbridled emission of worthless notes. These were deeply discounted by Eastern institutions. The Panic of 1837 closed many of the thinly capitalized banks. Treasury Secretary Chase, from Ohio, was familiar with the risks and perils of unregulated banks based on experience as a bank lawyer. He recommended that U.S. notes be legal tender and emitted through a national banking system.[89]

Secretary Chase's legal tender and banking recommendations of 1861 were initially rejected. After battlefield setbacks in 1862, the deficit and military back pay grew, causing Secretary Chase and Jay Cooke, Ohio investment banker, to campaign for banking reform. Advertisements in commercial centers detailed the benefits of the National Bank Act. Key provisions were a national currency, regional bank charters and fiscal agent. Conversion of existing state chartered banks into federal institutions was encouraged. Initially there were minimal additional requirements. State circulating notes were to be replaced with federal currency or be subject to tax.[90]

After the victories at Gettysburg and Vicksburg, Congress authorized another $250 million bond issue priced to yield 7 percent interest. The Treasury had already suspended gold redemption of circulating notes. Momentarily, the change dampened imports but improved the balance of payments. Early success convinced the New York Chamber of Commerce the changes were not detrimental to business. In fact, business in general was better off. The Treasury had to issue notes suitable for low value transactions because of the disappearance of change. After the suspension of specie payments, small coins were hoarded. Small change notes were treated similar to legal tender. Every day transactions, like the purchase of postal and revenue stamps, also required a medium of exchange.

U.S. Custom Houses required importers to pay duties in gold. Such specie supplemented California gold deliveries. Gold increased with the war and inflation. The South had no gold reserves and their bonds were "junk" in European bourses. Although the federal debt grew exponentially, rebel debt was even more out of hand. The Treasury sold gold reserves at substantial profits, adding more to the Treasury. The war was as economic as martial.[91]

After martial law was imposed in occupied New Orleans, banks were allowed to reopen after proving loyalty to the Union and giving the "Oath." New Orleans banks had suspended specie payments in September of 1861, forcing their customers to accept Confederate Treasury notes in payment for withdrawals. This caused "great distress, privation, suffering, hunger and even starvation." The discredited Confederate currency was worthless. Major General Benjamin Butler issued General Orders No. 30, May 19, 1862, ending the issuance of this "worthless stuff." In the future banks could only pay depositors with U.S. Treasury notes, their own currency or specie. Small change notes issued by banks could be in denominations between one and five dollars. Privately issued "shinplaster" in denominations between one and ten dollars had to be reserved with gold for 50 percent of the value.

Creditors preferred gold to money. Suspension of specie redemptions was never popular, however "greenbacks" were preferable to no payment at all. Sympathetic federal purchasing agents often allowed favored contractors to add "juice" to the contract to cover losses from inflation or delayed payment. New York banks on the average reported 12 percent return on capital, twice pre-war levels. State banks circulating notes were highly taxed. State chartered notes were $167 million in 1863, but were declining. State warrants and merchants scrip were discounted and also disappeared.[92]

Under the Currency Act of July 11, 1862, the U.S. Secretary was allowed $35 million in small change notes, ranging in denomination from one to five dollars, issued in August 1862. The notes, on their face, reminded the public such were lawful money "in payment of all debts, public and private, within the United States." (Fig. 56). Prior to that issue, five dollars had been the minimum denomination. Soon, counterfeiters appeared, especially for higher valued notes. Counterfeiting, a capital offense since the Revolution, was a felony, punishable by fifteen years in prison and a $5,000 fine. To substitute for the lack of small change, postal stamps were regularly used in retail transactions. Stamps were used for change as often as for postage.

Ohio Senator John Sherman, on January 8, 1863, delivered a speech entitled "Taxation of Bank Bills." He listed the benefits of a single currency during times of emergency. He recalled that both Alexander Hamilton and James Madison had come to that same conclusion. To silent "hard money" advocates, he promised that as soon as the Union was restored and normal commerce resumed, "greenbacks" would be withdrawn from circulation. The nation would resume specie redemptions. Senator Sherman acknowledged that Congress could "strike dead" all state notes, but he favored a softer solution. He proposed a 2 percent bank note penalty tax for state issues. For shinplasters and private fractional currency, he suggested a 10 percent tax.[93]

That same month, the U.S. Treasury issued an additional $250 million to meet "the exigencies of the public service, for the payment of the Army and Navy and other creditors of the Government." On March 3, 1863, Treasurer Frances E. Spinner issued "Postal Currency" as authorized by the Act of July 17, 1862. "Postal Currency" was good for all dues, other than customs, owed to the government if presented for debts less than five dollars (Fig. 57). A second series, termed "fractional currency," was part of the same bill. The fractional notes were to be furnished by Assistant Treasurers and Designated Depositories. These were "receivable for all United States Stamps." Contrary to tradition of not using the likeness of living persons on money or stamps, fractional currency carried portraits of Treasury Secretary William Fessenden and Treasurer Spinner (Fig. 58).

Senator Sherman's "Bank Bill Tax" was part of the National Bank Act of February 25, 1863. The penalty tax started at 1 percent. State chartered institutions began to convert to federal charters. Once chartered, the banks could issue greenbacks in their own name. Two other taxes, occupational licenses and income taxes were applied to banks, at relatively low rates. State bank currency was taxed. The office of Comptroller of Currency was charged with regulating, auditing and reporting on the national banking system. The semi- annual reports and statistics kept Congress and the Administration informed.[94]

To assure safety and soundness of the National Banking system, the law required banks to deposit United States bonds representing a third of their capital. Such reserves determined the amount of greenbacks a bank could issue.

National bank notes essentially were interest free loans to the Treasury. Lawmakers appreciated the disappearance of wildcat banks. Retained federal "reserves" allowed the Treasury to protect depositors and spread the risk of insolvency of troubled institutions. Annual reports to the Comptroller's Office, were filed with the Commissioner of Internal Revenue to assist collection of bank taxes, that ranged from ½ percent for community banks to 1 percent for larger.[95]

Hugh McCulloch, a former bank president from Indiana, was the first Comptroller of Currency, earning an annual salary of $5,000. Comptroller McCulloch furnished a surety bond of $100,000. In his message to Congress on December 8, 1863, President Lincoln stated that the National Banking System would support public credit to meet "all demands on the Treasury including the pay of the Army and Navy." National bank charters numbered sixty-six at the time. Regulated national banks, national currency and favorable markets all benefited the Treasury. By war's end, almost $300 million was in circulation, saving almost twenty million dollars a year in interest payments.[96]

The first bank to receive a national currency was the Bank of Philadelphia. By war's end, the number of charters exceeded five hundred. State banks, about 1,500 institutions before the act, dropped to twenty by 1866. National banks reported $1.5 billion in revenue. Large money center banks such as New York dominated the market. These largest institutions only moved money within their vaults to meet reserves rather than physical transfers. Redemption designated banks were required to have within their vaults a quarter of their statutory reserves. Reserves were defined as 40 percent of vault cash for small banks and 60 percent for redemption center banks.[97]

New York, Boston and Philadelphia deposits grew dramatically as the federal banking system grew. Taxing banks was easier for Congress. On July 30, 1864, the lawmakers increased the state bank note penalty to 10 percent. Closure of state chartered banks accelerated. After the war, only one such institution existed and that was in Mississippi. During Reconstruction, two-thirds of the federally chartered banks were domiciled in five states and responsible for half of the greenbacks in circulation. Redemption Center states were New York, Pennsylvania, Massachusetts, Ohio and Indiana.[98]

Bank failures dropped to five annually. Money center banks paid dividends to shareholders averaging 15 percent, more than twice the prewar payout. The 10 percent penalty tax, signed into law by President Lincoln just prior to his death, was modified by Congress July 13, 1866. The "excise" tax contributed over $140 million to the Treasury over the next forty years. The revenue covered engraving and printing costs. Actual expenses were only 12 percent of the tax collected. In 1869, the U.S. Supreme Court approved the bank currency tax.[99]

A subsequent Comptroller of Currency, John S. Williams of Virginia, remarked on the wartime banking experience in his 1917 Report to Congress. Comptroller Williams observed that during the national emergency, regulatory agencies seldom revealed policy or objectives behind administrative actions. He confirmed what had been long suspected. The Redemption Center banks charged up to 14 percent interest even to credit-worthy customers. Men of commerce only began to question the policy after peace. The Comptroller was of the opinion that it was a "well merited condemnation" of the industry. Congress had viewed banks as "utilities" dedicated to the public good during war. All expected federal oversight to curtail "profiteering." Such an assumption was false.[100]

Legal tender notes and national bank notes are often confused. Legal tender notes were part of a $300 million issue that could be fundable, at the option of the holder, into 6 percent bonds. The option to exchange into interest paying bonds was modified March 3, 1863, and placed a July 1, 1863, deadline on that privilege. Few notes were exchanged. The bulk of national currency was national bank notes with no conversion privilege. The Banking Act of June 30, 1874, retained the bank reserve requirements. The Superintendent of the National Bank Redemption Agency became the depository for U.S. bonds held in trust for chartered banks. Not until the bank cashier received notice from the Superintendent that the 5 percent reserve was fulfilled could banking operations begin.[101]

Chapter VII

Confederate States Taxes, 1863

As federal banking was taking shape, Confederate finances worsened. Tax programs successful in the North were duplicated but dissimilar conditions doomed most from the start. Inflation, the lack of gold, and unrestricted note and bond emissions precluded either a central bank or currency. Soldiers, suppliers and creditors were forced to accept fiat money with ever increasing devaluation. "Fiat money" beat no money at all. States also flooded the market with their own variety of scrip and warrants. The Confederate Congress was forced into refunding that was on a trajectory toward total debt repudiation. This was particularly embarrassing to a Congress that was against debt in all forms. A commodity-based economy founded on agricultural credits was incapable of funding a war once the blockade was effective.

Barter, exchange and oral promises replaced banking. Cotton enrollment agents encouraged planters and dealers to exchange cotton for produce loans. The Servier County, Arkansas, enrollment officer, Matthew W. Lock, appointed by the Chief of the Trans-Mississippi Cotton Department, W. Warren Johnson, was empowered by Special Order No. 4 of Major General Hindman on June 26, 1862, to gather cotton. Enroller Lock, at the conclusion of his transactions, receipted the bales taken, averaging five hundred pounds each. The son of cotton grower Nazareth Wilder turned over seventy-five bales to the cotton agent August 13, 1862, expecting produce loan bonds when printed (Fig. 59).

Suggestions from the press and public offered fixes to the Confederate Congress. Mississippi Senator Albert G. Brown, on February 4, 1862, suggested a "cotton tax" of $20 a bale at the grower level. Smaller farms would be exempted. Mississippi Representative J. W. Clapper on March 26, 1862, presented a plan that allowed producers to pay taxes with in-kind commodities. Neither motion made it out of committee. The bills did harken "Tithe" and "In Kind" taxes. These biblical levies held allure for the Bible Belt taxpayers who preferred "sharing" crops rather than paying taxes. As commodities rose in value, the willingness to share waned. Socialism was not a part of the Confederate creed.

More dreaded than collectors and enrollers were "impressment officers." These free agents could seize private property even from friendlies. Foodstuffs, fodder and draught animals were never safe. General Hindman instructed his Arkansas agents to seize tax collections. General H. E. McCulloch in Nacogdoches also ordered tax collectors to turn over funds so his paymaster could make payroll. Seizures became so common that Galveston Depositary James Sorely publicly apologized to creditors for delinquent payments. He explained that tax seizures precluded him from clearing accounts in a timely fashion. Sorely estimated the tax revenue loss to be $100,000. Sorely's complaint was made with risk. General McCulloch had threatened that any person resisting his orders would be treated as a traitor.[102]

The tax seizures reached the desks of the Confederate Secretaries of War and Treasury. Both Departments declined to comment, and referred the matter to Confederate Attorney General, T. H. Watts. He, too, elected to sidestep the issue, sensing political fallout. Watts did advise the remedy was a claim to the Treasury Department. General McCulloch continued and matters worsened. Martial law increased impressments. As much as a tenth of garden crops and livestock were taken from loyal citizens in some rural areas. Targeted small farmers were the most vulnerable.[103]

Public protest eventually forced the Confederate Congress to take action. The Impressment Acts of March 26, April 6 and April 27, 1863, addressed some of the complaints. Citizens suffering damages from impressments were given a new claims process. Compensation was available according to price schedule for each produce, animal and foodstuff. If posted prices were not agreed, the claimant could appeal to the State Claims Commission. Most accepted the scheduled prices because of ease and time. Each State Board was appointed by the President and Governor. Despite the effort, complaints persisted. The Army's Inspector General on April 6, 1863, reminded field commanders to impress only what is necessary and never deprive citizens of essentials. The order was read but not followed.[104]

Armies on the move outpaced supply trains. Foraging squads scouted the line of march in search of edibles and fodder. If in retreat, impressment agents took draft animals to replace those lost in combat. Protocols defined the limits of seizures but exigencies trumped the rules. General J. B.

Hood while at Petersburg, Virginia, ordered his agents to impress all draft animals available. Under his order of May 6, 1863, his Provost Marshal seized two horses and bridles, the property of James H. Herring. Conditions precluded value negotiations (Fig. 60). A year later, circumstances had worsened. General Polk's impressment officer, in March 1864, seized a mule then valued at $1,000. The owner was paid half in Confederate money, but had to file a claim with the Montgomery Commission for the balance (Fig. 61).

Chemicals and medicines were always in short supply. Created April 22, 1863, "The Niter and Mining Bureau," within the Confederate War Department, was charged with locating and securing mining and production of strategic minerals and chemicals. Agencies existed in Alabama, Georgia and Virginia. The Bureau had six chemists. Coal, iron and copper mines and foundries were included. The Bureau evolved into fourteen districts, one in the Trans-Mississippi run by chemist T. G. Clemson at San Antonio. It was common for Niter Bureau agents, such as Major Isaac Reid of Texas, to impress an entire mine or foundry. Georgia Governor Joseph E. Brown on November 9, 1863, complained to the Secretary of War about impressments of his state's facilities. He claimed the agents were "robbing contrary to the intentions of Congress." He complained "price schedules" for ores and chemicals were inadequate.[105]

Farmers realized hams, chickens and corn were an invitation to impressment agents. Whether seeking bacon for the commissary or oxen for the quartermaster, the Army was detrimental to the farmer's livelihood. Payment in "fiat money" was of little value to a small farmer losing his only mule. Hard assets had increasing value. The Virginia Impressment Claims Commission published a compensation schedule for the War Department December 4, 1863. The standard price for a horse was $250 and hiring a team was ten dollars a day. Beef cattle brought sixteen cents a pound, but exempted dairy and breeding animals. Congress, on March 24, 1864, responded to Governor Brown's complaints. In the future, small farmers could retain half their crops. A year later, Congress suspended all price schedules because inflation had rendered all unrealistic. Mules were up to $1,200.[106]

Cotton was most targeted of all commodities. Treasury agents were responsible for care, custody and transport of purchased, seized and tax-in-kind cotton. The second most seized property was slave labor. Even before Fort Sumter, planters loaned slaves for construction of harbor defenses. Compensation was set by official rates. Major General Dabney H. Maury, District of the Gulf, modified earlier schedules after the changes made by Congress in April 1863. Impressments were evidenced by duplicate receipts, one to the owner. The standard form had categories for tools, draft animals, wagons, forage and provisions. Owners could elect to provide food for their slaves and receive a higher day rate or accept government rations for a lower. Three slaves, Mark, Ezekiel and George, had meal and bacon provided according to his receipt of September 2, 1863 (Fig. 62). General Mercer's Provost at Americus, receipted $629.30 for slave laborers used in Georgia "defence" (Fig. 63). Impressment of slaves was taking of private property. Ironically, this was the central complaint of the secessionists before the war.

On May 18, 1863, the Confederate States Secretary of War had promulgated nationwide impressment prices provided by the Virginia Price Commission, consisting of E. W. Hubard, Robert Gibbons and William B. Harrison. These guidelines were about half retail value. The prices were announced through War Department General Order No. 65. Claimants could now appeal to State Commissions, who were notoriously tight-fisted and seldom awarded premiums. Schedule "A" of the circular covered commodities, foodstuffs and dry goods. Schedule "B" set rates for cotton, bagging, rope and hired wagons. Impressed slaves were valued at $2 a day or $40 a month if provisions provided. The Commissions advised impressment agents not to seize edibles if needed by locals. Price schedules were periodically updated but lagged behind inflation. Draft animals were the most expensive items impressed.

After the battlefield losses in Pennsylvania and Mississippi during the summer of 1863, the Confederate Treasury approached insolvency. Impressments only aggravated dispirited citizens. Government contractors demanded specie before they would provide services for printing, telegraph and transportation. The Secretary of State in an open letter stated that "the first great error was in attempting to carry on a great and expensive war, solely on credit—without taxation." His letter predicted that only with "comprehensive, simple and equal" system of taxation could government credit worthiness be maintained. A tax system had evolved to "foster vulgar prejudices ... frauds and perjuries." Impressment and forced funding were no substitute for economic policy. Some men of commerce realized the inevitable was approaching. Relocations and shifts in loyalty followed. If soldiers followed their lead, it was desertion.[107]

Congressmen needed a new tax plan. The public was hard to convince such would reduce inflation and impressments. The Tax Act of April 24, 1863, added excise, levies and licenses designed to capture revenue from all but the very poor, churches and schools. Ambiguities in the drafting hindered assessments. Profiteers and speculators operated "duty free" through subterfuge and fraud. Confederate tax officials always expected evasion. The dishonest benefited from shortages through the black market. Alexander Stevens in Augusta, Georgia, noted that the passage of another tax would not be welcomed, but understood the necessity. Trans-Mississippi General Kirby Smith wrote Richmond that he had not received any new tax assessors and collectors. Tax execution lagged behind enactment. Delays were never recoverable.[108]

On July 2, 1863, the Confederate Congress added an 8 percent property tax, a 10 percent tax excess profits tax, a luxury tax and a progressive income tax up to15 percent. Chief Tax Clerk Thomas Allen was promoted to Commissioner of the Tax Bureau. Soon collectors, assessors and their deputies exceeded five hundred people. A tenth of the tax districts were behind enemy lines. The most productive section of the new law was "Tax In Kind." The produce collected under the "Tithe Tax" was to be transferred to Assistant Quartermaster, Colonel Larkin Smith. Regional superintendents held the rank of major. Depot or "post" quartermasters, who oversaw warehouses, were captains. This tax borrowed from medieval Europe was the most effective fiscal act adopted by the Confederate Congress. It also, was the most evaded. It was never considered by the United States Congress.[109]

Section 11 of the July 2, 1863 "Tithe Tax" Act targeted planters, dealers, farmers and stockmen. The assessment process began while the crops were in the field. Producers negotiated with assessors as to yields and their family exemptions. The most valued crop was always cotton. If the owner failed to agree with the assessor, he could appeal, but the produce was collected. Tax In Kind precincts corresponded to Congressional Districts. Delivery of produce was sixty days from notice. Compliance varied with assessors. The more distant a taxpayer from the seat of government, the more flexible the collectors. Kinship, friendship and bribes were realities the Treasury was powerless to lessen.

Major Benjamin Botts, Chief of the Trans-Mississippi Tax Bureau, effective September 1, 1864, coordinated the impressments of cotton with the Treasury. He had the difficult task of competing with state agents. His agencies in Alexandria, Houston, San Antonio, Goliad and Brownsville had numerous post depots. Farmers avoided all collections. Post Quartermaster T. C. Clark, through agent M. Pearson, at Smith's Ferry, warned those in that district subject to Tax In Kind that failure to file estimates by the deadline would cause a 500 percent penalty (Fig. 64).

All produce and commodities were covered in forms "to lay taxes for the common defense and carry on the government of the Confederate States." For commercial centers, forms arrived in the fall. Specialized schedule, with instructions interpreting the law were available in Columbia, South Carolina, when Allen Davis negotiated with his assessor, S. Beard, his corn, hay and fodder. His "Tithe Tax" was $16.00, one-tenth the estimated yield as of November 27, 1863. Davis used his family exemption for garden crops that allowed fifty bushels of sweet and Irish potatoes, a hundred bushels of corn, fifty bushels of wheat, twenty bushels of peas and beans. The assessment when completed was sworn to by Davis (Fig. 65).

Under Section I, V and X of the Tax Act of April 24, 1863, businessmen had to swear that they had remitted true assessment Lists for:

List No. 1 (Naval Stores, Spirits)

On the value of all naval stores, salt, wine, spirituous liquors, tobacco, manufactured and unmanufactured cotton, flour, sugar, molasses, syrup, rice and other agricultural products, held or owned on the 1st July 1863, and not necessary for family consumption for the unexpired portion of the year and of the growth or production of any year proceeding the year 1863, a tax of eight per centum is levied, and, on all moneys, bank notes, or other currency on hand or on deposit, the value of all credits on which the interest has not been paid, held or owned on the 1st day of July 1863, and not employed in business, the income of which is taxed under said act, and on all moneys held, owned or deposited beyond the limits of the Confederate States, a tax of 1 percent is levied. All moneys owed, held or deposited beyond the limits of the Confederate States, are to be valued at the current rate of exchange in confederate treasury notes.

List No. 2 (License for Occupation)

Trades, business and occupations required to be registered and taxed and were subject to a tax upon gross receipts and sales, to wit: Bankers, auctioneers, wholesale dealers in liquors, wines, distilled spirits and fermented liquors of every kind. Retail dealers in liquors, wines, distilled spirits and fermented liquors. Retail dealers of goods, wares, groceries and merchandise of every description. Wholesale dealers of goods, wares, merchandise of every description and groceries. Pawnbrokers, distillers, brewers, keepers of hotels, inns, taverns and eating houses, brokers, commercial brokers or commission merchants, tobacconists, theaters, circuses, jugglers, bowling alleys, billiard tables, livery stable keepers, cattle brokers, butchers, peddlers, apothecaries, photographers, lawyers, physicians, surgeons and dentists actually engaged in the practice but not to include physicians and surgeons exclusively engaged in the confederate service and collections.

List No. 3 (Profits)

On all profits made by any person, partnership or corporation, during the year 1862, by the purchase within the Confederate States, and sale, during said year, of any flour, corn, bacon, pork, oats, hay, rice, salt, iron, or the manufacture of iron, sugar, molasses mad of cane, leather, woolen cloth, shoes, boots, blankets and cotton cloths, but not to apply to purchases and sales made in the due course of the retail business, a tax of ten per centum is to be levied and collected on the 1st day of July 1863, or as soon thereafter as practicable.

The Naval Stores and wine list was originally due July 1, 1863, but was delayed. Wealthy Virginia merchant John Purcell, of Richmond, agreed to values with assessor, A. P. Johnson, on September 15, 1863. The tax was $448 and included manufactured tobacco and canned turpentine. The retail storekeeper also reported $44,260 in gold, silver and cash for which he was assessed $442.60 for a total tax bill of $890.60. Purcell had earlier financed Purcell's Battery (Fig. 66). The Richmond standard forms never reached the Trans-Mississippi. After delays, General Kirby Smith instructed agents to use local job press forms, although crude. The Chief Purchasing Officer of the 7th District forwarded a sample of such forms to his Post Quartermasters (Fig. 67)

Tax In Kind was passed to reduce discretionary impressments, but had problems. After complaints, C.S. Secretary of War James Selden, on November 26, 1863, communicated to the President that although the "Tithe Tax" was passed "to obviate the issue of notes and the resort to impressments," the public was not pleased and impressments continued. The assessment process was slow and inflexible. The C.S. Adjutant General had earlier advised Post Quartermasters they could continue impressments "where the exigencies of the Army compel." Impressments did not decline. On April 24, 1864, the Attorney General withdrew that opinion. Secretary Selden by June 30, 1864, concluded that the Tax "has proved a more valuable resource for the subsistence of the armies." Collected tobacco bypassed Post Quartermasters and went directly to market. No free smokes for soldiers.[110]

The Confederate income tax was progressive. Above the personal exemption of $500, rates initially began at 5 percent. Businesses were allowed to deduct costs of sales and manufacturing, repairs, labor and a 10 percent depreciation allowance. Insurance companies could subtract losses paid to policy holders before computing tax on investment income and premiums collected. Corporations and joint stock companies had rates starting at ten and rising to a maximum of 20 percent. Mules, raised cattle and horses if not draft animals were assessed 1 percent of value. Beef cattle raisers paid sales taxes. Farm animals such as chickens, lambs and hogs raised for personal consumption were exempted.[111]

The Confederate Tax Act of April 24, 1863, had provisions for retail and wholesale merchants. Most were subject to sales and occupational taxes:

Business/Occupation	*License*	*Sales Tax*
Auction	$450	2½%
Wholesale Liquor	$200	5%
Retail Liquor	$100	10%
Distillers	$200	2½%
Brokers	$200	20%
Theaters	$500	2½%
Butchers and Bakers	$50	1%

Sales taxes were due quarterly and license annually. Other licensed professions included bankers ($50), lawyers ($50), physicians ($50), dentists ($50) and pawnbrokers ($200). Shows and livery stables paid $50. Pool halls and bowling alleys paid $40 per table or lane. Hotels, inns, restaurants and taverns were charged according to the quality of the facility. First- through third-class establishments paid $500, $300 and $200 respectively. Low-quality boarding houses paid only $30. Room upgrades from economy to first class had a tax cost.

Assessments and collections were interrupted by enemy action. Officials and records fell into enemy hands. Merchant and circus proprietor Henry S. Matlby, of Corpus Christi, Texas, delayed filing his quarterly sales tax and 1863 annual license because the Union Navy was offshore. He did not remit $2,500 in sales and $50 occupation fee until June 4, 1864. Late penalties were waived. Merchant Matlby's rate was 2½ percent (Fig. 68). Matlby also operated a circus and filed a "Certificate of Registry" costing $50, July 25, 1864.

States also imposed license fees, for distillers, ferrymen and auctioneers. A license in no way gave any right to conduct a business. It was simply an excise tax, not a permit. Business regulations were for state and municipal authorities. Anderson County, Texas, peddler D. H. Love, made payment of his annual fee on May 4, 1865, to District Collector J. H. McKnight. This was just prior to the surrender of the Department of the Trans-Mississippi. At that time, inflation was so high the peddler paid with $100 in Confederate money and $31.50 in Texas warrants. This was three times the fee, but Love needed to continue his livelihood (Fig. 69).

Confederate Treasury notes eventually arrived in Texas. Lack of personnel and funds had delayed implementation of the 1863 Tax Act. Emergency measures were imposed. To control smuggling into Mexico, custom stations along the Rio Grande collected cotton taxes. Flour merchant Major Simion Hart, of El Paso, oversaw the traffic through San Antonio. After lax enforcement, General Kirby Smith instructed Major Hart to strictly enforce tariffs for cotton being exported to Mexico. Peculiar to the Department were "Cotton Certificates" reflecting that the cotton tax had been paid. Cotton shipper O. C. Phelps paid $51.20 on his three bales to Collector J. W. Brooks November 10, 1863[112] (Fig. 70).

Cotton was so financially essential to the Trans-Mississippi

Department that a Cotton Bureau was created. Lieutenant Colonel W. A. Broad was in charge. Cotton planters, shippers and dealers were permitted to ship cotton on government vessels or transport bales into Mexico after taxes were paid. Smugglers and blockade runners avoided such duties. Competing with Colonel Broad were agents working for the Texas Military Board. Smugglers took advantage of the competing agencies. Dishonest agents allowed traffic tax free. Fraud prompted some planters to distill grains into moonshine rather than be impressed.

Chapter VIII

United States Taxes, 1864

George S. Boutwell, the U.S. Commissioner of Internal Revenue, assumed office the summer of 1862 and began organizing for implementation of the new tax laws. It is four Deputies were New Yorker C. F. Estee, responsible for regulations, rulings and Tax Guide. Second Deputy, Joseph J. Lewis of Pennsylvania, as legal counsel, worked with Congress. Businessman William Otren of New York used his experience in industry to solve practical problems. Administration was assigned to Deputy E. A. Rollins of New Hampshire, who was second in charge. Rollins nominated District Commissioners, Collectors and Assessors. Starting with only three field commissioners, that number grew to ten by the end of the war. Clerks grew from only 68 to over 3,000.[113]

Secretary Chase was most sensitive to political matters. On November 27, 1863, Secretary Chase informed "each tax collector in Missouri" that no U.S. Revenue Stamp would be required for oaths of delegates to the upcoming St. Louis Convention. "Iron Clad Oaths" would be revenue stamp free at this political convention, regardless of literal reading of the statute. A copy of Secretary Chase's telegram was forwarded to U.S. Representative H. T. Blow, a Missouri Republican Congressman, and member of the Joint Committee on Reconstruction. Tax questions, if of political consequence, were usually decided in the Secretary's office.

The U.S. Tax Bureau's meager five-million-dollar budget was soon consumed by printing, space, personnel and startup costs. Offices coast to coast and within occupied zones were manned by officials eager for lucrative jobs. The patronage positions were dispersed like booty. Qualifications were second to favors or nepotism. A postwar Tax Commission observed that the "Greatest weakness of the system in capacity of lower officers and dishonesty of higher ones." The Commission estimated the United States Treasury lost 40 percent of expected taxes because of evasion and under-reporting. Penalties were seldom imposed. The Commission suggested the Bureau be placed under a civil service system in lieu of appointments. It called for unfaithful agents to be dismissed.[114]

Tax forms late in the war were standardized. Recipients were instructed to make out a list or lists of all income, property, goods, wares, and merchandise, articles or objects owned by you, or of which you have the care and management, subject to duty or tax, together with the amount for license, under and in conformity with the Act of July 1, 1862. The only new tax mentioned in the 1863 tax instruction was a $10.00 billiard table tax. Curious was the conversion table used for calculating avoirdupois to troy ounces for gold and silver assessments. The conversion rate from avoirdupois was 91.2 percent into troy ounces used for assessments. An omission or negligence, under-reporting, evasion, fraud and failure to file was a fifth of each tax projections.

E. A. Rollins became U.S. Commissioner of Internal Revenue in 1866. He prepared a pamphlet for the Assessment of incomes, Articles in Schedule A (i.e., luxury goods) and Licenses. The Government Printing Office delivered those "Instructions" after April 26, 1866. The booklet (Series 2, No. 4) included frequently asked questions with sample answers. Some of the standard rulings were:

1. No deductions were allowed for labor of minor children, house servants or the unproductive.
2. Gains from the sale of lands or timber could be offset by the market value as of January 1, 1862.
3. Ditching and clearing land are capital improvements not deductions.
4. Only if an owner had made repairs to a building over five years, could current repairs be deducted.
5. Gifts were income tax free as were life insurance proceeds.
6. Citizens living abroad and resident aliens were subject to income tax.
7. Traveling shows and circuses required multiple licenses.
8. Annual license fee was not permission to operate.
9. Charity lotteries needed permission from the District Collector.
10. Farmers were not taxed for produce consumed by the family.
11. Loss in value of assets was not deductible until asset disposed.

Schedule of Forms—U.S. Internal Bureau, 1866

1. General Receipt for Taxes (with stubs)
2. Demand for Tax on Manufacturers (lotteries and slaughtered animals)
3. Manufacturer's Monthly Return
4. Monthly Return of Gross Receipts
5. Auctioneer's Monthly Return

6. Broker's Monthly Return
7. Quarterly Return of Receipt for Advertisements
8. Monthly Return of Slaughtered Animals
9. Demand for Tax and Annual Lists
10. Return by Paymasters and Disbursing Officers
11. Application for License
12. Notes by Manufacturers
13. Form of book to be kept by Distillers
14. Distiller's Tri-Monthly Account
15. Distiller's Monthly Account
16. Distiller's Receipt
17. Collector's Preliminary Notice
18. Brewer's Monthly Account
19. Receipt for Annual Taxes
20. Brewer's Receipt
21. General Demand for Taxes
22. Collector's Monthly Abstract
23. Assessor's Alphabetical List
24. Return of Annual Taxes
25. Form of book to be kept by Coal Oil Distillers
26. Coal Oil Distillers Tri-Monthly Account
27. Tri-Monthly Account of Crude Petroleum
28. Oath of Assessors and Assistant Assessors
29. Invoice for Fermenting Liquor
30. Distiller's Coal Oil Manufacturers Bond
31. Annual Return of Gross Amount of Sales By Dealer
32. Oath of Allegiance
33. Receipt for Legacy Tax
34. Succession Return
35. Return of Legacies
36. Assessors Statement/Return by Banks
37. Cotton Returns (Holder of Cotton)
38. Assessor's Monthly Report of Cigar Stamps
39. Tobacco, Snuff and Cigar Inspector's Bond
40. Tobacco, Snuff and Cigar Manufacturers Bond
41. Demand for Tax on Manufactured Tobacco
42. Estimate for Expenses (Due 5th of Each Month)
43. List of Deposits
44. Account Current of Collector Acting as Disbursing Agent
45. Rectifier's Return
46. Claim for Refunding of Taxes Improperly Collected
47. Claim for Remission of Taxes Uncollected (affidavit)
48. Schedule or Claims for Statement of Taxes
49. Daily Report of Collections
50. Tri-Monthly Report of Assistant Assessor in Charge of Distilling
51. Statement of Accounts Collected, Abated and Uncollected
52. Monthly Return by Foreign Banks (Association)
53. Schedule of Uncollected Taxes
54. Clerk's Bill (voucher for hired employee)
55. Monthly Return of Stamps Sold and on Hand
56. Abstract of Vouchers for Disbursements to Assistant Assessors
57. Assistant Assessor's Bill
58. Collector's Detailed Statement of Unassessed Penalties
59. Inspector's Return of Spirits and Coal Oil
60. Detailed Statement of Merchandise Placed in Bond
61. Aggregate Statement of Amounts of Merchandise Placed in Bond
62. Tobacco and Snuff Manufacturer's Return
63. [Blank]
64. Return by Insurance Companies of Premiums and Assessments
65. Return of Dividends (Due After Payment)
66. Return by Banks of Semi-Annual Profits
67. Return of Bank Circulation (Monthly)
68. Return of Railroad Companies of Bond Interest Paid
69. Warrant for Distress(For Collection of Taxes)
70. Inventory of Tobacco, Snuff and Cigars (Annual)
71. Cigar Maker's Permit
72. Cigar Manufacturer's Monthly Return
73. Cigar Maker's Account Book
74. Cigar Maker's Monthly Return
75. Assigner's Monthly Return
76. Permit for Manufacture of Tobacco
77. Abstract of Monthly Reports of Cigar Makers
78. Cigar Inspector's Monthly Report to Assessor
79. Collector's Quarterly Account
80. Revenue Inspector's Monthly Account
81. Demand for Tax on Licenses
82. Assessor's Schedule of Vouchers
83. Requisition for Stamps
84. Assistant Assessor's Account for Postage and Stationery
85. Collector's Schedule of Vouchers
86. Schedule of Lists
87. Statement of Corrected Footings (?)
88. Permit for Removal
89. Certificate for Payment
90. Transportation Bond

The most familiar tax official was the assessor, who was responsible for forms, guidance and assessments. If delinquent, taxpayers had twenty days to clear the delinquency. If not, the District Collectors would post notice. A distress sale at public auction would follow. Auctions were to be held in the county of the taxpayer within twenty days of the final notice. If fraud was suspected, the case could be assigned to a Revenue Detective. If spirits or tobacco was involved, Revenue Inspectors conducted audits. Costs of inspections were charged to owners of the inventory. Only a District Attorney could issue summons and warrants. Deposits of taxes collected were to be made monthly to a U.S. Depository. Assistant Treasurers could draft against these funds. Tax penalties were infrequent and minimal.[115]

The initial "Return of Annual Taxes" was ready in 1863. The four page "GPO" form explained income and deductions. The second page required the taxpayer to disclose each source of income. Allowable deductions were made on page three. After completion, the taxpayer certified all information as filed "is a true and faithful statement of the gains, profits on income." The tax was computed according to a schedule with five categories:

Income above exemption (3 percent tax)
Income in excess of $10,000 (5 percent tax)
Income from United States securities (1½ percent tax)
Income of citizens residing abroad (5 percent tax)
Income exceeding $10,000 with 3 percent withholding (2 percent tax).

Most evasion involved distillers, brewers and liquor dealers, as exampled by the New York "Whiskey Ring." A cottage moonshine industry prospered. Illegal stills, forged records and fictitious inventories were made possible by corrupt officials. Surplus corn, wheat, rye, barley and molasses were all used to distill New York "Moonshine Whiskey." Bribes were so common that standard charges were well known. Not until after the war did the Bureau seriously address illegal liquor. Ploys used included arson of bonded warehouses, false custom drawbacks and watered down liquor. Perhaps as much as a third of the expected revenue from liquor was untaxed. Even with that level of fraud, spirits and brewer taxes during the war were remarkable:

Year	*Liquor*	*Beer*
1863	$1.6 million	$71,000
1864	$2.2 million	$66,000
1865	$3.6 million	$77,000
TOTAL	$7.4 million	$214,000[116]

Voluntary compliance by the majority of the population was common. Disputes were locally mediated and settled usually in favor of neighbors, to the detriment of the Treasury. The most common violation was tardy renderings or assessments. Citizens accepted the small late penalty. The cost of the notice was also added to the tax bill. Lowell Dodge of Germantown, Pennsylvania, missed his 1863 deadline. After agreeing to a $20 tax, the District Collector added 1 percent (20 cents) for the notice to the October 1, 1864, bill which was paid February 2, 1865 (Fig. 71). A.O. Rigon, Trustee, was delinquent in paying his ward's 3 percent income tax for 1863 that was due November 22, 1864. A 5 percent ($12.60) failure to file penalty was added by New York District Collector N. O. Thayer (Fig. 72).

Assessed income taxes were due by May 1 and became delinquent on June 30. A grace period was allowed before the notice was sent. Failure to file or pay were negligent subject to a 5 percent penalty. Death or insolvency waived such penalties. For high-ranking federal employees, income taxes were withheld by paymasters. Military and federal officials earning more than $600 annually were subject to payroll tax withholding. When filing the annual income tax return, the official would take credit for any withheld at source tax. The taxpayer filed an affidavit with his district assessor allowing the withholding tax credit. The tax at that time officially was an "income duty" rather than "income tax," sidestepping the constitutional Direct Tax issue. The "George Washington" tax form used to remit withheld taxes was also present in occupied zones like New Orleans, where on December 17, 1864, such a form was forwarded to Washington (Fig. 73).

Withholding was also required for dividends paid by banks, trust and thrift institutions under Article 82. These were due after September 1, 1862. Banks were taxed on retained profits beginning March 3, 1863. Railroads paid tax on earnings but were allowed to deduct interest and dividends paid out. Railroads reported semiannually and remitted a standard 3 percent. Institutions were subject to a $500 penalty for failure to file or pay. Individual taxes were also 3 percent for incomes less than $10,000, but 5 percent if above. Under Article 90, citizens living abroad were charged the higher 5 percent. Few Americans, other than overseas government employees, paid taxes while living abroad.[117]

On July 30, 1864, Second Comptroller of the U.S. Treasury issued a "Circular" to disbursement officers of the Navy, Army and Marine Corps implementing Section 123 of the June 30, 1864, Act imposing a "duty" of 5 percent on salaries in excess of $600 on all civil, military and congressional officials. Specifically noted was taxability of Prize Money which was considered "income from salaries." The prize withholding tax would apply to income above two dollars a day or fifty dollars monthly. Taxes withheld were to be forwarded to the Commissioner of Internal Revenue, Washington, on "Form 10." In accordance with "tax usage of the Naval Service," the reduction in pay would be netted before computing charges for the Naval Hospital Fund. Commuted rations were taxable and subject to withholding, but not travel expenses.

The Acts of June 30 and July 4, 1864, increased personal income tax rates to a maximum of 10 percent. Few publically complained. Noted commentator and Victorian novelist Timothy Shay Arthur published a short story, "Growler's Income Tax," meant to shame tax protestors. He considered the "War Tax" patriotic. His fictional Midwestern farmer was outraged over a $40 assessment. A neighbor who had lost a son in battle scorned the old man. The story concluded, "Thousands and tens of thousands have given their sons and wives have given their husbands ... they are with the dead.... A grumble over this paltry war tax, for shame!"[118]

Volunteers in the regular army were given an enlistment bonus under the June 21, 1862, act. The recruit also earned a month's salary in advance if he extended for three years. The enlistment reward was not funded by Congress. Treasury realized it would be short of funds. By Joint Resolution Congress on July 4, 1863, passed a "Special Tax," or surcharge of 5 percent on incomes in excess of $600 for years ending after December 31, 1863. This surcharge was due October 1, 1864. Arthur O. Regan paid his "Special Tax" to New York Collector N. O. Thayer, 6th District, on December 21, 1864 (Fig. 74).[119]

Western States called up militias to protect frontiers after Army troops withdrew. Brigadier General John Bidwell of Chico, California, commanded such a state militia. One was at Camp Bidwell in Chico. The cavalry company was for the gold mining district of Butte County. The Sacramento River passed through the San Joaquin Valley nearby. The militia was supported by a local "Military Poll Taxes." Resident of

Butte County, T. Rogers was receipted for his 1865 military poll tax on May 12, 1865, as signed by the County Auditor, Treasurer and Controller. The capitation, or direct tax, of two dollars per head, passed the State Legislature April 25, 1863 (Fig. 75).

On March 3, 1865, the United States Congress again modified the income tax. The 5 percent bracket was lowered to $5,000. District Directors experienced more understatements. Assessors were instructed to closely consider facts and circumstances rather than relying upon taxpayer renditions. Appeals could be made to the District Collector. Deputy Collector N. O. Thayer of New York received for Collector M. B. Field of the Sixth New York District a 5 percent tax of $158.55 along with a three-dollar luxury tax for three watches. Because delinquent, a twenty cent notice was added. The Deputy Collector had to track down the reluctant taxpayer (Fig. 76).

Officials and politicians appreciated the labor saving advantage of self-assessment by willing taxpayers. Emphasized was the patriotic duty to pay their fair share. Incidents of the wealthy or powerful citizens evading taxes threatened the integrity of the entire system. A 25 percent penalty was ignored. Even the 50 percent fraud penalty had little effect. To quell public complaints, the Commissioner hired more inspectors for commercial centers to ferret out evaders. In 1864 Commissioner Boutwell opened to public view individual tax files. The New York *Tribune* ran lists of taxpayer returns. This sparked questions, but shocked the upper class. Press disclosures ceased after Congress, on July 14, 1870, and prohibited future publications of personal information. An effective compliance tool was abandoned in deference to the right of privacy to the wealthy. No one ever questioned a police blotter being open to the press.[120]

On April 27, 1872, Washington, D.C. Tax Assessor Walter Burr disclosed the 1863 tax return for President Lincoln. The return reported outside earnings of $1,183. His second withholding tax return was for a $25,000 presidential salary on which 5 percent was withheld. His combined taxable income, after a $600 exemption, resulted in a tax bill of $1,279.15. To this was added the "Special Surcharge" of 5 percent for soldier pay. Less than a thousand individual returns were filed that year. The number rose to 32,000 by the war's end. In comparison, seven thousand distilled spirits returns were received. Two years later, that number tripled. Between 1863 and 1865 tobacco tax returns grew from 3,000 to 11,000. In 1863, the national per capita income tax was $8.49 with a collection cost of two and half cents. By 1866 personal tax filings reached 56,000. With better monitoring, non-filers fell. Enemy occupation and distant location were no longer excuses.[121]

Tax collections in 1866 exceeded $300 million, a high mark before the U.S. Congress began to reduce or eliminate war taxes. Taxes continued for spirits and tobacco, and soon composed the majority of internal revenue. Income taxes contributed $3 million in 1863 and $20 million in 1864 and $32 million in 1865. The Special 5 percent surcharge of July 4, 1864, made a total of $84 million in war income taxes. The greatest collection year was 1866 totaling $73 million. Sixty percent of the taxes collected were from citizens in New York, Pennsylvania and Massachusetts. The 5 percent tax assessed against citizens living abroad yielded only $50,000 in 1864 and $170,000 in 1865. By region, the Mid-Atlantic States contributed 55 percent of all income tax, followed by New England (20 percent), Midwest (15 percent), Far West (4 percent), Plains (3 percent) and South (3 percent).[122]

United States tax collections for the year ending June 30, 1864, exceeded projections as a result of enhanced coverage and increased rates:

Revenue Source	*Estimate*	*Actual*
Customs	$72 million	$102 million
Land Sales	$.4 million	$.6 million
Direct Tax	———	$.5 million
Excise Tax	$78 million	$101 million
Miscellaneous Taxes	$5 million	$18 million
Captured Rebel Property	———	$2 million
Premium from Gold Sales	———	$19 million
Admirality Prizes	———	$4 million
Other Payments	———	$4 million
TOTALS	$155.4 million	$251.1 million

Even with a tax surplus, the Treasury needed another $600 million in new bonds. The 5 percent "Special Tax" was a surprising windfall. Occupational taxes accounted to 20 percent of the sums collected. As other categories improved, occupational licenses as a percentage dropped to 7 percent.[123]

Professionals and traders usually complied with license, registration and sales reporting rules. If not, the business could be closed. Commercial brokers under the law of July 1, 1862, needed a fifty-dollar license. This category included builders, real estate and rental agencies. A June 30, 1864 amendment set the licensed term from May 1 to April 30. After Charleston was occupied in the spring of 1865, all merchants applied for licenses so that they could continue doing business. With the influx of federal troops, housing prices were rapidly rising. Loyalty oaths were a prerequisite to any permit. Occupation taxes were date prorated. Charleston realtor B. Oakes, located downtown at No. 4 Broad Street, received a realtor's license April 2, 1866. Almost three thousand licenses had already been issued (Fig. 77).

Manufacturers, other than distillers, brewers and tobacconists were subject to a ten-dollar fee if their annual production exceeded $1,000 under Article 64 of the July 1, 1862, Act as modified June 30, 1864. Manufacturers included jewelers, job printers, stone cutters but not mechanics, carpenters, masons or house painters. In occupied zones, locals could only apply for the license after being adjudged loyal and taking the loyalty oath. Newberry, South Carolina, manufacturer Elisha E. Kinard Schumpert satisfied Deputy Collector James H. Dennis, 3rd District, on February 3, 1868, that he was loyal and was allowed to pay a $30.00 license covering the years 1866, 1867 and 1868. The license had been delayed until loyalty could be established (Fig. 78). Peddlers selling out of push carts were also covered. By 1878, a Special Tax for the Business of Peddler had evolved into four classes. The lowest, a push cart, Fourth Class Peddler, cost only ten dollars (Fig. 79).

Until occupied, Southern businessmen were free of U.S. taxes. Federal tax collections in occupied zones in Tennessee, Louisiana, South Carolina and Virginia were slow to occur. Direct Tax in occupied zones under the August 5, 1861, Act was as follows:

Year	*United States Direct Tax Collected*
1862	$1.8 million
1863	$1.5 million
1864	$.5 million
1865	$1.2 million
POST WAR	$10.4 million

In comparison, war time bank taxes amounted to thirteen million dollars. Revenue stamps contributed twenty million dollars, even after the commission to retailers.[124]

Inherited personal property was taxable under Article 11, legacy tax. Small estates valued less than a thousand dollar were exempt. The death tax applied to inheritance by will or intestacy. Gifts or donations were also included. Until paid, the executor was personally encumbered by a tax lien. The legacy tax rate depended on degree of kinship. The act, as amended June 30, 1864, added real estate property. Rates then ranged from none for widows, 1 percent for children and up to 6 percent for unrelated heirs including surviving husbands. Legacy tax receipts were only $52,000 for 1862 but soon increased. Failure to pay the tax subjected the estate and executor to a 5 percent penalty. Before the law was enacted, the Treasury estimated death taxes could raise about a million dollars annually but this was too optimistic. No evidence has come to light indicating the estate tax of President Lincoln or income taxes for the year of the assassination.[125]

Gambling such as poker, horseracing and wagering was virtually tax-free. New Orleans had always had an active lottery business. An Augusta lottery dealer advertised $100,000 grand prizes every third Saturday. Tickets cost $20. Drawings three times a month offered a $50,000 grand prize in return for a $10 half chance ticket. New Orleans dealer Charles T. Howard advertised his lottery in the "Texas Almanac of 1860." The U.S. Tax Act of March 3, 1863, required a $1,000 lottery occupation tax and revenue stamps for every ticket. Only three dealers paid for such a permit in 1864. The license fee was lowered to $100 on June 30, 1864. Over 400 ticket sellers then obtained permits. The act added a 5 percent business income tax on lottery establishments. The law precluded deducting prizes, "hits," commissions or expenses. Few reported; even fewer paid. Deductions became immaterial if not filing.

The apparent disregard for gambling seems puzzling. The apathy toward lottery dealers suggests the effect of lobbyists. Taking the well-publicized Augusta lottery alone, this indicates an overlooked bonanza for the Treasury. Besides the $1,000 license fees and 50 percent penalty for failure to file, a 5 percent gross revenue tax would have caused a substantial tax bill. This single example indicates lost revenue in excess of $500 per establishment or up to $500,000 annually. Every lottery ticket required a revenue stamp of at least two cents. This loss amounted to about $2,000 per dealer or another million dollars. This industry could have exceeded liquor and tobacco businesses.

The Temperance Movement frowned on gambling and was used as a cover to lawmakers wishing to avoid the entire subject. Lotteries had historically funded prestigious universities, such as Yale, Harvard and Brown. The public knew many lottery dealers pocketed the proceeds. The U.S. Post Office eventually prohibited using the mail to support gambling. The U.S. Supreme Court noted lotteries were demoralizing. Gambling was prevalent at every army camp and navy yard. It seems curious that liquor and tobacco were so heavily war taxed while gambling was ignored.

After the legacy tax was converted to a death tax including real estate, the term "succession tax" was substituted for the legacy excise. Deceased Confederates were subject to federal death taxes. Charleston Acting District Collector W. R. Cloutman received $12.50 from the administrator of Dr. Samuel Gourdin's estate, including his valuable Buckhall Plantation in Saint John's Parish. Dr. Gourdin' taxable estate, after the war, had declined to only $1,250 for the transfer to a distant relative (Fig. 80). Death taxes provided about $900,000, of which only 20 percent was from the earlier legacy tax.[126]

Chapter IX

Confederate States Taxes, 1864–1865

Confederates were hampered with few options for more revenue. On February 6, 1864, Secretary Memminger delivered the preliminary results of the latest tax efforts. Only a million dollars had come in, a third of projections, from Richmond, Augusta and Mobile. Commissioner of Taxes, Thompson Allen, apologized for the incomplete numbers and none from the Trans-Mississippi. In the Eastern District, only through "onerous labour," had tax in kind been collected. A Senate Report recommended that the President appoint an Assistant Secretary of the Treasury for the Trans-Mississippi Department. This "Agency" would be under General Kirby Smith, and function as a Western Treasury.[127]

The "Tax In Kind" of April 24, 1863, under Colonel Larkin Smith, Assistant Quartermaster General, was responsible for gathering, storing and dispensing commodities. Post quartermasters in charge of warehouses divided goods among quartermasters, commissariats and treasury agents. If perishable, the articles were sent to market as soon as possible. Mindful of waste and spoilage, Congress on December 23, 1862, had allowed taxpayers to commute perishable produce in lieu of delivery. Family allowances were increased by Congress February 17 and June 10, 1864. Crops were more valuable than money. Tax credits were allowed for crops lost to enemy action. Georgia, North Carolina and Alabama provided two-thirds of all "Tax In Kind" collected.[128]

Tax In Kind procedures under the February 17, 1864, Act required estimates of agricultural products be made before September 1. "Form No. 1" listed wheat, oats, rye, hay and wool quantity, quality and tithe. The form was signed and sworn to by taxpayer or his agent. A. C. Shealey of Lexington, South Carolina, through his attorney, executed the form on September 24, 1864. The bottom was the receipt (Fig. 81). "Form No. 2" was for products such as corn, rice, fodder, molasses and peas. This was to be returned before January 1 (Fig. 82). Tax In Kind "Form No. 3" covered all other items. Enemy incursions delayed deadlines. Penalties were few and mostly waived. Noncompliance in western regions was widespread.

Tobacco, cotton and bacon required special handling by Post Quartermasters. William Lindsey, Agent of Reidsville, Rockingham County, North Carolina, posted his procedures when announcing he was ready to receive wheat and oat because the "Government needs it." Time was of the essence as stores were running low. Grain bags for shelled oats were available for pick-up. Delivery three months after September 19 would cause a 500 percent penalty plus costs and warrant of distress. Taxpayers were reminded that tobacco was to be packed in boxes and cotton ginned, bagged and roped. Transportation was only free for eight miles (Fig. 83).

Quartermasters and commissariats withdrew stores from Post Depots. The small tax-in-kind collections in 1863 grew six times the next year. More taxpayers elected to commute their In-Kind produce with money payments. Congress, on January 27, 1864, allowed Texas and Louisiana to divert depots stores for the troops. Auctions were suspended.[129]

Major James R. Arnold of Nacogdoches, Chief Post Quartermaster for Texas, supervised six Post Depots. On May 10, 1864, the Treasury Agent announced that all liable for "Tithe Tax" could take a credit for impressed produce in the future. No mention was made for seizures made by state collectors. The more westward the farms and ranches, the less strict "Tax in Kind" was enforced. Even officials skirted assessments. Quartermaster Major Simeon Hart of San Antonio, according to reports published in the newspaper at Fort Brown, moved three thousand Merino sheep to Mexico. The Post Quartermaster at Sequin, Captain R. W. Brahan, also reported avoidance. Houston's depot under Captain John S. Sellers covered twenty-eight counties. The depot at Bonham covered twenty-four counties and was under Captain R. G. Harper. The Austin, Crockett and Marshal depots each had fewer than twenty depots.

As valuable as wheat, corn and livestock were, none could replenish a depleted treasury. The Confederate Congress passed the greatest tax and funding act of the war on February 17, 1864. Essential was controlling inflation. Forced funding of currency into bonds and debt repudiation, were enacted. The public after enactment of the massive Act, distrusted the concoction of currency scale downs, forced funding and more taxes. The complex Confederate statute did little more than add another layer of receipts, exchanges and reissues. More process did not create more funds.[130]

The taxable property base included slave property valued

at a billion dollars. Secretary Memminger had proposed a 5 percent ad valorem tax. Few opposed. Increased also were business and license fees under Section 1 of the Act. Section 4 addressed distillers and brewers. Gross receipts tax applied to almost every business under Section 5. Attempts were made to withhold payroll tax similar to the federal procedure for high paid officials earning over $1,500 annually. Confederate withholding under Section 6 was seldom effective. Pay was always in arrears. The Tax Act in Section 10 explained that these measures were absolutely necessary for the survival of the government.[131]

Agricultural land, slaves, cotton and tobacco were now assessed at values on June 1, 1862, rather than prewar levels. Gold, coins and trade credits were taxed at 5 percent. Bank bills, shinplasters and currency (except Confederate) were taxed at 25 percent. Ten percent was due on business profits. A surcharge of 25 percent applied to banks paying profits in excess of 25 percent of capital. The personal exemption was increased by $100 for each minor child and son in the military, even if deceased, plus an additional $500 for every new recruit. A $1,000 hardship exemption was allowed surviving widows, orphans and disabled veterans. District tax collectors could grant relief if a taxpayer's property was destroyed by the enemy. Military and government salaries up to $1,000 annually were exempt. Confederate Judges were not subject to tax on their salaries because to do so would violate the separation of power provision of the Constitution. Also excluded were partnerships engaged in manufacturing, but joint stock companies doing the same activity were taxable. Such inconsistencies could only be cured by lawmakers. State loans, even if stated tax free, were subject to Confederate taxes. Most taxes owed were satisfied with Depository Receipts issued for forced funding or currency scale downs. Little new money came to the Treasury. The nation's capacity to withstand more levies was exhausted. The 1864 Tax Law had more propaganda value than fiscal worth.

To account for the variety of taxes imposed, an official "Confederate States Tax Registry Book," a double page ledger was printed. Costs and difficulty in distributing forestalled use. The discarded tax journal had ten columns:

1. Name of person, firm or corporation
2. Residence
3. Business conducted
4. Names
5. Capital
6. Specific tax
7. Gross sales
8. Gross receipts
9. Tax due
10. Remarks

Most assessors created personal registers. Upon occupation, these incriminating papers were usually destroyed. Evidence of rebel complicity was dangerous if treason trials were brought before Military Commissions.

In spite of Louisiana's occupation, the Northwest counties had fourteen Confederate Tax officials. Sheriff Jack S. Meredith, Tax Collector for Caldwell Parish, south of Alexandria, at Columbia, collected taxes late in the war. Taxpayer E. H. Martin was assessed on $10,523 of real estate, which was taxed at 5 percent for a total of $526.15. Another $50.00 was owed on personal property. A "special tax" surcharge, similar to the federal, was added to help pay soldiers. This surcharge increased his tax bill $105.23. All was cleared with almost worthless Treasury notes (Fig. 84).

Arkansas Representative Hugh Thompson proposed that Congress amend the new tax act exempting $1,200 for servicemen. He urged Congress to grant such relief because thousands remained unpaid. Even after the "Special Tax" soldier tax, the problem persisted. Union County, Arkansas, Tax Collector, receipted the normal and special tax on December 27, 1864, from minor taxpayer Henry C. Murphy, through his guardian. Collector J. M. McRae issued a receipt for $149.59 and the funds remained in the Trans-Mississippi (Fig. 85).

Peter W. Gray was appointed Confederate Treasury Agent of the Trans-Mississippi Department effective March 2, 1864, but delayed establishing his office at Marshall until July. His jurisdiction included Texas, Arkansas and Western Louisiana. David F. Shall was his auditor and Thomas H. Kennedy served as Comptroller. Captain W. C. Black was in charge of the Foreign Supply Office, which was responsible for cotton exports. The Treasury Agency functioned through May 22, 1865. Acting Treasurer M. J. Hall, principal depositary at Marshall, was active because no banks existed in Texas or Arkansas. General Kirby Smith, Commander of the Department, without Richmond's approval, stamped and reissued withdrawn Confederate money, because currency had completely dried up. Banks east of the Mississippi took a bank holiday before the March 28, 1864 date, for a scale-down and forced refunding under the February 17, 1864, Act. States west of the river had three additional months. Special depository forms were not available west of the Mississippi.[132]

Lithographer "Archer," of Richmond, Virginia, printed an impressive "Certificate of Deposit" for exchange of the old for new issue currency, dated April 2, 1864. Printing delays limited use to only three cities: Fincastle, Christianburg and Richmond. Old treasury notes surrendered were two-thirds exchangeable into "New Issue." The one-third loss was a "tax" (Fig. 86). The Tyler, Texas, Depositary issued a December 17, 1864, "Exchange Certificate" of old for new issue. He wrote that the payment of the estimated $3,000 entitled the taxpayer to $2,000 in "New Issue." The Texas receipt was a product of E. M. Cushing & Co., Houston (Fig. 87).

Texans were notified of the refunding mechanisms by newspaper in Houston, Galveston, San Antonio, Shreveport, Huntsville, Austin, Crockett and Dallas:

> Notice is given to all holder of Treasury Notes not bearing interest, that they may exchange them at the office of any Depository of the Treasury, for Certificates which will entitle them to Four per cent bonds, until the first day of July next. After that date, all Notes over the denomination of Five Dollars are taxed thirty-three and one-third per cent, and can only be funded if received for taxes at 66½ cent on the dollar; and One Hundred Dollar Notes will, after that date not be receivable for public dues, and can be funded only subject to an additional tax and reduction of ten per cent per month. On the first of October next, Five Dollar notes will also be subject to the tax of 33½ per cent; and after the first of January, 1865, all Treasury Notes of the present issues cease to be fundable or receivable for public dues.
>
> The Certificates issued, and Bonds for which they may be exchanged, are receivable of taxes due and payable during the year 1864, at the full amount expressed on their face without interest; and are not subject to the tax imposed for that year on other bonds and credits.
>
> For convenience in funding, additional Depositories will be appointed, and several Depositories of the Treasury are authorized to appoint Deputies in counties convenient to them, to receive deposits for funding, to whom the principal Depositories will forward Certificates for the amounts received.
>
> The short time allowed for funding should admonish all holders promptly to present their note, and not risk the chance of exclusion by the pressure which will occur at the end of the month of June.
>
> Collectors of Customs are notified that Treasury Notes are no longer receivable for Import Duties. Both Export and Import Duties must be paid in coin by all parties.
> P. W. GRAY
> Agent of Treasury, Trans-Mississippi Department[133]

Confederate Depositaries and collectors were responsible for making exchanges under the Tax Refunding Act of February 17, 1864. Treasury Agent Peter W, Gray had the following depositories: Edward Cross, Washington; H. J. G. Battle, Shreveport; Samuel F. Mosley, Jefferson; J. W. Smith, Dallas; James Sorely, Houston; D. M. Stapp, Victoria; and George W. Palmer, San Antonio. The agent responsible for exchanging postal funds was James H. Starr. Military agents handled for troops. He hired three dozen "Deputy Depositories." The practical solution was questioned as soon as Treasury officials learned of his pragmatic accommodation. Richmond, had not appropriated funds and ordered the practice to cease. Some were dismissed, but others continued.[134]

The Depository at Jefferson forwarded instructions to subagents May 20, 1864:

> Your duties are simple, being those only appertaining to the funding of the currency under the recent Act of Congress, the terms of which are succinctly set forth in the notice of Judge Gray, a copy of which I enclose, and to which I beg your careful attention:
>
> You will receive deposits of Treasury Notes, from parties desiring to fund giving you receipts a per form herewith; and to report to me weekly, with the funds, the names of depositors, and amounts deposited; on receipt of which I will forward to you my official certificates to be exchanged for your receipts.
>
> As there are many counterfeits in circulation, you will have to exercise great care to prevent the imposition of these upon you; and, as a precaution, I will advise that you number the receipts and write with ink on the back of each Treasury Note the number of the receipt.
>
> Deposits can only be received for sums which are the multiple of One Hundred Dollars. You will give only one receipt to any party for his entire deposit made at one time, unless where he may desire to divide his funds one portion to cover his taxes, and the other for bonds in which case you can give two receipts, one for each amount.
>
> It is not intended that you will attend to any other duties of a Depository such as paying interest, etc.
>
> Your appointment is for one year, or until further notice and your compensation is a commission fixed by law, not exceeding Fifteen Hundred Dollars per annum.

Additional guidance from Depositary Mosely's was forwarded on May 26:

1. Your receipts for all monies deposited must be for a sum for which 100 is a perfect division, whether for Taxes or Bonds.
2. Certificates from this Office only, will pay Taxes for 1864, and are negotiable Bonds when issued are transferable only on the books of the Treasury Department.
3. The Public will be advised forthwith after the new Issue is received for exchange for the old Issue after the 1st of July, next.
4. Deputy Depositaries have no authority to issue receipts for interest due on Treasury Notes of Coupon bonds.
5. Certificates will not be issued from this office upon receipts of Depositaries until the money is deposited here by the Depositary receiving it.
6. The Secretary of the Treasury only is authorized to negotiate for new Loans.[135]

Many Confederate deputy collectors continued to make exchanges through the end of the year despite ordered closure. Their $125 a month salary was taken from petty cash, because not authorized by Richmond. Mosely had sent the deputy depository closure order in September 1864:

> By instructions from the Treasury Department, your functions as Deputy Depositary will cease on the 1st of October 1864. So soon as practicable, after that time, you will make out your account for salary, at the rate of $1500 per annum, for the time actually occupied by you in office, and all necessary expenses incurred for the use of your office, accompanied with vouchers, from No. one up, giving the items and prices paid for the same, you will make out your account in duplicates for each. The first from the date of your qualification to the 30th June, 1864. The other from the 1st July to the 1st October, next; and sworn to as per form herewith enclosed. You will return them with the funds deposited since the first of July, with report of business done since that date; and deliver the same at this office as soon as practicable after first October next.[136]

The two for three scale down also applied to State held Confederate currency in the Treasuries. Texas, for example, as of June 30, 1864, had $2,800,000 in old issue currency. Because of a complex conversion table the amount States were entitled to under the Act of June 14, 1864, depended on denominations and dates redeemed. Full value was given for one hundred dollar notes if exchanged for twenty year, 5 percent bonds. Additional haircuts were taken if submitted afterwards. Texas was to receive new currency only when available:

Held in Texas Treasury	*Rounded*
Bonds, 4%, 20 year	$1,300,000
New Issue notes	$1,500,000
Total exchanged	$2,800,000

Depending upon the denomination of Confederate Treasury notes and the physical location of the depositor, the exchange table was a confounding matrix. Holders west of the Mississippi had three months longer to comply. The table was overwhelming for farmers and soldiers in the field:

Treasury Note Final Compulsory Funding Table (Act of February 17, 1864)

	Note Denomination			
	50 cents, $1 & $2	*$5*	*$10, $20 & $50*	*$100 No Interest*
Cis-Mississippi				
1. Remain current and receivable	X			
2. Fundable into 4% registered bonds				
a. At full value if by April 1, 1864			X	X
b. At full value if by July 31, 1864		X		
c. At 66⅔% of value if by December 31, 1864			X	
3. Exchangeable into New Issue 2 for 3				
a. After April 1, 1864			X	
b. After July 1, 1864		X		
4. Taxed an additional 10% per month				X
5. Taxed at 100% after December 31, 1864		X	X	X
Trans-Mississippi				
1. Remain current and receivable	X			
2. Fundable into 4% registered bonds				
a. At full value if by July 1, 1864				X
b. At full value if by October 1, 1864			X	
c. At 66⅔% of value if by December 31, 1864		X		
3. Exchangeable into New Issue 2 for 3				
a. After July 1, 1864			X	
b. After October 1, 1864		X		
4. Taxed an additional 10% per month				X
5. Taxed at 100% after December 31, 1864		X	X	X

The Confederate Commissioner of Taxes paid assessors and collectors by draft drawn on regional depositories. The Assessor for the 21st District of North Carolina received his salary, $223.35, on March 8, 1864. This was only the seventeenth check written by A. L. Edwards, Richmond Disbursement Clerk. The check was drawn against Wilmington Depositary Henry R. Savage (Fig. 88). On May 25, of that year, Depositary Savage certified to Clerk Edwards that he had received $1,000.00 from Richmond covering salaries, printing, stationery, and contingent expenses (Fig. 89). Later many collectors deducted their salaries from funds on hand. Control and accountability had broken down. Depositary John Brown in the Camden, Arkansas, started exchanging old issues for new on July 6. By September, Judge Brown had redeemed $2,000,000 in old money. Major Shall, his predecessor, had converted another $3,000,000 before going to Texas to be the Agency auditor. Clerks, such as Judge Brown's son, Hugh, transported bundles of old currency to Marshall for cancellation. Judge Brown confessed in his diary that he paid himself in federal greenbacks, exchanged at a 500 percent premium, even though dealing in enemy currency was a felony, punishable by three years in prison. Brown was never charged. The Confederacy was out of money. President Davis on May 2, 1864, lamented: "In our present circumstances I know of no mode of providing for the public wants which would entail sacrifices so great as a fresh issue of Treasury notes." The farther a depository was from Richmond, the more serendipitous the process. The depository at Victoria, Texas, was issuing exchange certificates at the time of Appomattox, despite the fact the deadline had long expired.[137]

The Confederate Treasury also relaxed controls and normally rigid reporting rules. The Treasurer deposited $3,000.00 from the Eleventh District for Virginia War Taxes directly into the Treasury. Virginia Chief Tax Collector Thomas C. Green was bypassed. Treasurer Elsmore receipted the deposit personally (Fig. 90). In Augusta, Georgia, the correct procedures were followed. Chief Tax Collector, E. G. Cabaness, on July 7, 1864, deposited $108,277.05 with the Depositary at Augusta. Amazingly, included was $48.26 in coin. No longer was a 5 percent rebate given for paying early as announced May 15, 1863. The term "War Tax" had become generic, no longer simply meaning the "Direct Tax" (Fig. 91).

The Confederate Indian Nations had special status because of their independent sovereignty. None of the Direct Tax was apportioned to tribal governments by either side. After secession, Confederate agents negotiated treaties with some tribes within the Indian Territory. The Tax Act of February 17, 1864, ignored this tax free status for refunding and scale downs. The Rev. Israel Folsom, a Cumberland Presbyterian Minister, at Armstrong Academy, Choctaw Nation, brought $67,215 in tribal held "old issue" Treasury notes to the Marshall depository, on December 31, 1864, the last day for conversion. The Reverend received a depository receipt for $44,810 to be held for the benefit of the Choctaws and other "Friendly Indians." A third was lost to taxes.[138]

Treasury and banking personnel spent the last half of 1864 completing the complex exchange. Agent Peter Gray described that exercise as the "most arduous task" of his tenure. The burdensome provision allowing taxpayers to satisfy tax bills with depository receipts complicated the matter. With the scarcity of specie, high inflation and little currency, taxes could only be paid with depository receipts. Agent Gray estimated he would withdraw up to twenty million dollars of the old currency from circulation by the end of the year. Notices were posted in French, Spanish and German. Tax Collector Adolph Weiss of Gillespie County, Texas, nailed to the courthouse door a German version that May (Fig. 92).

Collector Weiss held several government positions. He devoted time in his capacity as the District's Commissary Agent. The Officer in Charge of Commissary Purchases at San Antonio, notified Agent Weiss August 1, 1864, to contract as much produce as possible before Tax In Kind began. Specifically needed was corn, soap and candles. Also short was beef. Weiss was instructed to promise "new issue" currency to cattlemen and wheat farmers. He was always on the lookout for any willing to make soap for the army.

Agent Gray issued no "new issue" currency in 1864 according to his summarized activities filed October 1, 1864:

Bonds Issued	
4% Bonds, Act Feb. 17, 1864 (Public)	$46,469,100.00
4% Bonds, Act June 14, 1864 (States)	413,500.00
Revenue Collected	
Taxes	5,758,457.42
Sequestration	1,336,012.95
Draft substitutes	10,000.00
Customs	56,278.51
Export duty	9,012.15
Light house money	130.15
Currency scale down	649,175.34
Disbursing officers scale down	32,173,865.32
New issue notes received	8,000,000.00
Total Receipts	$94,915,621.84[139]

Funds forwarded to the Agency were designated for war, $5,950,000, navy, $156,000, and civil, $315,000. The numbers reveal how little was available to pay suppliers and contractors:

New issue received	$1,255,486.07
Old issue notes held for cancellation	74,383,652.69
Drafts drawn on Richmond Treasury	12,790,000.00
Coin and bond coupons redeemed for customs	65,610.81
Funds held in Agency	$88,494,649.57

Richmond had little intelligence from the Treasury Agency. Commissioner of Taxes Allen, remained confident in Judge Gray's ability as he stated October 28, 1864:

> Owing to the difficulty of communication with the Trans-Mississippi Department, little was known as to the condition or progress of the tax business. Ample instructions had been sent to Judge Gray, State collectors were directed to report to him, and Agent Gray was to forward periodical reports.[140]

Quartermaster General Larkin Smith in his report to Congress concerning the Trans-Mississippi was also optimistic. Although tax in kind information in Texas was unknown, the seven million dollars expected was hopeful. Perhaps as much as three million dollars in commodities were at post depots in Arkansas and Louisiana. The Austin Chief Tax Collector reported $37 million in taxes received, but this was before the currency scale down. The Texas Chief Collector estimated that for the fiscal year he expected:

	Tax
Property values of $381,944,005 (assessment of 5%)	$19,097,200
Jewelry and watches luxury tax	50,000
Less reduction due to enemy occupation	<3,829,440>
Less Tax In Kind credit	<10,211,840>
Less income tax credit	<1,531,776>
Income and Occupation taxes	4,100,000
Soldier Surcharge 5%	3,883,552
Total tax expected from Texas	$11,557,696[141]

Treasury Agent Gray was autonomous after February 1865 when he was granted authority to function as a bureau. Gray made appointments, without approval. The Auditor, Controller and Treasurer, were commensurate in authority with their Eastern counterparts. The agency had incurred operating expenses of $80,000, including $30,000 in salaries. That was only 10 percent of the costs in Richmond. The agency was behind $320 million in bond funding due to taxpayers. As of November, the agency reported the following to Richmond:

Treasury Notes Sent to Regional Depositories

San Antonio	$16,700,000
Houston	1,000,000
Shreveport	34,000,000
Total	$51,700,000

Funds Forwarded to Agency at Marshall

Treasury notes sent between June and November 1864	$20,000,000
Six per cent non-taxable bonds sent between June and November 1864	$6,000,000
Four per cent bonds sent between June and November 1864	$9,000,000
Certificates of indebtedness sent between June and November 1864	12,000,000
Total to Treasury Agency	$47,000,000
Reported Forwarded from Richmond	$98,700,000[142]

In November about fourteen million dollars in taxes had come to various depositaries. Custom receipts were only $50,000 despite increased cotton shipments overseas. By year end the Confederate debt had passed a half billion dollars. Outstanding warrants, back pay and general claims were staggering. Scheduled interest and contractual commitments of $300 million were in default. Gold payments were impossible. By 1865, the Confederacy's credit worthiness was junk. The financial houses of Europe closed to more rebel financing.[143]

The Sequin, Texas, Tax Collector, on February 28, 1865, detailed a particularly complicated transaction. The official was presented payments from several family members related to John L. Durham, then deceased. Three taxpayers owed $302.50. A commuted 1863 Tithe tax of $368.71 was also due. They remitted $15.00 in specie as partial payment. This was credited at seventeen times face value. A $1,000 bond certificate (4 percent) was due to the group under the refunding law. The $88.79 overpayment was cleared by refunding $60.00 in new currency after the scale down. The balance was credited to "Soldiers Tax" owed. The "intra office" accounting hints at the burden placed upon officials. Few were trained in banking or accounting.

As the Confederate government abandoned Richmond in March 1865, Congress passed final emergency measures. Tax rates were raised, extended and moved up. Taxes In Kind could now be offset against agricultural property taxes. Bank specie, coin and foreign bills of exchange were taxed at 20 percent. Excess profits were taxed between 10 and 25 percent. Another Soldiers Tax surcharge of 12½ percent was added. Richmond banks were assessed 25 percent "In Kind" for all vault coin, gold and foreign exchange, regardless of ownership. Private property was no longer sacred. No court could challenge the survival measures.[144]

President Davis had earlier assented to a long-overdue agreement among the War, Navy and Treasury Departments for the transport of cotton, tobacco and naval stores overseas. The Army assumed control of inland commodities under the April 18, 1864, memorandum. The Treasury took custody of produce destined for shipment overseas. A purchase fund of $20 million was for commodities, especially cotton, to be provided to Lieutenant Colonel Thomas L. Bayne at the Foreign Supply Office. Almost 300,000 bales of cotton were shipped by that Supply Office. Henry Sampson of Houston was responsible for 9,000 bales from Texas. The counties of Leon, Brazoria, Robertson, Colorado, Fort Bend and Washington accounted for two-thirds of that shipments.[145]

Henry Sampson, head of the Texas Cotton office, summarized his impressed and "Tithe" cotton transactions warehoused in Houston. The purchased cotton averaged 12½ cents a pound. Half the fifteen thousand bales were from the plantations of R. and D. E. Mills of Houston. Both Houston Depositary James Sorely and Sampson shipped private cotton in their own names aboard government transports. The favorable cotton numbers benefited individuals as often as government. Cotton passed into Mexico at Laredo and Del Rio after Fort Brown was Union occupied. Cotton depots at Goliad and San Antonio inspected, graded and registered exports to Mexico. All was according to the plan of April 3, 1864.[146]

As more land came under Union control, the Confederate Treasury suffered more. Louisiana Congressman L. J. Dupre was disturbed because his farmer and merchant voters were insolvent. Secretary of the Treasury, George A. Treholm, only response was that "Thousands have suffered by depredation of the enemy" and compared to "injuries by some of our Treasury agents" was of no consequence compared to the loss of life and property wrought by the enemy. He reminded Dupre that if funds were given based on sufferings, the national revenue would immediately evaporate. The "pitiful sum" that might be awarded is "unfortunate but not so much as the thousands of those [who] have lost all they had." Whether to friend or foe, the loss was the same.[147]

Georgia and Mississippi suspended tax collections. Missouri, West Virginia and Southern Louisiana shut down as Union troops advanced. North and South Carolina were barely operational. Richmond's source of funds was exhausted.[148]

Editor G. G. Carmon, of the *Loyal National Union Journal* at Brownsville, resumed circulation of his occupation newspaper July 18, 1864. In that issue he stressed the "interests of the army, the people, and the election of Abraham Lincoln." He encouraged all to support "reconstruction and reduction in the price of tobacco." Half of that July issue was devoted to a Spanish reprint of President Lincoln's Amnesty Proclamation dated December 1, 1863. The edition also noted escaping Confederates taking up residence in Monterey, Mexico, and the hot spring resort known as "Topo." Included among the "non-combatant reserves of Dixie" who were "in a place of safety for a rainy day" were Treasury, cotton and purchasing agents. The Monterey rebels fed stories to the English-language *Morning Star* encouraging continued support for the Confederacy and slavery. Union Editor Carmon assured readers that the Mexican people were "Republicans" at heart and supported the United States.

Insolvency, hyperinflation, and credit unworthiness doomed the Confederate Treasury. States withdrew trust funds, such as the Louisiana Levee Fund and Texas Education endowments for war purposes. The most effective Confederate tax was "In Kind" collections. Actual numbers for Confederate taxes do not exist. An estimate made by historian Richard Cecil Todd was:

Import Duty	$3 million
Export Duty*	NIL
Tax Acts	
Direct Taxes	$18 million
Indirect Taxes	$119 million
Tax In Kind	$62 million
Tax Not Remitted from Trans-Mississippi	$6 million
Estimated Total	$208 million[149]

*Only $30,000

The only taxes of actual value were $65 million, consisting of customs dues and "Tithed" produce and commodities. The majority was scale downs, forced funding and fees paid with worthless depository receipts and fiat money adding nothing to the Treasury.

Chapter X

United States Taxes, 1865

When the United States war tax ledgers closed, the numbers revealed that five loyal states contributed three-quarters of the U.S. Internal Revenue. A third was drawn from New York alone and closely followed by Pennsylvania, Ohio, Massachusetts and Illinois. Territories Nebraska, Colorado, Utah, Nevada and Washington added only two hundred thousand dollars. Opponents of progressive taxes became vocal as the war's conclusion neared. It had always been politically necessary to convince the public that the wealthy were also suffering. The passport tax, never of revenue consequence, escaped criticism. "Sin" taxes raised large sums without controversy. Radical Republicans continued their drive for the rebels to bear the cost of the war. Traitors were punished by confiscating their estates.[150]

Government subsidized care for freedmen and refugees waned after the victory parades. The care for Union veterans was a budget of unknown dollars. Interest free greenbacks and increasing tariffs, momentarily concealed the expected short falls after the war. The Treasury needed $600 million to cover its cash shortage of one hundred million dollars monthly. A Revenue Circular dated June 2, 1865, eased the tax burden of rebels then in poverty. Assessments of taxes from the defeated would not begin until collection districts were designated. The former rebels were reminded that this should not be considered a waiver of their tax obligations, only a delay. Border States like Kentucky, West Virginia, Delaware and Maryland, were already being taxed and did not qualify for postponement.[151]

Wartime passports were critical to security during the war. The travel documents were first handled by the Department of Foreign Affairs during the Confederation pre–Constitution era. The U.S. State Department later issued papers of safe conduct along with passports. Between 1800 and 1850, only a thousand passports were issued annually. The passport contained a description of the bearer below the official coat of arms of the United States. By 1846, evidence of U.S. citizenship was required in the passport application. At that time, "free blacks" were issued "certificates" in lieu of passports, because they were not "citizens" of a state. Costing one dollar and valid for a year, the fee only offset expenses.

Passport control through the U.S. State Department applied to both domestic and foreign travelers. The U.S. Passport Office, created July 1, 1862, charged three dollars as a duty. The charge subsidized the minimal State Department budget. Loyalty, current oaths and draft status were checked. Purpose for travel, except for officials under orders, was required. As applications increased, administrative costs rose and the fee was raised to five dollars effective June 30, 1864. Again it was considered a "duty" and continued until the summer of 1870. Over ten thousand passports were issued during the war adding about $50,000 to the State Department. The first year after the war, six thousand domestic passports were processed. Northerners were relocating.[152]

Travelers first entered the Port Royal enclave in 1862, soon after Union occupation. The following year, Nashville and Knoxville also admitted northern officials, merchants and missionaries. Senator Andrew Johnson was appointed Tennessee's Military Governor January 26, 1864, and opened his government at Nashville. Loyal officials could resume city business. Simultaneously, all men and women had to take an oath of loyalty to the United States within six months if they wished to remain. A State Convention was scheduled that May to restore self-rule, in anticipation of the November national election. The Post commander was instructed to "clean up" the city. A boatload of prostitutes were transported to Lewisville and Cincinnati, but were rejected by town fathers as "miserable cargo" and returned to Nashville.[153]

The premier "sin tax" was a prostitute license. A city, under martial rule, was policed by provost marshals. Before being granted a license "to do business," women of the night were informed of work rules, physically examined and certified free of disease, if seeking a permit for "active service." The five dollar "whore tax" was renewable every six months. Women, orphans and soldiers "pest houses" were supported by the fifty cent prostitute tax. The Nashville soldier "pest house" had sixty patients that first year. Records indicate over four hundred Nashville prostitutes registered. This was double the Census count a year before the war. The license read "A Public Woman to Pursue her Occupation in the City of Nashville." Unlicensed prostitutes were subject to a thirty-day jail term (Fig. 93).

United States Collectors within occupied zones contributed little revenue, but the propaganda was priceless. Loyal taxpayers relished knowing hot-headed rebels were paying for their disloyalty. Taxes were indifferent in rural occupied zones. In Missouri, local taxes were eventually "piggy backed" by adding a 3 percent surcharge. Some citizens in Virginia, Tennessee, Louisiana and Kentucky paid greater sums each year. Nashville Collector H. L. Norvell received $5.13 from James Montgomery on September 4, 1864, along with eleven hundred other tax returns. J. T. S. Fill located at College and Union Streets printed the form (Fig. 94). An 1866 federal tax was paid in Thomasville, Georgia, on November 15, 1867, as documented for the 5 percent income tax and a watch tax (Fig. 95).

The most familiar tax to post war Southerners were federal revenue stamps. After the loyal community of Barbour County, West Virginia, voted to award a hundred-dollar bounty to all who answered the President's call for men, the Board of Supervisors was surprised to learn that a quarter revenue stamp was due on each bonus check. In nearby Wythe County, Virginia, couples wishing to marry had to add a nickel revenue stamp to their license and another to the marriage certificate. Probate wills required revenue stamps even if death occurred before occupation. The amount of revenue stamps varied with the value of the estate. Surety bonds for estate administrators required stamps based on the property, subject to court supervision. One Revenue Stamp for a Virginia surety bond was not affixed until July 10, 1867, long after the death of the person in question (Fig. 96).

One of the smallest federal tax districts was occupied Beaufort, South Carolina. Thirty-nine loyal merchants, missionaries and officials paid $2,500 in 1864 for income and excise taxes, plus some penalties. Merchant Jonathan C. Alexander paid $752.10 for his income that was over $15,000 (5 percent). Departmental Photographer Samuel A. Cooley paid $220 on $4,400. Port Royal Railroad builder Stephen C. Millet incurred a penalty of 25 percent for failure to remit his taxes in timely fashion. Another merchant, Edgar F. Nichols,was charged with fraud but only fined a 100 percent penalty of $250. Four post offices were included in Collection District No. 32, Division No. 8. J. C. Alexander paid a luxury tax for his yacht of ten tons ($5.00) and a gold watch ($1.00). Twenty others paid the watch tax. Tax Commissioner W. E. Wording had the most expensive timepiece in town according to that assessment. Two residents, David F. Thorpe of Saint Helena's Island, and Freedmen's Bank President Nelson R. Scovil, paid on luxury town carriages. Scovil also was assessed for family silver. The fraudster, Mr. Nichols, also owed on a piano ($2.00), as did merchant C. W. Dennis. Union officials had payroll taxes withheld by the paymasters.

Table
1864 United States Tax Roll
Occupied Beaufort, South Carolina
Taxpayers Assessed

Post Office Name	*Income*	*Gold Watch*	*Yacht*	*Carriage*	*Piano*	*Silver*	*Penalty*
Beaufort							
Alexander, J. C.	$752.10	$1.00	$5.00				
Allen, Alden S.	40.90						
Brisbane, Wm. Henry	0.00	1.00					
Cooley, Sam'l. A.	220.00						
Dudley, E. G.	2.75						
French, W. M.	0.00	1.00					
Fuller, Walter	20.60						
Fyler, Franklin F.	0.00	1.00					
Hall, K.	20.00						
Hamilton, A. H.	15.40	1.00					
Hammond, R.	3.25	1.00					
Hentschel, A. F.	15.00						
Holmes, George	8.85	1.00					
Hutchinson, E. P.	56.85	1.00					
Jackson, Wm. W.	10.00						
Jenniman, Henry	177.00	1.00					
Kendall, Chas. P.	0.00	1.00					
Millett, S. C. Jr.	174.75						$43.69
Nichols, Edgar F.	250.00	1.00			$2.00		$250

Table (continued)
1864 United States Tax Roll
Occupied Beaufort, South Carolina
Taxpayers Assessed

Post Office Name	*Income*	*Gold Watch*	*Yacht*	*Carriage*	*Piano*	*Silver*	*Penalty*
Nichols, John J.	133.35						
Nickerson, F. H.	15.65	1.00					
Poelling, Charles	24.05						
Reed, Wm.	0.00	1.00					
Scovil, Nelson R.	0.00	1.00		$1.00		$1.20	
Tucker, J. D.	0.00	1.00					
Waterhouse, George	52.00						
Wording, W. E.	46.10	3.00					
Bluffton							
Verdier, F. U.		$1.00					
Dataw Island							
Carey, D. R.	60.00						
Davis, C. A.	10.00						
Dennis, C. W.	77.80	1.00			$2.00		
Riddell, E. S.	166.25	1.00					
Roberts, Benj. S.	0.00	1.00					
Wakefield, Peter	20.75	1.00					
Ladies Island							
Phelps, E. W.	0.00	1.00					
Saint Helena Island							
Hunn, John	20.00						
Randolph, W. J.	24.05						
Thorpe, David F.	76.25				$3.00		

Source: U.S. National Archives, U.S. Treasury, Internal Revenue Service, 1864 Assessment, Division #8, Collections District 32 (Roll R W #1435).

The U.S. Direct Tax in South Carolina started in 1863. Enforcement was dissimilar to any other state. Although passed as a revenue measure, propaganda was more important. It was a means to punish rebel landowners. The impact was enormous, the aftermath lasted decades. The Direct Tax lingered longer than any other war tax. Of the twenty million dollars legislated, less than three-quarters was credited, discounted, waived or offset. Actual monetary receipts were less than expected. Two million dollars in prepayment discount occurred early. Collections continued through 1888 but the books were not closed until the turn of the century. All loyal states, except Delaware, assumed the Direct Tax obligation for their citizens. After statehood, West Virginia was allowed to pay a portion of disloyal Virginia's allocation.[154]

Implementation of the U.S. Direct Tax was scheduled to begin August 1, 1862. For "persons residing in insurrectionary states" collection was suspended until Union Forces re-established federal control. The levy was a national property or "ad valorem" tax, based on state real property assessments complete with normal appeals, collection and enforcement provisions. The major difference from state to state was the constitutionally mandated allocation based on census numbers. This resulted in each state's true rates being different. The Direct Tax had little effect on loyal taxpayers because it was paid for them. Tax foreclosures for delinquent taxes only had occurred in occupied territory. Twenty-day grace periods, redemption, tax foreclosures and auctions were followed by forty years of claims by disloyals. Tax deeds "in fee simple, free and discharged of all prior liens" were given by Direct Tax Commissioners to auction buyers. Titles were deemed good and marketable to third party purchasers.[155]

President Lincoln, as authorized by Congress June 7, 1862, appointed Boards of Direct Tax Commissioners after federal order returned. Battlefield shifts precluded most of Direct Taxes in rebel states. Occupied counties in South Carolina, Florida, Virginia, Tennessee and Arkansas endured the process. Coverage was spotty. No complaints were made that owners were assessed differently because of where property was located. Fair and equal was of no concern for rebel owners.[156]

Commodore Samuel F. Du Pont's Navy and General Thomas Sherman's Expeditionary Forces captured Forts Beauregard and Walker at the Battle of Port Royal on November 7, 1861. White residents on the surrounding lowcountry islands of Port Royal, Hilton Head and Saint Helena evacuated to the mainland. Within a year the Direct Tax Commission for the Beaufort District was operational. Secretary Chase recommended abolitionist attorney Abram D. Smith, formerly of South Carolina and a slave owner, William H. Brisbane and William E. Wording. The Tax Office opened in the waterfront Rhett Mansion. South Carolina's share of the National Direct Tax was $363,570 of which only $11,911.04 was due from occupied Beaufort. This "3 percent" tax created unsurpassed bureaucracy, surveys, foreclosures and costs. Never had so much enforcement produced so little tax. Any Beaufort plantation owner could have cleared the direct tax liens for a small sum if only the Commissioners would have accepted payment from a disloyal. Only a few tried.[157]

The tax allocation was little more than guesswork. In fact, it was considered by the Secretary "comparatively immaterial what the total amount of assess value for the State [South Carolina], providing all its parts were proportionally assessed and taxed." Old tax rolls of owners of town lots and rural lands were available. Surveys were redrawn using the "federal township, range and section" protocol. This obliterated traditional property lines. On November 3, 1862, the Commissioners gave notice that Direct Taxes were due by January 2, 1863. Unpaid taxes would result in foreclosures. If delinquent properties were passed at auction, such could be struck off in the name of the United States. The tax auction of February 11, 1863, had most properties bid in by the government. Subsequently, plantation lands were sold at Hilton Head Island. The few purchasers received tax deeds titled as a "Commissioner Certificates." Owners had a redemption period, but this was seldom used because they were absent and disloyal.[158]

The Tax Commission gave notice in both local and national papers. If taxes remained outstanding sixty days after notice, foreclosure proceedings began. Should an owner clear the balance after the deadline, a 50 percent penalty was added. The first auction covered 241 Beaufort town lots, dwellings and commercial. This was followed by an auction of 208 island plantations. That land was assessed at four dollars an acre, under a long-standing South Carolina fixed appraisal law. All were below market because this was some of the most valuable agricultural land in the country. The initial Direct Tax for Beaufort was doubled by the $5,955.52 in penalties, $1,432.81 in interest and $1,220.87 for notices. This was still below market value, and the bargain was noticed by speculators.[159]

Speculators flooded to Beaufort to bid on valuable cotton land. The February 11, 1863, auction was postponed because such "sharpies" concerned the military Governor. General Saxton even considered using the "Cotton Fund" held in New York to purchase farms for the freedmen needing shelter and a livelihood. The President instructed the Beaufort Tax Commissioners to hold back property that might be useful to the military, naval and other public purposes such as care of freedmen and refugees. Exempted from sale were churches, schools, cemeteries, civic buildings, the jail and arsenal. The sale took place two weeks later on February 25, 1863, at the steps of the Rhett Mansion. Included were properties belonging to Beaufort's "free blacks" community downtown. Three freedmen purchased small lots on the "Point," one for $13.34 for use as a dock. Loyal postmaster John Fyler and farmer David L. Thompson, and three loyal Beauforteans living North, along with six free blacks, paid their tax and retained ownership. Sixty-one plantations passed over the auctioneer's block to Northern speculators.[160]

The President's directive spared island timberlands from commercial loggers. Hunting and Saint Phillips Islands were declared reserves. Sixteen island plantations on Coosaw, Saint Helena, Ladies, Parris and Port Royal were later designated reserves for freedmen settlement villages. Lincoln's instructions provided small farms available as pre-emption land grants. The General Land Office decades before had offered pre-emption land to lure pioneers to the Western wilderness. The pre-emption homestead was priced at $1.25 an acre for up to twenty acres. In a Circular dated November 3, 1863, General Saxton increased the acreage. School lands were set aside, the rental of which was dedicated to public education. Commissioners lowered the minimum price if property was passed at auction to a third of its original value. This did not affect the homesteaders $1.25 fixed price. The Administration was testing a model designed to make available parcels of rebel lands to freedmen, whereby they might support themselves.[161]

U.S. Tax Commissioners began to deliver "Tax Sale Certificates" to third party purchasers in the name of the U.S. government. Certificate No. 154 giving tax title for Old Fort Plantation on the southern side of Port Royal Island, dated April 2, 1863, and included the ruins of the 1730s Fort Frederick on the Beaufort River, just west of town. Owned by rebel planter John Joyner Smith, it had been a campground for the First South Carolina Volunteers commanded by Colonel Thomas W. Higginson. The seven-hundred-acre plantation was purchased for $1,000 (Fig. 97). The Emancipation Proclamation, read January 1, 1863, was delivered there to a large audience of soldiers, missionaries and freedmen. The Direct Tax created no tax benefit to the Treasury but did spark homesteads and a land rush to wealthy Boston speculators.

Tax Commissioners were aware of the consequences of tax foreclosures. Sheriff sales of tax delinquent property was common in America. Notices, grace periods and rights of redemption were procedural niceties necessary for valid deeds to the third parties. After the auction closed, unsold parcels could be sold by private treaty at lower prices. Full payment was required at auction. Later, terms were available for veterans but not for pre-emption homesteaders.

The nation had always awarded donation land to veterans. Army and naval active personnel along with veterans and their families could purchase, with a 25 percent down payment, auction lands, and could pay the balance over three years with no personal liability. An auction announced in the *Free South* newspaper November 21, 1863, listed over five hundred town tracts scheduled for sale on January 19, 1864. The average price was five hundred dollars which was an increase. General Rufus Saxton used his veteran benefits to purchase the Governor's mansion. The much improved Heyward Mansion had been his official residence. By April 17, 1865, almost half the tax properties had been purchased by third parties. Rural land went as high as $10.00 an acre. Forty percent of the veterans' purchases were later foreclosed for non-payment. After the troops withdrew, prices dropped and the resale market collapsed.[162]

The Beaufort U.S. Tax Commission conducted an auction April 6, 1866, of tracts no longer reserved for military, medical or revenue purposes. Some were transferred to the newly created Freedmen's Bureau. Two Beaufortians residing in the North, who remained loyal during the war, the Rev. Richard Fuller and Edward Pritchard, retained their family plantations. Both had given loyalty oaths to the Union. A Boston consortium acquired 6,030 acres of cotton lands divided among eleven plantations. These Massachusetts speculators, including the State's Governor and industrialist John Forbes, netted over one hundred thousand dollars from "free labor" cotton. Another venture, the Sea Island Company, incorporated in 1864, sold five plantations to the United States Cotton Company for a hefty profit shortly after their purchase. Some New England abolitionists were more effective at land profiteering than social work. Most returned North, but a few remained and contributed to the recovery and progress of island freedmen.[163]

The last auction of Low Country farmlands grossed $87,669 from ninety-one plantations containing ten thousand acres, realizing nine dollars an acre. Veterans purchased 7,147 acres, civilians 2,225 and 650 acres to freedmen farmers exercising pre-emption rights. Freedmen paid $25.00 for twenty acres. This sum was first saved at the Freedmen's Thrift of Beaufort. Government surveyors had earlier laid out the "New City of Port Royal" at Lands End next to the repair facility of the South Atlantic Blockading Squadron. This was more a commercial venture than freedmen community. The town had a grid of loyal street names, starting with Adams and ending with Yates. The town center was to have three squares, town lots measuring 66' × 115', a community garden serving sixty-four blocks of neighborhoods. The cashier of the Beaufort Freedmen's Bank, S. L. Harris, controlled sales and in the process, reserved prime locations for associates.[164]

Governor Saxton also was responsible for Northern Florida. The Florida U.S. Direct Tax Commission included political opportunist, L. D. Stickney, who had been Superintendent of Freedmen of African Descent in Florida. He imported from New York goods for the Florida Black Regiments, selling them at a hefty profit. Stickney and his brother John owned *The Peninsula* press, the official newspaper for tax notices. The rates were higher than all others. The other Florida Tax Commissioners were John. S. Sommes and Harrison Reed. Commissioner Stickney's law partner became the U.S. Attorney for Northern Florida, C. P. Chamberlain. They provided legal services to the Tax Commission. Professional fees were paid in addition to costs. Audit, reviews and pre-approvals were absent.[165]

The Stickney and Chamberlain Law Firm also represented a Florida railroad in a confiscation case. None complained of the conflict of interest. Although Commissioner Stickney was paid $3,000 for his Treasury Commissioner job, his legal, commercial and newspaper businesses exceeded this salary. He was seldom present in Florida. To appraise the property for direct tax assessment, Commissioner Stickney hired William A. Davis. The process took only three days. *The Peninsula* gave notice that the Fernadina Auction was to begin June 15, 1863. Prior to the sale, some were allowed to redeem posted property by paying tax, penalties and interest amounting to $304.13. Auction results were mixed. Ninety-three lots brought in $16,002.00. Most buyers were friends, family and associates of the three Commissioners. Commissioner Reed acquired forty-three town lots. President Lincoln's private secretary, Major John Hay, acquired a beachside mansion. Stickney bought former U.S. Senator David Levy Yulee's expensive mansion on Fernadina for $19,329.[166]

Watchdogs in Washington questioned the Florida tax auctions, forcing half the transactions be rescinded. Fraud was apparent, so the Secretary appointed Austin Smith, Special Treasury Agent, to audit the Florida Direct Tax Commission. Agent Smith's report of July 30, 1864, concluded that Lyman Stickney had engaged in private speculation as an official and "gave very little attention to the actual duties of his office." Commissioner Reed was deemed "culpable." The report concluded the Florida Tax Commission accomplished little besides the enrichment of officials. Reed and Sommes were replaced by "Union Men," William Alsop and Buckingham Smith. Although Stickney was accused of felonies by the inspector general, no indictment followed. In June 1864, the Treasury's Solicitor, Edward Jordan, released Stickney's two bondsmen, precluding any recovery.[167]

Another South Carolina auction was planned for Prince Williams Parish but was suspended. President Andrew Johnson questioned the entire program. Suspensions were ordered. In Virginia, only 350 town lots and 6,400 rural acres passed under the auctioneers hammer during the war. Proceeds were a respectable $110,417. The Beaufort tax sales were the pride of the Treasury.[168]

Abolitionists recognized the available opportunity of the tax foreclosures in providing lands for freedmen farmers. Governor Saxton was one of the first to realize the importance of those twenty acre plots. U.S. Senator James R. Doolittle of Wisconsin, too, viewed the foreclosures as a "most efficient" way to empower freedmen. The "New South" should be "founded on principals broad and equitable for all." Despite progressive program proponents, all ceased with the death of President Lincoln. General Saxton's dedicated stewardship was just too radical. He was replaced in 1866. Before departure, President Andrew Johnson instructed the Tax Commission to suspend any more property seizures. Rebel owners could now recover lost lands.

The Freedmen's Bureau Land Division was charged with restoring property to any "who could show constant loyalty, past as well as present." This required an "Iron Clad" oath of loyalty, assuring past and future fealty. The Land Division controlled three-hundred-thousand acres of abandoned or confiscated lands. Two-thirds was in South Carolina. In addition, hundreds of acres in Georgia were made available to freedmen under General W. T. Sherman's Special Field Orders No. 15. Supporters of the freedmen expected Congress to enact legislation making permanent Sherman's Field Orders No. 15. Instead President Johnson withdrew Sherman's Field Orders No. 15 and instructed the Bureau to return lands to loyal owners even if occupied by freedmen. The only exceptions were for titles already passing to third parties holding "Certificates of Titles" in Beaufort. Head of the Freedmen's Bureau, General O. O. Howard, was ordered to evict those occupying farms under Sherman's Field Orders No. 15. Most became sharecroppers after signing contracts with owners, often their prior masters. The labor contracts were similar to indenture contracts.

The Beaufort Direct Tax Commission issued a thousand tax deeds to freedmen by the end of 1865. Before closed, another two thousand titles were executed if pre-emption prices were fully paid. Some lost land to sharpies and squatters. "School lands" were released for sale and on January 11, 1867, three thousand acres were auctioned for a minimum price of ten dollars an acre—too high for subsistence farmers. On November 15, 1867, Secretary of War U.S. Grant released lands remaining in inventory and not claimed by rebel owners. Disloyals in "contempt of government" remained excluded from reclaiming.

The suspensions of auctions did not terminate the Direct Tax Commissions. Although on May 17, 1865, the U.S. Commissioner of Internal Revenue instructed the Commissions "to suspend all sales of land for taxes until otherwise ordered," other functions continued. Secretary of the Treasury William P. Fessenden recommended that tax foreclosures remain in effect until all states paid their share of the 1861 Direct Tax. Congress on July 28, 1866, extended the foreclosure suspension through 1867. By Joint Resolution, Congress on July 23, 1868, finally terminated the foreclosure provisions of the Act, thereby ending the punitive sections. Collections and redemptions were still processed monthly. The Commissioners workload lessened but the salaries continued.

The Georgia U.S. Direct Tax Commission opened June 1865, and collected about $82,000 before the State Legislature tried to assume the balance on behalf of its citizens. In Virginia, the ancestral home of Robert E. Lee, "Arlington Hall," was foreclosed and transferred to the Government for a National Cemetery. After years, the Lee family descendants eventually were awarded $150,000 in damages by Congress. In Arkansas, Commissioners added the Direct Tax to its annual State ad valorem tax bill.

Seven states had foreclosure sales after the war. The South Carolina federal office did not close until October 28, 1870. Commissioners collected two-thirds of the original apportionment of $363,570 of the state allocation. The balance of other funds held by the South Carolina Tax Commission was transferred to the Freedmen's Bureau. Rachel Barrett, widow of the President of the Charleston Hebrew Benevolent Society, paid her Direct Tax bill for downtown property. Tax Commissioner Cooley receipted payment May 5, 1865. Interest, penalty and costs were waived without explanation (Fig. 98). The District Collector in Helena, Arkansas, on December 1, 1865, received payment of $2.22 for three lots owned by George Porter (Fig. 99). The Tax Commissioner for Arkansas, Charles Stoddard, collected over $154,000 of the state's share of the Direct Tax.

William Hurt of Cleveland, Tennessee, Direct Tax Collector for the State, received $1.68 from M. W. Legg of Bradley County in January 1866 for eighty acres valued at $480. Tennessee collected over half its allotment of $669,498 before being dissolved April 30, 1867 (Fig. 100). Acting Collector A. H. Grahams for the Texas Commission receipted $7.35 for Elisha Allens' land in Milam, Williamson and Brown counties (Fig. 101). The Texas Commission was disbanded February 28, 1867, after depositing about half of its $355,000 allotment.

The Charleston Direct Tax office closed three years after Virginia and Tennessee were shuttered. The U.S. Congressional Joint Committee on Reconstruction, chaired by

Thaddeus Stevens, continued to favor a more punitive approach rather than restoring rebel land. The Joint Committee agreed that it was just that disloyals pay taxes similar to loyal citizens. A few members of the Joint Committee disapproved, delays seeming a "premium for insurrection," their poverty or not. Congress concluded that rebels should not benefit from "wickedness and folly."[169]

The South Carolina U.S. Tax Commission also collected $50,000 from "school lands" leased for farming in Beaufort. The Freedmen's Bureau received the balance of those funds but without designating benefit for Sea Islanders. The Beaufort District Tax Commission closed its ledgers December 31, 1865, and filed a "Summary of Revenue Collected from land Rents and Fee and Disbursements Paid Out." Rent, farm leases and pre-emption sales totaled almost one hundred thousand dollars. Direct costs, including surveys, clerks and fees consumed 30 percent of the revenue or $28,583.61. Twenty-five thousand of the balance went for teachers, schools and supplies. With creative accounting, the $60,000 in Commissioner salaries for six years were sidestepped. If deducted, the program was a loss. None questioned the effectiveness after the report was laid on the table of Congress.

Low Country hero, Robert Smalls, invested his admiralty prize for capturing the rebel steamer *The Planter* by buying tax auction property. The U.S. Supreme Court had deferred tax cases with economic impact during the war. Robert Smalls tax purchase of a home in Beaufort, was decided in *De Treville v. Smalls* (1878) 98 U.S. 571. The Court held that the purchase of a townhome for only $238 at auction (one-tenth the value) under the Act of March 13, 1863, had completely transferred title. "Tax Certificate" was prima facie evidence that purchased rights were superior to prior debts, liens or encumbrances. This settled the question of titles issued by the Commission to auction buyers.

The *Beaufort Republican* newspaper, owned by General Saxton's brother-in-law, who had been a Brooks' Farm missionary before the war. James G. Thompson ran a editorials in 1870 criticizing fellow "visionary enthusiasts and fanatics, who imagined that they had a humanitarian mission to pursue and while professing a desire to bless only succeeded in cursing the country with the silliest projects, half carried out." He accused the Tax Commission of unnecessarily complicating traditional property lines by resurveying. If the entire tax process had been managed by "sensible, practical men" much hardship would have been averted and more good accomplished. Thompson ran a self-help piece titled "How to Get Back Your Land." He recounted the successful redemption of an Elliott's commercial property. They had good political connections. He observed that no single veteran had received a deed even after paying the mortgage. The veterans had "neither land nor money." Many in frustration, had sold to land speculators.

The remaining government land in Beaufort was disposed under the Acts of June 8, 1872, and February 8, 1875. Auctions were held December 20, 1872 and January 12, 1876, of parcels returned after veterans defaulted. Purchases were made by Edgar F. Nichols and eight other Beaufort realtors. Afterwards, Hunting Island Lighthouse, National Cemetery and public docks remained federal hands. Although only $6,017.00 was received from these two auctions, at least the parcels were returned to the tax rolls. This was suggested by editor Thompson. On October 27, 1872, Thompson had pointed out that local government could not tax or raze government tenements that

Summary of South Carolina Tax Commissioner Rents and Fees and Disbursements

January 1, 1870

Revenue		
Rents (Act of June 7, 1862)	$21,899.70	
School farm leases (Acts of September 16, 1863, and July 16, 1866)	26,015.73	
Special rents (Commissioner of Internal Revenue Instructions of 1866)	17,987.80	
Certificate fees	4,289.50	
Miscellaneous	971.62	
Head of household preemption claims (Acts of September 16, 1863, and July 16, 1866)	34,243.28	
Total		$105,407.63
Disbursements		
Surveys	$3,801.57	
Clerks	15,810.79	
Messengers and servants	2,216.97	
Certificates	4,055.47	
Incidentals	2,698.81	
Total		28,583.61
Net Revenue Collected		$76,824.02
Distribution of Net Revenue		
Teachers, schools and educational expenses (Presidential Instruction dated September 16, 1863)	$23,496.44	
Balance transferred to Bureau of Refugees, Freedmen, and Abandoned Lands (Presidential Instruction dated June 3, 1865)	54,765.69	
Less unpaid expenses	(1,455.11)	
Total Distributed		$76,817.02

were "eyesores and fire hazards." "The United States will not pay taxes, will not repair, will not remove, will not clear," and will not do anything but hold.

Soon after the tax decision in *De Treville v Smalls*, R. F. Patterson, Superintendent of Sales, Memphis Tax Office, published notice of a "Sale of Direct Tax Lands" for May 1, 1878, in Shelby County. All but three parcels were rural. The Commissioner of Internal Revenue was disposing of those lands as provided by Section 4 of the June 8, 1872, Act. Terms were cash due upon delivery of a certificate of purchase, only conveying whatever title possessed by the United States. The government reserved the right to bid on any parcel.

An unintended consequence benefited a few rebel mansion owners. Because many Beaufort mansions were reserved for hospitals, schools and headquarters, the residences were spared the tax auction. Some of the staunchest rebels were better positioned after the war than Beaufort free blacks, poor loyals and non–slave owning whites. In some instances property was even improved, such as Miss Elliott's waterfront home used by the Departmental Medical Director. The O'Connor's Beaufort Hotel sold to Colonel Henry Ware and Lieutenant H. W. Case for $10,000.00, the highest price ever. The officers took advantage of veteran payments over three years. After the military withdrew, the property was defaulted back to the government. The O'Connor family, on September 18, 1882, received $4,637.13 in damages through the efforts of South Carolina Congressman M. P. O. Connor, the son of the original owner (Fig. 102). The U.S. Government only received $2,500 from the officers but paid out almost $5,000 to the family as damages, again evidencing the pointless effort of the Commissioners.

First families of Beaufort subsequently received damages through the Court of Claims. Heirs were scattered across the nation, but cash settlements were preferable because real estate values had declined. Over seventy claims were stymied. The Fullers, Johnsons, Pointels, Perryclears, Stuarts, Talbirds and Leveretts did not receive checks until after the century.

The Commissioner of Internal Revenue in his Annual Report of July 11, 1870, concluded:

> The land acquired in the South by the United States, under tax sales, have proven to be rather a source of embarrassment than of profit. For that reason, and because the real object of a tax is to obtain the tax imposed, it seems advisable that a system of redemption of these lands by the delinquent owners should be provided. From this system it would probably be necessary to except the lands so purchased in South Carolina, since they have been to a large extent settled upon by the freedmen, at the instance of the government.

Results of Beaufort Tax Sales

		Percentage
Proceeds from Auctions Held 1863–1865		
Net of assessed tax, interest and penalties totaling $20,411.36	$7,820.93	2.4%
Property Sales		
Army, Navy and veterans	144,460.76	44.6
Head of family Pre-Emptions	33,375.40	10.3
General public	54,529.17	16.9
School land	83,312,47	25.8
Gross proceeds	323,498.79	100.0%
Expenses (estimated)	150,0000.00	46.4
Net proceeds from foreclosed lands in the Beaufort District through January 31, 1882	$173,498.79	53.6%

The financial failure of the program was confirmed by an accounting of foreclosed property in Beaufort. More than half the proceeds were consumed by expenses, of which no detailed accounting was provided.

Although repeatedly requested by the U.S. Congress, the South Carolina Direct Tax Commissioners failed to forward details of disbursements. Prior to 1868, accounts were audited by Fifth Auditor who excused Commissioners under Section 6 of the, March 3, 1865, Act which permitted the deduction of expenses from rents and sales as provided in Section 9, of the June 7, 1862, act. The auditors allowed the Commissioners to offset expenses against proceeds without approval from Washington. Even more curious was the small sum actually transferred to the Treasury. Over $320,000 in proceeds produced only $20,411.36 in Direct Taxes, penalties and interest. That was all the Treasury got. The disposition of the other $300,000.00 is a mystery. Only a small balance from School Lands was transferred to the Freedmen's Bureau.

Secretary of War, William W. Belknap, requested that some tax-foreclosed properties scheduled for sale under the Act of June 10, 1872, be excluded. Arsenals at Shreveport, Chattahoochee, and military posts in Marshall, Jefferson and Jeff Davis, Texas, were deemed of value to the Army. Sales proceeds were to be dedicated for the purchase of land for an Atlantic Coast arsenal. The Attorney General on October 8, 1872, concluded that Texas posts could not be retained by the government because it never acquired "marketable title" since such posts were leased from private owners. Private owners had not been tax foreclosed. The federal government held no public domain in the "Lone Star State."

Section 12 of the Direct Tax Act directed the deposition of the tax auction proceeds:

1. A quarter was for loyal citizens suffering enemy losses.
2. A quarter for deportation and colonization of former slaves offshore.
3. Half to the U.S. Army's budget.

Most auctions occurred in South Carolina and in 1882 the South Carolina Legislature applied for a quarter of the auction proceeds to cover losses sustained by loyal citizens. The first Comptroller of the Army, William Lawrence, with few words ruled that "no state has any right to payment under Section 12 of the Jan. 7, 1862 act." The audacity of the Palmetto State legislators repulsed the auditor. The Comptroller's excuse for denial was that Emancipation had made the point moot. No slavery existed and colonial deportations after the Emancipation Proclamation did not occur.

The Secretary of the Treasury was directed by Congress on March 2, 1891, to settle claims of heirs of direct tax foreclosed property. Congress appropriated a half million dollars and later approved $498,038 in claims. Over time, almost twenty million dollars in Direct Taxes was credited. As a revenue producing mechanism, the Direct Tax was a boondoggle. Administrative costs exceeded collections. Even as a punitive measure, it was costly and burdensome and discretionary. The only value was propaganda, which waned as years passed. Congress overestimated the efficacy of Direct Taxes.

After the South Carolina Direct Tax Commission closed, Beaufort's Congressman, William Elliott, pursued claims on behalf of voters. Property passing to third parties was beyond recovery, but damages approved by the Court of Claims continued. Successful families receiving damages before the turn of the century included the first families of Beaufort: Barnwell, Smith, Rhodes, Capers, Chaplain, de Saussure, Fripp, Fuller, Heyward, Rhett, Means, Stuart, Seabrook, Semes, Pinckney, Morcock and Coffin. Plantations' former owners receiving money were the heirs of "Old Fort," "Jereco," "Cherry Hill," "Fairfield," "Barton Hill," "Cedar Grove," "Shell Point," and "Frogmore." No records indicate if any Beaufort tradesmen, laborers or "free blacks" received compensation for their losses. Political connections rather than merits often determined recompense.

Chapter XI

Post-War United States Taxes, 1866–1900

With the surrender of Lee's Army of Northern Virginia at Appomattox on April 9, 1865, the Confederate States were no more. Surrenders of Georgia, the Carolinas, Louisiana and Texas followed. Field commanders "discharged" companies and irregulars sparing troops the indignity of capture. Only if rebel soldiers were formally paroled were they given food, medical and transportation home. Escaping rebels were outside the law. Proof of a parole and an "Iron Clad Oath," allowed former rebels the vote, office or claims. The day of President Lincoln's assassination, Union troops raised the flag over Fort Sumter, where the rebellion began. The President's funeral followed that Wednesday.[170]

After the assassination, the nation was less forgiving of their prodigal cousins. Radical Republicans had never agreed with the President's "forgive and forget" policy. Punishment for treason and citizenship for the emancipated became the Radical Republican's mantra. Accordingly, "oaths of loyalty" transmuted into complicated affirmations of past, present and future allegiance. The "Iron Clad Oath" precluded most from readmission. Radicals wanted to eliminate all remnants of planter society to establish a "New South," in the image of Brook Farm. A home to sober, loyal, free labor voters. The only Southern district that resembled that model was Beaufort, South Carolina. Locals absent, freedmen were the majority and were joined by northern merchants.

The co-chairs of the Joint Committee for Reconstruction charged with drafting a plan were Senators Thaddeus Stevens and William P. Fessender. Stevens tried to limit presidential amnesties and pardons. Stevens supported General Rufus Saxton's pre-emption land for freedmen farmers as necessary to citizenship. The Bureau of Freedmen, Refugees and Abandoned Lands, to Stevens' dismay, was directed by President Johnson to cancel Sherman's Special Field Order No. 15 granting homesteads. Disloyals could reclaim farms. Thousands of plantations that could have been set aside for freedmen farmers was returned to rebels.[171]

The "Congressional Globe" on March 10, 1866, reprinted Thaddeus Stevens' speech demanding that "bloody estates" of planters be "stripped away." He proposed amendments to the Confiscation Acts calling for more forfeitures of rebel property. His bill would have added the seized estates to the public domain and be administered by the General Land Office. He proposed forty-acre farms for pre-emption homesteads. Further, he suggested a fifty dollar "grub stake" for freedmen. Stevens' bill was the type of legislation General Sherman expected of Congress after declaring his Special Field Orders No. 15. Smaller rebel farms, valued at less than $5,000 on March 4, 1865, would have been excluded by Stevens. His target was the planters, not yeoman farmers. Most in Congress considered Stevens' bill an affront to private property rights. Although rebellion was treason, property rights were sacred. The Fifth Amendment guaranteed that private property would not be taken "for public use without just compensation." Ironically this was one of the causes for secession. Loyalties and positions were shifting.[172]

The Bureau of Refugees, Freedmen and Abandoned Property, within the War Department, relied on the defense budget for funding. After the War, Congress was tepid to social programs, including benefits for veterans. Stevens' forty-acre farms were deemed land giveaways. Priced at 6 percent of pre-war land values was close to market. Abandoned or confiscated lands were transferred to the Freedmen Bureau under War Department General Order No. 110, June 2, 1865, but was soon withdrawn.[173]

Commercial traffic down the Mississippi River began in June 1865. Treasury Secretary McCulloch on May 9 announced that his office would accept new requests for trading licenses within occupied territories. Applicants had to give evidence of loyalty, an oath and pay fees. Most used political connections. West of the Mississippi, ports opened May 16 in Arkansas and Louisiana. By Proclamations on June 13 and 24, the blockades of Galveston, LaSalle, Brazos de Santiago, Point Isabel and Brownsville, Texas, were lifted. A Texas editor noted that Texas, with unbuilt railroads, cheap land and almost untouched by war, was prime for a rebound. Property values were 20 percent of pre-war assessments. Tax collections ceased. Only with outside capital would recovery occur.[174]

Because the "Iron Clad Oath" precluded most southern officials from federal positions, patronage rather than recruitment filled positions. Custom personnel remained political appointments. Indiana Representative Henry Smith Lane, on June 6, 1865, recommended for the Collector at Indianola, Major General Milton Stapp, then living in Indiana. Stapp, a Union man, left Goliad, Texas, during the war. Congressman Lane wrote to Treasury Secretary Hugh McCulloch that General Stapp, a veteran of the Mexican-American War, was "a true, brave and loyal man" who had suffered greatly after leaving Texas. Because the candidate was "honest and competent," in 1869, General Stapp became Collector at Galveston, a lucrative position.

The August 5, 1865, editorial of the *Boston Daily Advertiser* mentioned "many openings for Northern enterprise" in the war-torn states. Massachusetts Governor John A. Andrew along with a Boston cabal known as the "American Land Company and Agency" had long speculated in prime cotton lands in the Low Country. Their preferred purchase was tax foreclosure auctions. The abolitionist investors promoted "free cotton" from "free labor." In Texas, another Bostonian, wrote his brother to come to Texas and join his Houston trading company months after the surrender of the Trans-Mississippi. The July 23, 1865, letter was tempting:

> I have stayed here through the war to protect my property.... There is a good chance to make some money on cotton here. I know the condition of cotton in this state & Red River as well as any man in the state. The Gov't will not let the cotton go out yet unless the shipper can show a clear title.... I can get [a] permit to take out all the cotton that I can get money to purchase & it is but a little money I can raise. Have you not got some man that you can send out here with $10,000 or $20,000 ... you can deposit in Boston & draw on it as you make purchases.... I can get good cotton here now for ten cents ... per pound and I can get it shipped to New York or Boston for three cents ... for my trouble I will ask one half the profit after you get you money.... I am satisfied that all the permits I ask for will be granted & no one can take out cotton yet without first getting a permit.... I shall ship some cotton from Shreveport down [the] Red River to New Orleans.[175]

While speculative profits flowed north, locals suffered the lack of civil government. All rebel Treasuries were broke. In Alabama, less than a thousand dollars of "real" money existed. Texas had a thousand dollars specie but owed nine million dollars. Texas had "borrowed" a million dollars from its "Educational Trust Funds." Arkansas's Provisional Governor Isaac Murphy asked for help from Northern friends. All needed food, housing and clothing. Georgia had suspended property tax collections altogether. On January 18, 1866, the reconstructed Legislature at Milledgeville announced it was unable pass a Tax Act. Surety bonds for State Tax Collectors were suspended. The Comptroller General could not borrow until a Tax Act was passed (Fig. 103). In Charleston, Mrs. Abbey A. Legare, on May 26, 1866, managed to pay $7.60 for past due taxes and penalties (Fig. 104). The following year the Union Bank of South Carolina paid its Parish Tax of $120.80 plus a late penalty. Bank President William B. Smith had followed John Pope, who had resigned that position to become the State's Chief Tax Collector.[176]

Southern governments endured the consequences of defeat. State Conventions convened to ratify Constitutional Amendments necessary for readmission to Congress. Military rule was costly. The Panola County, Mississippi, assessor charged the Estate of T. B. Middleton for 1861 paupers and military taxes. The taxes were split a third to the County and the balance to the State (Fig 105). In Texas, General Winfield Scott Hancock, Fifth Military District, authorized a State Convention. The delegates, because of the "Iron Clad Oath," were primarily freed blacks, foreign born– and transplanted loyals. The Convention assembled in Austin on June 1, 1868, but had to adjourn for lack of funds. The counties collected a "Constitution Tax" before reopening that fall. Grayson County Collector J. P. Hopson collected $3.20 from the Estate of Willis Holmes. The delegates reassembled after collecting $100,000 for the Convention (Fig. 106).

Before the War, the Texas Legislature on February 14, 1860, had forwarded a Joint Resolution before the war to their Congressmen "to procure the reimbursement to the State of Texas of funds expended for the protection of the frontier." Included were requests for indemnification of private property losses from Indian raids along the Rio Grande as well as incursions from the Cortina Mexican Rebels. Also requested was a federal law prohibiting buying stolen Texas horses in New Mexico and the Indian Territory. A muster into United States service of the existing Texas Rangers was also requested.

Texas passed its Ordinance of Dissolution from the United States on February 1, 1861. Specifically, Texas considered the annexation compact with the United States had "failed in purpose." The only specific example of breach was the federal failure to protect people and property "upon an exposed frontier." The first war bond was a Frontier Defense loan. During Reconstruction, Constitutional Conventions, between 1866 and 1875, repeated the need for better border defense. A precursor of the Texas Rangers, the Frontier Battalion, was funded by a Frontier Loan of $750,000 on August 5, 1870. It was to be repaid by a surcharge against property owners. The Sheriff of Grayson County issued a receipt to G. W. Newcome and Andrew Willis Holmes for their $1.20 Frontier Tax on June 23, 1871 (Fig. 107). Included among the plenary powers provided by the 1876 Texas Constitution was "Protection of the Frontier," Section 48, Article III. The frontier security issue never went away.

The Texas reconstruction constitution contained Article III, Section 48, that allowed taxation only for the "economical administration of the government." Examples included bond debt, education, asylums, public buildings, grounds and cemeteries. Necessary health and civic expenses were allowed. Curiously, despite prohibition of paying war debts, Section 5, Article III of the Texas Constitution provided a tax for "Confederate Soldiers and Sailors and Their Widows." Doubtless, the lawmakers deemed this a "donation" rather than a debt. The veterans pension was only available to the indigent and disabled. No Union vets need apply.

The United States unintentionally granted other relief to broken Southern Treasuries. Debts paralyzed the defeated South. The nullification of all War Debts was part of the Fourteenth Amendment adopted July 21, 1868. Section 4 declared "null and void" all rebel, civil and military debt in and between January 28, 1861, and August 5, 1865. Such relief was similar to the post World War II "Marshall Plan" of 1948. Post–World War II relief also went to Great Britain and France. No relief was intended by the repudiation of Confederate debt. It was meant to be punitive, to Confederate creditors. The unintended beneficiaries were broken Southern Treasuries.

The magnitude of the unintended relief is seldom appreciated. The majority of the debt was to unpaid soldiers, contractors and civil servants. Bondholders in France and Great Britain lodged complaints about the financial impact of the Fourteenth Amendment. The "Public Debt" section of the Fourteenth Amendment was clear:

> The validity of the public debt of the United States, authorized by law, including debts incurred for payment of pensions and bounties for services in suppressing insurrection or rebellion, shall not be questioned. But neither shall the United States, nor any state, assume or pay any debt or obligation incurred in aid of insurrection or rebellion against the United States, or any claim for the loss of emancipation of any slave, but all such debts, obligation and claims shall be held illegal and void.

On Juneteenth (June 19, 1865), General Gordon Granger, in Texas had issued an "Important Order" restating President Lincoln's January 1, 1863, Emancipation Proclamation, declaring slaves in Texas free. Granger's order also directed Texans to deliver property of the so-called Confederate State or Texas to United States officials. On July 3, 1865, Special Treasury Agent T. J. Conalty demanded all to relinquish government cotton to his agents. The "Whom It May Concern" announcement named C. B. Alexander as the subagent at Milam, Texas. Alexander's territory included seventeen North Texas counties. The broadside by the *Inquirer Print* at Brenham considered all cotton to be contraband. Owners had to prove that their cotton was private and owners loyal. Only "loyal cotton" sold, and then only after the "cotton tax" was paid (Fig. 108).

The U.S. Cotton Tax continued after the war. Cotton growers, factors and dealers paid an excise tax that ranged between 2½¢ to 3¢ a pound. A proposal to increase to a nickel a pound failed to pass Congress. Cotton Tax contributed $350,000 in 1863 and rose to $800,000 by 1865. When repealed on February 3, 1868, cotton taxes had generated between $18 and $24 million annually. The tax collection process however was plagued by fraud and bribes. Commissioner David A. Welles just prior to the Act's repeal, concluded that "fraud and incompetence" permeated the system and deprived the Treasury of hundreds of millions of dollars. Collector S. C. Cochram for the Second District, Mississippi, at Canton on October 20, 1866, issued McFarland & Stinson a Cotton Permit after paying the tax (Fig. 109).[177]

Before the war, America produced 85 percent of the world's cotton. Commercial mills processing that cotton in England and Europe consumed most, leaving only 20 percent for domestic use. The United States had exported 1,400,000 pounds of cotton annually. Although Confederate cotton tax did not meet projections, United States cotton tax was significant after the war. Both Treasuries realized the wisdom of Alexander Hamilton's prediction that high duties inevitably increase smuggling.

Planters and mill owners complained about the punitive nature of the cotton tax after the war ended. The "specific industry" penalty was questioned. Some argued it violated Article 1, Section 9 of the Constitution because it was a prohibited export tax on unprocessed agricultural products. The law excluded cotton from interstate commerce until the tax was paid. Others alleged the cotton tax was a Direct Tax and that should be apportioned among the states based on population. New York dealers stood by that position. The *New York Times*, on March 11, 1872, claimed that cotton taxes were regressive because the consumer paid in higher prices. Another tax was considered after the original cotton tax was repealed in 1868. The New York Chamber of Commerce successfully led the campaign to end any more cotton taxes.

Alabama lawmakers sent a Memorial to Congress requesting a full refund of all cotton taxes collected in their state. The lawmakers cited a New York Cotton Board Resolution that condemned the tax because it gave advantage to cheaper cotton from Egypt and India. The 1872 Alabama Memorial relied on the standard Direct Tax reasoning. The U.S. Treasury subsequently processed millions of dollars in claims for rebel cotton seized and auctioned in New York and St. Louis. Claims were forwarded to the U.S. Court of Claims for adjudication after approval. That Court, created in 1855, consisted of five appointed judges who made recommendations to Congress for appropriations to pay valid claims.[178]

Treasury Special Agent Oscar G. Burbridge, brother of Union General Stephen G. Burbridge, in March 1866, had seized cotton at Shreveport as contraband. Subsequently, the cotton was shipped to New York and sold. Later it proved not to be contraband. Agent Burbridge was replaced for numerous fraudulent seizures. The damaged owner filed a claim that was decided by the U.S. Supreme Court. The High Court held in favor of the owner in *Flanders v. Tweed* 15 U.S. 569 (1872). The opinion concluded the property was private and not the rebel government. Damages were awarded. Benjamin Flanders was the Treasury Agent in New Orleans at the time of the unlawful taking. Another New Orleans case, involved cotton factor J. E. Jordan. New York Cotton Exchange director, Samuel G. Ferguson, used his influence to keep Jordan's cotton in a New Orleans warehouse until ownership was determined. Treasury Agent Flanders tried unsuccessfully to bypass the stay order and ship to New York for auction. Ultimately, Jordan retrieved two-thirds of the bales seized. "Disloyals" were seldom successful in recovering cotton illegally seized by government agents. Those bales benefited the United States and agents, even if acquired as a result of fraud.[179]

The Charleston Board of Trade made internal improvements necessary for the rebirth of the port. The "Taxpayer Convention of South Carolina," between May 9 and May 12, 1871, met in Columbia. Chamber of Commerce President W. D. Porter presided. Other delegates included George A. Trenholm, former Confederate Secretary of Treasury, and Colonel Richard Lathers. The assembly agreed that their economy was in shambles, "bowed down by hard realities." Loans to finance improvements were lacking. A $16,000 debenture bond was authorized and issued December 7, 1870. Creditors were forced to accept two-thirds of the balance due by a bankruptcy court in 1876. Earlier, Major General Robert K. Scott met with a Committee of Eleven from the Chamber and Board of Trades. Obvious was that the fact only sixty thousand voters paid any state tax. So-called "minority representation" of the Reconstruction Legislature borrowed twelve million dollars. Governor Scott delayed the scheduled property tax assessment for 1871 until March 1872 after declaring a moratorium on public debt until sorted out.

Major General Scott served as South Carolina's governor until 1872. He was succeeded by Governor Franklin I. Moses, who served a single term. A committee of the Legislature sent a memorial to Governor Moses complaining that taxpayers had no voice in government or officials. More importantly, they were forced to pay exorbitant property taxes. Moses responded that they had no one to blame but themselves. State taxes had always favored planters over tradesmen, professionals and laborers. Agricultural lands were assessed a percentage of value. President U.S. Grant on March 30, 1874, expressed sympathy for over taxed Carolinians and taxes became paramount in elections. More postwar farmers lost land through state foreclosures than during the war to the U.S. Direct Tax Commission. Small farmers of both races suffered.[180]

Governor Moses delivered a "Message" to the State Assembly in October 1873. Prompted by defaulted creditors, a judge had ordered the Comptroller General to levy additional taxes in November 1873 to pay the $3,700,000 bonds. An extra session of the Legislature addressed the debt crisis. Governor Moses gave an analysis of the state's system of taxation after conceding that "no civilized community exist without taxation." He stated all taxation involved "the taking of private property for public use." He urged a more uniform and equitable system. He noted that Carolinians paid $3.92 per capita in taxes, while the prosperous citizens of Massachusetts paid an average of $16.94. While the average tax burden in loyal states was 20 percent, Carolinians only paid 11 percent. Although poor, the average citizen could stand an increase in the rates even if doubled. The problem was not resolved.

Cotton claims continued into the twentieth century. Half were from South Carolina and a tenth from Texas. Houston law firm Jones & Garnett filed cotton claims on behalf their client, Barnard and Reichmann, of Independence, Texas. As the process came to a conclusion, the Treasury reported it held $31 million in escrow to satisfy such claims awaiting determination. Twenty million dollars had already been disbursed to owners proving loyalty and ownership. Texans had ten million dollars in limbo. Northern Congressmen were unwilling to help "disloyal planters, who suffered in confiscation." After the turn of the century, the "Iron Clad Oath" was relaxed. Texas Congressman Samuel B. Cooper, a member of the Committee on War Claims, predicted that in the future during a "fat year" cotton claims would be paid. Republicans still yelled that "You fellows kicked up the war, you ought to pay for it." Like the Direct Tax fiasco, much of the Cotton Tax was returned to rebel owners. The loss of revenue was dwarfed by thousands in lawyers, administrative and court costs.[181]

Postwar revenue collections exceeded those during the rebellion. The first year of the war, excise taxes were merely $36 million. By war's end, that number was $109 million and in 1866 had grown to $300 million. Liquor, tobacco and cotton taxes reached $500 million. All excises except distilled spirits and tobacco were repealed July 14, 1870. The Treasury had always assured Congress that war taxes would stop as soon as the Union was restored.[182]

Municipalities resumed programs of safety, sanitation and welfare that had been suspended during the war. Recognition for military service reduced some taxes. In Indiana, veterans were spared poll taxes if honorably discharged, served a year and were not a draft substitute. Matthias Bechdor was exempted on January 20, 1866 (Fig. 110). In New Jersey, another tax benefit recognized service: Soldiers were credited with $4.00 against their property tax (Fig. 111). Firemen received 10 percent tax credit (Fig. 112). Although Alexander Hamilton was no proponent of poll taxes, in Federalist No. 36, he conceded their popularity because of ease of collections and uniformity. The Texas 1876 Constitution allowed poll taxes. As the war came to a close, the Tax Receiver for the Seventh Ward, Newark, New Jersey, collected poll, lamp, military, dog and property taxes. The ad valorem assessments amounted to $2.15 per hundred dollar valuation. The poll, dog and military taxes were assessments. Early payers received a 3 percent discount (Fig. 113).

Americans paid $300 million in internal taxes and another $180 million in customs. The national debt reached three billion dollars, but was liquidated by 1886. The Bank Act of July 1, 1866, had virtually ended state bank notes. Income taxes grew to $300 million before repeal. Land sales resumed with added homestead and veterans programs as first signed by President Lincoln. Most Internal Taxes were from Spirits (59 percent), Tobacco (32 percent), and Revenue Stamps (7 percent). Peacetime expenditures included 36 percent for interest, 21 percent for veterans and 19 percent defense related. War debts were retired and a budget surplus followed.[183]

U.S. Senator John Sherman, reflecting back on war tariffs, noted that adjectives such as "protective," "revenue" or "free trade" deceived the fact that all were costs to consumers. His ideal tariff would be discretionary against targets like imported wines and silks. Excises for pleasure or "comforts" such as sugar, tea and coffee were preferable. All were regressive, but if elective purchases for sin or luxury, few complained. Secretary Sherman, in a January 23, 1867, speech, dismissed the notion that tariffs should protect domestic industry from foreign imports. The Treasury collected duty on imported goods of $300 million annually but foreign goods were less than 5 percent of the national product. The Treasury had expended $140 million in gold reserves to service debts. Custom duties collected in gold were no longer essential after the national debt was paid off.

The most imaginative fiscal innovations of the War were the Confederate's "Tax in Kind" and the Union's "National Bank Acts." Plagued by no specie reserves, redundant debt and fiat money, the southern collectors had little beyond "Tithes" and promises to fund the Treasury. The United States "legal tender" notes and a national banking system, controlled inflation and supported bond markets. A corollary of less bankruptcies, audits and quarterly reporting encouraged better banking compared to state chartered institutions. Although state banks at the end of the war still outnumbered national, total deposits and reserves were mostly held by federal institutions. However, one notable exception stained the record.[184]

An outgrowth of the army savings banks systems within occupied zones, the Freedmen's Saving and Trust Company (Freedman's Bank) was chartered by Congress and signed by President Lincoln March 3, 1865, to encourage thrift among slaves. Existing between 1865 and 1874, the institution was plagued by fraud, mismanagement and waste. The New York chartered institution followed thrifts in New Orleans and Beaufort during the war. For political reasons the Bank moved to Washington, D.C., in 1867. Freed farmers and veterans deposited earnings and bonuses to buy homesteads. Speculative land ventures, contrary to the charter, forced the Thrift into bankruptcy after the Panic of 1873. Almost 61,000 depositors lost a third of their savings. Congressional inquiries continued for years. Most blame was placed on General O. O. Howard, head of the Freedmen Bureau. The real culprits were land speculators.[185]

The U.S. Comptroller of Currency, responsible for winding down the affairs of the Freedmen's Savings Bank, did not end its charge until 1899. During the initial term, Hugh McCulloch, Secretary of the Treasury, was well versed in state banking and managed the audits. In his first Annual Report of the Treasury, Secretary McCulloch also encouraged retirement of national bank notes and for a return to the gold standard. Congress had started a reduction of four million dollars, but the act was repealed February 4, 1868. The Secretary between 1870 and 1876 was a partner in the investment banking firm of Jay Cooke, McCulloch & Company, New York. He returned as Secretary of the Treasury for President Chester A. Arthur serving from October of 1884 to March 1885. He continued to lobby for a return to the gold standard as promised during the war.

In his final report to Congress, Secretary McCulloch reminded lawmakers that greenbacks were emergency measures never intended to be permanent. Higher tariffs were also only temporary. He wrote "Like our currency laws, our tariff laws are a legacy of war ... unnecessary after twenty years of peace...." He observed over four thousand articles subject to duty. Regional and district collectors, appraisers, examiners, gaugers, weighers and countless dockhands and clerks were paid handsomely. The Congressional Tariff Commission described the system as "injurious to the interests supposed to be benefitted." The bureaucracy had a life of its own, separate from origin and purpose. Ports of delivery sometimes cost more to man than the duties collected.[186]

Senator Sherman, during the debate regarding Internal Taxes approved January 25, 1871, addressed taxpayer complaints. He agreed that there is nothing more pleasing to a Congressman than to repeal taxes, but resisted the urge to "hurry through." He defended the 2½ percent income tax (earnings over $2,000) as being equivalent to an ad valorem assessment on $30,000 on real estate. The income tax is essentially an excise tax of one and a half mills. He suggested future taxes be divided between levies on consumption and property taxes. Custom duties contributed $175,000,000 annually compared to $126,000,000 from internal revenue. Internal revenue consisted of excise on spirits, tobacco, income and stamps.

The tax legacy of the War is the "IRS." Commissioners George S. Boutwell (1863–1865); Joseph J. Lewis (1863–1865); William Orten (1865); and Edward Rollins (1865) served terms with reputations intact. Their combined service formed our tax framework. Reliance on self-assessment was key. The Tax Act of 1862 made it the duty of every taxpayer "to mark a loss or return" with the assessor by the deadline. By 1872, the Treasury Building east of the White House at "F" and "15th" Streets, was full of tax men and women. There were five divisions: law, direct, stamps, spirits and tobacco. Each year more collectors, assessors and deputies were hired. The nation had nine substations, located at Baltimore, Boston, Chicago, Cincinnati, New York, Philadelphia, New Orleans, Saint Louis and San Francisco. New York remained the most active office.

The income tax law repealed in 1872 was restored. A tax case from 1864 involving an Illinois attorney refusing to pay tax on professional fees and interest income was not decided until 1881. Treasury agents had seized the attorney's property and held a distress sale. The taxpayer appealed to the U.S. Supreme Court, where justices in *Springfield v. U.S.* 102 U.S. 586 (1881) held the income tax was not prohibited as a Direct Tax. The majority characterized the tax as a "duty" or "excise." Earlier, the High Court ruled in *Pacific Insurance Company v. Soule*, 74 U.S. 433 (1868) and *Veazie Bank v. Fenno* 75 U.S. 533 (1869) that income tax was not an ad valorem, poll or capitation tax. Thus, no apportionment required, clearing the way for future income taxes.

After the war, U.S. District Assessors were distributing tax returns, such as one styled "Detailed Statement of Income, Gains and Profits ... during the year 1868, and of Carriages, etc. owned or kept by him, March 1, 1869." Form 24 came with instructions and a "Take Notice" warning that failure to comply within ten days would result in a 50 percent penalty. Fiduciaries used the same form for wards or estates. Gold, gold bonds and interest coupons were taxed at specie value. To compute value of gold, the form included a conversion table for avoirdupois to Troy ounces. One avoirdupois ounce equaled .912 Troy ounces. Corporations and associations filed at the location of each business. Short term bond profits, less than the year holding period, were simple income as a dealer. The tax exemption was $1,000 (Fig. 114).

After the rate was lowered to 2½ percent in 1870, compliance improved. Deputy Collector of the Second District, Division No. 7, receipted taxpayer Ed. J. Wilson on October 2, 1871, for $187.50 on his income of $5,000. The taxpayer was assessed only $125.00 but had failed to timely file and was fined a 50 percent penalty. Fines and penalties became more common, but tracking was crude. Only in financial centers was enforcement stringent. Northwestern loggers, prairie farmers and western ranchers seldom paid federal taxes for their mostly cash businesses (Fig. 115).

A decade after the war, the Register of the Treasury distributed an "Alphabetized List of the Ports of the United States" listing the three types of customs offices. Ports of Entry were full service. The smaller Ports of Delivery only had an assistant collector or inspector. The third, Hailing Ports, were simply entry points where a vessel could dock but had no custom officers. In 1875 there were 113 districts: Atlantic (68); Gulf Coast (14); Pacific Coast (7); Northern Lakes (20); and Interior (4). The Gulf Coast ports were at Brazos de Santiago, Galveston, Corpus Christi, Indianola and Saluria. Also in Texas was the Interior Ports, located at Frontera and Paso del Norte. Hailing and Delivery Ports in Texas included Aransas; Brownsville; Matagorda; Coranchue (Jackson County); Cedar Bayou (Harris County); Clarksville (Red River County); Clear Lake (Harris County); Copano (Refugio County); Eagle Pass (Maverick County); Lamar (Aransas); Lavaca; Old River (Brazoria); Orange; Palacios; Point Isabel; Red Bluff (San Saba); Rockport: Sabine Pass; San Antonio; San Benard; San Elizario; Saint Maria (Refugio); Velasco; and Wallaceville (Chambers). Most hailing and delivery ports were staffed with part-time clerks and kept irregular hours.

Federal tax forms were modified over time. Commissioner E. A. Rollins on January 1, 1866, released "Instructions to Assess and Collectors and Schedule of Blank Forms" including "blank forms" available for the convenience of officers. Also released were instructions for Assessments (Series 2, No. 1). The guidance covered license and special tax assessments. Mention was made of taxes on slaughtered animals, stagecoaches, lotteries, theaters, petroleum, legacies and successions. Slaughterhouses and lotteries were subject to the same monthly filings as manufacturers. No notice was required to impose late penalties. If notice was given, it was gratuitous and not a requirement. States had outlawed lotteries except in Louisiana. Texas even prohibited in its 1876 Constitution in Section 47 of Article III lotteries, sale of tickets and the awarding of gambling winnings.

Secretary John Sherman, in his Report to Congress delivered December 2, 1878, favorably summarized the national banking experiment of the Civil War. The public embraced the commercial advantage of legal tender notes which reduced counterfeiting. Security and soundness of national banks was encouraged by director participation, examination by federal auditors and quarterly reporting. Takeovers of troubled institutions gave confidence to depositors. The first charters of 1863 renewed at the expiration of twenty-years, when Secretary Sherman declared the national banking system is "good policy" and should be continued.

The Spanish-American War caused lawmakers to return to emergency revenue measures. A new act imposed an "excise" tax on gains, profits and income in excess of $4,000. Reinstated was the income tax on wages, business, rents, interest and dividends at 2 percent. On June 17, 1898, one industry, refining companies, had its tax status reviewed by the Supreme Court in *Sponeckels Sugar Refinery v. McClaen* 192 U.S. 397, (1904). Editors for years had debated the efficacy of future income taxes. The Perry Mason & Co. publication *Youth's Companion* joined in the discussion. Its March 2, 1895, edition ran an article arguing that the 2 percent income tax was a Direct Tax and the Supreme Court should rule on its constitutionality as soon as possible. The Court would come full circle on the income tax issue.

The same year as the *Youth's Companion* article, the Supreme Court agreed with the editor. In *Pollock v. Farmers' Loan & Trust Company*, 157 U.S. 429, (1895), the majority held that portions of the 1894 Wilson-Gorman Tariff Act were unconstitutional because Direct Taxes without proper apportionment. The unlawful sections related only to assessments on interest, dividends and rents. The Court concluded such was an "ad valorem" or property (Direct Tax). The opinion distinguished between indirect taxes (tariffs) and direct taxes (polls.) National taxes under the Constitution had two permissible classes. The first, direct, included polls, capitation and ad valorem. The second was duties, imports, tariffs and excise. All the Constitution required of "indirect taxes" was "uniformity." Direct taxes were to be apportioned by state based on census numbers. The tax was not ruled totally improper, just those sections that assessed a levy on passive income from rent, interest and dividends.

As expected, Congress responded to the High Court's rebuff of the income tax. The Sixty-first Congress, during its first session, in March 1909, prepared a Constitutional Amendment permitting the income tax. The amendment permitted direct taxation without apportionment. The proposed amendment was ratified by a majority of the States and signed into law as the Sixteenth Amendment in 1913 prior to World War I. As worded "The Congress should have the power to lay and collect taxes on incomes, from whatever source derived, without apportionment among the several States and without regard to any census as enumeration."

Rates began at 1 percent for incomes greater than $3,800 for single taxpayers and $4,000 for married. For wealthy taxpayers earning in excess of $20,000, the rates increased to 6 percent. The Revenue Service had two forms: one for lower incomes, Form 1040A, and another for the higher, Form 1040. District Directors assigned taxpayer's identification numbers for better record keeping. The filing deadline remained March 15. The returns included explanatory paragraphs with columns for amounts. Typical inquires included: Did you file last year?; Do spouse and children have taxable income?; Any Charity deductions? All was sworn to by taxpayers. Businessmen could deduct cost of goods sold, payrolls, interest, taxes and bad debts. Capital gains could be reduced by an assets market value at March 1, 1913 (Fig. 116). Withholding at source continued for government salaries, rents and profits in excess of $3,000 annually. Form 1042 was used to take credit for withheld taxes (Fig. 117).

The U.S. Tax Code after passage of the Sixteenth Amendment was substantially revised in 1939, prior to World War II and the Korean War in 1954. Politicians, commentators and the public at large pleaded for lower rates, simplification and clarity. Congress experimented with "excess profits taxes," "luxury taxes," "investment credits," and some rates approached 90 percent. During the Viet Nam conflict, Congress returned to "surtaxes" for higher incomes. Such extraordinary measures trace back to the Civil War. Like Victorian politicians, twentieth century Congressmen realized there were limits even to patriotic American tax tolerance after peace is restored The Whiskey Rebellion and Nullification Movement are early examples of tax protest. Outcries grew: "The More you Work, the More you must Pay" (see Fig. 1). Two elements of effective taxation in a free society are voluntary assessment and compliance.

Conclusion

Just prior to secession, Attorney General James L. Petigru of South Carolina made a gibe: "South Carolina is too small for a republic and too large for an insane asylum." He knew King Cotton could not forever support their culture or a war. After the losses of Vicksburg and Gettysburg, others realized the same. The Confederate Congress failed to appreciate the fragility of their financial model. More Congressional time was consumed over flags, seals and mottos than their cotton-dependent economy. Although both sides borrowed to cover tax shortfalls, the South avoided real taxation until too late. Local government had traditionally been tight fisted with public funds for education, health and welfare. Of necessity, all that changed after the War.

When the rebel government's sustainability became questionable, civil rights became secondary to survival. Courts judiciously avoided decisions involving press, assembly and speech that might affect the war effort. Property rights are suspended during martial rule. Taxation without appeal or review becomes acceptable. Impressment officers have latitude during war that is never tolerated during peacetime.

D. Appleton and Company of New York published in 1861 the first manual for the U.S. Direct and Excise Taxes. In the book, the effectiveness of the direct tax was doubted. None expected any collections from the rebels. The Treasury allowed states to offset with counterclaims and costs of state expenses. Most loyal states assumed their share of the U.S. tax in return for a 15 percent discount. In some cases, the federal government owed money back. The New York editor concluded "the only effect" of the Act was fruitless effort. The following year Congress suspended any more direct taxes until after April 1, 1865. Federal excise taxes substituted for direct taxes.

Excise taxes tapped every consumption, trade, business, luxury and vice. Death and marriage became more expensive. Discretionary compliance was always a concern. Although failure to file was subject to penalty, few were charged. Tax offices did agree that excise and licenses were easier to collect than direct taxes. Sprits, beer and tobacco were the most productive with the least cost, but more susceptible to fraud. Citizens with no post office were invisible to most assessors. A "barter" economy operated tax-free. Excess profit taxes due from strategic contractors were added to the contract costs. Railroads and telegraph companies paid less as a vital industry and were free to raise prices as necessary. Soldier and farmers had no market power. Their only relief was a family exemption.

The federal treasury entered the war with sound credit, minimal debt and a stream of gold from California. The Confederate Treasury, in contrast, had few lenders, a single-commodity economy and little industry. Financial panics had left three states without banks. The South collected only a fifth of the federal revenue. Nevertheless, the Southern lawmakers duplicated almost every federal statute. The Confederate tax effort was sustained by taxes in kind and impressments. All Confederate Treasuries were broken, half the businesses bankrupt, southern ports and rails destroyed. The victorious North enjoyed the spoils, while the vanquished South endured the spoilage. A failed rebellion has economic consequences.

The saving grace of the defeated Confederate Treasuries was the Fourteenth Amendment. Never intended by Congress, this amendment repudiated all Confederate national, state and municipal bonds, notes and claims. Texas, virtually unoccupied, soon experienced rises in land prices, new businesses, railroad construction and immigration. Arkansans and Mississippians instead barely survived through public and private charity. Subsistence sharecropping was little different from Antebellum slavery. Poverty was widespread, but disproportionately shared.

The Civil War forever changed the methods of American taxation. No longer was customs the primary source of federal revenue. Direct taxes as an emergency war measure were no longer used. "Sin taxes" became a permanent excise. The middle class provided an ever-growing portion of federal revenue. The Tax Code was dependent on self-assessment and voluntary timely compliance. Progressive rates and luxury levies provided a semblance of fairness. Perceptions of equity were more important than what others paid or how the tax was computed.

The National Bank Acts proved effective, even though a national monetary system had critics. President Andrew

Jackson distrusted bankers in general. He believed the mischief of a national bank outweighed any advantages. Texas, Mississippi and Arkansas were no longer "bankless" after receiving federal charters. When the economy is most stressed, credit tightens and collections decline. "Rainy day" surplus reserves had supporters but were difficult to retain.

When President Lincoln delivered his Message to Congress on Independence Day the first year of the war, he reasoned, "If a state may secede, so may another, and when all should have seceded, none is left to pay the debts." He pondered, "If this is quite just to creditors?" This was a pragmatic analysis of the consequences of secession. A sovereign without credit is vulnerable. On December 4, 1865, President Johnson asserted that, "No favored class shall demand freedom from assessment, and the taxes should be distributed as not to fall unduly on the poor but rather on the accumulated wealth of the country." Jeffersonian equality was ever-present. The Treasury modeled budgets with little empirical evidence. The market's direction was subject to panic, fear and inflation and not national priorities or partisan politics. Taxes were reactive despite the government's desire to appear predictive.

Today American monetary policies are the standard in contrast to its antiquated tax system. The Civil War saw every conceivable duty and excise, but lessons learned have been forgotten. President George Washington, in his "Farewell Address," conceded taxes were unpleasant but essential. Thomas Jefferson believed it was tyranny to tax for projects contrary to the wants of the people. Abraham Lincoln knew that to delay taxation until fully fair to all would defer needed collections. Ulysses S. Grant wanted not to exempt any enterprise except churches and cemeteries. Only if supported by self-assessment can any tax survive long. Lawmakers silently accepted that a fifth of taxes are avoided. Expected evasion was factored in the projections.

Primordial fears of Old Testament tax collectors were imagined after the war's first year. After peace, Americans were intolerant of war taxes that were promised to be temporary. Reminiscent of George Washington's warnings, taxes took private property. Heirs of the Boston Tea Party, Whiskey Rebellion and Nullification Crisis were wary of national takings for amorphous purposes. Doomsday war taxes are necessary for survival. Taxation, broadly defined as the lawful taking of private property by a sovereign for public purposes, is always without just compensation. Emancipation was the grandest tax of all, although never debated as a fiscal measure. Victory, not largess, was popularly supported. A peaceful nation needs no war taxes.

The Civil War experience provides suggestions regarding tax administration. Perhaps Congress should reconsider publically disclosing individual taxes. The privacy argument is hollow. In criminal and civil matters, all is already discoverable by subpoena. Real estate values are matters of public record. Probate files already reveal personal estates. Even more transparent are divorce proceedings. "Taxable income" is no more private. Tax evaders might be exposed. Another Congressional consideration would be the elimination of the corporate tax for dividends distributed to shareholders. Shareholders would assume the role of tax examiners, because it is their money the Company is holding. The expansion of withholding to all passive income such as rents, dividends, interest and royalties would eliminate a good portion of the slippage. Even at minimal rates, non-filers could no longer escape some taxes. The only costs would be the "use of money." Most have forgotten that Legal Tender is an interest free loan to the Treasury.

If enacted, the above proposals would reduce unreported income, encourage shareholder oversight and reduce evasion. These are measures learned from the Civil War experience. Doubtless many would be entitled to refunds, especially tax exempts. The estimated tax interest free money provided to the Treasury would only be an extension of National Bank Act legal tender solutions. Obviously, politics are more powerful than logic. The reduction in the collection of taxes could lessen the sting of universal withholding.

One fiscal loss of the Civil War was the reliance on Direct Taxes to fund national emergencies. Since the War, the distinction between permanent excise and temporary taxes has blurred. After the Sixteenth Amendment, a hodgepodge of internal taxes was passed, but few repealed. A labyrinth of rulings and regulations cloud the purpose, lacking any strategy other than revenue. The purpose of a "War Tax" is clear. It should be reserved for a crisis. War budgets are primarily financed with debt, but require assured taxes to service that debt. If a "War Tax" had a triggering device, lead time would be shorter. A "Tax Board," similar to the Federal Reserve, might be the solution for rapid "War Tax" activation.

The temporary suspension of charitable and retirement contributions could be the emergency tax mechanism. A "Tax Board" could declare implementation. The suspended deductions would increase withholding and higher tax brackets immediately. Duration of the suspension would end when the "Tax Board" proclaimed the crisis over. The deductions would be carried forward against future taxable income over time. Such forced funding of a war budget would affect mostly higher incomes.

Similar to the Federal Reserve Board, "Tax Boards" would befriend few, despite the practical necessity. Those with vested interests, such as tax attorneys, pension advisors and trust companies would be most critical of such a board. Already benefiting from ERISA (1974), Sarbanes-Oxley (2002) and Dodd-Frank (2010), their professions would survive. Although the Civil War changed the American tax system, the lessons learned should not be forgotten. War taxes are for a temporary emergency. Regular taxes for all else.

Illustrations

Figure 1. "The More You Work, The More Taxes You Must Pay," *Harper's Weekly*, March 2, 1878.

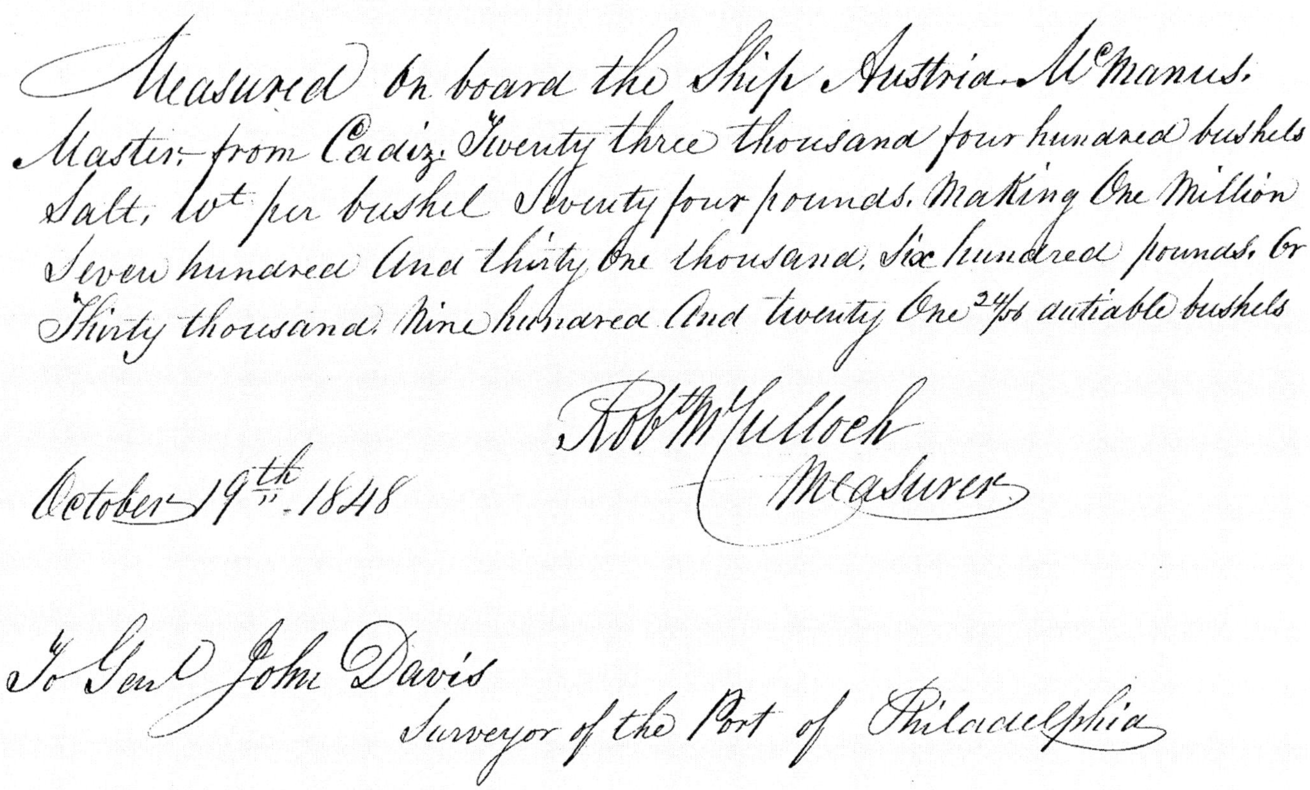

Measured On board the Ship Austria McManus.
Master from Cadiz. Twenty three thousand four hundred bushels
Salt, wt per bushel Seventy four pounds. Making One Million
Seven hundred And thirty One thousand, Six hundred pounds. Or
Thirty thousand. Nine hundred And twenty One 24/56 dutiable bushels

Robt McCulloch
October 19th 1848 Measurer

To Genl John Davis
Surveyor of the Port of Philadelphia

Figure 2. Certification for Customs Duty Measurer. Philadelphia, 1848.

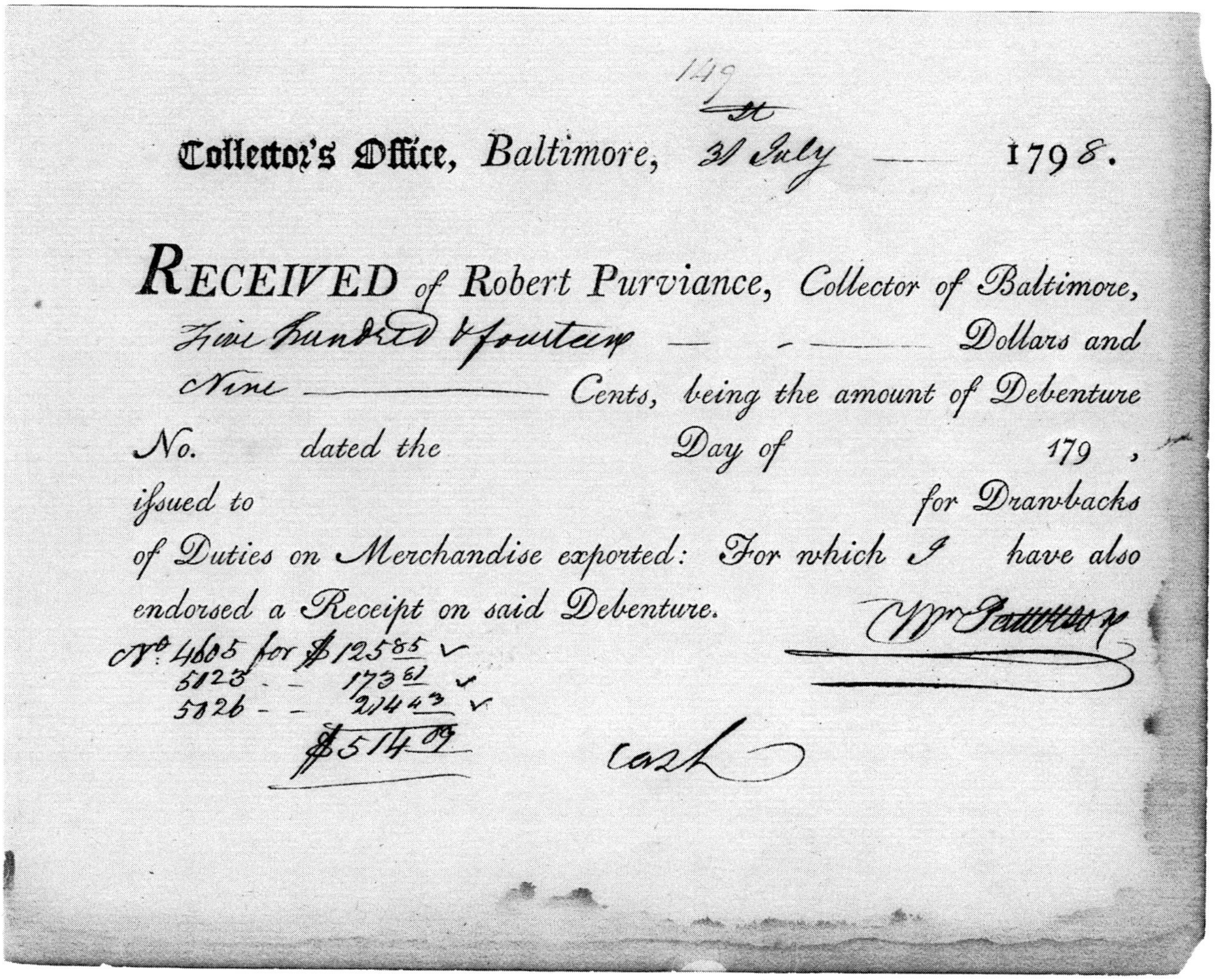

149

Collector's Office, Baltimore, 31 July —— 1798.

RECEIVED of Robert Purviance, Collector of Baltimore, Five hundred & fourteen —— Dollars and Nine —— Cents, being the amount of Debenture No. dated the Day of 179 , issued to for Drawbacks of Duties on Merchandise exported: For which I have also endorsed a Receipt on said Debenture.

No. 4605 for $125.85
5123 – – 173.61
5126 – – 214.43
$514.09

cash

Figure 3. "Drawback" Security Bond for Duty on Exports, Collector. Baltimore, 1798.

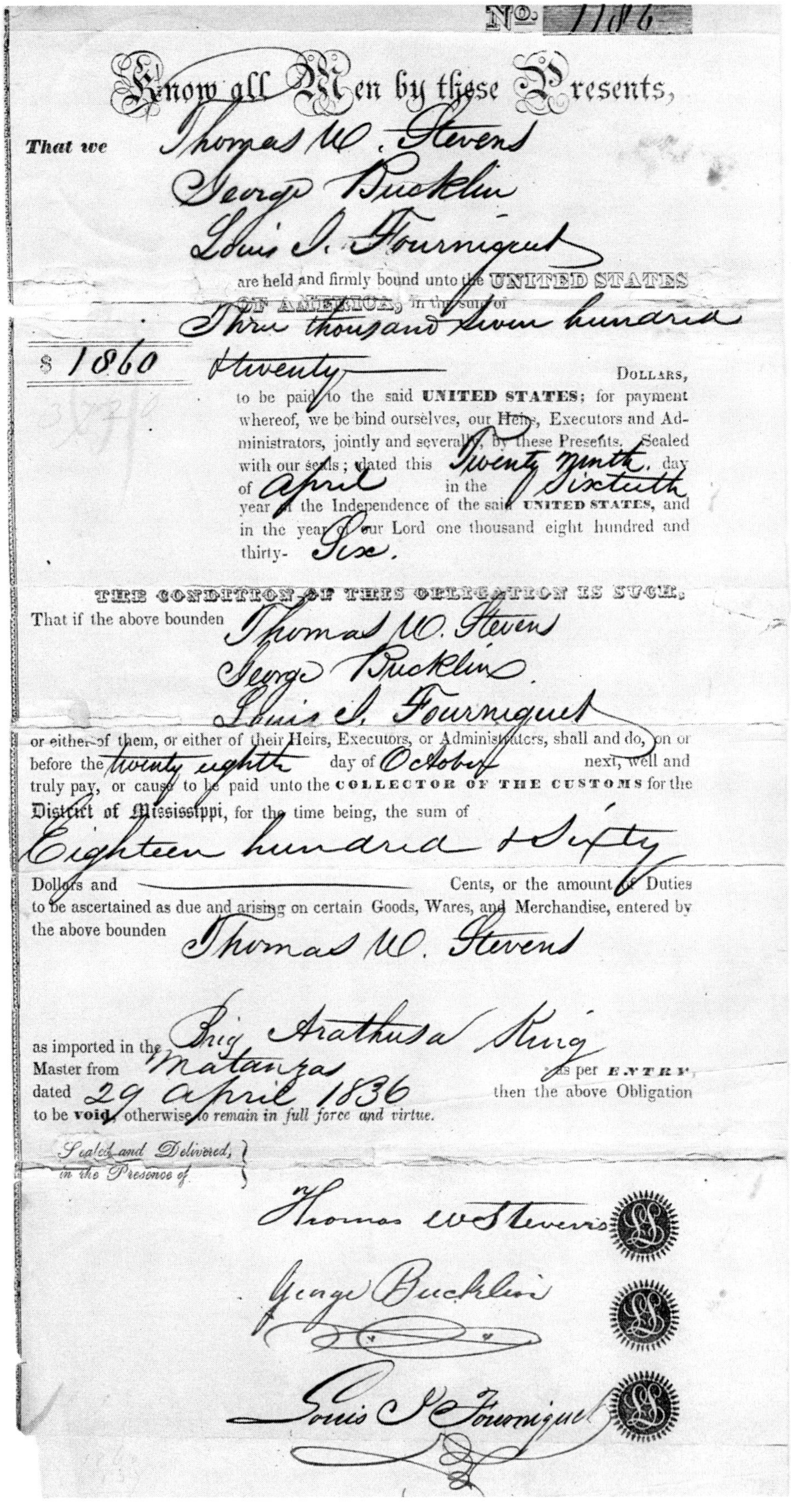

No. 1186

Know all Men by these Presents,

That we Thomas W. Stevens
George Bucklin
Louis I. Fourniquet

are held and firmly bound unto the UNITED STATES OF AMERICA, in the sum of
Three thousand seven hundred

$ 1860 & twenty Dollars,

to be paid to the said UNITED STATES; for payment whereof, we be bind ourselves, our Heirs, Executors and Administrators, jointly and severally, by these Presents. Sealed with our seals; dated this Twenty ninth day of April in the Sixtieth year of the Independence of the said UNITED STATES, and in the year of our Lord one thousand eight hundred and thirty-Six.

THE CONDITION OF THIS OBLIGATION IS SUCH,

That if the above bounden Thomas W. Stevens
George Bucklin
Louis I. Fourniquet

or either of them, or either of their Heirs, Executors, or Administrators, shall and do, on or before the twenty eighth day of October next, well and truly pay, or cause to be paid unto the COLLECTOR OF THE CUSTOMS for the District of Mississippi, for the time being, the sum of

Eighteen hundred & Sixty

Dollars and ——— Cents, or the amount of Duties to be ascertained as due and arising on certain Goods, Wares, and Merchandise, entered by the above bounden Thomas W. Stevens

as imported in the Brig Arathusa King Master from Matanzas as per ENTRY, dated 29 April 1836 then the above Obligation to be void, otherwise to remain in full force and virtue.

Sealed and Delivered, in the Presence of

Thomas W Stevens [L.S.]

George Bucklin [L.S.]

Louis I Fourniquet [L.S.]

Figure 4. Customs Duty, New Orleans. 1836.

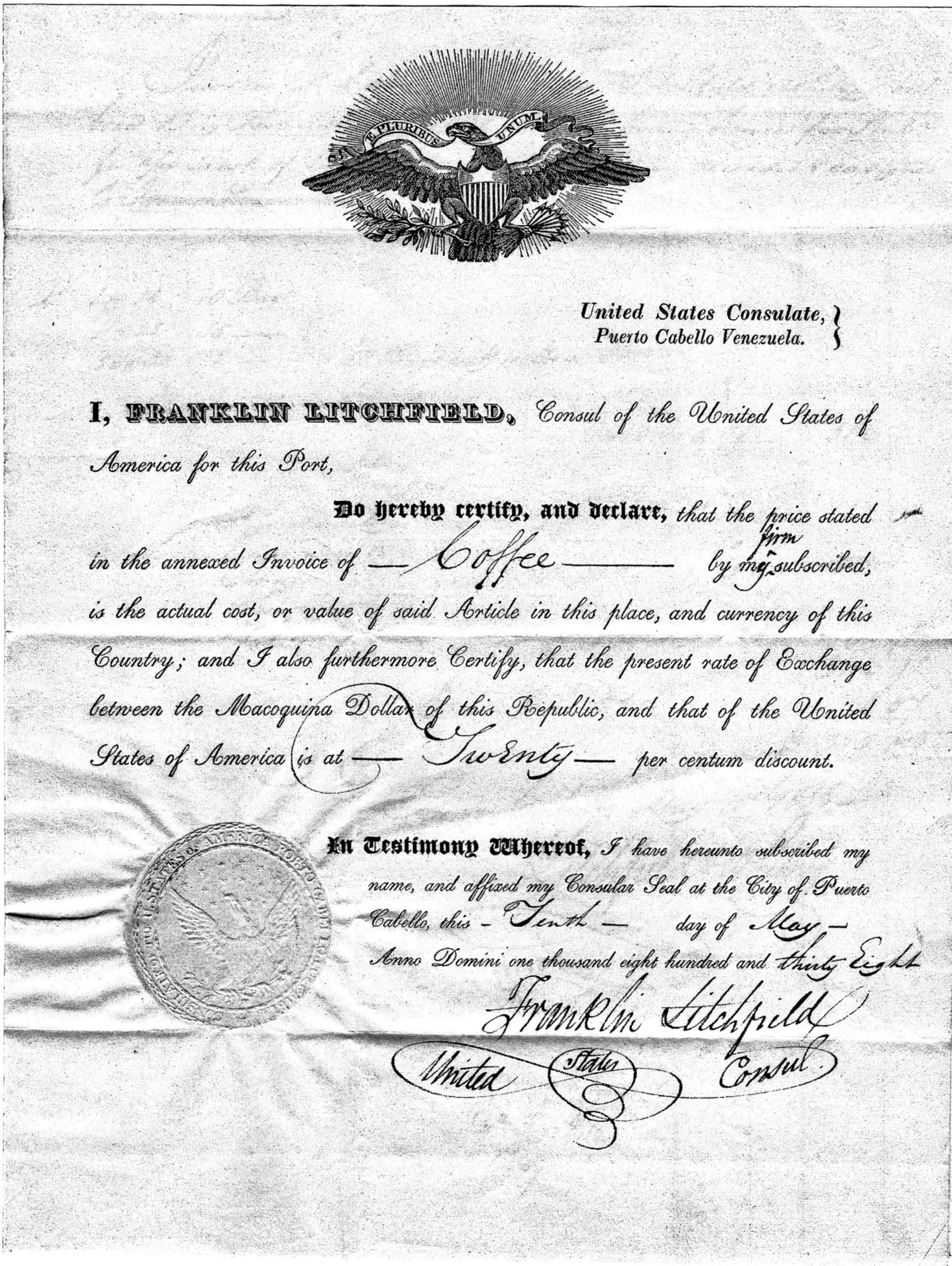

E PLURIBUS UNUM

United States Consulate,
Puerto Cabello Venezuela.

I, FRANKLIN LITCHFIELD, Consul of the United States of America for this Port,

Do hereby certify, and declare, that the price stated in the annexed Invoice of — Coffee —— by my firm subscribed, is the actual cost, or value of said Article in this place, and currency of this Country; and I also furthermore Certify, that the present rate of Exchange between the Macoquina Dollar of this Republic, and that of the United States of America is at — Twenty — per centum discount.

In Testimony Whereof, I have hereunto subscribed my name, and affixed my Consular Seal at the City of Puerto Cabello, this - Tenth - day of May - Anno Domini one thousand eight hundred and thirty Eight

Franklin Litchfield
United States Consul

Figure 5. Certification of Foreign Exchange and Duty, U.S. Consul, Puerto Cabello, Venezuela, 1838.

TREASURY DEPARTMENT,
OCTOBER 13th, 1814.

SIR,

IN obedience to the resolutions of the House of Representatives, of the 10th instant, I have the honor to transmit the accompanying statements.

In compliance with the first resolution, the statement (A) is rendered, shewing the amount of the valuations of lands, dwelling houses and slaves, and the assessments founded upon them, as made under the acts of July 22d, and August 2d, 1813, so far as returns have been received at the Treasury.

The statement (B) furnishes, as far as the materials existing at the Treasury admit, the information required by the second resolution. In the collection districts in regard to which no information is given, either the assessment is not ascertained to have been completed, or has been so recently completed, as to have allowed little time for collecting the tax. The sums annexed to those districts in which the collection is completed or in progress, are the amounts ascertained to have been received by the collectors. As the returns of the collectors made in the month of September, have been but partially received, and as in that month the collections appear to have been made with great activity, a much larger aggregate amount than that stated, is believed to have been received.

The statement (C) furnishes, as far as the accounts rendered admit, the information required by the third resolution. These accounts do not supply the materials for a statement in which the amount actually received on account of *each* duty can, at present, be exhibited.

To comply the more fully with the scope of the resolution, two views are presented; the first, of the amounts of the several Internal Duties, distinctly exhibited, that have *accrued* for the two first quarters of the present year, in each collection district, so far as returns have been made by the collectors; the second, of the aggregate amounts of duties ascertained on the 10th of October, 1814, to have been *received* in each state or territory, the former being derived from quarterly, and the latter from monthly returns made by the collectors. In those districts from which the returns for the two quarters have not been received, the period of time for which returns have been rendered is stated. Monthly returns have been received from all the collection districts, except the 1st of Louisiana, in which there is yet no collector.

I have the honor to be,
Sir,
Your obedient servant,
SAMUEL H. SMITH,
Acting Secretary of the Treasury.

Honorable the Speaker
of the House of Representatives.

Figure 6 (this page and page following). Direct Tax and Internal Duties Assessed, Secretary of the Treasury, 1814.

AGGREGATE amounts of Internal Duties ascertained, on the 10th of October, 1814, to have been received in each state or territory.

	DOLLS.	CTS.
New Hampshire,	24,604	65
Massachusetts,	170,911	75
Vermont,	21,359	06
Rhode Island,	31,555	52
Connecticut,	58,875	97
New York,	303,694	27
New Jersey,	54,202	92
Pennsylvania,	279,983	09
Delaware,	18,779	93
Maryland,	99,797	04
Virginia,	136,568	16
North Carolina,	62,067	94
Ohio,	32,099	81
Kentucky,	32,935	46
South Carolina,	60,132	97
Tennessee,	18,185	85
Georgia,	28,425	48
Louisiana,	20,156	97
Illinois territory,	1,047	37
Michigan territory,	1,312	18
Indiana territory,	2,065	07
Missouri territory,	1,525	60
Mississippi territory,	4,928	77
District of Columbia,	26,169	80
Total, . Dollars,	1,491,385	63

LETTER

FROM THE

Secretary of the Treasury,

TRANSMITTING

A STATEMENT

OF

THE EMOLUMENTS OF THE OFFICERS

EMPLOYED

IN THE COLLECTION OF THE CUSTOMS FOR THE YEAR 1815.

February 24, 1816,
Read, and Ordered to lie upon the Table.

WASHINGTON:

PRINTED BY WILLIAM A. DAVIS.

.....

1816.

Figure 7 (this page and page following). Emoluments of Officers, Acting Secretary of the Treasury, Treasurer, Washington, 1815.

TREASURY DEPARTMENT,

Comptroller's Office, 21*st February,* 1816.

SIR,

I have the honour to transmit, herewith, duplicate abstracts of the official emoluments and expenditures for the year 1815, of those Officers of the Customs of the United States, who have rendered the statements required of them by the 2d section of the act of the 2d March, 1799, entitled "An act to establish the compensation of the officers employed in the collection of the duties on imports and tonnage, and for other purposes."

With great respect,

(Signed) JOSEPH ANDERSON.

Hon. A. J. Dallas.

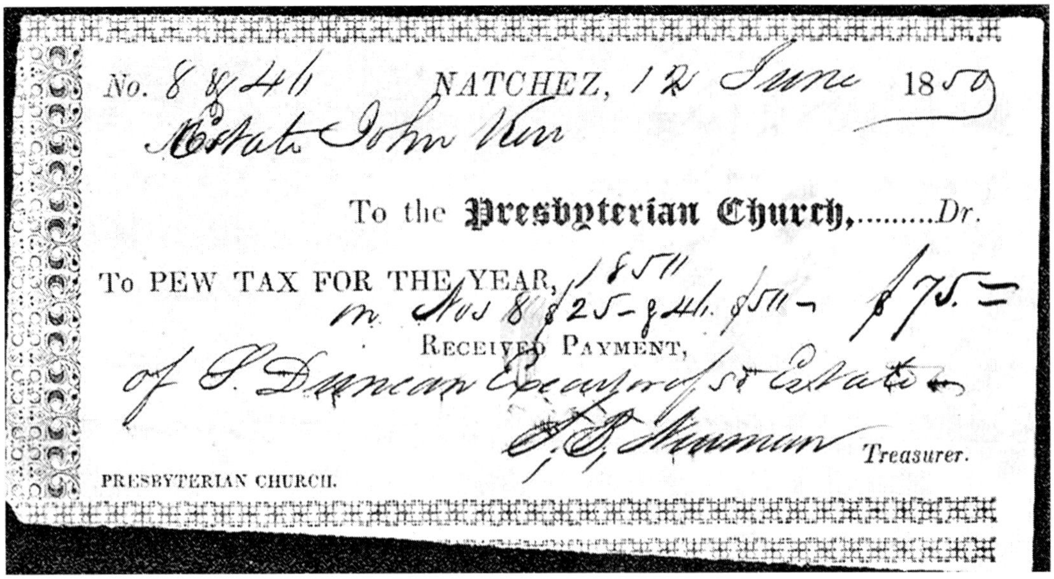
No. 8846 NATCHEZ, 12 June 1850

Estate John Ker

To the Presbyterian Church, ...Dr.

To PEW TAX FOR THE YEAR, 1850

RECEIVED PAYMENT,

Treasurer.

PRESBYTERIAN CHURCH.

Figure 8. Pew Tax Receipt. Property Commissioner of Revenue, Natchez, Mississippi, 1850.

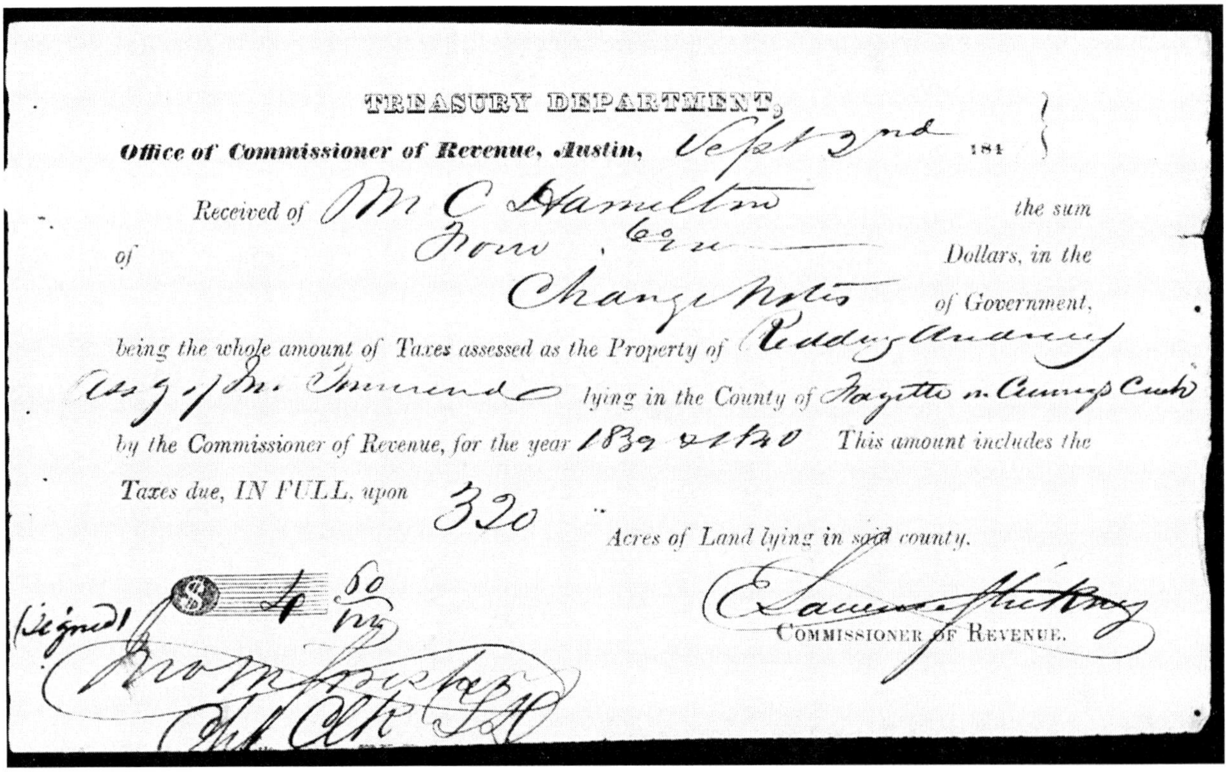
TREASURY DEPARTMENT,

Office of Commissioner of Revenue, Austin, Sept 2nd 184

Received of M C Hamilton *the sum*

of Four 60/100 *Dollars, in the*

Change Notes *of Government,*

being the whole amount of Taxes assessed as the Property of

lying in the County of Fayette

by the Commissioner of Revenue, for the year 1839 & 1840 *This amount includes the*

Taxes due, IN FULL, upon 320

Acres of Land lying in said county.

$ 4 60/100

(Signed)

COMMISSIONER OF REVENUE.

Figure 9. Real Estate Tax Receipt. Austin, Republic of Texas, 1841.

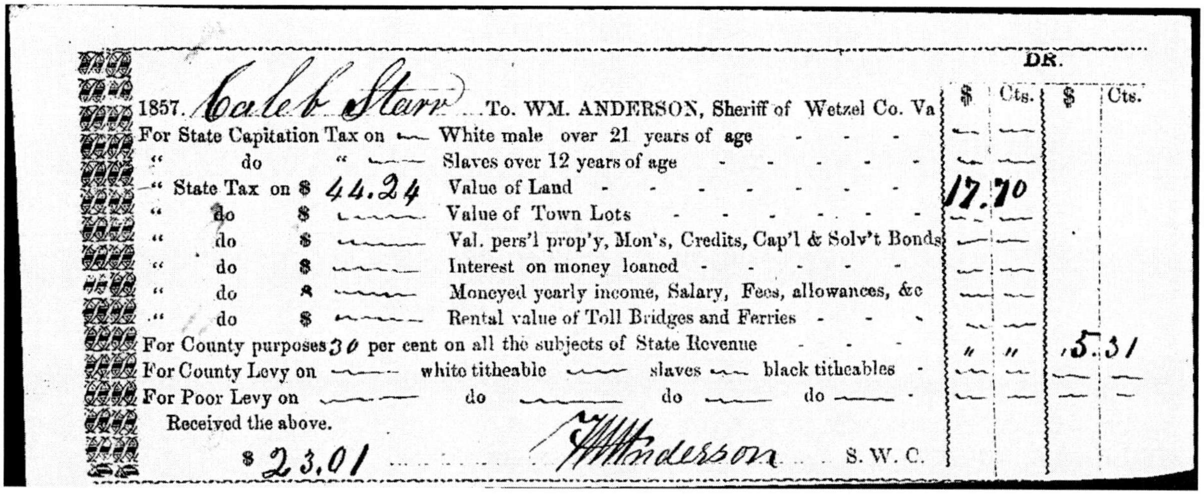

1857. Caleb Starr ...To. WM. ANDERSON, Sheriff of Wetzel Co. Va

	$	Cts.	$	Cts.
For State Capitation Tax on — White male over 21 years of age	—	—		
" do " — Slaves over 12 years of age	—	—		
" State Tax on $ 44.24 Value of Land	17.	70		
" do $ — Value of Town Lots	—	—		
" do $ — Val. pers'l prop'y, Mon's, Credits, Cap'l & Solv't Bonds	—	—		
" do $ — Interest on money loaned	—	—		
" do $ — Moneyed yearly income, Salary, Fees, allowances, &c	—	—		
" do $ — Rental value of Toll Bridges and Ferries	—	—		
For County purposes 30 per cent on all the subjects of State Revenue	"	"	5.	31
For County Levy on — white titheable — slaves — black titheables	—	—	—	—
For Poor Levy on — do — do — do —	—	—	—	—

Received the above.

$ 23.01 ... W. M. Anderson ... S. W. C.

Figure 10. Capitation and Poor Tax Receipt, Sheriff, Wetzel County, Virginia, 1857.

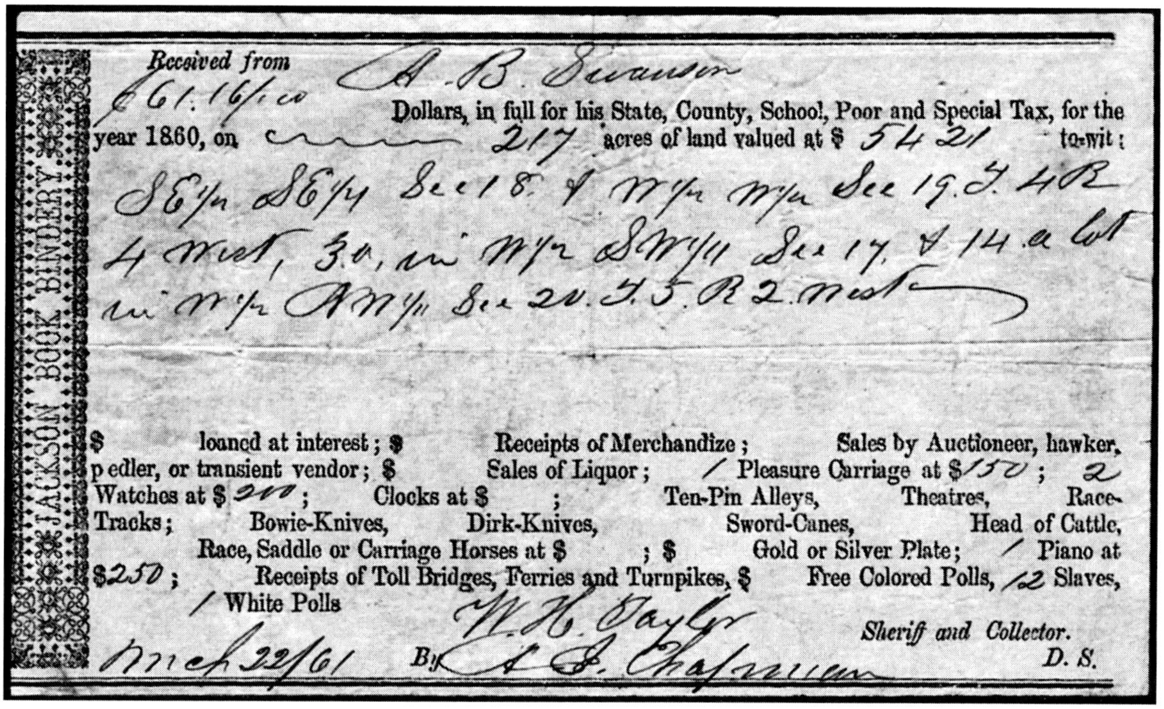

JACKSON BOOK BINDERY

Received from A. B. Swanson

$61.16/100 Dollars, in full for his State, County, School, Poor and Special Tax, for the year 1860, on — 217 acres of land valued at $ 5421 to-wit:

SE¼ SE¼ Sec 18 & W½ W½ Sec 19. T. 4 R 4 West, 30 a. in W½ SW¼ Sec 17, & 14 a lot in W½ NW¼ Sec 20. T. 5 R 2 west

$ loaned at interest; $ Receipts of Merchandize; Sales by Auctioneer, hawker, pedler, or transient vendor; $ Sales of Liquor; 1 Pleasure Carriage at $150; 2 Watches at $200; Clocks at $; Ten-Pin Alleys, Theatres, Race-Tracks; Bowie-Knives, Dirk-Knives, Sword-Canes, Head of Cattle, Race, Saddle or Carriage Horses at $; $ Gold or Silver Plate; 1 Piano at $250; Receipts of Toll Bridges, Ferries and Turnpikes, $ Free Colored Polls, 12 Slaves, 1 White Polls

W. H. Taylor *Sheriff and Collector.*

Mch 22/61 By A. S. Chapman *D. S.*

Figure 11. Property, Poor, Special, Polls, Sales Tax and License, Collector, Jackson, Mississippi, 1860.

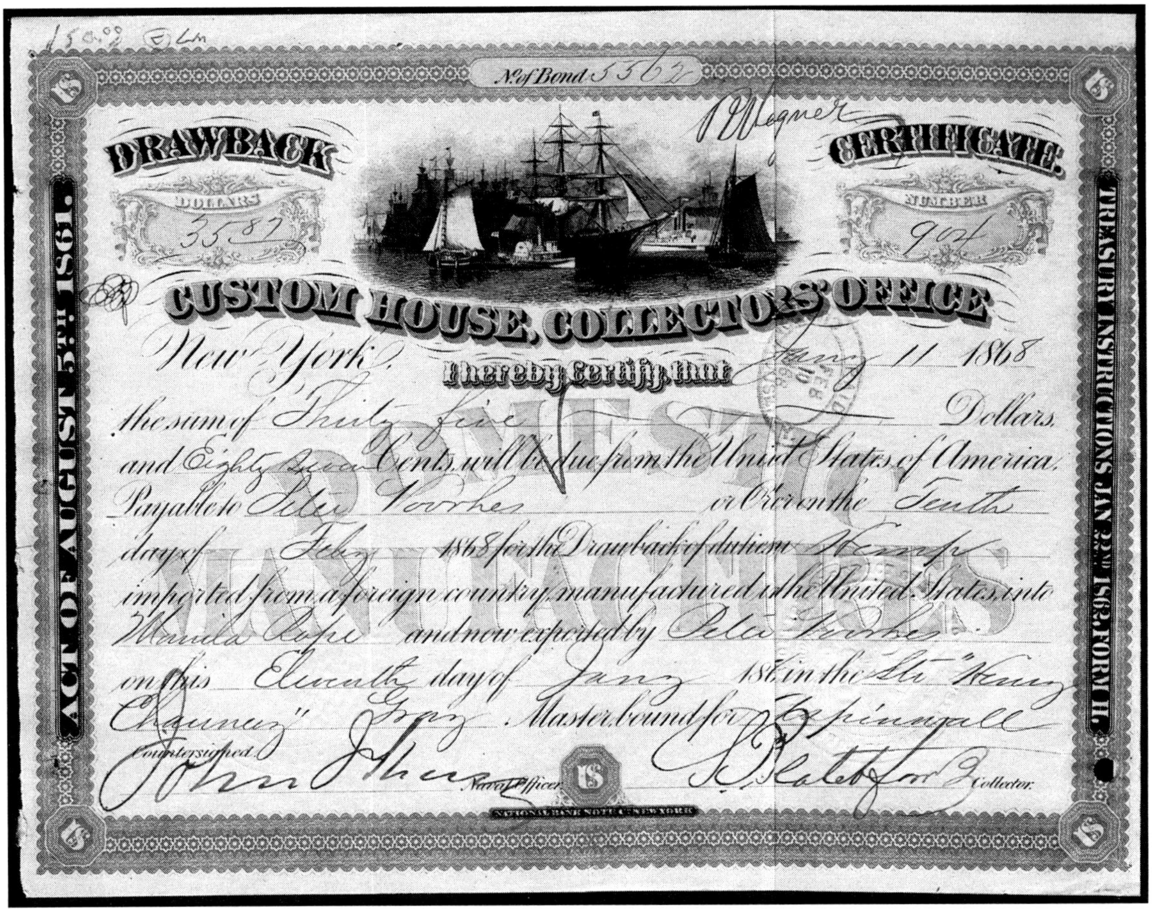
No. of Bond 3562

DRAWBACK CERTIFICATE

DOLLARS 35.87

NUMBER 904

ACT OF AUGUST 5th 1861.

TREASURY INSTRUCTIONS JAN 22nd 1862. FORM H.

CUSTOM HOUSE, COLLECTORS' OFFICE

New York, I hereby Certify that Jany 11 1868

the sum of Thirty five Dollars and Eighty seven Cents, will be due from the United States of America, Payable to Peter Voorhes or Order on the Tenth day of Feby 1868 for the Drawback of duties on Hemp imported from a foreign country, manufactured in the United States, into Manila Rope and now exported by Peter Voorhes on this Eleventh day of Jany 186 in the Str "Henry Chauncey" Gray Master bound for Aspinwall

Countersigned John J. [illegible] Naval Officer H. Blatchford Collector.

NATIONAL BANK NOTE CO. NEW YORK

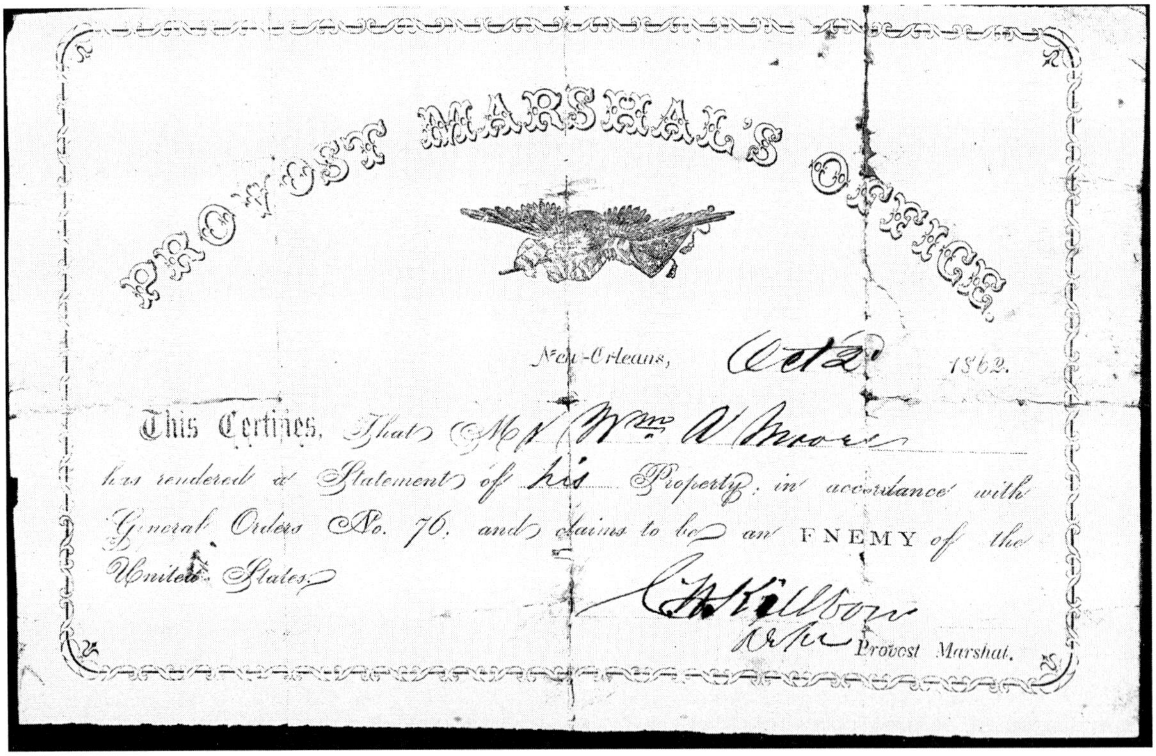
PROVOST MARSHAL'S OFFICE

New-Orleans, Oct 2 1862.

This Certifies, That Mr Wm. A Moore has rendered a Statement of his Property, in accordance with General Orders No. 76, and claims to be an ENEMY of the United States.

Provost Marshal.

Top: **Figure 12. Customs Drawback Certificate Act of August 5, 1861, Collector. New York, January 11, 1868.** ***Bottom:*** **Figure 13. Certificate for "Enemy of the United States" Provost Marshall. New Orleans, October 2, 1862.**

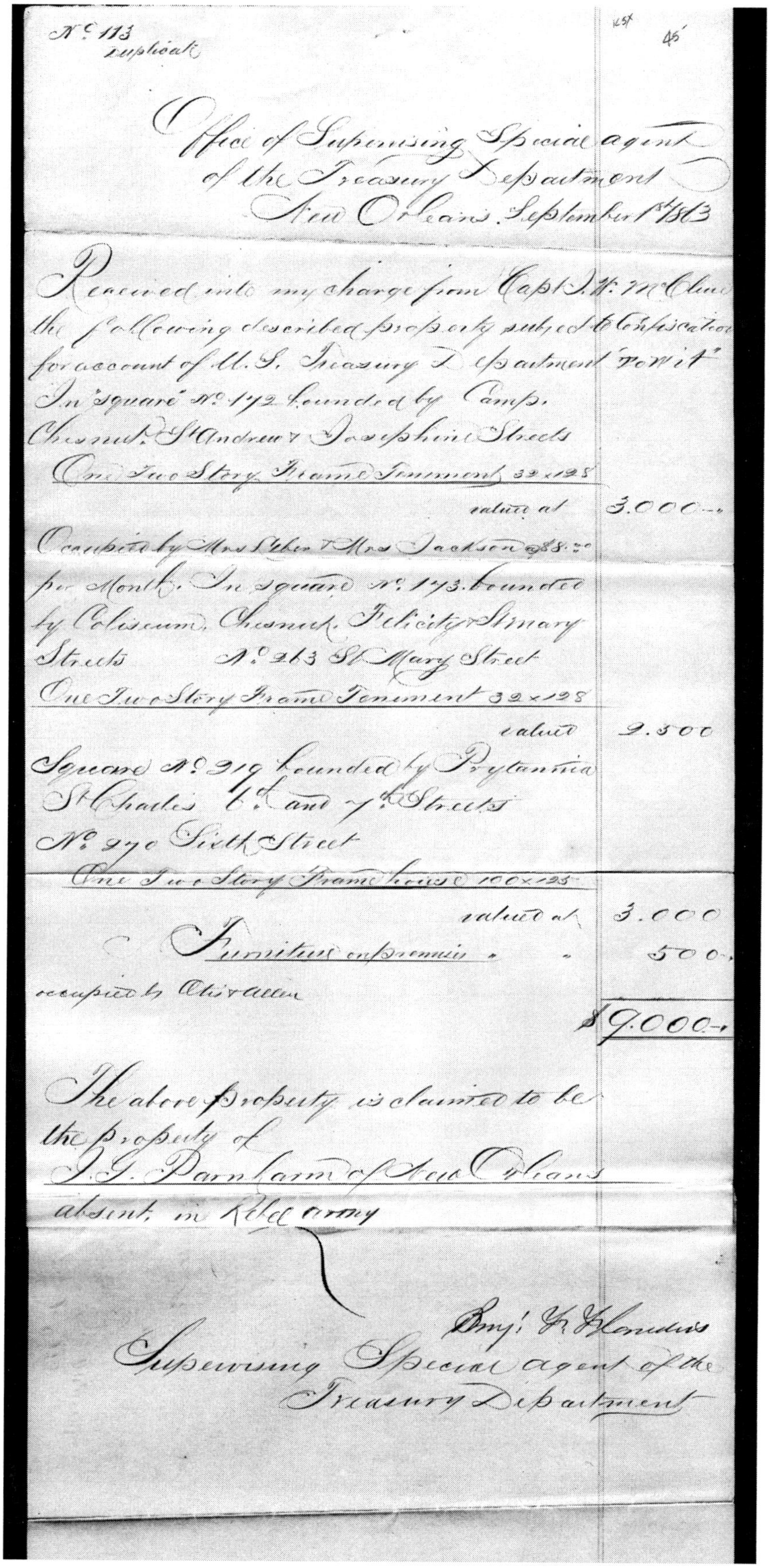

No. 113
duplicate

Office of Supervising Special Agent
of the Treasury Department
New Orleans September 1st 1863

Received into my charge from Capt J. W. McClure
the following described property subject to Confiscation
for account of U.S. Treasury Department to wit
In "square" No. 172 bounded by Camp,
Chesnut, St Andrew & Josephine Streets
One Two Story Frame Tenement 32 x 128
valued at 3.000

Occupied by Mrs Lehr & Mrs Jackson @ $8.00
per Month. In square No. 173. bounded
by Coliseum, Chesnut, Felicity & St Mary
Streets No. 263 St Mary Street
One Two Story Frame Tenement 32 x 128
valued 2.500

Square No. 219 bounded by Prytannia
St Charles 6th and 7th Streets
No. 270 Sixth Street
One Two Story Frame house 100 x 125
valued at 3.000
Furniture on premises 500
occupied by Otis & Allen
$9.000

The above property is claimed to be
the property of
J. G. Parnham of New Orleans
absent in Rebel army

Benj. F. Flanders
Supervising Special Agent of the
Treasury Department

Figure 14. Confiscation Receipt for Rebel Soldier, Supervising Special Agent, New Orleans, September 1, 1863.

Figure 15

Office Assistant Quartermaster,
Bureau Refugees, Freedmen and Abandoned Lands,
STATE OF LOUISIANA
No. 82 Carondelet st.

New Orleans, April 8th 1866

This is to certify that from the records of this Office it appears that the property of John A. Stevenson situated and described as follows, to-wit; In the 1st Dist of this City, in Sq. 217. Dwelling House & Lots No 226 Carondelet St, & in Sq. 3. Three Store Houses & Lots Nos. 37. 39. & 41 Front St. was under siezure by the United States Government and in charge of the Agents of the United States from the 15th day of August. 1863. to the 31st day of March 1866.

W. B. Armstrong.
Capt & A. Q. M. Bureau
R. F. & A. L. La.

No. 342

THE STATE OF LOUISIANA.
FIRST DISTRICT, CITY OF NEW ORLEANS.

Received, of M Jno A. Stevenson the sum of One hundred & two 25/100 Dollars,

STATE TAX FOR THE YEAR 1865, *on the property designated on the other side in conformity to law.* cond't per p. by W. A. Sept

New Orleans, Sept 26 1866.

Collector.

$ 102 25/100

"REA'S STEAM PRESS"

Figure 15. Affidavit and Tax Receipt Freedmans Bureau, Property Not Subject to State Taxes, State Collector, and A.Q.M., R.F. of A.L., LA., New Orleans, 1866.

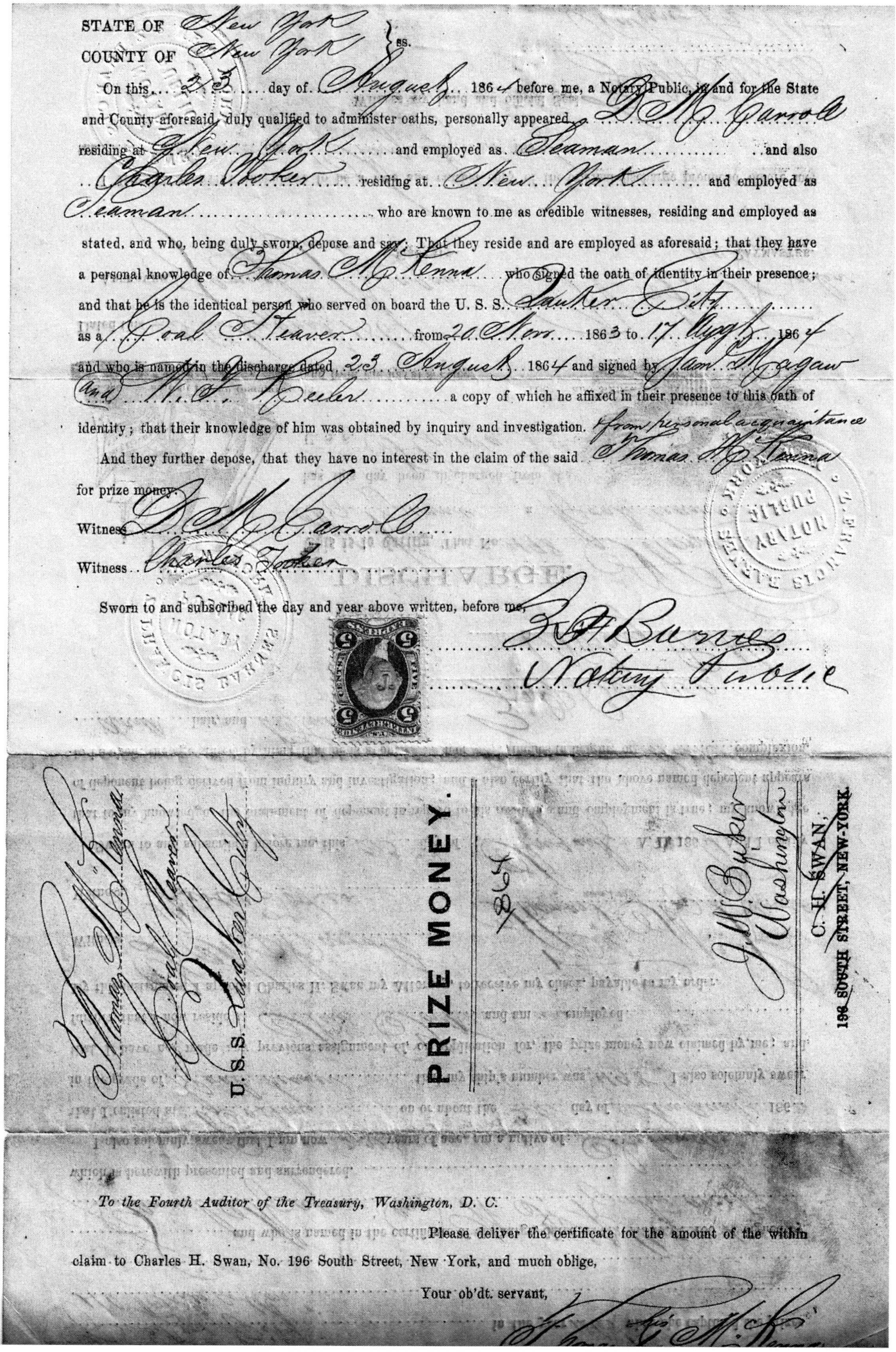

STATE OF New York
COUNTY OF New York } ss.

On this 23 day of August 1864 before me, a Notary Public, in and for the State and County aforesaid, duly qualified to administer oaths, personally appeared D. M. Carroll residing at New York and employed as Seaman and also Charles Tooker residing at New York and employed as Seaman who are known to me as credible witnesses, residing and employed as stated, and who, being duly sworn, depose and say: That they reside and are employed as aforesaid; that they have a personal knowledge of Thomas McKenna who signed the oath of identity in their presence; and that he is the identical person who served on board the U. S. S. Quaker City as a Coal Heaver from 20 Nov 1863 to 17 Aug 1864 and who is named in the discharge dated 23 August 1864 and signed by Jam. Magaw and W. F. Keeler a copy of which he affixed in their presence to this oath of identity; that their knowledge of him was obtained by inquiry and investigation. from personal acquaintance

And they further depose, that they have no interest in the claim of the said Thomas McKenna for prize money.

Witness D. M. Carroll

Witness Charles Tooker

Sworn to and subscribed the day and year above written, before me, F. H. Barnes Notary Public

Thomas McKenna
Coal Heaver
U.S.S. Quaker City

PRIZE MONEY.

1864

J. W. Burkin
Washington

C. H. SWAN,
196 SOUTH STREET, NEW-YORK.

To the Fourth Auditor of the Treasury, Washington, D. C.

Please deliver the certificate for the amount of the within claim to Charles H. Swan, No. 196 South Street, New York, and much oblige,

Your ob'dt. servant,

Thomas McKenna

Figure 16 (this page and page following). Prize Money Affidavit and Claim, 40 Bales of Cotton, Sailor USS *Quaker City*. August 23, 1864.

I, Thomas McKenna do solemnly swear, that I am the identical person who served by that name as a Coal heaver on board the U. S. Ship "Quaker City" in the year 1863 1864 when she captured the prizes "40 Bales cotton"

and who is named in the certificate of discharge, dated 23 Aug. 1864 signed by Samuel A. Magaw and W. F. Keeler a copy of which is herewith presented and surrendered.

I also solemnly swear that I am now 21 years of age, am a native of Ireland that I enlisted at Boston on or about the 22 day of August 1863 in the grade of Coal heaver that my ship's number was 498 I also solemnly swear that I have not made any previous assignment of, or application for, the prize money now claimed by me; and further, that I now reside at New York and am unemployed

By this instrument I appoint Charles H. Swan my Attorney, to receive my check, payable to my order.

Witness D. M. Carroll

Witness Charles Tookes

Thomas his X mark McKenna

Sworn to and subscribed before me, this 23 day of August A. D. 1864 And I certify that to my knowledge, the statement of deponent in regard to his residence and employment is true; my knowledge of deponent being derived from inquiry and investigation; and I also certify that the above named deponent appears to be about the age stated by him; that he is about 5 feet 8 inches in height, of dark complexion, dark hair, and Blue eyes.

Z. H. Barnes
Notary Public

DISCHARGE.

This is to Certify, That No. 498 Thomas McKenna a Coal heaver has this day been discharged from the U. S. S. Florida and from the naval service.

Dated this 23 August 1864

APPROVED, Samuel A. Magaw Lt. Comdr CAPTAIN.

W. F. Keeler a.a. PAYMASTER.

I HEREBY CERTIFY the above to be a true and correct copy of the original discharge produced before me,

TREASURY DEPARTMENT,

OFFICE OF INTERNAL REVENUE,

WASHINGTON, *December* 30, 1867.

A. H. MECHLIN, ESQ., GEORGETOWN, D. C.,

Sir: Your letter of 10th inst., has been received, relative to that provision of Sec. 123, Act of June 30th, 1864, which declares " that payments of prize money shall be regarded as income from salaries, and the duty thereon shall be adjusted and collected in like manner."

You inquire whether this provision refers to payments of prize money for captures made before the passage of that law, or whether it is restricted to the payments of prize money which accrued from captures made after the enactment of said provision.

In reply, I would state, that the tax of five per cent. should be withheld from all payments on account of prize money, without regard to the time when the captures were made, whether previous to the passage of the Act of June 30th, 1864, or not. Section 116 imposes the Income Tax upon the gains, profits, and *income* of every person residing in the United States, or of any citizen of the United States residing abroad, whether derived from any kind of property, rents, interest, dividends, or salaries, &c.; but Section 123 provides for a salary tax upon all salaries paid to persons in the civil, military, naval or *other* employment or *service of the United States*, and in accordance with its first proviso, which you quoted, *payments of prize money* shall be regarded as income from salaries. Your attention is called to those two sections, because, in your letter you seem to think that Sec. 123 is a repetition of Sec. 116; whereas, the law, in Sec. 123, contemplates only *salaries* paid by the *United States;* but in the 116th Section the *entire income, gains or profits.* Provision is then made in the returns of personal income for a deduction of any portion thereof of any individual which has been subject to the first per cent. tax.

The fact that the law is silent as to the point raised by you, whether prize money for captures previous to June 30th, 1864, should be subject to tax, leaves the office no option, but to construe the Section according to the evident intention of the law-makers. It is, therefore, the rule of the office, that the five per cent. tax should be withheld from all *payments* of prize money, without regard to the time *when* the captures were made.

Very Respectfully,

E. A. ROLLINS, *Commissioner.*

Figure 17. Opinion Taxability of Admiralty Prizes. Commissioner of Internal Revenue Washington, December 30, 1867.

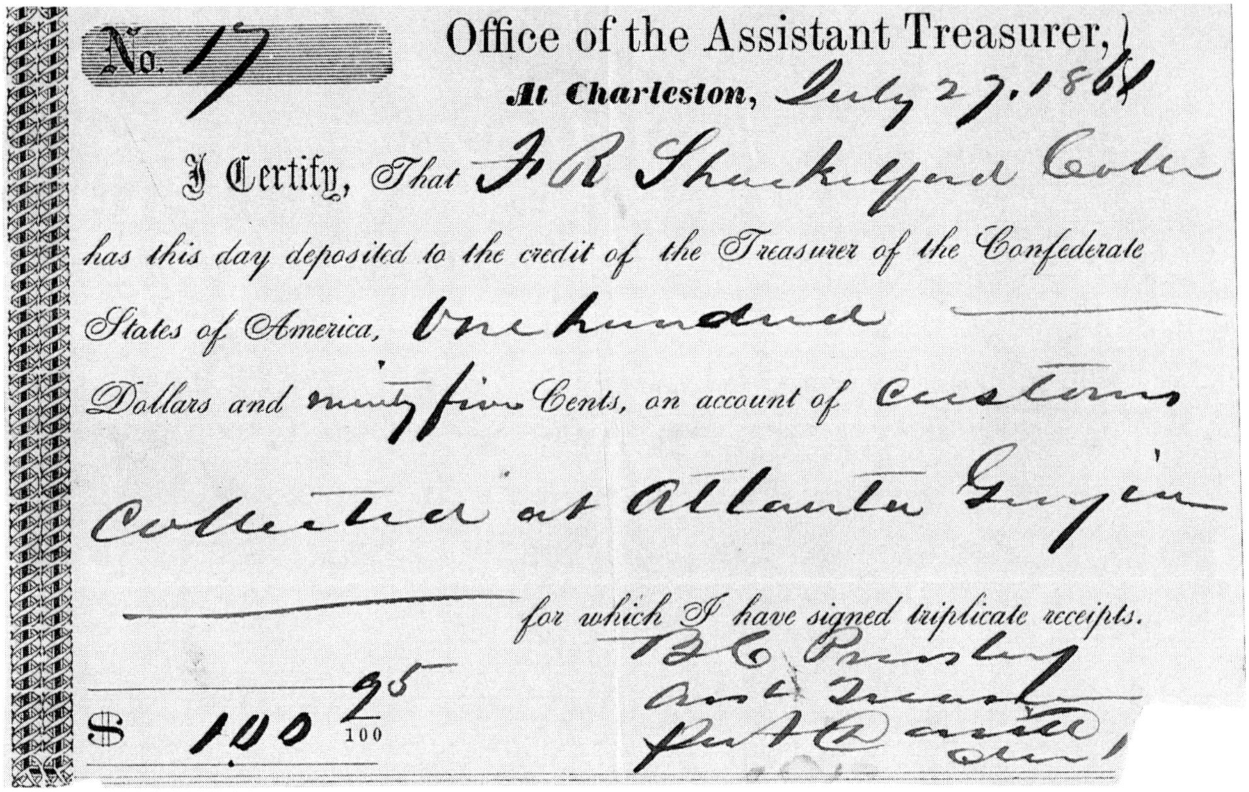
No. 17

Office of the Assistant Treasurer,
At Charleston, July 27. 1861

I Certify, That F R Shackelford Collr
has this day deposited to the credit of the Treasurer of the Confederate
States of America, One hundred ———
Dollars and ninety five Cents, on account of Customs
Collected at Atlanta Georgia

——— for which I have signed triplicate receipts.
B C Pressley
Asst Treasr
Pr A [illegible]
Clerk

$ 100 95/100

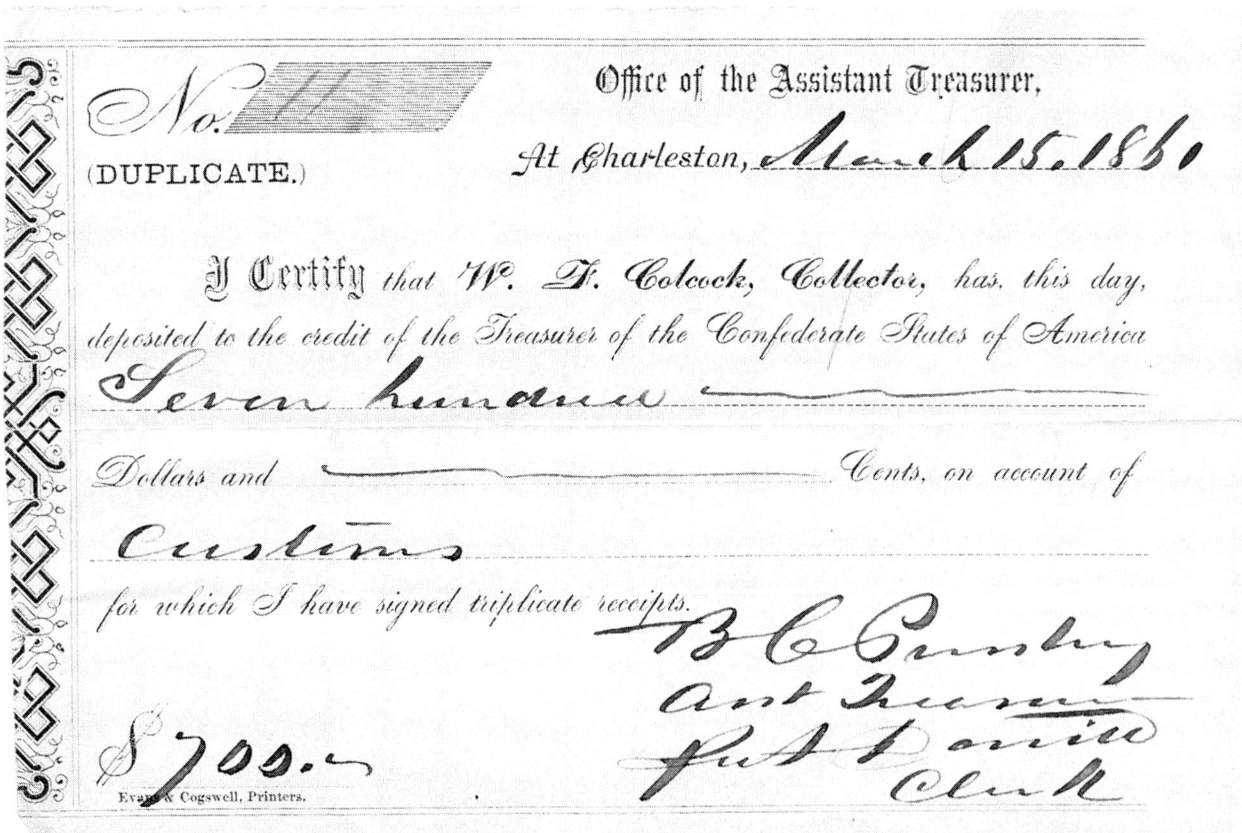
No.
(DUPLICATE.)

Office of the Assistant Treasurer,
At Charleston, March 15. 1861

I Certify that Wm. F. Colcock, Collector, has, this day,
deposited to the credit of the Treasurer of the Confederate States of America
Seven hundred ———
Dollars and ——— Cents, on account of
Customs

for which I have signed triplicate receipts.
B C Pressley
Asst Treasurer
Pr A [illegible]
Clerk

$700.—

Evans & Cogswell, Printers.

Top: **Figure 18. Certificate of Deposit of Inland Customs, Assistant Treasurer. Atlanta, July 27, 1861.** ***Bottom:*** **Figure 19. Certificate of Deposit of Customs, Assistant Treasurer. Charleston, March 15, 1861.**

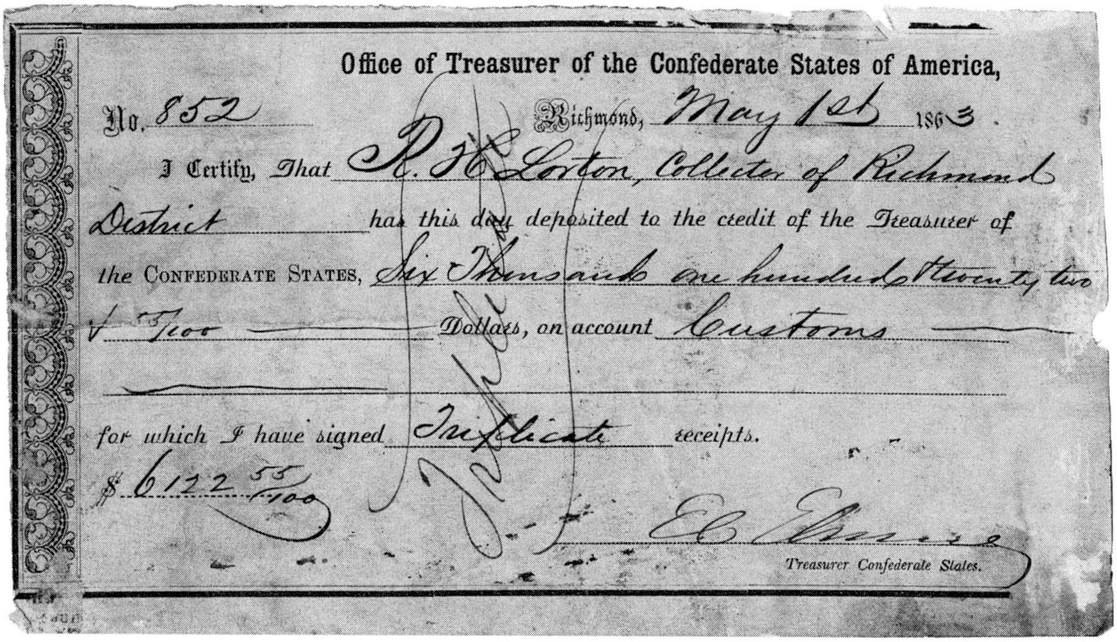

Office of Treasurer of the Confederate States of America,

No. 852 Richmond, May 1st 1863.

I Certify, That R. H. Lorton, Collector of Richmond District has this day deposited to the credit of the Treasurer of the Confederate States, Six Thousand one hundred & twenty two & 55/100 Dollars, on account Customs

for which I have signed Triplicate receipts.

$6122 55/100

Treasurer Confederate States.

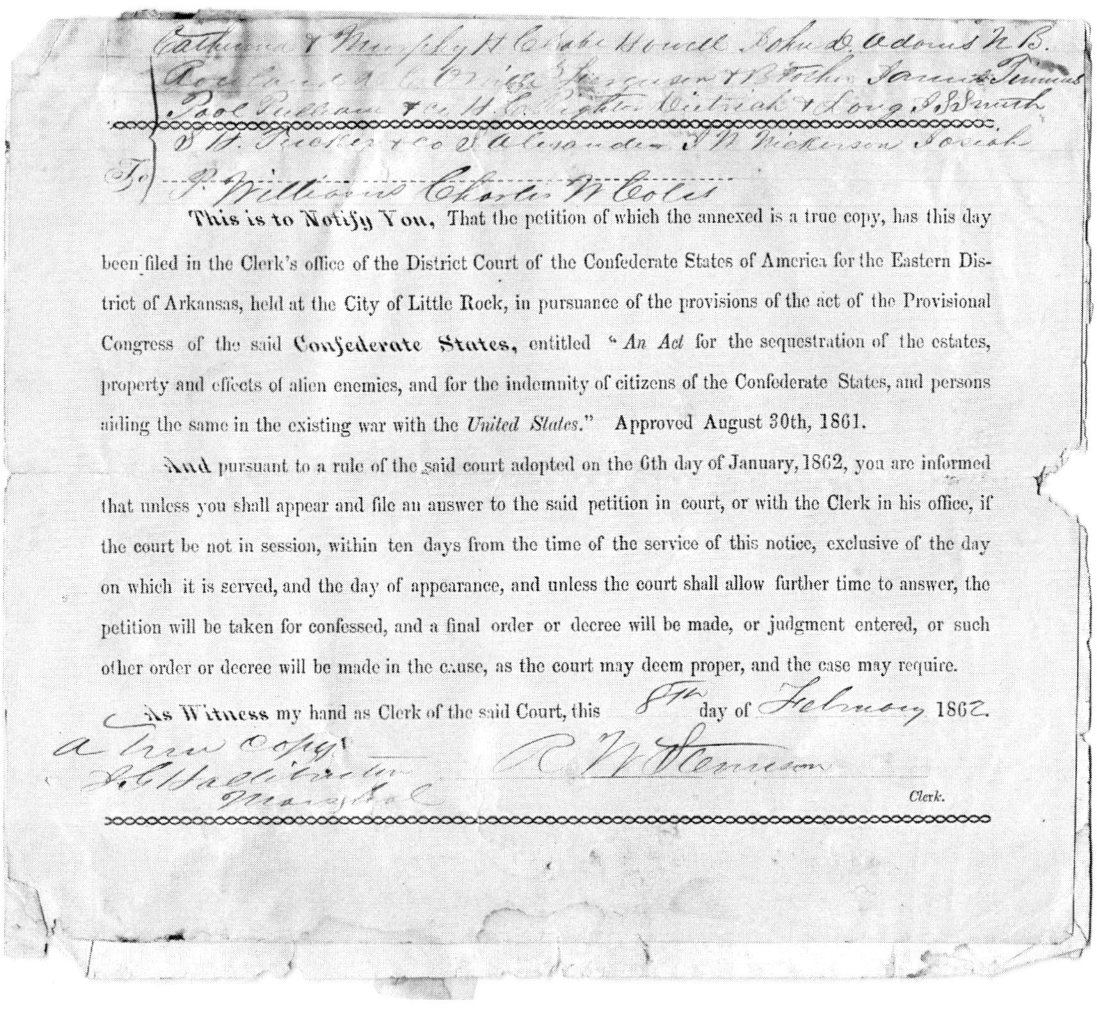

To

This is to Notify You, That the petition of which the annexed is a true copy, has this day been filed in the Clerk's office of the District Court of the Confederate States of America for the Eastern District of Arkansas, held at the City of Little Rock, in pursuance of the provisions of the act of the Provisional Congress of the said Confederate States, entitled "*An Act* for the sequestration of the estates, property and effects of alien enemies, and for the indemnity of citizens of the Confederate States, and persons aiding the same in the existing war with the *United States*." Approved August 30th, 1861.

And pursuant to a rule of the said court adopted on the 6th day of January, 1862, you are informed that unless you shall appear and file an answer to the said petition in court, or with the Clerk in his office, if the court be not in session, within ten days from the time of the service of this notice, exclusive of the day on which it is served, and the day of appearance, and unless the court shall allow further time to answer, the petition will be taken for confessed, and a final order or decree will be made, or judgment entered, or such other order or decree will be made in the cause, as the court may deem proper, and the case may require.

As Witness my hand as Clerk of the said Court, this 8th day of February 1862.

A true copy

Marshal

Clerk.

Top: **Figure 20. Certificate of Deposit of Customs, Treasurer. Richmond, May 1, 1863.** ***Bottom:*** **Figure 21. Notice by District Judge for Sequestration Informing "Alien Enemies to Relinquish Property," Clerk. Little Rock, February 8, 1862.**

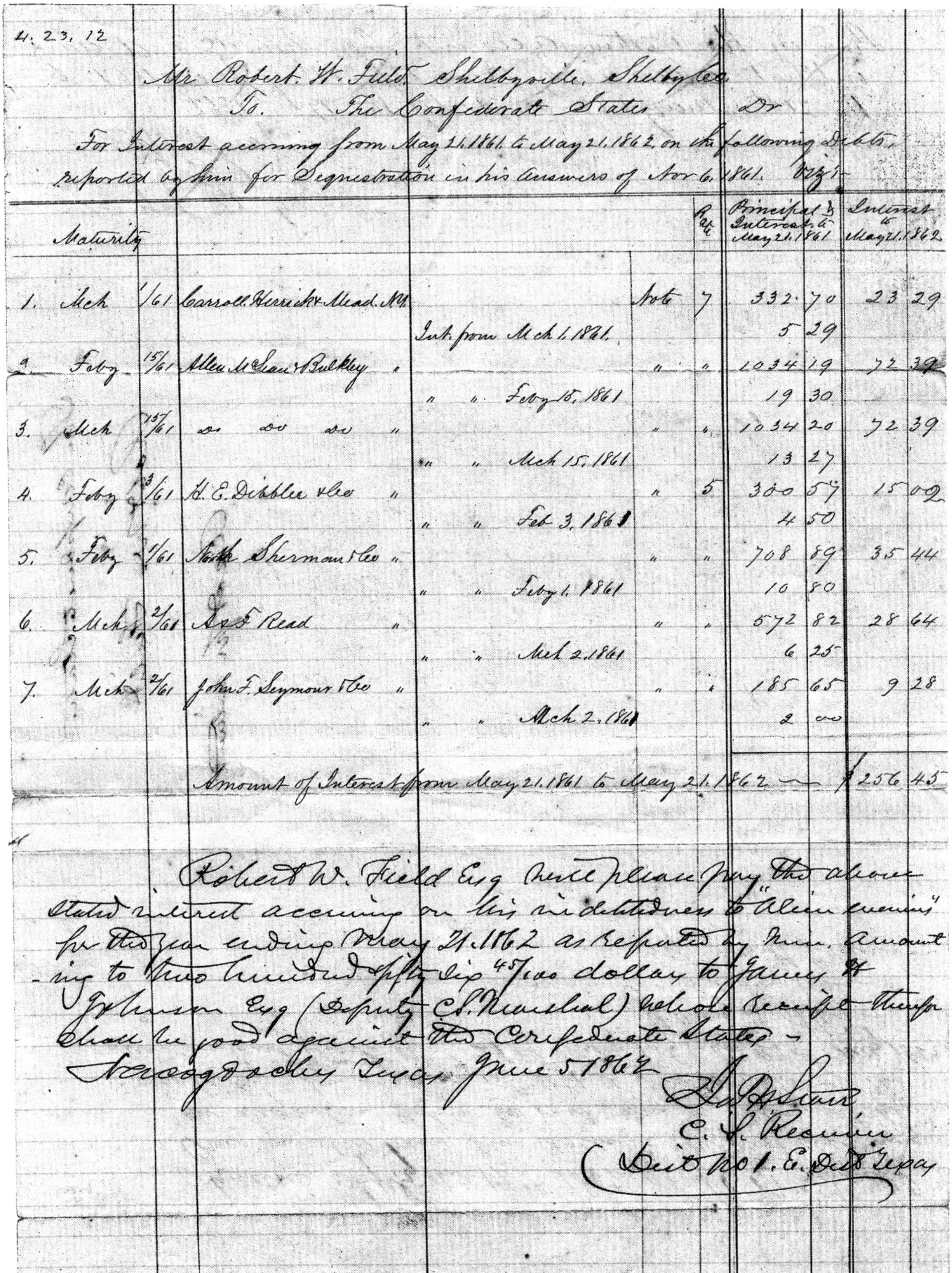

4.23.12

Mr. Robert W. Field Shelbyville, Shelby Co.
To The Confederate States Dr

For Interest accruing from May 21.1861 to May 21.1862 on the following Debts reported by him for Sequestration in his Answers of Nov 6. 1861. Viz:-

	Maturity					Rate	Principal & Interest to May 21.1861	Interest to May 21.1862
1.	Mch	1/61	Carroll Herrick & Mead Ny.		Note	7	332.70	23.29
				Int. from Mch 1. 1861.			5.29	
2.	Feby	15/61	Allen McLean & Bulkley	"	"	"	1034.19	72.39
				" " Feby 15. 1861			19.30	
3.	Mch	15/61	do do do	"	"	"	1034.20	72.39
				" " Mch 15. 1861			13.27	
4.	Feby	3/61	H. E. Dibblee & Co	"	"	5	300.57	15.02
				" " Feb 3. 1861			4.50	
5.	Feby	1/61	North Sherman & Co	"	"	"	708.89	35.44
				" " Feby 1. 1861			10.80	
6.	Mch	2/61	Asa F. Read	"	"	"	572.82	28.64
				" " Mch 2. 1861			6.25	
7.	Mch	2/61	John F. Seymour & Co	"	"	"	185.65	9.28
				" " Mch 2. 1861			2.00	

Amount of Interest from May 21.1861 to May 21.1862 — $256.45

Robert W. Field Esq will please pay the above stated interest accruing on his indebtedness to "Alien enemies" for the year ending May 21.1862 as reported by him, amounting to two hundred fifty six 45/100 dollars to James H. Johnson Esq (Deputy C.S. Marshal) whose receipt therefor shall be good against the Confederate States —
Nacogdoches Texas June 5 1862

[illegible]
C.S. Receiver
(Dist No 1. E. Dist Texas

Figure 22. Schedule of Sequestered Interest of "Alien Enemies," Receiver. Nacogdoches, June 5, 1862.

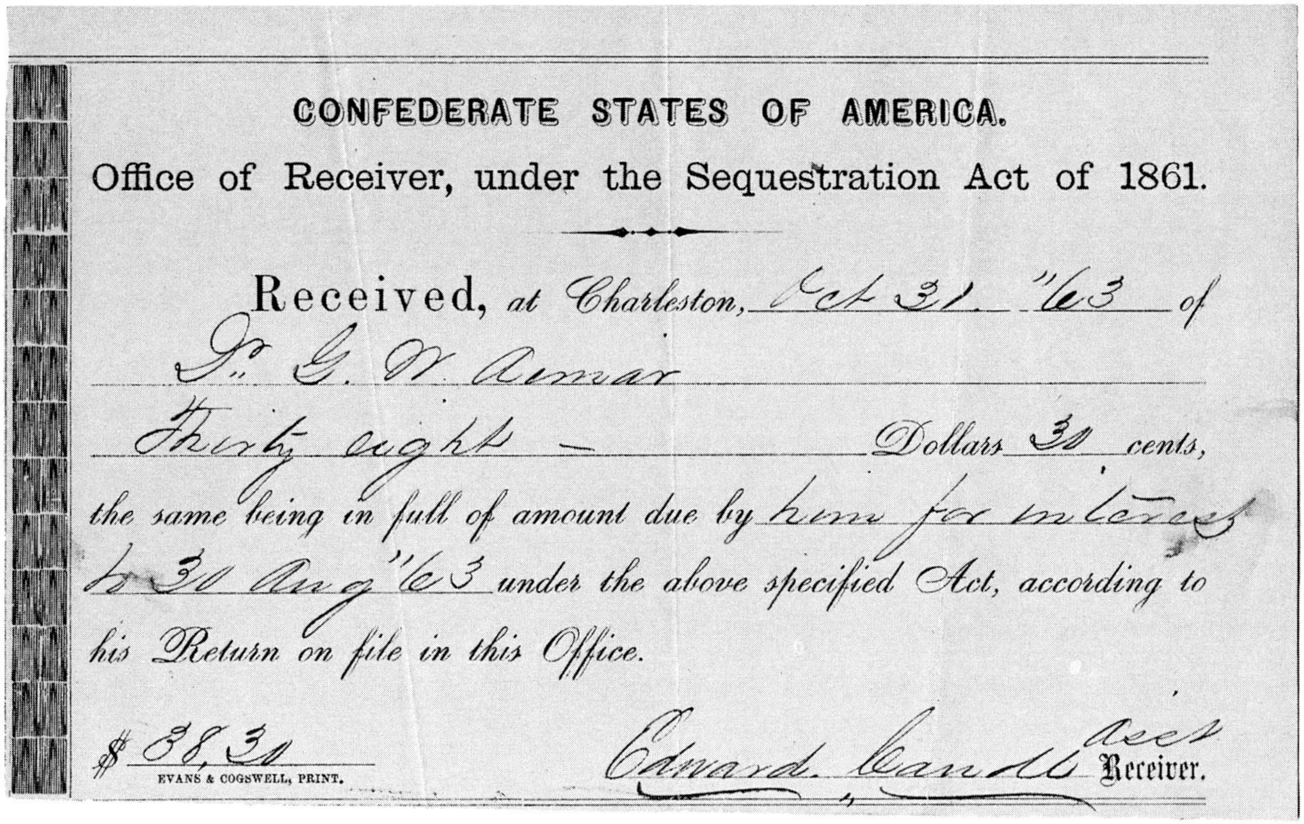

CONFEDERATE STATES OF AMERICA.

Office of Receiver, under the Sequestration Act of 1861.

Received, at Charleston, Oct 31 "63 of

Dr. G. W. Aimar

Thirty eight — Dollars 30 cents,

the same being in full of amount due by him for interest to 30 Aug "63 under the above specified Act, according to his Return on file in this Office.

$ 38.30

EVANS & COGSWELL, PRINT.

Edward Candl Asst Receiver.

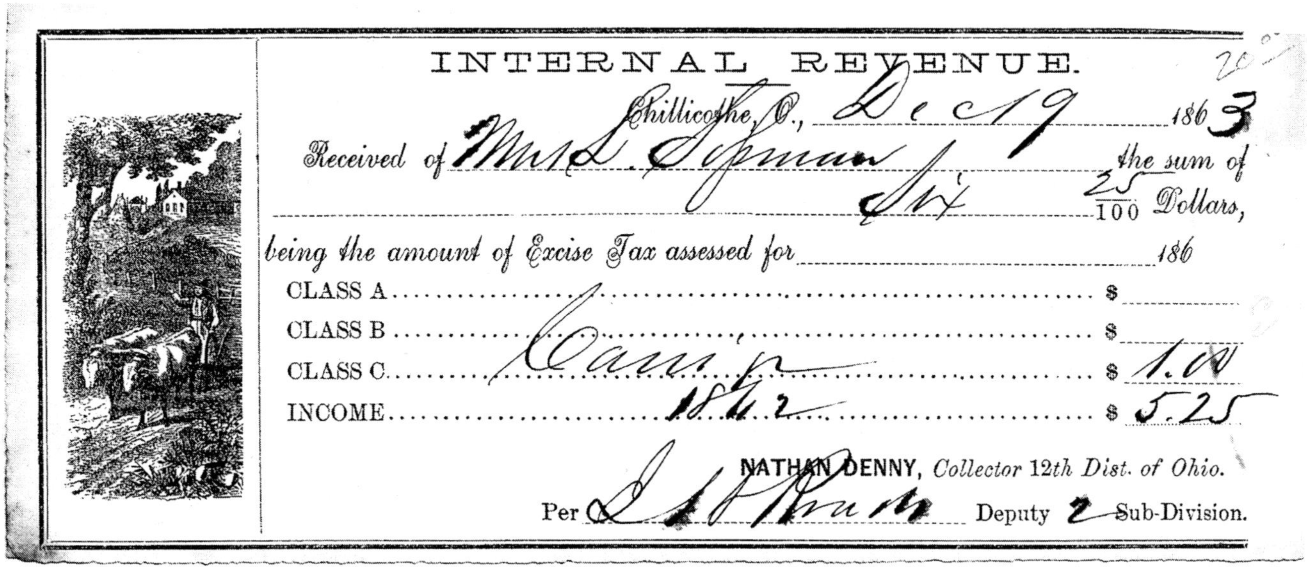

INTERNAL REVENUE.

Chillicothe, O., Dec 19 1863

Received of Wm L. Lofman the sum of Six 25/100 Dollars,

being the amount of Excise Tax assessed for 186

CLASS A	$
CLASS B	$
CLASS C Carriage	$ 1.00
INCOME 1862	$ 5.25

NATHAN DENNY, Collector 12th Dist. of Ohio.

Per J. S. P. Rudy Deputy 2 Sub-Division.

Top: **Figure 23. Sequestration Receipt for Interest Collected, Receiver, Charleston, October 31, 1863. *Bottom:* Figure 24. Income and Carriage Tax Receipt, Collector. Chillicothe, Ohio, December, 19, 1863.**

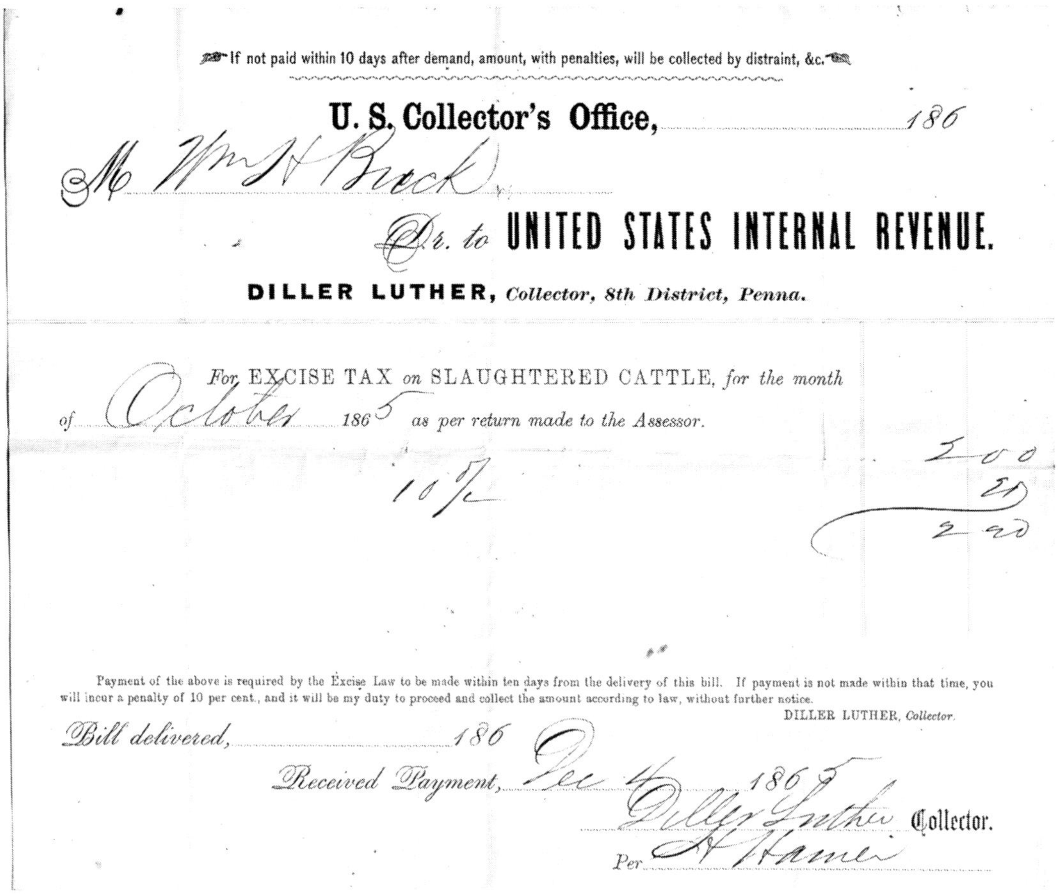

If not paid within 10 days after demand, amount, with penalties, will be collected by distraint, &c.

U. S. Collector's Office, 186

M Wm H Buck

Dr. to **UNITED STATES INTERNAL REVENUE.**

DILLER LUTHER, *Collector, 8th District, Penna.*

For EXCISE TAX on SLAUGHTERED CATTLE, *for the month of* October 1865 *as per return made to the Assessor.*

10% 2 00
20
2 20

Payment of the above is required by the Excise Law to be made within ten days from the delivery of this bill. If payment is not made within that time, you will incur a penalty of 10 per cent., and it will be my duty to proceed and collect the amount according to law, without further notice.

DILLER LUTHER, *Collector.*

Bill delivered, 186

Received Payment, Dec 4 1865

Diller Luther Collector.

Per H Hamer

Nov. 1, 1862.] FRANK LESLIE'S ILLUSTRATED NEWSPAPER. 89

THE NEW TAX LAW—INTERIOR OF A NEW YORK ASSESSOR'S OFFICE (M. PEMBROKE GILBERT'S), BROADWAY, NEW YORK.

MRS. JEFFERSON DAVIS.

The interest which naturally attaches to the wife of the rebel President has induced us to publish her portrait, which is taken from a photograph by Brady. She is the granddaughter of Governor Howell, of New Jersey, whose heroic sacrifices in the

manager, arguing with his companion the comparative merits of "legs and lungs." Here stood also the learned apothecary, who does not know the difference betwen arsenic and soda, or oxalic acid and epsom salts, while scattered around, in glorious confusion, were brewers, rectifiers, horsedealers, confectioners, tallow-chandlers, circus-keepers, and the whole etcetera of human swindling and

Bear Creek, in Baltimore county, Maryland, was so elated at the late rebel incursion in Maryland, that he determined to visit 'our deliverers,' and for that purpose hooked up his horse and wagon and started all agog. He alighted at a hotel near Frederick, and was drinking a bumper to Jeff., when a Confederate officer came in and inquired for the

***Top:* Figure 25. Excise Tax Receipt on Slaughtered Cattle, Collector, 8th District, Pennsylvania, December 4, 1865. *Bottom:* Figure 26. "Scenes in the Tax Collection Offices, New York City." *Frank Leslie's Illustrated Newspaper*, November 1, 1862.**

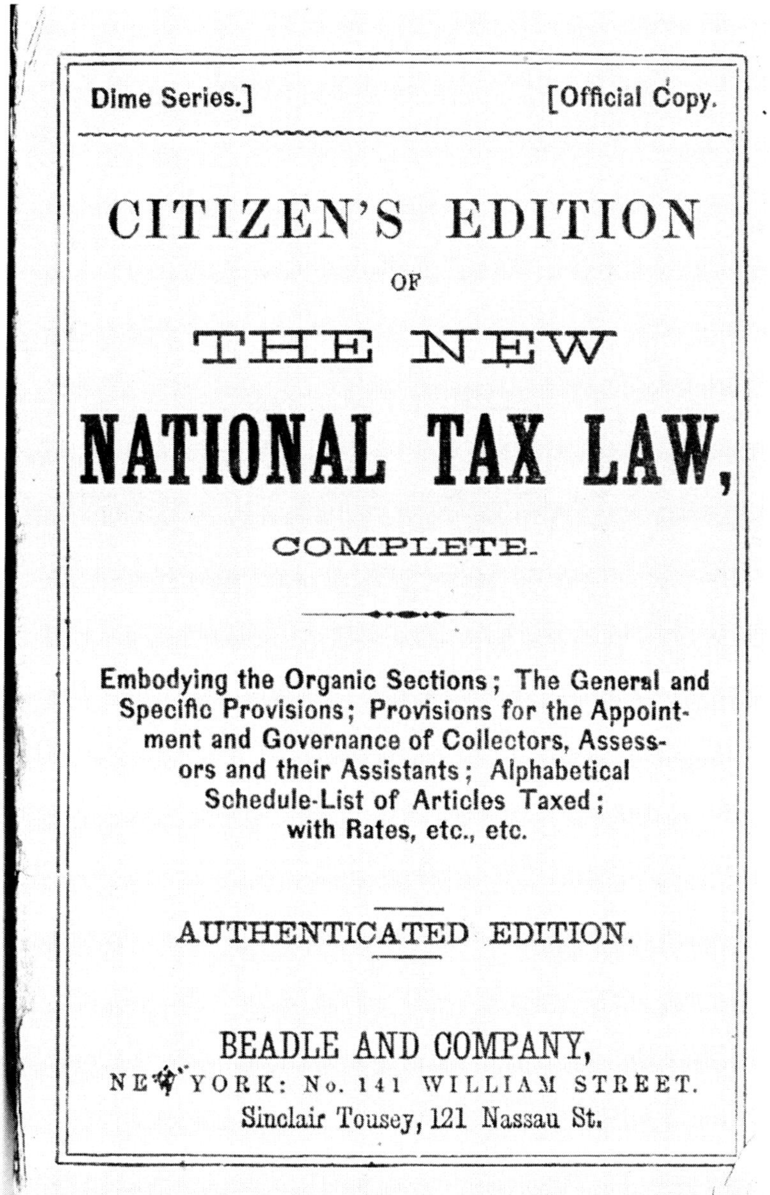

Dime Series.] [Official Copy.

CITIZEN'S EDITION

OF

THE NEW

NATIONAL TAX LAW,

COMPLETE.

Embodying the Organic Sections; The General and Specific Provisions; Provisions for the Appointment and Governance of Collectors, Assessors and their Assistants; Alphabetical Schedule-List of Articles Taxed; with Rates, etc., etc.

AUTHENTICATED EDITION.

BEADLE AND COMPANY,

NEW YORK: No. 141 WILLIAM STREET.

Sinclair Tousey, 121 Nassau St.

Top: Figure 27. *Citizens Edition of the New National Tax Law,* Beadle and Company, New York, 1862. *Bottom:* Figure 28. U.S. Revenue Stamps. Contracts (10¢); Inland Exchange (40¢); Entry of Goods (50¢); Foreign Exchange Conveyance ($1.00), 1862.

REVENUE STAMPS!

F. B. LEVIS, *with a view to better accommodate the public with Revenue Stamps, has effected an arrange=ment with* J. FRED LAUMASTER, *by which, in future, Stamps of all denominations, and in any a=mount, will be sold at the*

POST OFFICE IN MOUNT HOLLY,

at Philadelphia rates. Orders addressed by mail, or otherwise, to either of the undersigned, will be promptly attended to.

FRANK B. LEVIS,
J. FRED LAUMASTER.

Mt. Holly, Dec. 11, 1865.

Figure 29. "Revenue Stamps!" Broadside, Post Office. Mount Holly, Pennsylvania, 1865.

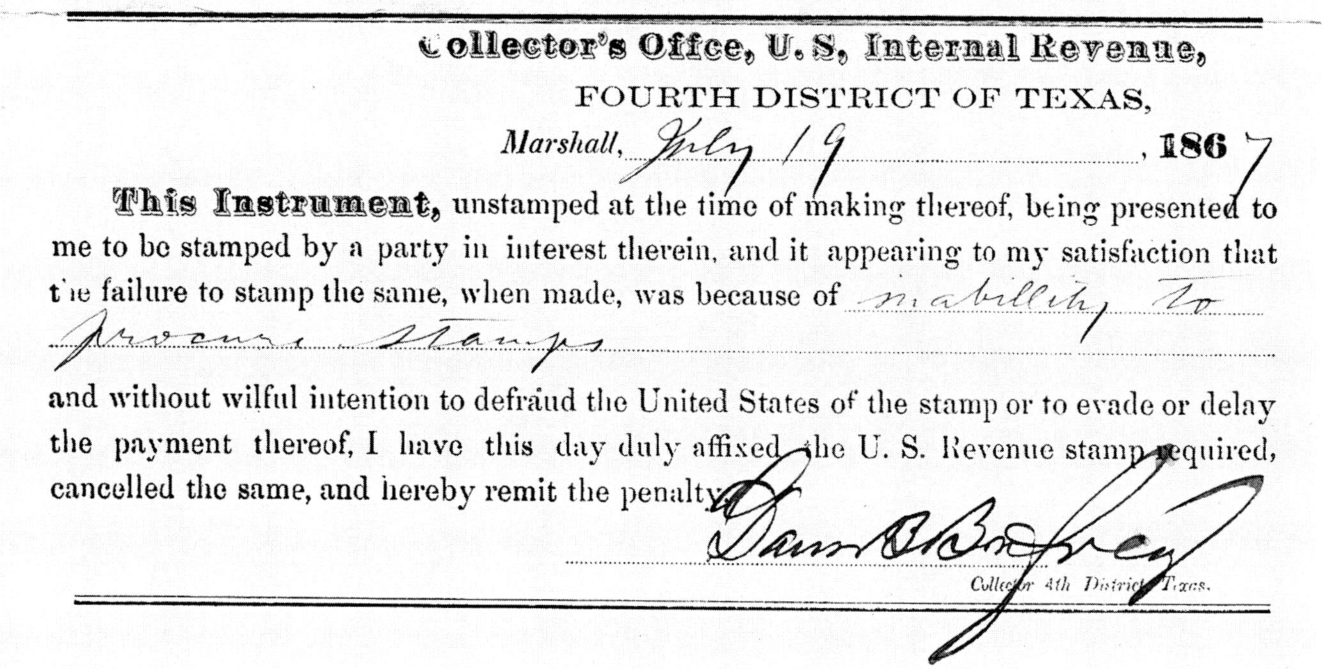

Collector's Office, U. S, Internal Revenue,

FOURTH DISTRICT OF TEXAS,

Marshall, July 19, **186**7

This Instrument, unstamped at the time of making thereof, being presented to me to be stamped by a party in interest therein, and it appearing to my satisfaction that the failure to stamp the same, when made, was because of inability to procure stamps and without wilful intention to defraud the United States of the stamp or to evade or delay the payment thereof, I have this day duly affixed the U. S. Revenue stamp required, cancelled the same, and hereby remit the penalty.

Collector 4th District Texas.

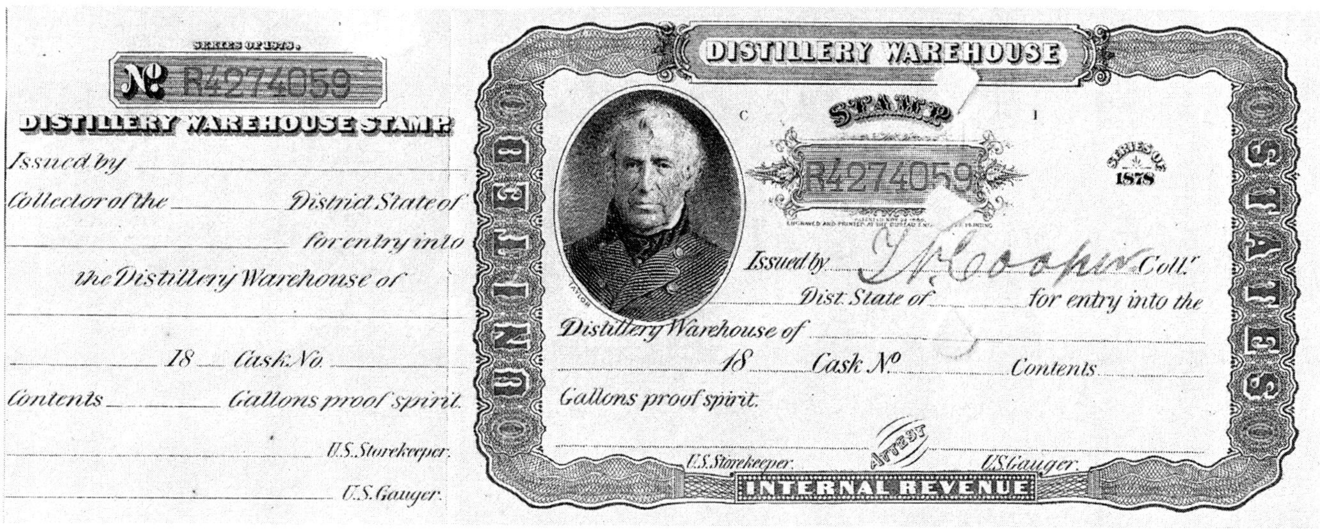

Top: **Figure 30. Remission of Penalty for Unstamped Instrument, Collector, Marshall, Texas, July 19, 1867.** ***Bottom:*** **Figure 31. "Distillery Warehouse Stamp." Collector, Storekeeper and Gauger [Blank], 1878.**

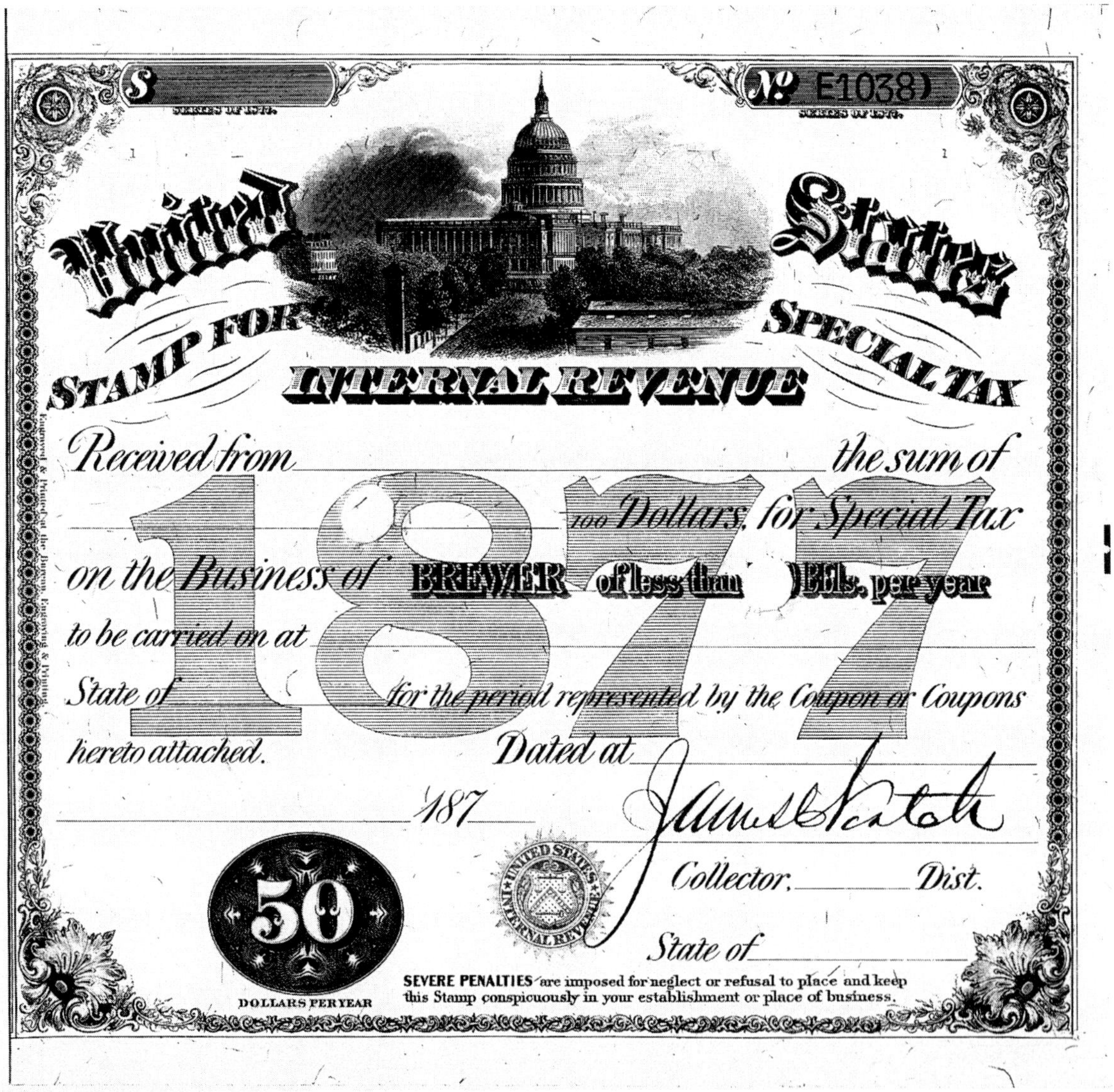

Top: **Figure 32. Stamp for Special Tax. Retail Liquor Dealer, [Blank], 1875.** ***Bottom:*** **Figure 33. Stamp for $50.00 Special Tax, Brewer of less than 500 barrels per year, [Blank], 1877.**

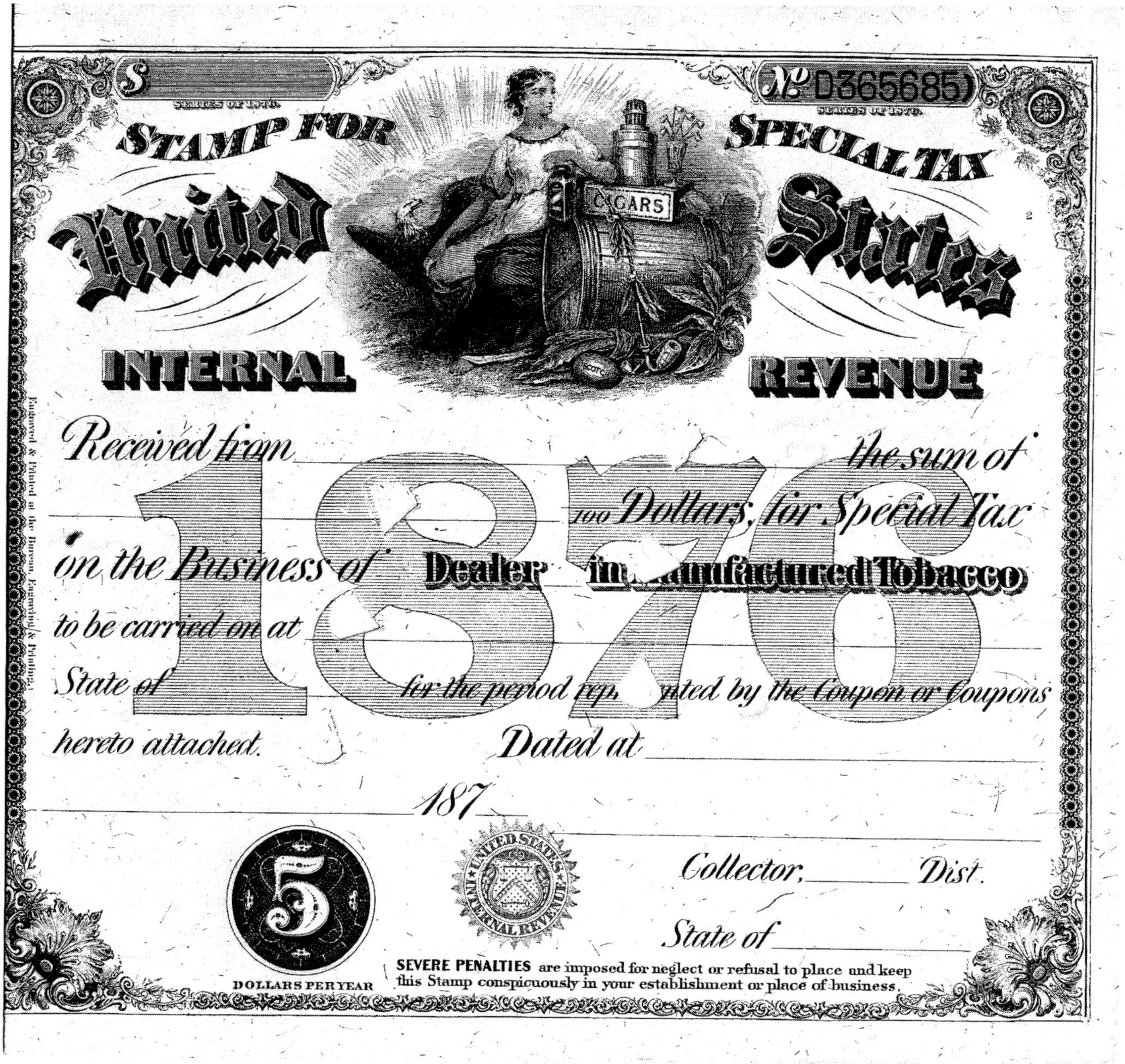

Figure 34. Stamp for $5.00 Special Tax, Dealer in Manufactured Tobacco, [Blank], 1876.

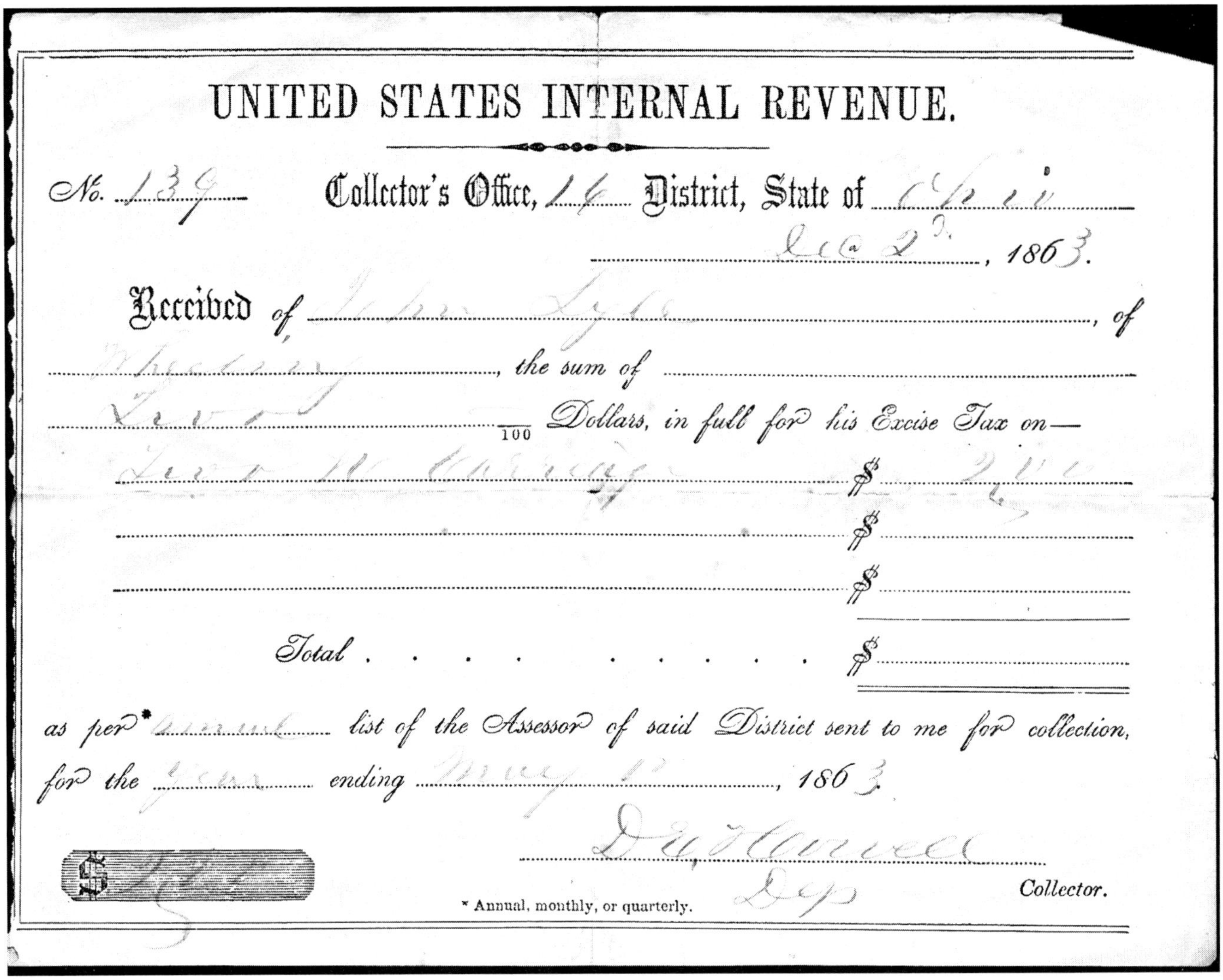

UNITED STATES INTERNAL REVENUE.

No. .... Collector's Office, ... District, State of ....

........, 186 .

Received of ...., of .... the sum of .... $\frac{}{100}$ Dollars, in full for his Excise Tax on—

.... $ ....

.... $ ....

.... $ ....

Total . . . . $ ....

as per* .... list of the Assessor of said District sent to me for collection, for the .... ending ...., 186 .

.... Collector.

* Annual, monthly, or quarterly.

Figure 35. Excise Tax Receipt for Collector. Wheeling, Ohio, May 1, 1863.

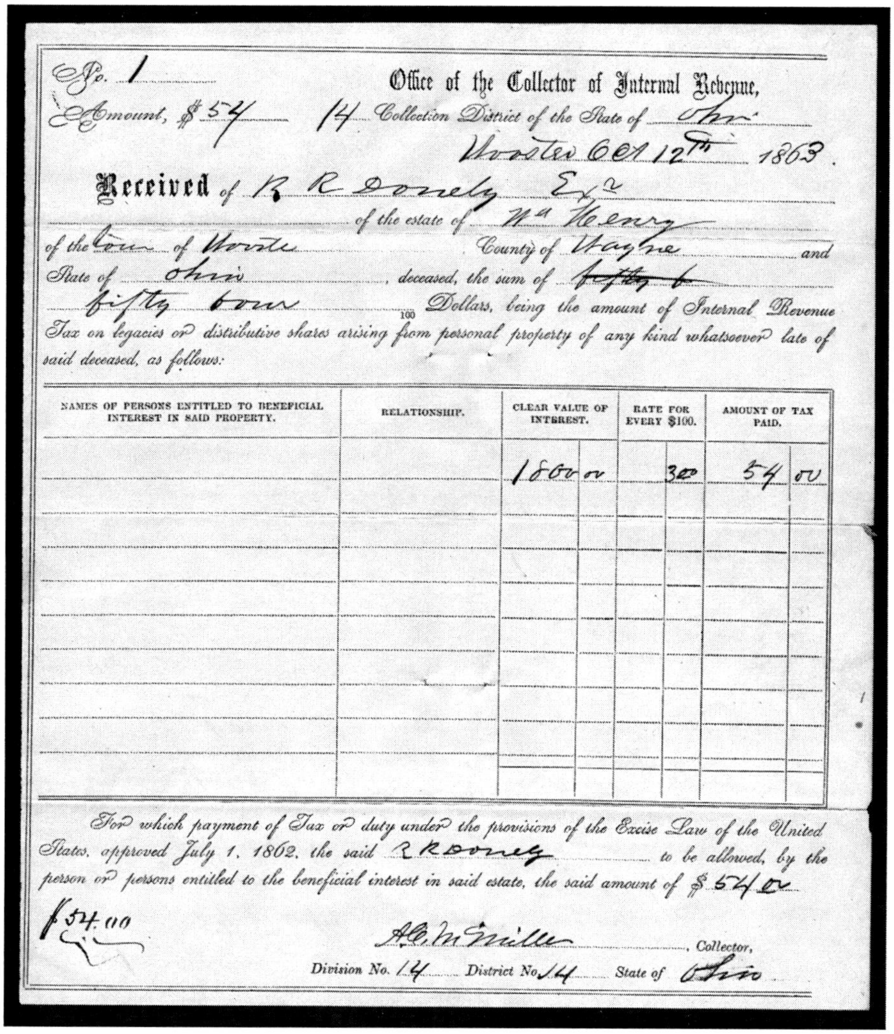

No. 1 — Office of the Collector of Internal Revenue,

Amount, $54 — 14 Collection District of the State of Ohio

Wooster Oct 12th 1863.

Received of R R Donely Exr of the estate of Wm Henry of the town of Wooster County of Wayne and State of Ohio, deceased, the sum of ~~fifty 6~~ fifty four $\frac{}{100}$ Dollars, being the amount of Internal Revenue Tax on legacies or distributive shares arising from personal property of any kind whatsoever late of said deceased, as follows:

NAMES OF PERSONS ENTITLED TO BENEFICIAL INTEREST IN SAID PROPERTY.	RELATIONSHIP.	CLEAR VALUE OF INTEREST.	RATE FOR EVERY $100.	AMOUNT OF TAX PAID.
		1800 00	300	54 00

For which payment of Tax or duty under the provisions of the Excise Law of the United States, approved July 1, 1862, the said R R Donely to be allowed, by the person or persons entitled to the beneficial interest in said estate, the said amount of $54 00

$54.00

A. C. McMiller, Collector,

Division No. 14 District No 14 State of Ohio

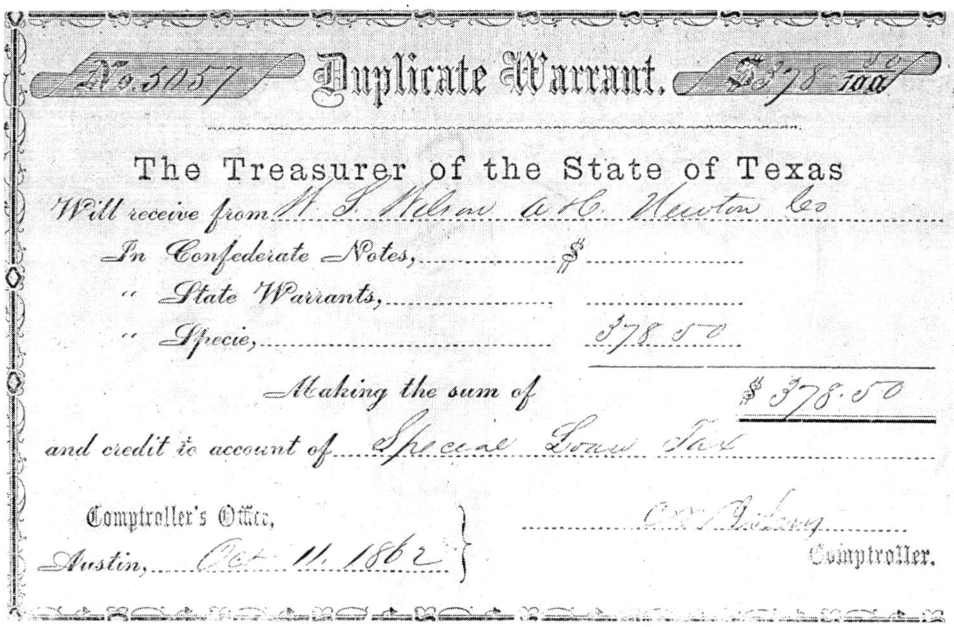

No. 5057 **Duplicate Warrant.** $378 $\frac{50}{100}$

The Treasurer of the State of Texas

Will receive from W. S. Wilson A & C. Newton Co

In Confederate Notes, $

" State Warrants,

" Specie, 378 50

Making the sum of $378.50

and credit to account of Special Loan Tax

Comptroller's Office,

Austin, Oct 11, 1862

Comptroller.

Top: **Figure 36. Legacies Tax Receipt Collector. Wayne County, Ohio, October 12, 1863.** ***Bottom:*** **Figure 37. Duplicate Warrant "Special Loan Tax," Treasurer. Austin, Texas, October 11, 1862.**

Auditor's Office, Little Rock,

May 30*th*, 1861.

SIR: Below you will find a copy of section two of "*An Ordinance to provide revenue for the State of Arkansas*," adopted May 28th, 1861,

You will observe that you are required to issue a warrant to the collector of your county, commanding him to collect the supplemental *tax* levied by the Ordinance. It is not absolutely necessary to make out a new tax-book, or new extentions or calculations, the warrant being sufficient authority for the collection of the tax.

Yours respectfully, WM. R. MILLER, *Auditor*.

SECTION 2. "A State tax for the year 1862, shall be levied on all the objects of taxation enumerated in sections one and two of Gould's Digest, and on all sums of money, over and above his liabilities, on hand at the time of the assessment, amounting to one-third of one per centum on the assessed value thereof for the said year, and supplemental tax of one-sixth of one per centum shall be levied, as a State tax, on all such objects of taxation, for the year 1861, and it shall be the *duty of each Clerk of the County Court to issue his warrant to the collector of his county, commanding him to collect a supplemental tax of one-sixth of one per centum on all objects assessed for taxation, for State purposes, for the year* 1861, and such collectors shall collect and account for the same in the manner now required by law."

ADOPTED, May 28th, 1861.

Figure 38. Notice of Supplemental Tax Auditors Office, Little Rock, May 28, 1861.

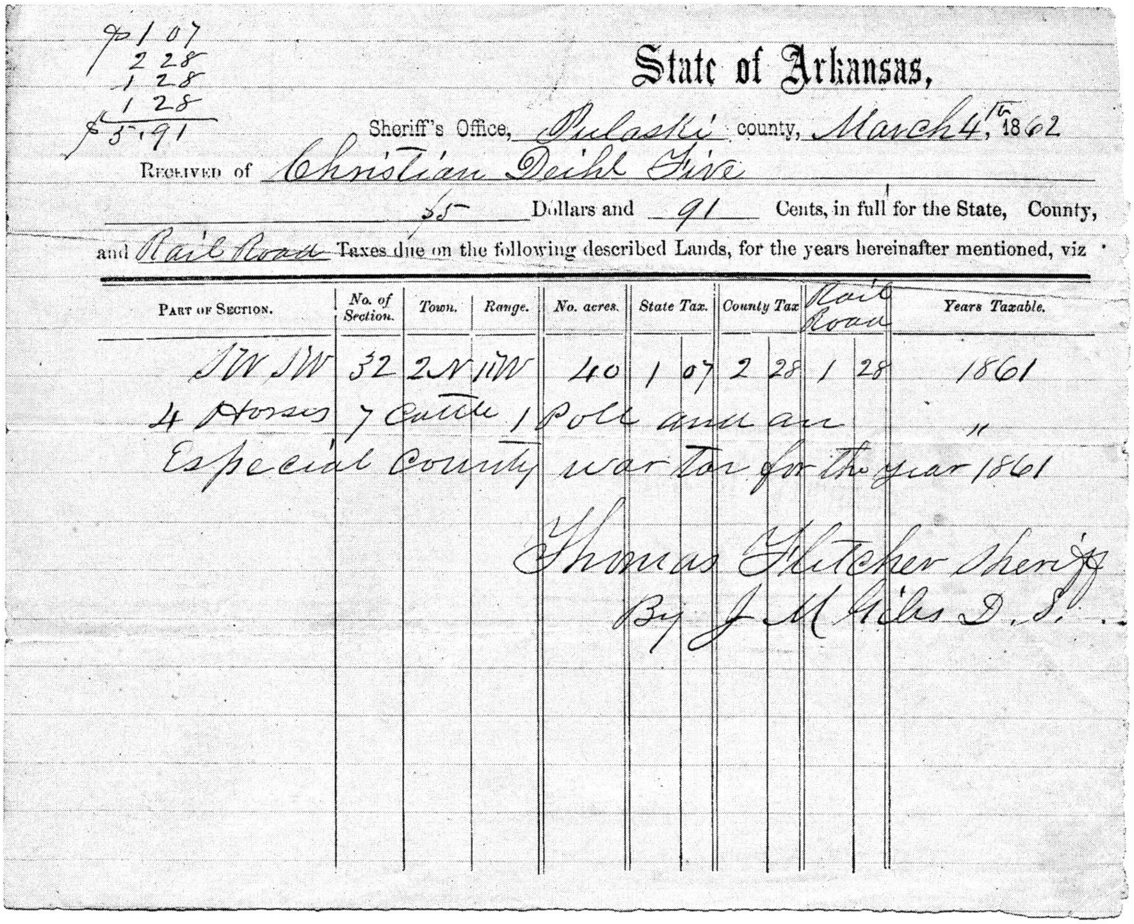

$1 07
2 28
1 28
1 28
$5.91

State of Arkansas,

Sheriff's Office, Pulaski county, March 4th 1862

Received of Christian Deihl Five

$5 Dollars and 91 Cents, in full for the State, County, and Rail Road Taxes due on the following described Lands, for the years hereinafter mentioned, viz

Part of Section.	No. of Section.	Town.	Range.	No. acres.	State Tax.	County Tax	Rail Road	Years Taxable.
SW SW	32	2 N	11 W	40	1 07	2 28	1 28	1861
4 Horses	7 Cattle	1 Poll and an						"
Especial County war tax for the year 1861								

Thomas Fletcher Sheriff
By J M Giles D. S.

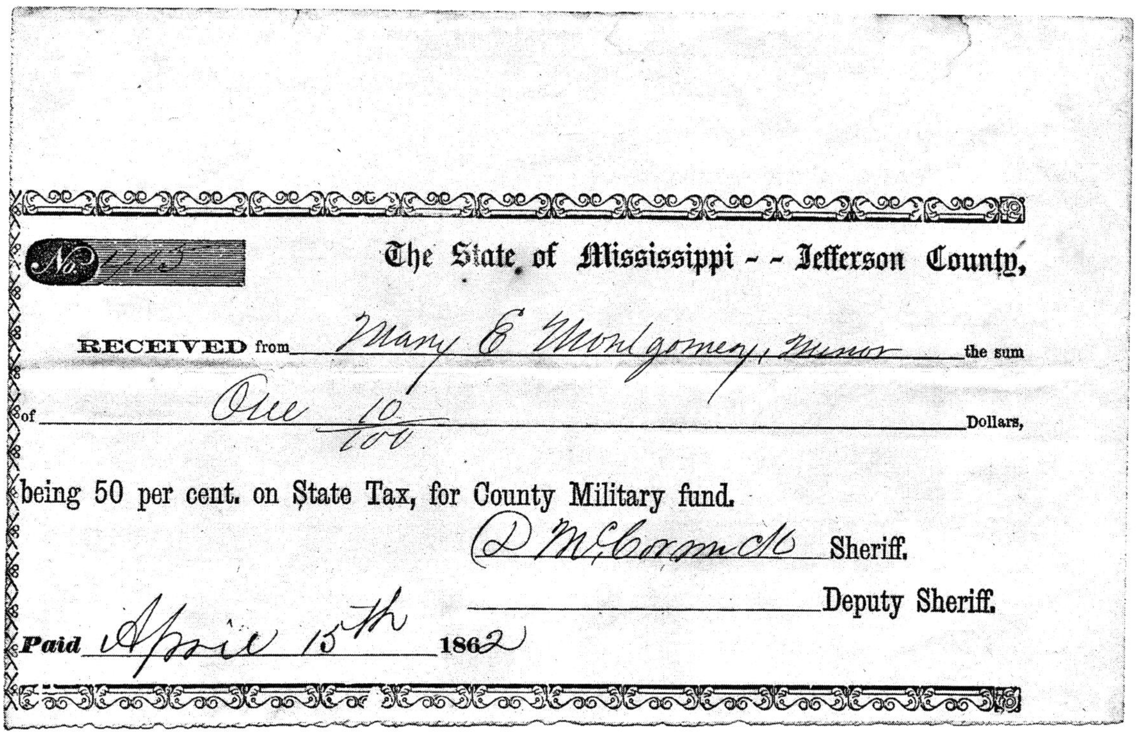

No. 403 **The State of Mississippi - - Jefferson County,**

RECEIVED from Mary E Montgomery, Minor the sum of One 10/100 Dollars,

being 50 per cent. on State Tax, for County Military fund.

D McCormick Sheriff.

Deputy Sheriff.

Paid April 15th 1862

Top: **Figure 39. "Especial" War Tax Receipt, Sheriff, Pulaski County, Arkansas. March 4, 1862.** ***Bottom:*** **Figure 40. "Military Fund" Surtax, Sheriff. Jefferson County, Mississippi, April 15, 1862.**

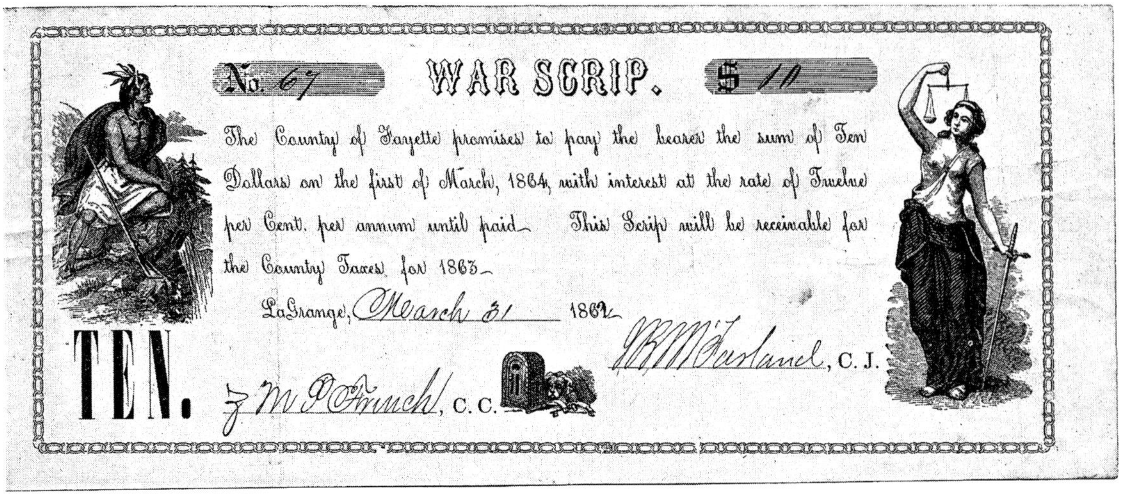

No. 67 WAR SCRIP. $ 10

The County of Fayette promises to pay the bearer the sum of Ten Dollars on the first of March, 1864, with interest at the rate of Twelve per Cent. per annum until paid. This Scrip will be receivable for the County Taxes for 1863.

LaGrange, March 31 1862

W. M. McFarland, C. J.

TEN.

F. M. P. French, C. C.

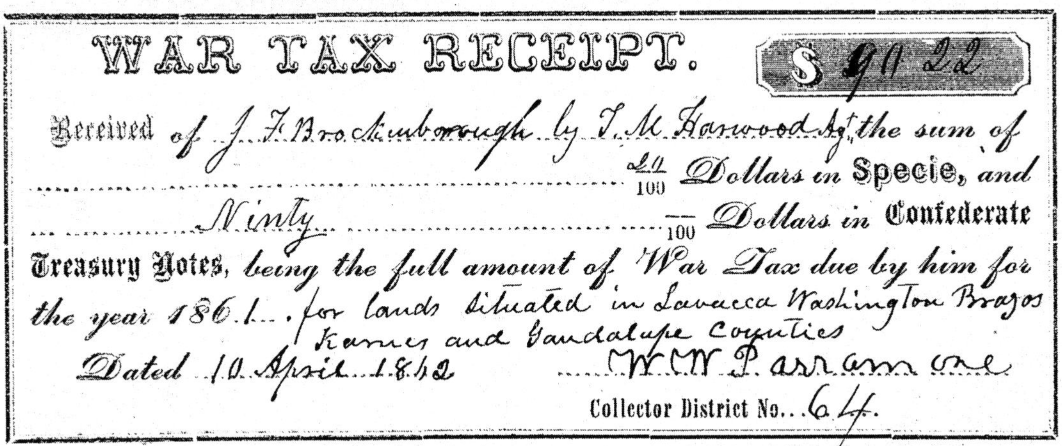

WAR TAX RECEIPT. $ 90 22

Received of J. F. Brockenbrough by T. M. Harwood Agt. the sum of 22/100 Dollars in Specie, and Ninety /100 Dollars in Confederate Treasury Notes, being the full amount of War Tax due by him for the year 1861 for lands situated in Lavacca Washington Brazos Karnes and Gaudalupe Counties

Dated 10 April 1862 W. W. Parramore

Collector District No. 64.

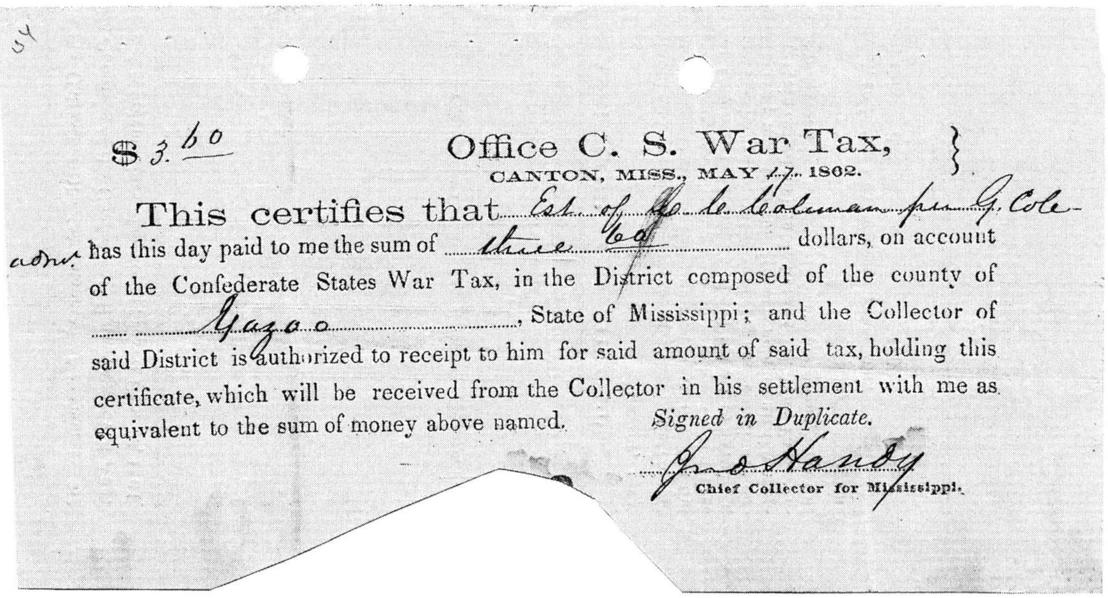

$ 3.60 Office C. S. War Tax,

CANTON, MISS., MAY 17 1862.

This certifies that Est. of G. C. Coleman per G. Cole admr. has this day paid to me the sum of three 60 dollars, on account of the Confederate States War Tax, in the District composed of the county of Yazoo, State of Mississippi; and the Collector of said District is authorized to receipt to him for said amount of said tax, holding this certificate, which will be received from the Collector in his settlement with me as equivalent to the sum of money above named. *Signed in Duplicate.*

Jno. Handy

Chief Collector for Mississippi.

Top: Figure 41. $10.00 "War Scrip" County Judge. La Grange, Fayette County, Texas, March 31, 1862. _Middle:_ Figure 42. War Tax Receipt, Collector, No. 64. Lavaca, Washington, Brazos, Karnes and Guadalupe Counties, Texas, April 10, 1862. _Bottom:_ Figure 43. War Tax. Chief Collector for Mississippi. Canton, Yazoo County, May 17, 1862.

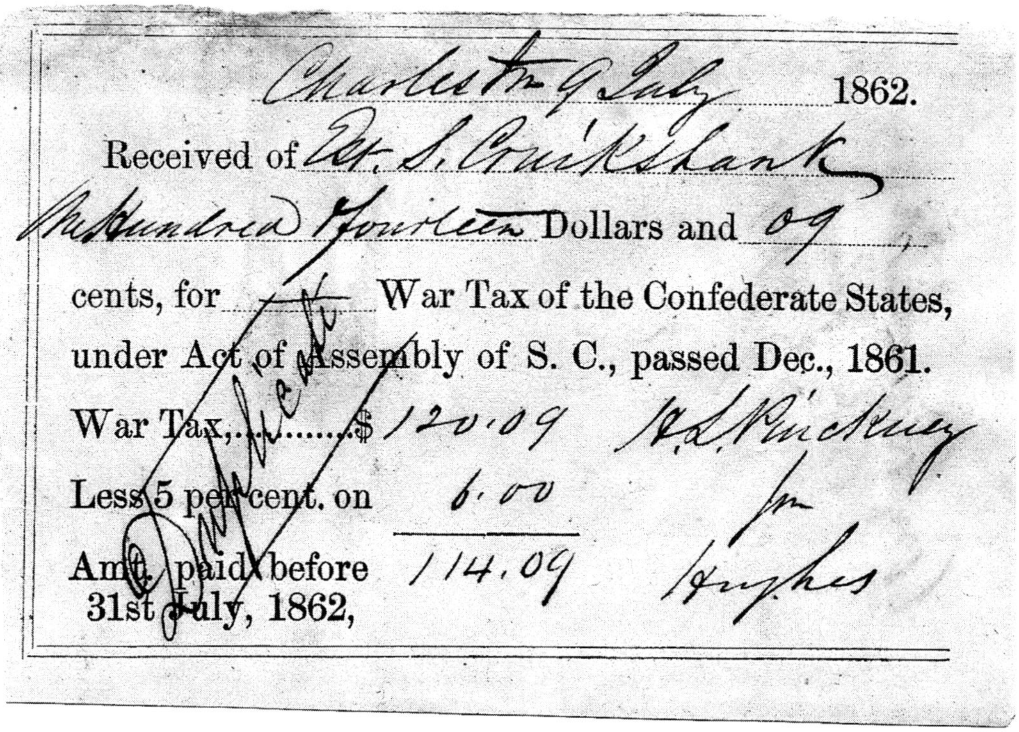
Charleston 9 July 1862.

Received of W. S. Cruikshank

One Hundred & fourteen Dollars and 09

cents, for — War Tax of the Confederate States, under Act of Assembly of S. C., passed Dec., 1861.

War Tax,........$ 120.09 H. L. Pinckney

Less 5 per cent. on 6.00 pr

Amt. paid before 31st July, 1862, 114.09 Hughes

Duplicate

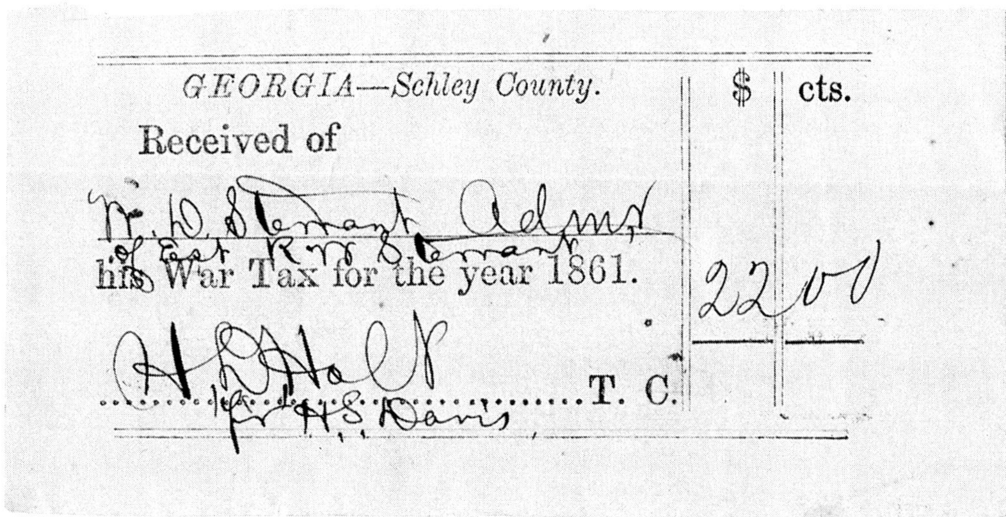
GEORGIA—Schley County. | $ | cts.

Received of

W. D. Stewart Admr of Est R. S. Stewart

his War Tax for the year 1861. 22 00

H. L. Hall T. C.

pr H. S. Davis

Top: **Figure 44. War Tax, South Carolina Act of December 1861 [State Collector]. Charleston, July 9, 1862.** ***Bottom:*** **Figure 45. War Tax [Tax Collector]. Schley County, Georgia, [1862].**

OFFICE OF STATE COLLECTOR OF VIRGINIA,

Richmond, 28th July 1863.

SIR:—You have been appointed one of the assessors for District No. 76, composed of the County of

Greenbrier

You will, if you accept the place, at once take the enclosed oath before some Justice of the Peace, and deliver it to James C. Spotts the Collector of your District. He will supply you with proper forms to begin your work; you will do so at once, having taken the oath of office. Confine your acts to the District of the Commissioner of the Revenue in which you live, or which may be assigned to you by the District Collector. Notify me of your acceptance or declination at once, and let me know your Post-office.

Very respectfully,

Thomas Green
State Collector for
Va

Figure 46. Notice of Assessor Appointment for County of Greenbrier, Virginia. State Collector, July 28, 1863.

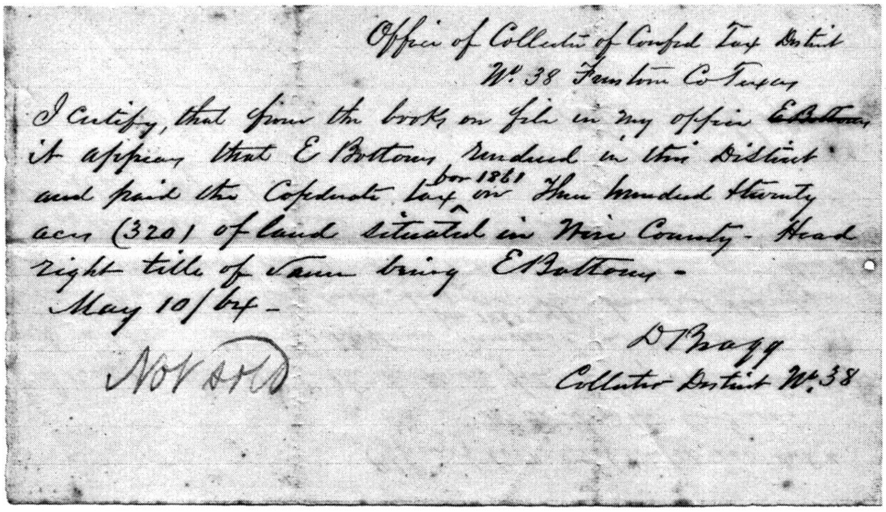

Office of Collector of Confed Tax District
No. 38 Freestone Co Texas
I Certify, that from the books on file in my office E Bottoms,
it appears that E Bottoms rendered in this District
and paid the Confederate tax for 1861 on Three hundred twenty
acres (320) of land situated in Wise County - Head
right title of same being E Bottoms -
May 10/64 -

[illegible]

D Bragg
Collector District No. 38

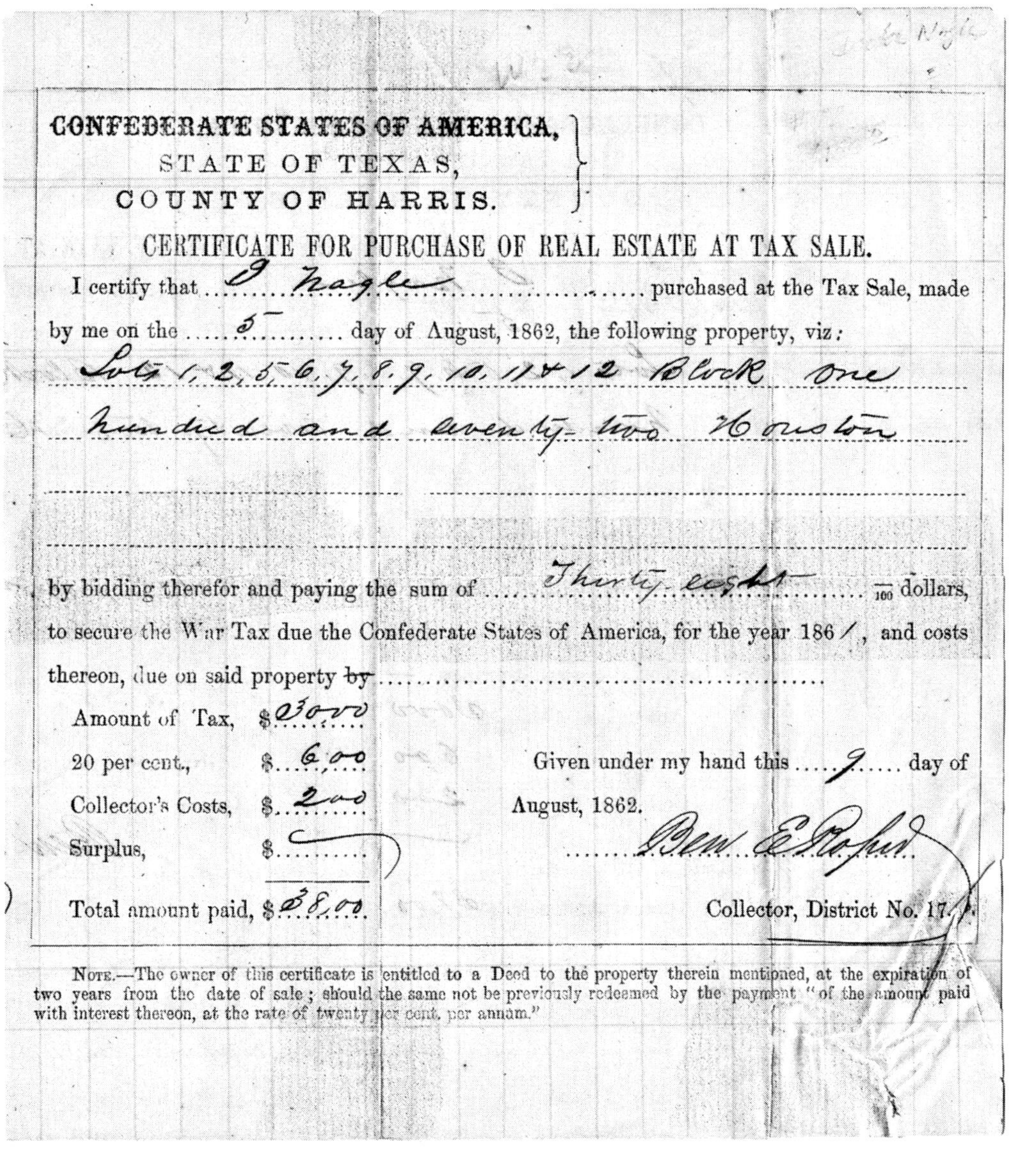

CONFEDERATE STATES OF AMERICA,
STATE OF TEXAS,
COUNTY OF HARRIS.

CERTIFICATE FOR PURCHASE OF REAL ESTATE AT TAX SALE.

I certify that J. Nagle purchased at the Tax Sale, made by me on the 5 day of August, 1862, the following property, viz: Lots 1, 2, 5, 6, 7, 8, 9, 10, 11 & 12 Block one hundred and seventy-two Houston

by bidding therefor and paying the sum of Thirty eight $\frac{}{100}$ dollars, to secure the War Tax due the Confederate States of America, for the year 1861, and costs thereon, due on said property ~~by~~ ....

Amount of Tax,	$30.00
20 per cent.,	$6.00
Collector's Costs,	$2.00
Surplus,	$—
Total amount paid,	$38.00

Given under my hand this 9 day of August, 1862.

Ben. E. Ropers

Collector, District No. 17.

NOTE.—The owner of this certificate is entitled to a Deed to the property therein mentioned, at the expiration of two years from the date of sale; should the same not be previously redeemed by the payment "of the amount paid with interest thereon, at the rate of twenty per cent. per annum."

Top: **Figure 47. Affidavit from Collector Certifying War Tax paid, Freestone County, Texas, May 10, 1864.** ***Bottom:*** **Figure 48. Certificate for War Tax foreclosed/purchased, Collector, Harris County, Texas, August 9, 1862.**

(FORM OF DEED, FOR UNRENDERED LAND SOLD FOR TAX OF 1861.)

The Confederate States of America, } COUNTY OF Bosque

STATE OF TEXAS.

Whereas, by an assessment made in conformity with An Act "to authorize the issue of Treasury Notes nd to provide a War Tax for their redemption" approved August 19th, 1861, there was due and owing to the onfederate States of America, the sum of Five & 40/100 Dollars, the same being the tax assessed for the year 1861, and twenty per cent. thereon, on the following escribed tracts of lands, situated in the County of Bosque viz:

NO. ON ABSTRACT.	NAME OF ORIGINAL GRANTEE.	NO. OF ACRES PURCHASED.	DESCRIPTION.
458	W. S. Rather	320	

r a more particular identification of which, reference is made to the Certificate, Field Notes and Title on ecord, in the General Land Office, which are hereby made part of this conveyance, and the same being offered r sale at public outcry, to the highest bidder B. F. Weeks became the urchaser thereof, by bidding the sum of Five & 40/100 ollars, which was duly paid over to the Collector of the War Tax for said County, as is evidenced by e Certificate of Purchase now surrendered; **AND WHEREAS,** the owner or owners, (the same not being in e Military service of the Confederate States) or any person in his, or their behalf, not having redeemed the me, by the payment of the above sum, and twenty per cent. interest per annum thereon, and two years aving expired since the date of purchase and sale, I hereby convey unto B. F. Weeks the purchaser thereof, and his heirs and assigns **FOREVER,** all the right and title of the rmer owner or owners thereto.

Witness, my hand as District Collector of the Confederate Tax, for the County of Bosque this 28th day of Dec 1864.

John Armstrong

Figure 49. Deed for Unrendered Land Sold for 1861 War Tax. Collector, Bosque County, Texas, December 28, 1864.

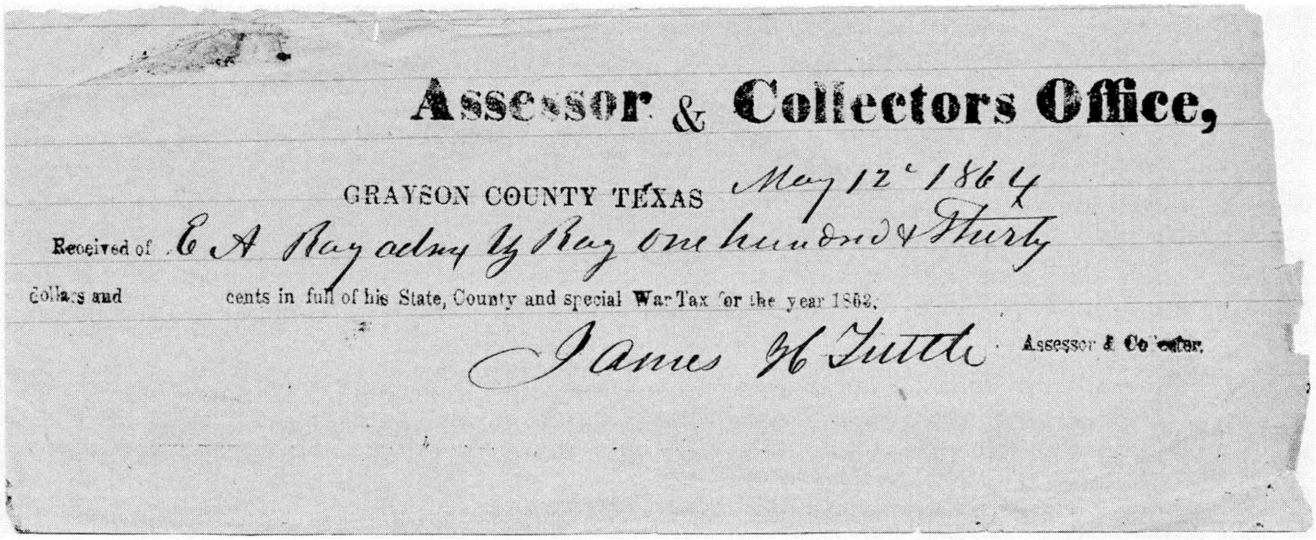

Assessor & Collectors Office,

GRAYSON COUNTY TEXAS May 12th 1864

Received of E A Ray adm[r] of Ray one hundred & thirty

dollars and cents in full of his State, County and special War Tax for the year 1863.

James H Tuttle Assessor & Collector.

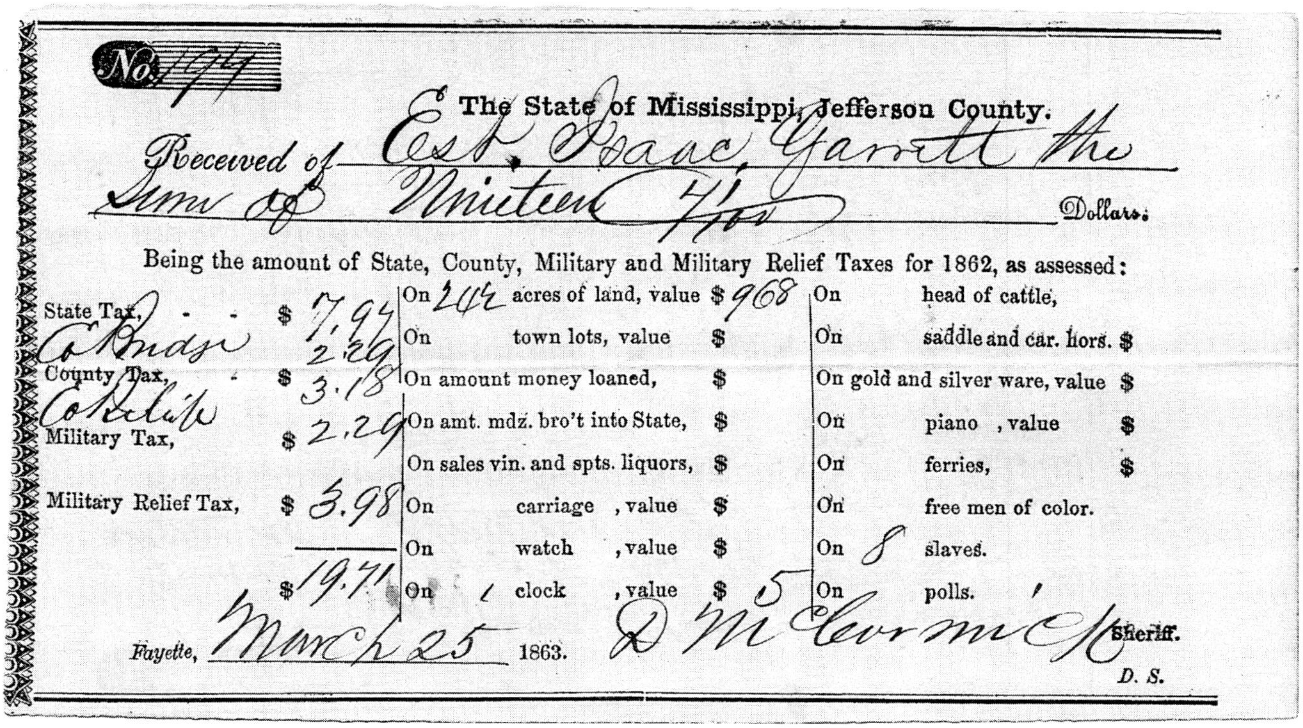

No. 174

The State of Mississippi, Jefferson County.

Received of Est. Isaac Garrett the Sum of Nineteen 71/100 Dollars.

Being the amount of State, County, Military and Military Relief Taxes for 1862, as assessed:

State Tax, . . . $ 7.94	On 242 acres of land, value $ 968	On head of cattle,	
C Bridge 2.29	On town lots, value $	On saddle and car. hors. $	
County Tax, $ 3.18	On amount money loaned, $	On gold and silver ware, value $	
Co Relief 2.29	On amt. mdz. bro't into State, $	On piano, value $	
Military Tax, $	On sales vin. and spts. liquors, $	On ferries, $	
Military Relief Tax, $ 3.98	On carriage, value $	On free men of color.	
	On watch, value $	On 8 slaves.	
$ 19.71	On 1 clock, value $ 5	On polls.	

Fayette, March 25 1863. D McCormick Sheriff. D. S.

Top: Figure 50. Receipt for Special War Tax, Collector, Grayson County, Texas, May 12, 1864. *Bottom:* Figure 51. Receipt for State, County, Military and Relief Taxes. Sheriff, Jefferson County, Mississippi, March 25, 1863.

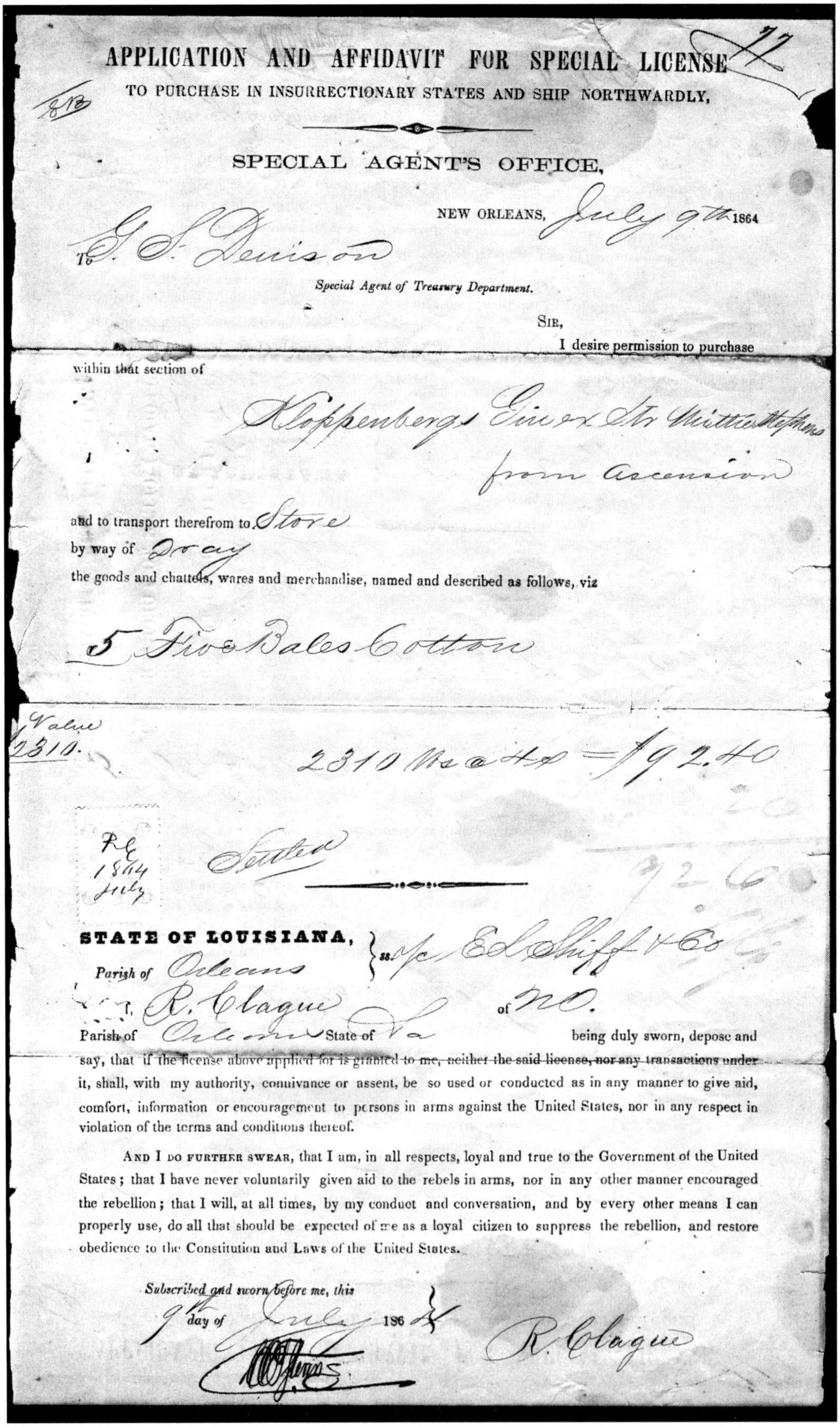

APPLICATION AND AFFIDAVIT FOR SPECIAL LICENSE 77

TO PURCHASE IN INSURRECTIONARY STATES AND SHIP NORTHWARDLY,

818

SPECIAL AGENT'S OFFICE,

NEW ORLEANS, July 9th 1864

To G. S. Denison

Special Agent of Treasury Department.

SIR,

I desire permission to purchase within that section of

Kloppenbergs Gin & Str Mittie Stephens

from Ascension

and to transport therefrom to Store

by way of Dray

the goods and chattels, wares and merchandise, named and described as follows, viz

5 Five Bales Cotton

Value

2310.

2310 lbs @ 4c = $92.40

Settled

STATE OF LOUISIANA, } ss. a/c E. L. Shiff & Co

Parish of Orleans

I, R. Clague of N.O.

Parish of Orleans State of La being duly sworn, depose and say, that if the license above applied for is granted to me, neither the said license, nor any transactions under it, shall, with my authority, connivance or assent, be so used or conducted as in any manner to give aid, comfort, information or encouragement to persons in arms against the United States, nor in any respect in violation of the terms and conditions thereof.

AND I DO FURTHER SWEAR, that I am, in all respects, loyal and true to the Government of the United States; that I have never voluntarily given aid to the rebels in arms, nor in any other manner encouraged the rebellion; that I will, at all times, by my conduct and conversation, and by every other means I can properly use, do all that should be expected of me as a loyal citizen to suppress the rebellion, and restore obedience to the Constitution and Laws of the United States.

Subscribed and sworn before me, this 9th day of July 1864

R. Clague

Figure 52. "Application and Affidavit for License to Purchase in Rebel States." Special Agent Treasury. New Orleans, July 9, 1864.

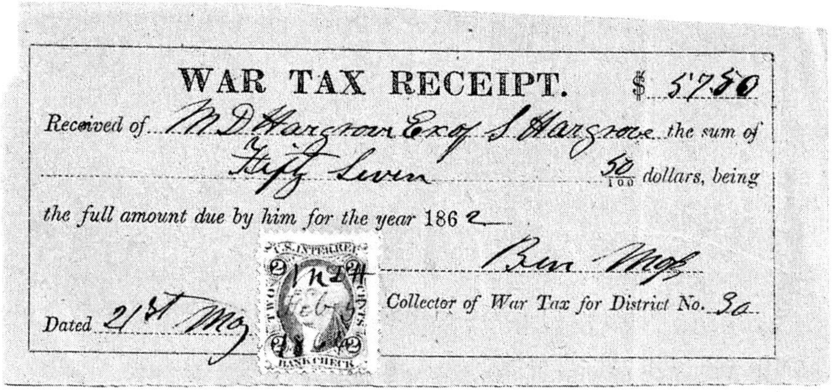

WAR TAX RECEIPT. $ 57.50

Received of M D Hargrove Exr of S Hargrove *the sum of* Fifty Seven 50/100 *dollars, being the full amount due by him for the year* 1862.

Dated 21st May — *Collector of War Tax for District No.* 30

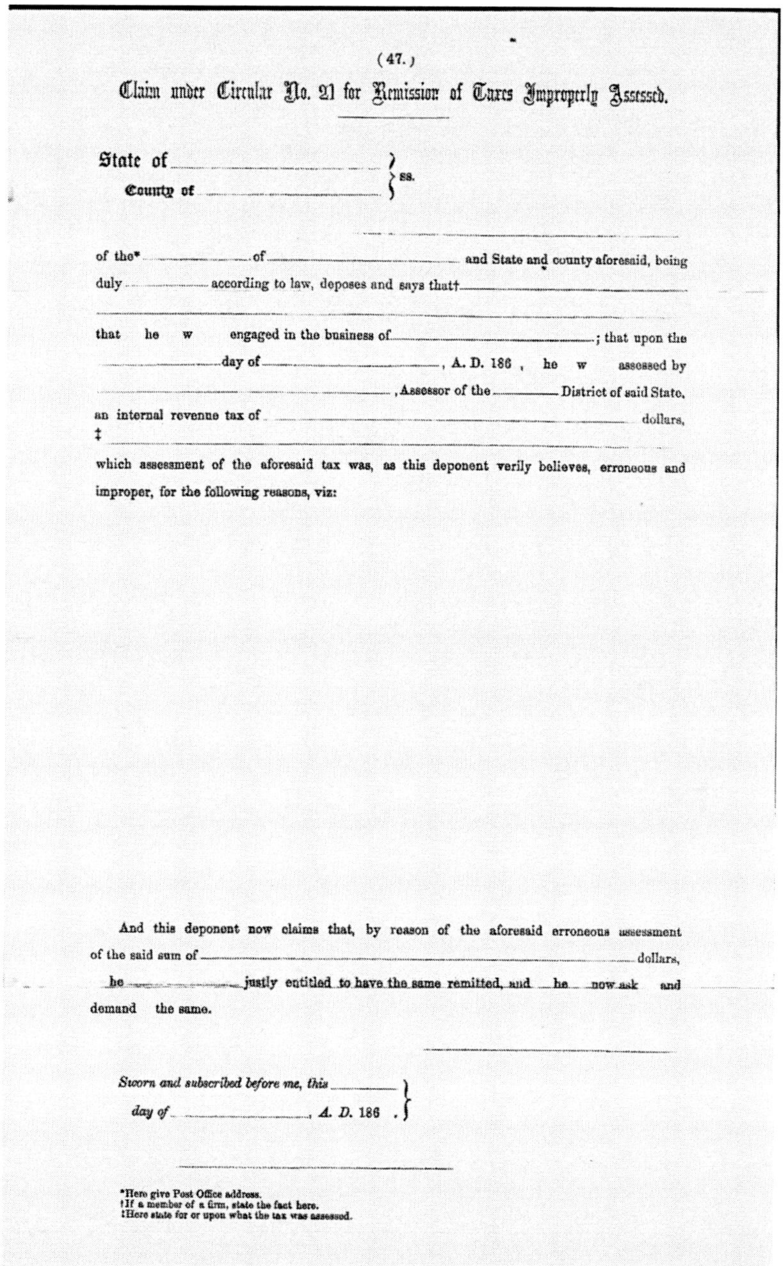

(47.)

Claim under Circular No. 21 for Remission of Taxes Improperly Assessed.

State of ______ } ss.
County of ______

of the* ______ of ______ and State and county aforesaid, being duly ______ according to law, deposes and says that† ______

that he w engaged in the business of ______; that upon the ______ day of ______, A. D. 186 , he w assessed by ______, Assessor of the ______ District of said State, an internal revenue tax of ______ dollars, ‡ ______

which assessment of the aforesaid tax was, as this deponent verily believes, erroneous and improper, for the following reasons, viz:

And this deponent now claims that, by reason of the aforesaid erroneous assessment of the said sum of ______ dollars, he ______ justly entitled to have the same remitted, and he now ask and demand the same.

Sworn and subscribed before me, this ______ *day of* ______, *A. D.* 186 .

*Here give Post Office address.
†If a member of a firm, state the fact here.
‡Here state for or upon what the tax was assessed.

Top: **Figure 53. Confederate States War Tax Receipt. May 21, 1863. U.S. Stamp attached, June 24, 1864 [Florida].** ***Bottom:*** **Figure 54. Claim for Remission of Taxes Improperly Assessed. [Blank] (Form 47).**

Head-Quarters District of Vicksburg,
On board Str "Ida Handy"
Natchez, Miss. Oct 5th 1864

Lt Col C. T. Christensen
Asst Adj. Genl.
Mil. Div. of West Miss.,

Colonel:

I send you, under arrest, in charge of a guard, Mr. George Moore, and Mr Elisha Tracy, of New Orleans, agents, associates and partners of Messrs G. W. Graham and Company, of New Orleans. The officer of the guard has also two packages of papers taken from their persons and valises, which explain the manner of their unwarranted and traitorous traffic with the enemy, for cotton, in defiance of laws, regulations and reiterated orders.

It is not with any desire of avoiding or dodging responsibility or labor that they are sent to you; but "the head and front of their offending" is in New Orleans—officers appear to be their intimates, and the proper place for their appearance and arraignment ~~appears~~ seemed to be New Orleans—at the Head Quarters of the Division.

I have reviewed all the papers, and have made my own pencil remarks merely to facilitate the investigation which may be thought best in the judgment of the Major General Comdg. I do not wish to disguise the opinion I entertain that all the parties named in these papers, are among the traitors and

Figure 55 (this page and 2 pages following). Letter, Commander of USS Steamer *Ida Handy*, District of Vicksburg, Natchez, October 5, 1864.

2.

Enemies of the country. These two men, Moore and Tracy, who appear to be intimately associated with officers both of the Army and Navy, and who are instruments of Graham and Company of New Orleans, and partners in their guilt, came on board of this boat, which I had taken as part of the transportation which landed my expedition at Tunica, this morning, under the impression that we were bound to New Orleans. They are disappointed. I have arrested them, and Moore has stated that he landed at a point two miles below Ft Adams and was taken prisoner in bed (?) and carried to Liberty, to the Head Quarters of General Hodges, commanding the rebel District of Southwest Mississippi and Eastern Louisiana, who generously released him. He then returned to the gunboat Chillicothe at Fort Adams, and thence came aboard of me. His associate, Tracy, came to Fort Adams, to meet him.

There is a small boat, of the class called "Cotton-thief," there, named "Golden Gate", which belongs to Graham, also, on which they were. There is cotton on the bank. I have ordered my troops, on their arrival there, to seize both. If they do not, it will be because the gunboat "Chillicothe" which I notified, has let the "Golden Gate" know the intentions.

The papers of these men, which I send herewith, will show you that the game of the tricksters, is to get papers from some insignificant authority at a Provost Marshal's Office in New Orleans, for Vicksburg and Natchez,

Figure 55c

3

their land on a gunboat, or be sent ashore, beyond the lines, with lots of money to buy cotton. This game these two worthies have long practiced in fraud and cunning. Their positions in society are presumed to be respectable. I have had them in close confinement. They are only a sample of a multitude ~~of~~ which have long infested this valley, to the great injury of the nation and of the cause for which our troops are shedding their blood.

Their papers are worthy of close and careful attention by an officer who would not permit a sycophantic or designing speculator to ~~approach~~ comes towards him with a smile or a favor. It is natural I should feel warmly in the matter, when I consider that I have this day sent my brave men to arrest the very traitor whose hospitality one of them has shared, and whose forces have perchance been concentrated, by means of information from just such traitors as these, to meet them in superior force.

I have the honor to be, Colonel,
Very respectfully, etc

J. May Gene.

Top: **Figure 56. $1.00 National Bank Note Act of July 11, 1862. Washington, August 1, 1862.** *Middle:* **Figure 57. $50.00 Legal Tender Note Under Act of March 3, 1863. Washington, March 10, 1863.** *Bottom:* **Figure 58. 25¢ Fractional Currency Act of March 3, 1863. "Receivable for all Stamps." Washington Assistant Treasurers and Designated Depositories.**

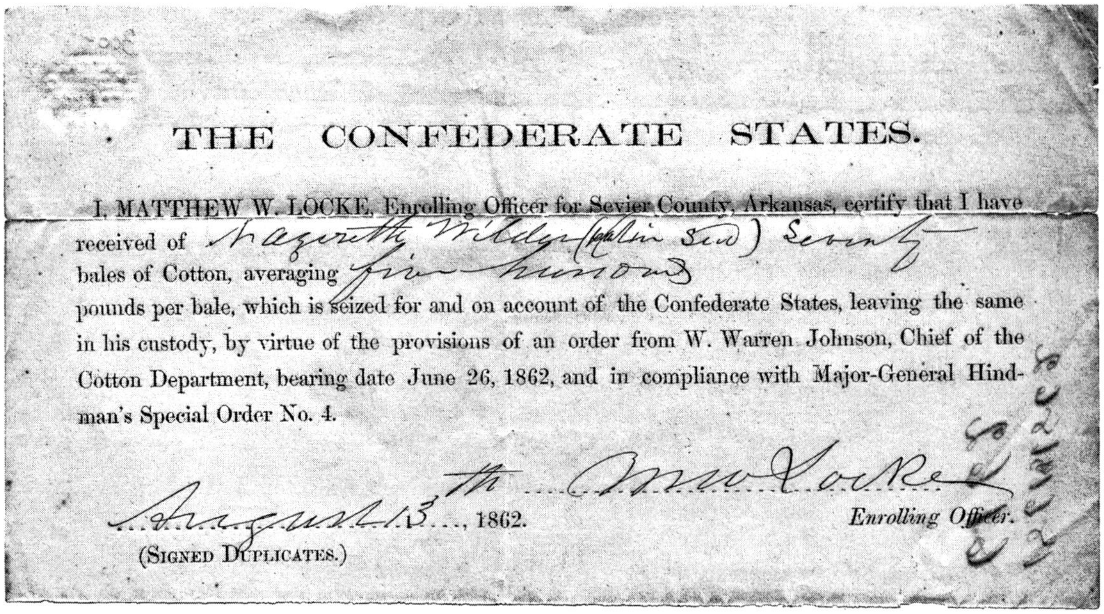

THE CONFEDERATE STATES.

I, MATTHEW W. LOCKE, Enrolling Officer for Sevier County, Arkansas, certify that I have received of Nazareth Mildyn (cotton seed) Seventy bales of Cotton, averaging five hundred pounds per bale, which is seized for and on account of the Confederate States, leaving the same in his custody, by virtue of the provisions of an order from W. Warren Johnson, Chief of the Cotton Department, bearing date June 26, 1862, and in compliance with Major-General Hindman's Special Order No. 4.

August 13th, 1862. M W Locke, Enrolling Officer.

(SIGNED DUPLICATES.)

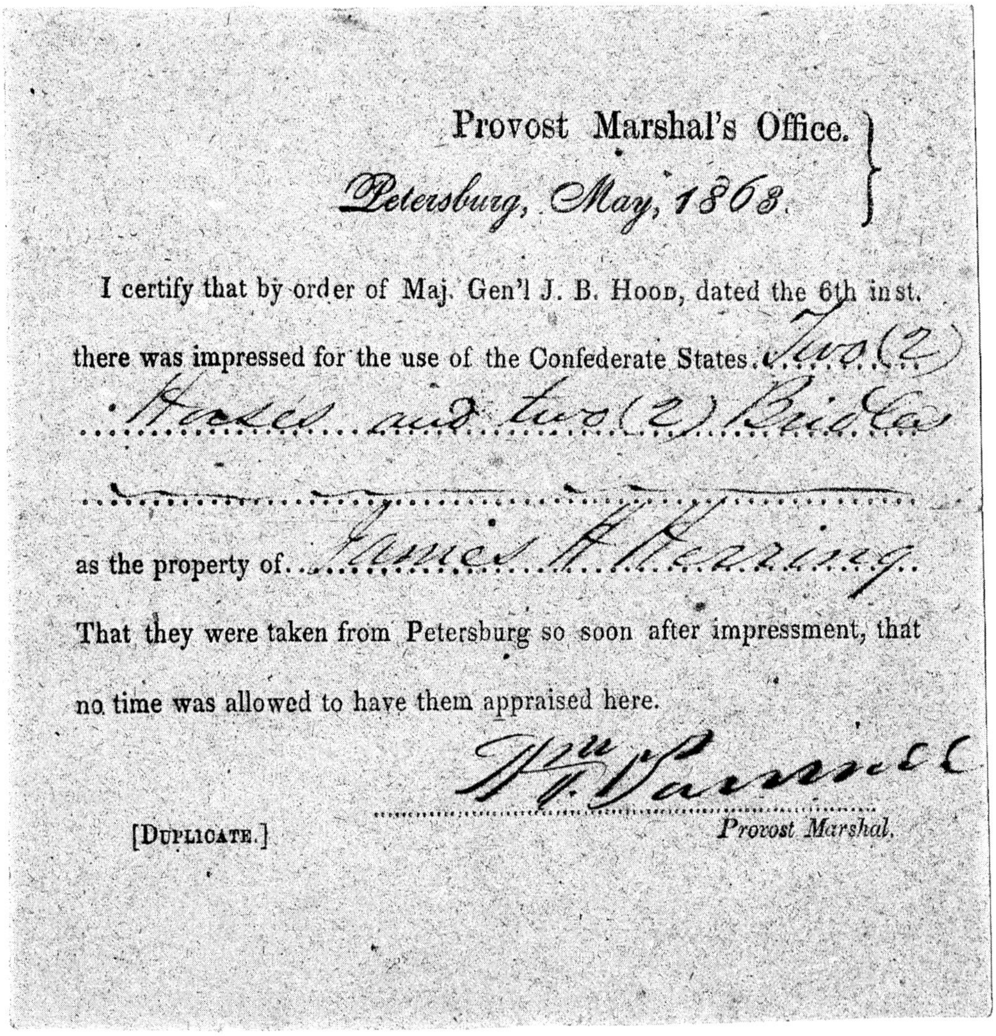

Provost Marshal's Office.
Petersburg, May, 1863.

I certify that by order of Maj. Gen'l J. B. HOOD, dated the 6th inst. there was impressed for the use of the Confederate States Two (2) Horses and two (2) Bridles

as the property of James H. Herring.

That they were taken from Petersburg so soon after impressment, that no time was allowed to have them appraised here.

Wm. Parnell, Provost Marshal.

[DUPLICATE.]

Top: **Figure 59. Receipt for Cotton Seized by Enrolling Officer, Sevier County, Arkansas, August 13, 1862.** ***Bottom:*** **Figure 60. Receipt for Impressment of Horses and Bridles. Provost Marshal, Petersburg, Virginia, May 6, 1863.**

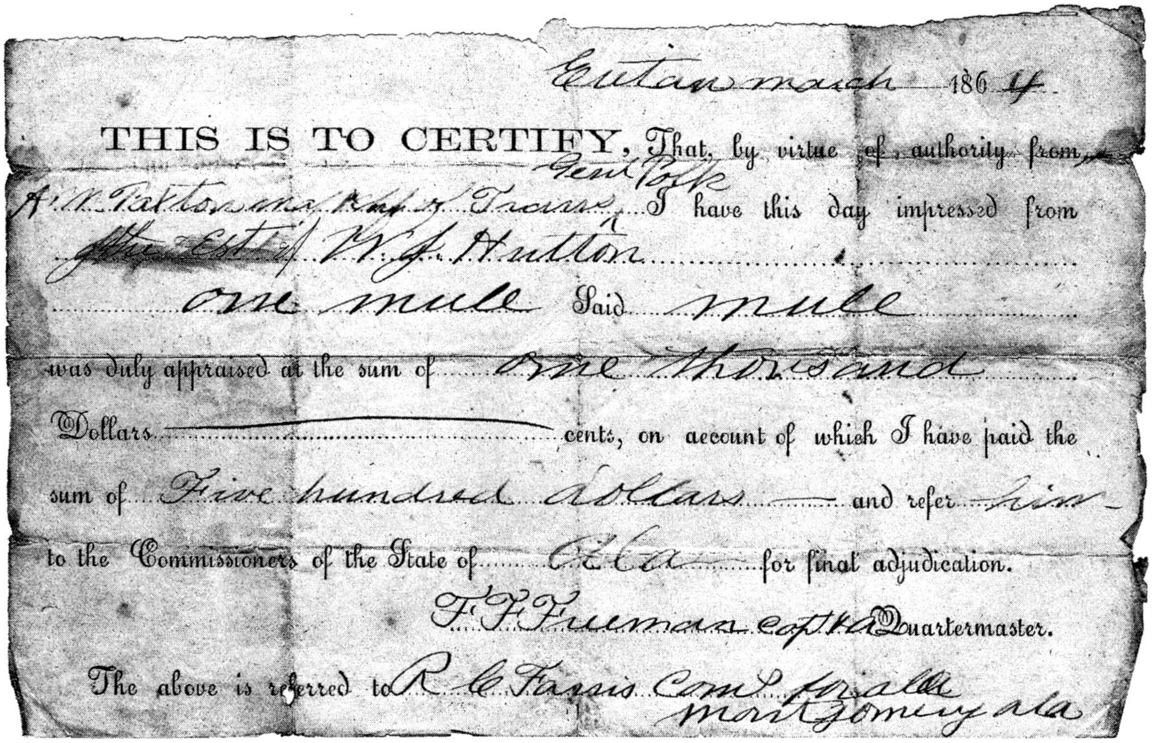

Eutaw March 1864

THIS IS TO CERTIFY, That, by virtue of authority from Genl Polk

A. M. Patterson Chf of Trans I have this day impressed from

the Est of W. J. Hutton

one mule Said mule

was duly appraised at the sum of One thousand

Dollars ——— cents, on account of which I have paid the

sum of Five hundred dollars —— and refer him

to the Commissioners of the State of Ala for final adjudication.

F. F. Freeman Capt & A Quartermaster.

The above is referred to R C Farris Comr for Ala Montgomery Ala

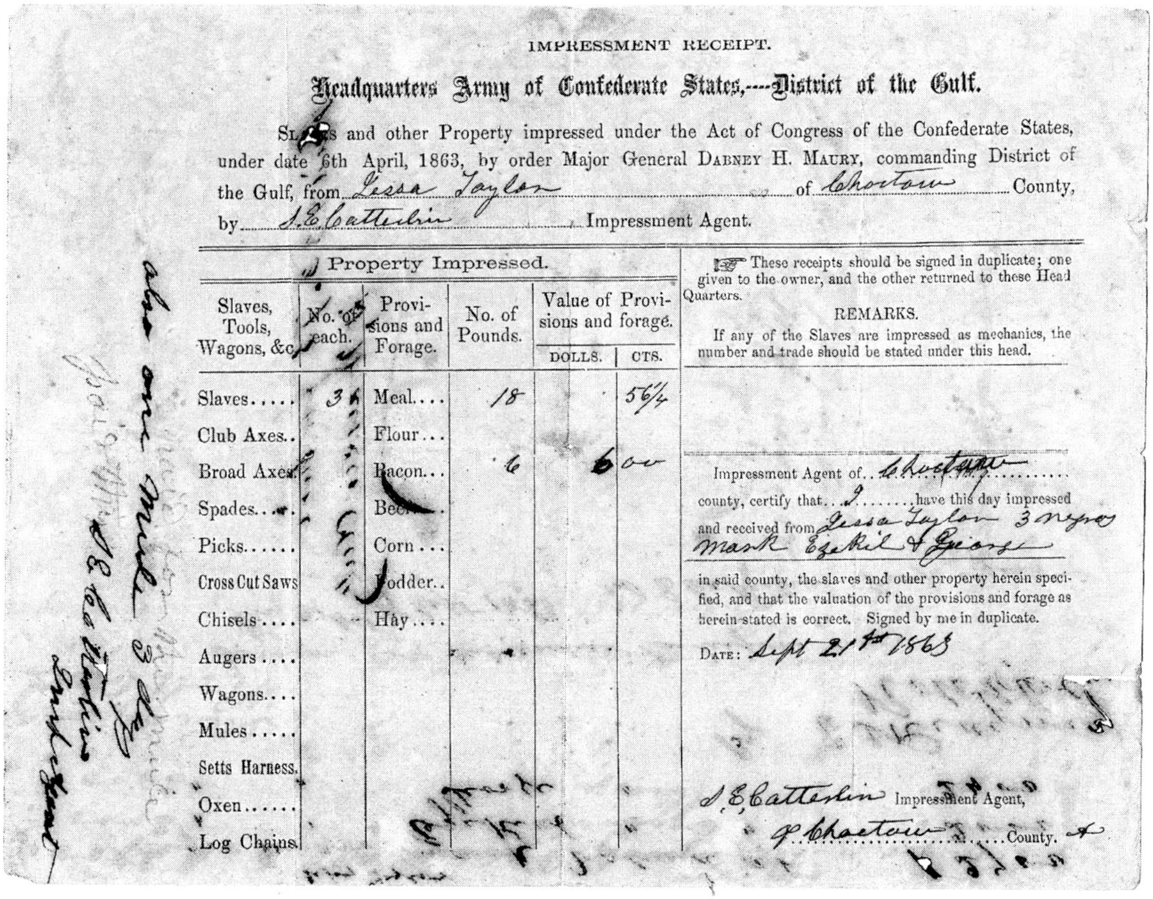

IMPRESSMENT RECEIPT.

Headquarters Army of Confederate States,—District of the Gulf.

Slaves and other Property impressed under the Act of Congress of the Confederate States, under date 6th April, 1863, by order Major General Dabney H. Maury, commanding District of the Gulf, from Jessa Taylor of Choctaw County, by S. E. Catterlin Impressment Agent.

Property Impressed.					
Slaves, Tools, Wagons, &c.	No. of each.	Provisions and Forage.	No. of Pounds.	Value of Provisions and forage. DOLLS.	CTS.
Slaves	3	Meal	18		56¼
Club Axes		Flour			
Broad Axes		Bacon	6	6	00
Spades		Beef			
Picks		Corn			
Cross Cut Saws		Fodder			
Chisels		Hay			
Augers					
Wagons					
Mules					
Setts Harness					
Oxen					
Log Chains					

☞ These receipts should be signed in duplicate; one given to the owner, and the other returned to these Head Quarters.

REMARKS.

If any of the Slaves are impressed as mechanics, the number and trade should be stated under this head.

Impressment Agent of Choctaw county, certify that I have this day impressed and received from Jessa Taylor 3 negros Mark Ezekiel & George in said county, the slaves and other property herein specified, and that the valuation of the provisions and forage as herein stated is correct. Signed by me in duplicate.

Date: Sept 21st 1863

S. E. Catterlin Impressment Agent, of Choctaw County.

also one mule 3 day ... Impressment

Top: **Figure 61. Receipt for Impressment of Mule. Quartermaster, Eutaw, Alabama, March 1, 1864.** ***Bottom:*** **Figure 62. Receipt for Impressment of Slaves. Act of April 6, 1863. Agent, Choctaw County, Alabama, September 21, 1863.**

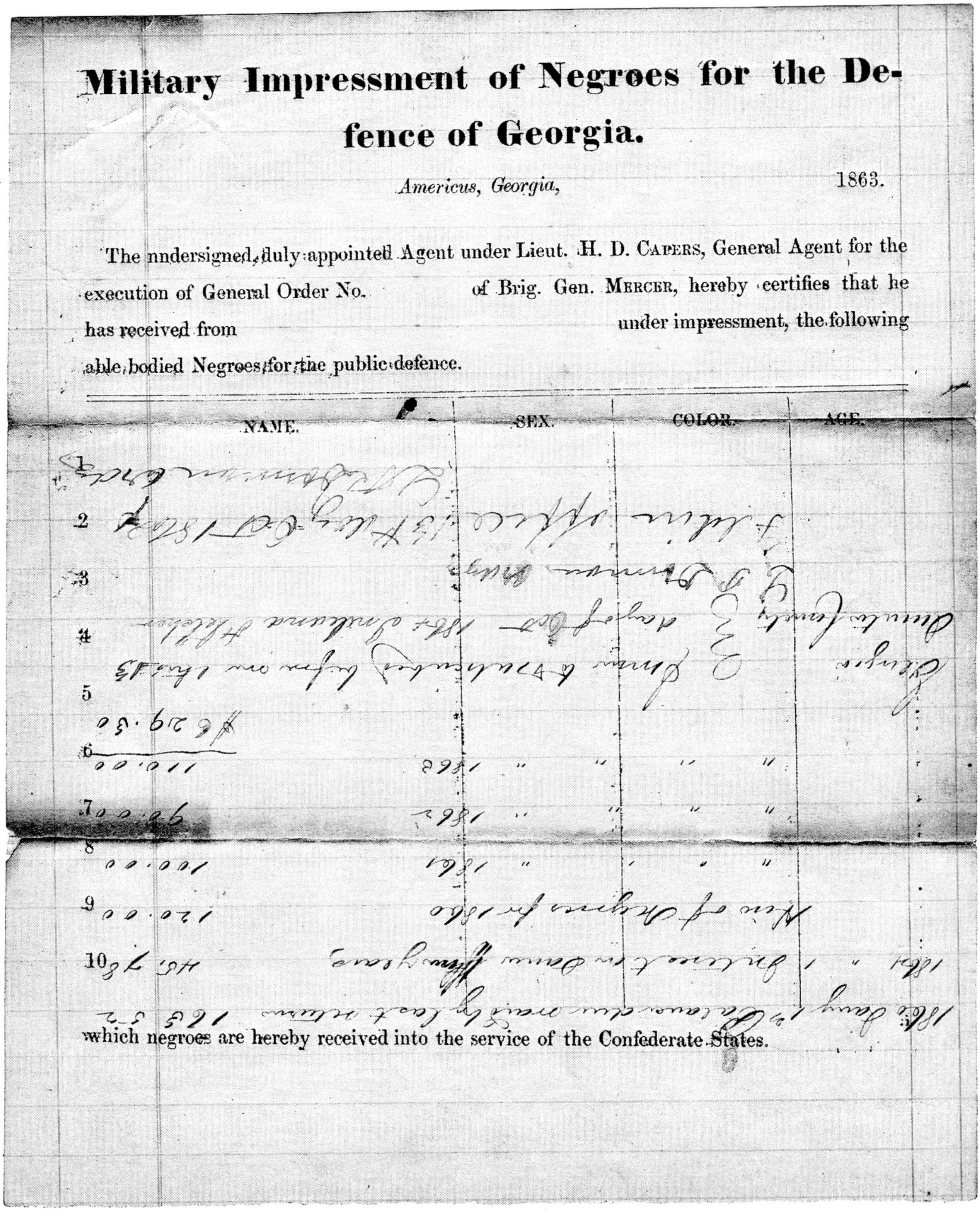

Military Impressment of Negroes for the Defence of Georgia.

Americus, Georgia, 1863.

The undersigned, duly appointed Agent under Lieut. H. D. Capers, General Agent for the execution of General Order No. of Brig. Gen. Mercer, hereby certifies that he has received from under impressment, the following able bodied Negroes for the public defence.

	NAME.	SEX.	COLOR.	AGE.
1				
2				
3				
4				
5				
6				
7				
8				
9				
10				

which negroes are hereby received into the service of the Confederate States.

Figure 63. "Military Impressment of Negroes for the Defence of Georgia." Agent, Americus, Georgia [1863].

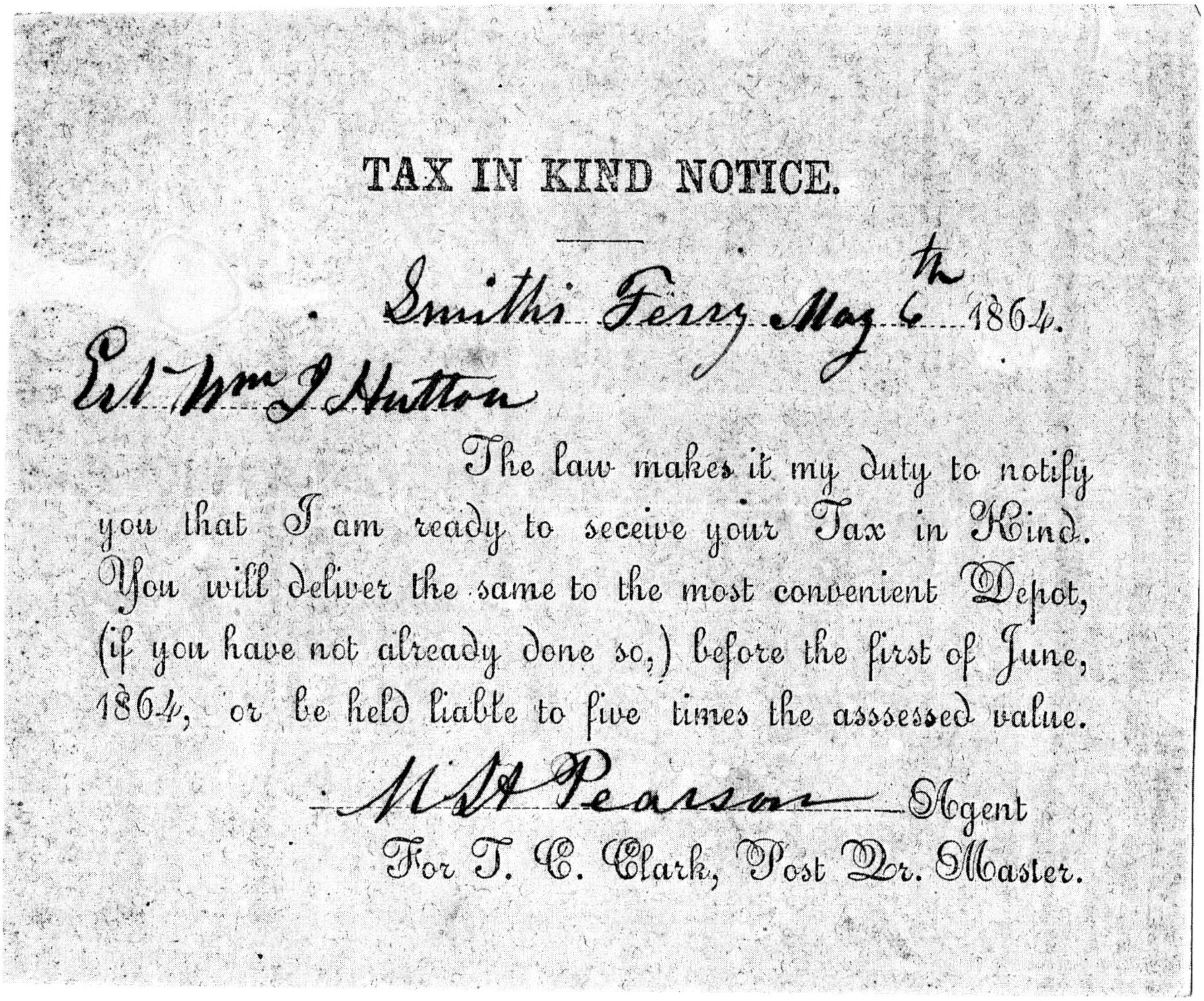

TAX IN KIND NOTICE.

Smiths Ferry May 6th 1864.

Est Wm J Hutton

The law makes it my duty to notify you that I am ready to seceive your Tax in Kind. You will deliver the same to the most convenient Depot, (if you have not already done so,) before the first of June, 1864, or be held liable to five times the asssessed value.

M A Pearson Agent

For T. C. Clark, Post Qr. Master.

Figure 64. "Tax In Kind Notice," Agent for Post Quartermaster. Smith's Ferry [Texas]. May 6, 1864.

No. 4.

Form of the Estimate and Assessment of Agricultural products agreed upon by the Assessor and the Tax-payer, and the value of the portion thereof to which the government is entitled, which are taxed in kind, in accordance with the provisions of section 11, of "an act to lay taxes for the common defence and carry on the government of the Confederate States," said estimate and assessment to be made as soon as the crops are made ready for market.

	Quantity of Gross Crop.	Quality.	Tithe or One tenth.	Value of one tenth.
WHEAT				
CORN	25 Bu	Good	2½	$10.00
OATS				
RYE				
BUCKWHEAT				
RICE				
SWEET POTATOES				
IRISH POTATOES				
CURED HAY	200 lbs	Ordinary	20 lbs	60
CURED FODDER	2000 lbs	Good	200 lbs	6.00
SUGAR				
MOLASSES MADE OF CANE				
COTTON				
WOOL				
TOBACCO				
PEAS				
BEANS				
GROUND PEAS				

I, *Allen Davis* of the *Dist* of *Richland* and State of *So Ca* do swear that the above is a true statement and estimate of all the agricultural products produced by me during the year 186*3*, which are taxable by the provisions of the 11th section of the above stated act, including what may have been sold or consumed by me, and of the value of that portion of said crops to which the Government is entitled.

Sworn to and subscribed before me the *27"* day of *Nov* 186*3*, and I further certify that the above estimate and assessment has been agreed upon by said *Allen Davis* and myself as a correct and true statement of the amount of his crops and the value of the portion to which the Government is entitled.

Allen Davis

Saml Beard Assessor.

Note.—Each farmer and planter has the privilege of reserving fifty bushels of sweet potatoes, fifty bushels of Irish potatoes, one hundred bushels of corn, or fifty bushels of wheat produced in year 1863, and twenty bushels of peas or beans, but not more than twenty bushels of both for his own use. In making the estimate and assessment, therefore, these quantities of the articles mentioned will be excluded therefrom.

Figure 65. Estimate and Assessment for Tax In Kind. Assessor, Richland County, South Carolina, November 27, 1863.

LIST No. 1.

Tax on Naval Stores, Wines, &c., and Agricultural Products,

The production of any year preceding 1863, to be returned on 1st day of July 1863, or as soon thereafter as practicable, and payable 1st day of October; including also, moneys, bank notes or other currency, on hand or on deposit on 1st day of July 1863, and the amount and value of all credits on which the interest has not been paid, held or owned by any person, copartnership or corporation, on said 1st day of July 1863, either at home or abroad.

NAVAL STORES, AGRICULTURAL PRODUCTS, ETC.							VALUE.	RATE.	TAX.
Manufactured Tobacco —							5400	8	432.0
galls Spts Turpentine —							200		16
									448

MONEYS AND CREDITS.	Amount.	Value of credits and coin.	Aggregate.	Rate.	Tax.
Gold coin [illegible] hand or on deposit, - - - - -	4300 @8/	34400			
Silver coin on hand or on deposit, - - - - -	1400 @70	980			
Bank notes or other currency on hand, - - - -	500	1500			
Bank notes or other currency on deposit, —— -	7880	7880	44260	1/10	442.60
Credits within Confederate States, - - - -					
Credits beyond limits of Confederate States, - -					
Money deposited beyond limits of Confederate States,					

442.
890

I, John Purcell of the City of Richmond and State of Virginia, do swear, that the above list contains a true statement of all the naval stores, salt, wine, spirituous liquors, manufactured and unmanufactured tobacco, cotton, wool, flour, sugar, molasses, syrup, rice and other agricultural products, not necessary for family consumption for the unexpired portion of the year 1863; and of all moneys, bank notes or other currency, on hand or on deposit, at home or beyond the limits of the Confederate States, including all gold and silver coin, and the amount and true value of all credits on which the interest has not been paid, and not employed in a business the income of which is taxed under the provisions of the following act, held or owned by me, either in my own right or in the right of any other person, corporation or firm, in accordance with the provisions of the act "to lay taxes for the common defence and carry on the government of the Confederate States."

Sworn to and subscribed before me, this 15 day of Sept 1863.

Assessor.

Figure 66. "Tax on Naval Stores and Agricultural Products." List No. 1, Assessor. Richmond, Virginia, September 15, 1863.

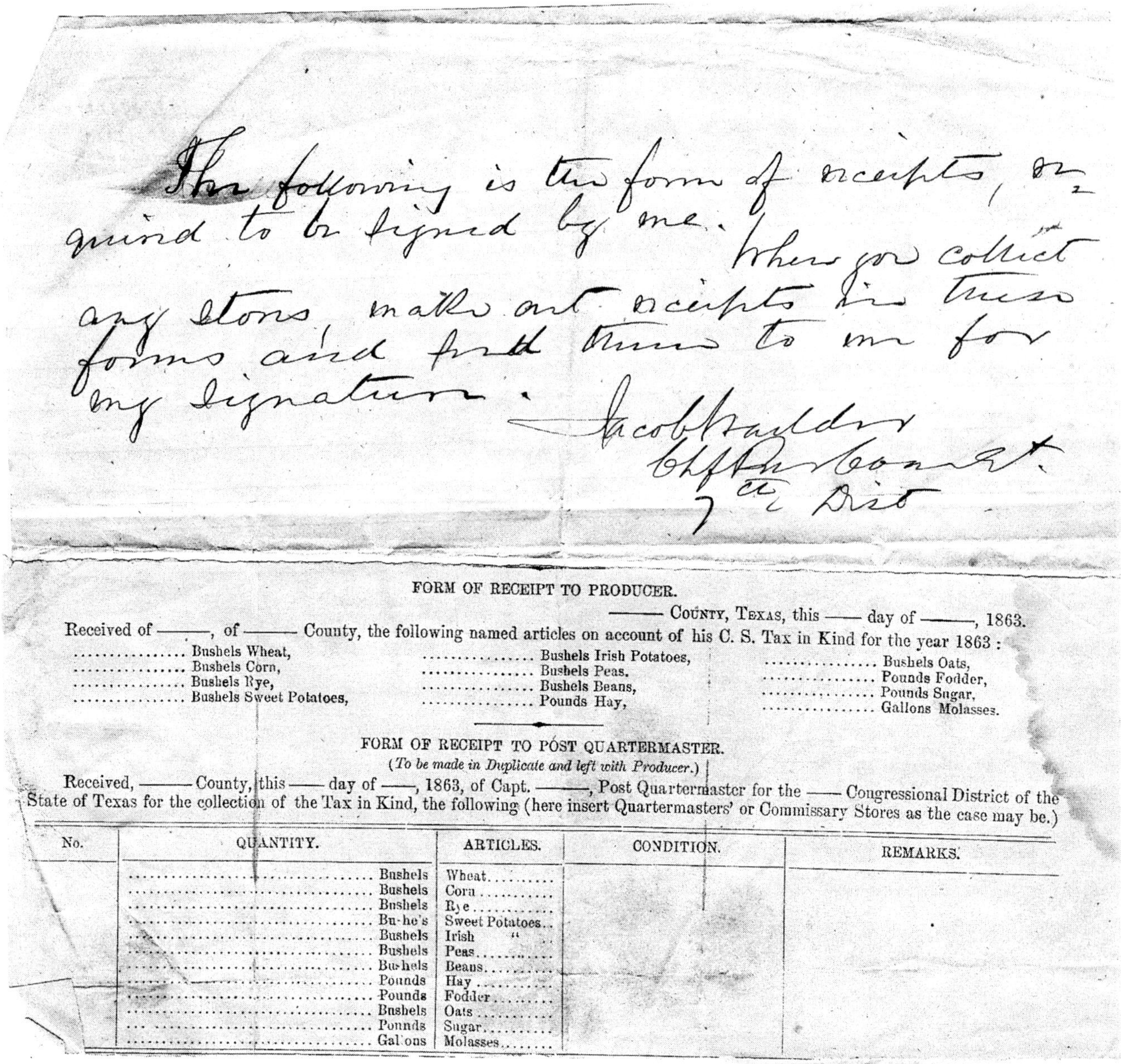
The following is the form of receipts, required to be signed by me. When you collect any stores, make out receipts in these forms and forward them to me for my signature.

Jacob Waelder
Chf Tax Comr.
7th Dist

FORM OF RECEIPT TO PRODUCER.

——— County, Texas, this —— day of ———, 1863.

Received of ———, of ——— County, the following named articles on account of his C. S. Tax in Kind for the year 1863:

.... Bushels Wheat,
.... Bushels Corn,
.... Bushels Rye,
.... Bushels Sweet Potatoes,
.... Bushels Irish Potatoes,
.... Bushels Peas,
.... Bushels Beans,
.... Pounds Hay,
.... Bushels Oats,
.... Pounds Fodder,
.... Pounds Sugar,
.... Gallons Molasses.

FORM OF RECEIPT TO POST QUARTERMASTER.

(*To be made in Duplicate and left with Producer.*)

Received, ——— County, this —— day of ——, 1863, of Capt. ———, Post Quartermaster for the —— Congressional District of the State of Texas for the collection of the Tax in Kind, the following (here insert Quartermasters' or Commissary Stores as the case may be.)

No.	QUANTITY.	ARTICLES.	CONDITION.	REMARKS.
	.... Bushels	Wheat..........		
	.... Bushels	Corn..........		
	.... Bushels	Rye..........		
	.... Bushels	Sweet Potatoes..		
	.... Bushels	Irish "		
	.... Bushels	Peas..........		
	.... Bushels	Beans..........		
	.... Pounds	Hay..........		
	.... Pounds	Fodder..........		
	.... Bushels	Oats..........		
	.... Pounds	Sugar..........		
	.... Gallons	Molasses........		

Figure 67. "Forms for Receipt to Producers and Post Quartermaster" [Blank]. Texas, Post Quartermasters, 1863.

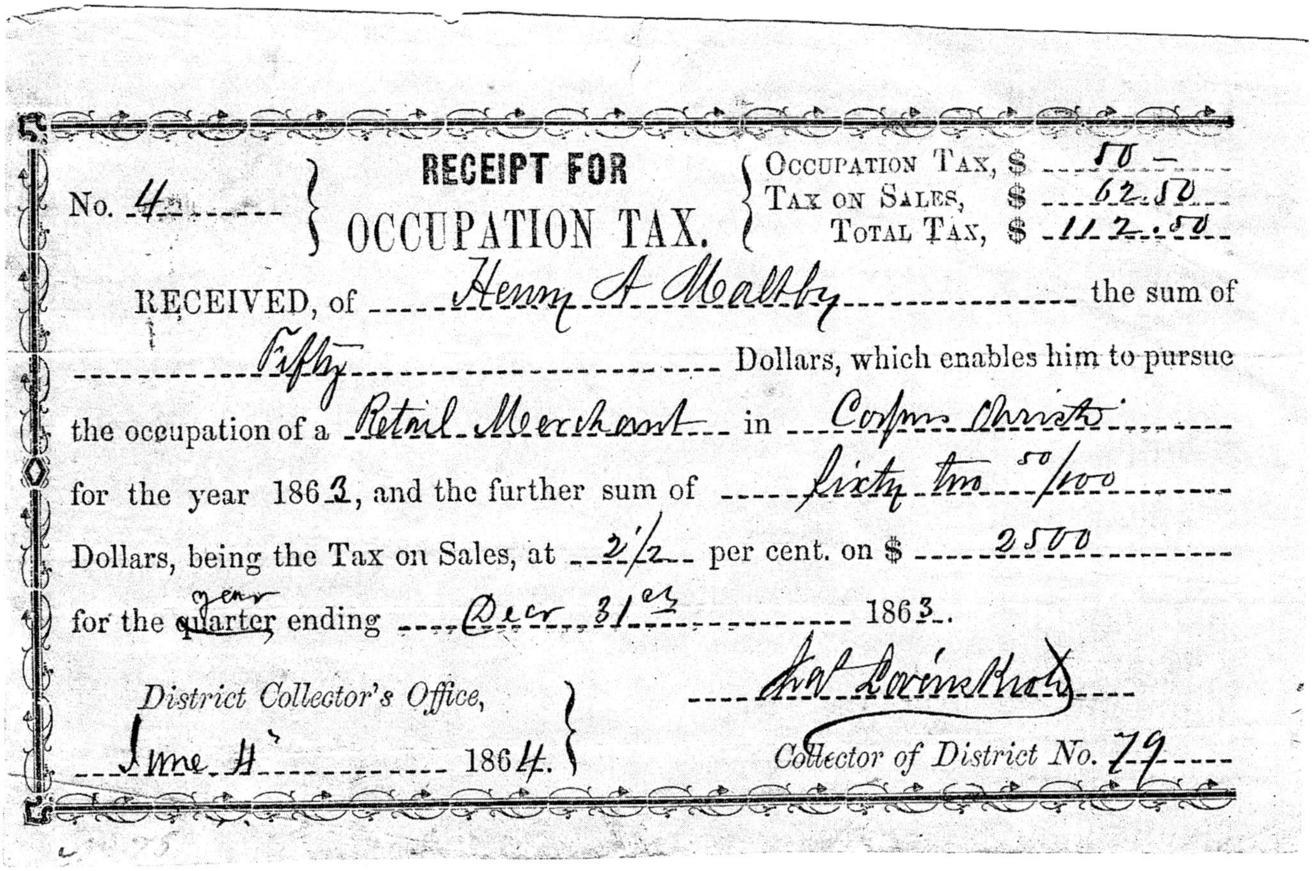

No. 4 } **RECEIPT FOR OCCUPATION TAX.** { OCCUPATION TAX, $ 50 — TAX ON SALES, $ 62.50 TOTAL TAX, $ 112.50

RECEIVED, of Henry A Maltby the sum of Fifty Dollars, which enables him to pursue the occupation of a Retail Merchant in Corpus Christi for the year 1863, and the further sum of Sixty two 50/100 Dollars, being the Tax on Sales, at 2½ per cent. on $ 2500 for the ~~quarter~~ year ending Decr 31st 1863.

District Collector's Office, June 4th 1864. } [illegible] *Collector of District No.* 79

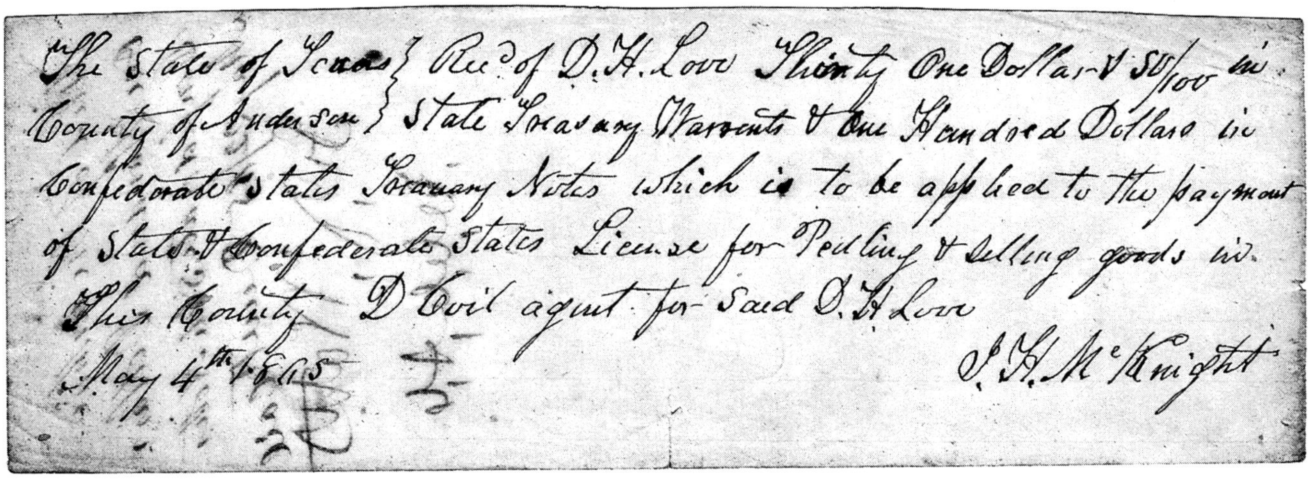

The State of Texas } Recd of D. H. Love Thirty One Dollar & 50/100 in
County of Anderson } State Treasury Warrents & One Hundred Dollars in
Confederate States Treasury Notes which is to be applied to the payment
of State & Confederate States License for Pedling & selling goods in
this County D Coil agent for Said D. H. Love
May 4th 1865
J. H. McKnight

Top: **Figure 68. "Receipt for Occupation and Sales Tax." Collector, Corpus Christi, June 4, 1864.** *Bottom:* **Figure 69. Receipt for Peddlers License. Collector, Anderson County, Texas, May 4, 1865.**

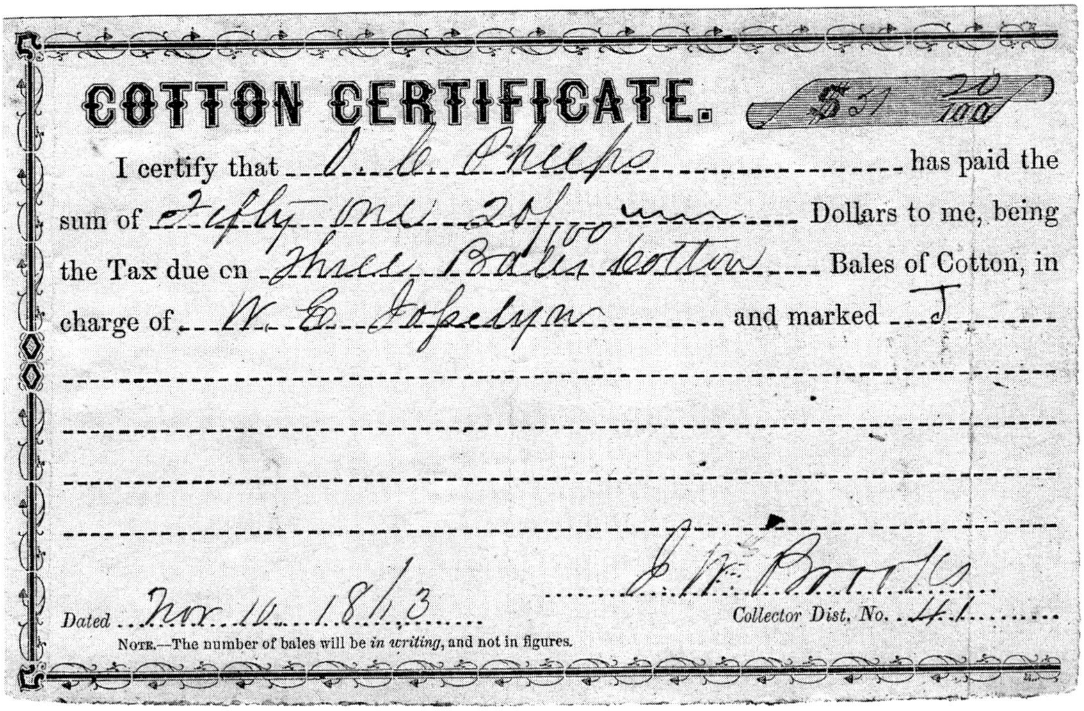

COTTON CERTIFICATE. $51 20/100

I certify that O. C. Phelps has paid the sum of Fifty one 20/100 Dollars to me, being the Tax due on Three Bales Cotton Bales of Cotton, in charge of W. E. Joselyn and marked J

Dated Nov 10 1863 J. W. Brooks Collector Dist. No. 41

NOTE.—The number of bales will be *in writing*, and not in figures.

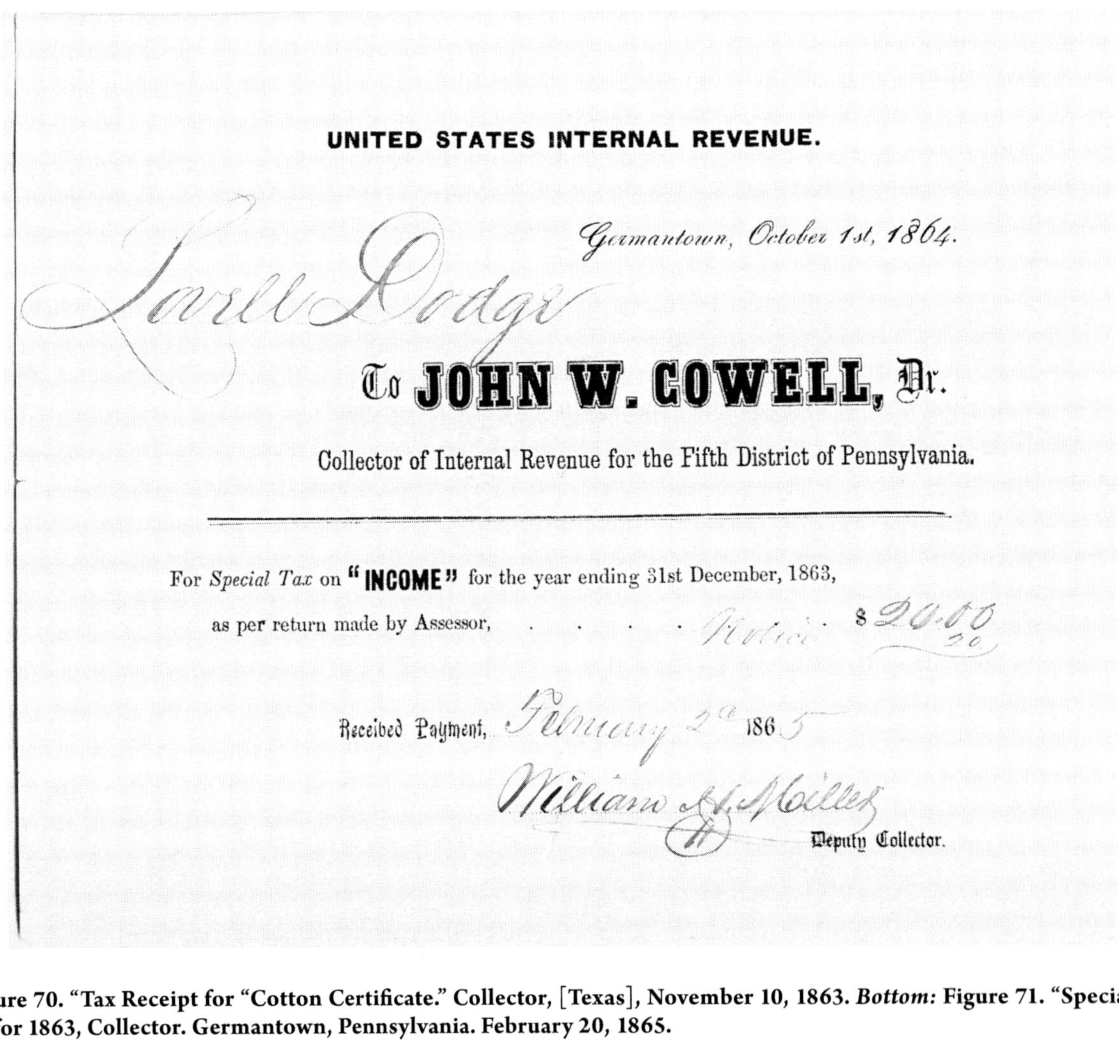

UNITED STATES INTERNAL REVENUE.

Germantown, October 1st, 1864.

Lovell Dodge

To JOHN W. COWELL, Dr.

Collector of Internal Revenue for the Fifth District of Pennsylvania.

For *Special Tax* on "INCOME" for the year ending 31st December, 1863,

as per return made by Assessor, ... Notice . $20.00

Received Payment, February 20 1865

William H. Miller

Deputy Collector.

Top: **Figure 70. "Tax Receipt for "Cotton Certificate." Collector, [Texas], November 10, 1863.** ***Bottom:*** **Figure 71. "Special Tax" on Income for 1863, Collector. Germantown, Pennsylvania. February 20, 1865.**

5844
…ion No. ....

Office of Internal Revenue,
6th DISTRICT OF NEW YORK.

Nov 22 1864.

I hereby Certify, *that the sum of*

Twelve 60/100 *Dollars,*

being the amount of tax on the income of Edwd J Wilson Trustee

for the year 1863, returned to me by the Assessor as follows, viz: A. O Regan

SOURCES OF INCOME.	AMOUNTS.		RATE.	AMOUNT TAX.	
From all sources, when the total is less than $10,000,	420	00	3 %	12	60
" " " " " *exceeds* $10,000,			5 "		
" *interest upon notes, bonds, or other securities of the United States,*			1½ "		
" *property in the United States, owned by a citizen thereof, residing abroad,*			5 "		
" *Income exceeding* $10,000, *upon a portion of which a tax of* 3 *per cent. has already been paid,*			2 "		
and on the following articles, for the year ending May 1st, 1865:					
.... *Carriage,*					
Billiard Table, kept for use or hire,					
.... *ozs. Troy of Plate of Silver, at* 3 *cents per oz.,*					
		Penalty			63

Total, ... $ 13.23

Figure 72. Certificate for 1863 Income Tax and Penalties, Collector. New York, November 22, 1864.

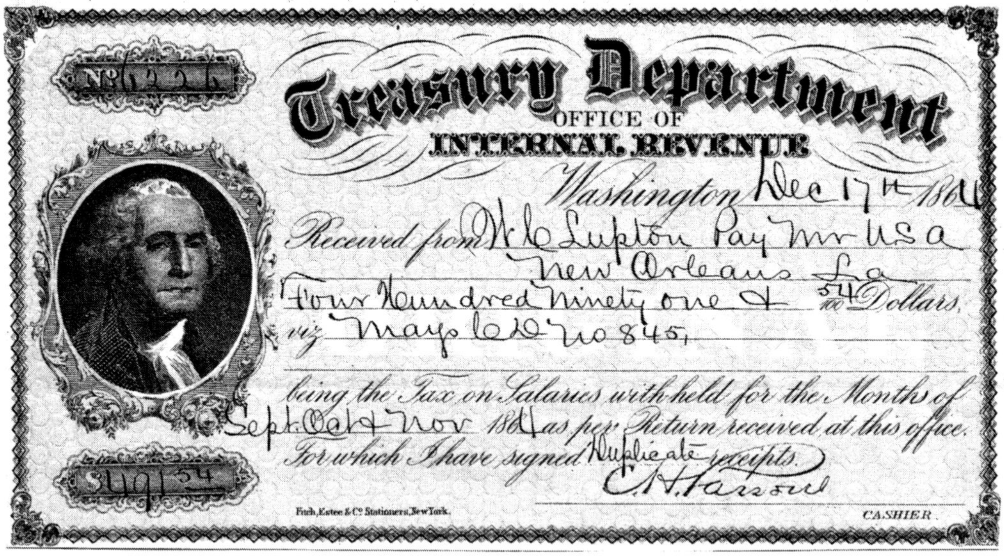

No. 6226

Treasury Department
OFFICE OF
INTERNAL REVENUE

Washington Dec 17th 1864

Received from W. C. Lupton Pay Mr U.S.A.
New Orleans La
Four Hundred Ninety one & 54/100 Dollars,
viz May 6 D No 845,

being the Tax on Salaries with-held for the Months of
Sept. Oct & Nov 1864 as per Return received at this office.
For which I have signed Duplicate receipts.

C. H. Parsons
CASHIER.

$491.54

Fitch, Estee & Co. Stationers, New York.

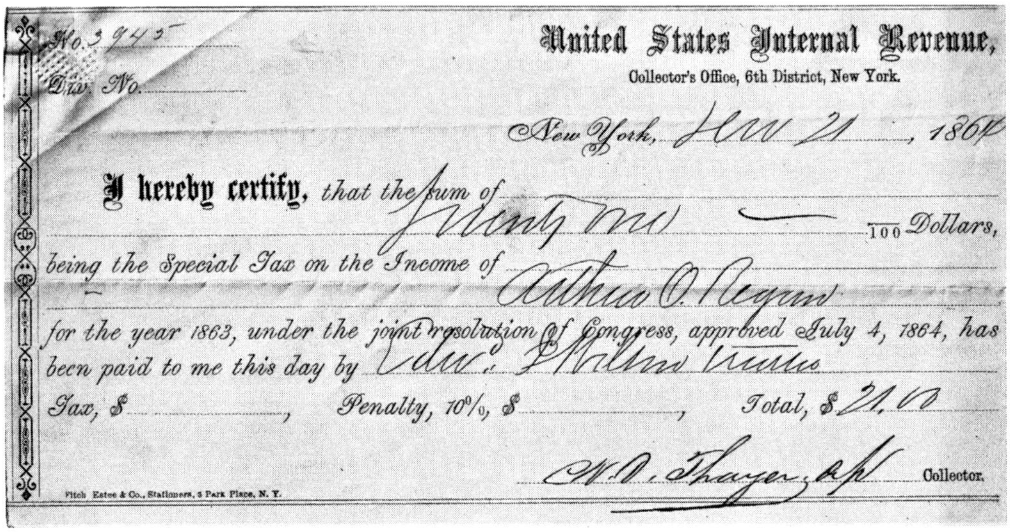

No. 3945
Div. No.

United States Internal Revenue,
Collector's Office, 6th District, New York.

New York, Dec 21, 1864

I hereby certify, that the sum of Twenty one ——— 100 Dollars,
being the Special Tax on the Income of Arthur O. Regan
for the year 1863, under the joint resolution of Congress, approved July 4, 1864, has
been paid to me this day by

Tax, $, Penalty, 10%, $, Total, $21.00

W. O. Thayer, asst Collector.

Fitch Estee & Co., Stationers, 5 Park Place, N. Y.

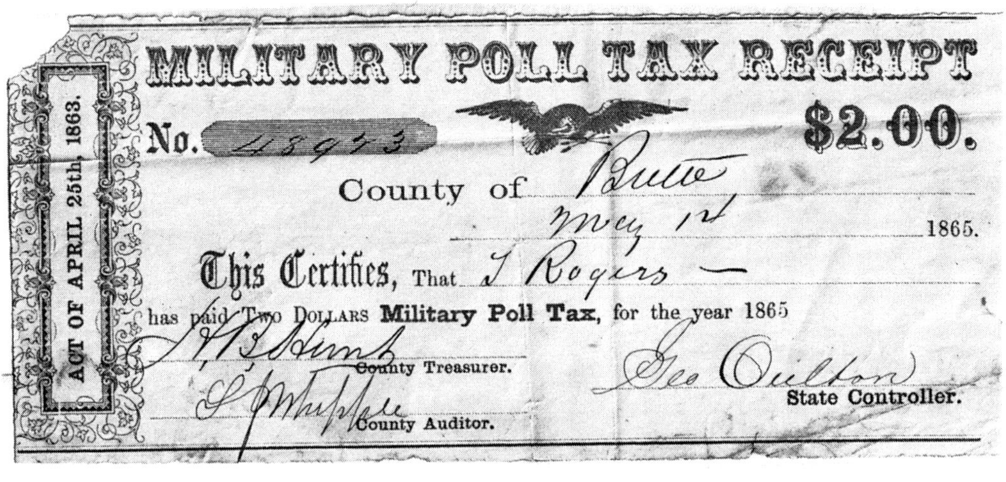

MILITARY POLL TAX RECEIPT

ACT OF APRIL 25th, 1863.

No. 43943

$2.00.

County of Butte

May 12 1865.

This Certifies, That I. Rogers —
has paid Two Dollars Military Poll Tax, for the year 1865

A. B. Hunt County Treasurer.

S. J. Whipple County Auditor.

Geo Oulton State Controller.

Top: Figure 73. Receipt for Tax Withheld on Salary Withheld for Quarter, November 1864, Paymaster. New Orleans. December 17, 1864. *Middle:*Figure 74. Certificate for "Special Tax" Paid by Fiduciary, Collector. New York, December 21, 1864. *Bottom:* Figure 75. Military $2.00 Poll Tax, State Controller. Butte County, California, May 12, 1865.

(19)

UNITED STATES INTERNAL REVENUE.

Sixth District, State of New York,

Div. No. 13 List Am — Oct. 31st, 1866.

Collector's Office, No. 187 West 14th St.

Mr. E. J. Wilson
91 W. 11th

To U. S. Internal Revenue, Dr.

M. B. FIELD, Collector.

			AMOUNT TAX.	
Tax on income for the year 1865, viz:				
Income not exceeding $5,000: Amount, $ 3171 *at 5 per cent.*			158	55
" *exceeding 5,000:* " *$ ...... " 10* "				
Total . . .				
Tax withheld . . .				
Tax on the following articles, for the year ending May 1, 1867:	RATE.	ABSTRACT NO.		
......*Billiard Tables, kept for private use*	*$10 each.*	261		
......*Carriages, valuation over $50 and not over $100*	1 "	262		
...... " " " 100 " " 200	2 "	263		
...... " " " 200 " " 300	3 "	264		
...... " " " 300 " " 500	6 "	265		
...... " " " 500	10 "	266		
......*Pianofortes, &c., valuation over $100 and not over $200*	2 "	267		
...... " " " 200 " " 400	4 "	268		
...... " " " 400	6 "	269		
......*oz. Gold Plate, kept for use ...... oz.*	*50c. per oz.*	270		
......*oz. Silver Plate,* " " *...... oz.*	*5c.* "	271		
1 ......*Gold Watches, kept for use, valuation not over $100*	*$1 each.*	272	1	
1 ...... " " " *over 100*	2 "	273	2	
......*Yachts,*	Notice			20

Amount of Tax .... $ 161.75

Received Payment,

W. O. Thorpe
Deputy Collector.

Figure 76. Receipt for 1865 Tax on Income and Watches, Collector. New York, February 1, 1866.

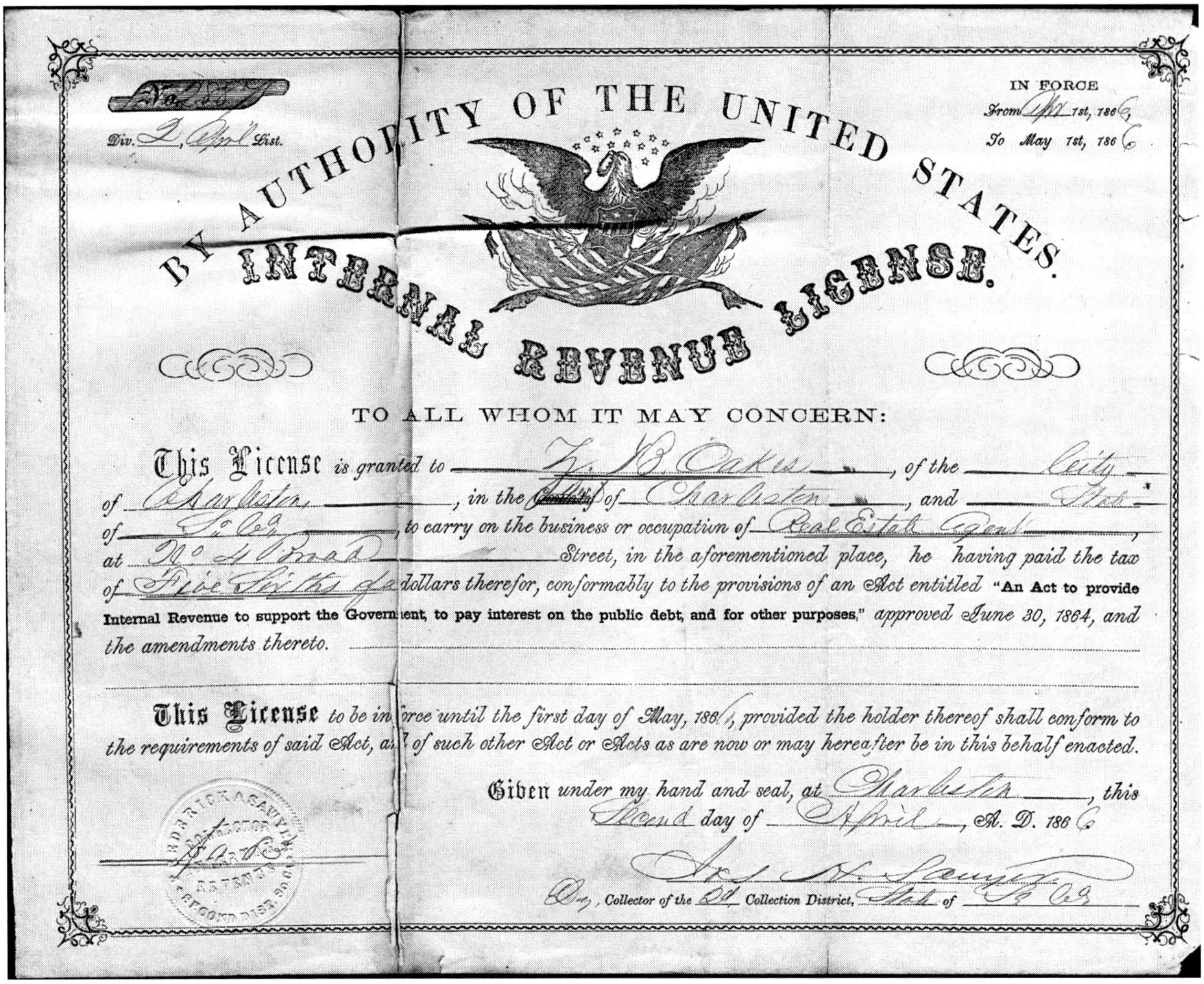

No. 237

Div. 2, April List.

IN FORCE
From April 1st, 1866
To May 1st, 1866

BY AUTHORITY OF THE UNITED STATES.

INTERNAL REVENUE LICENSE.

TO ALL WHOM IT MAY CONCERN:

This License is granted to F. B. Oakes, of the City of Charleston, in the County of Charleston, and State of S. Ca., to carry on the business or occupation of Real Estate Agent, at No 4 Broad Street, in the aforementioned place, he having paid the tax of Five Dollars dollars therefor, conformably to the provisions of an Act entitled "An Act to provide Internal Revenue to support the Government, to pay interest on the public debt, and for other purposes," approved June 30, 1864, and the amendments thereto.

This License to be in force until the first day of May, 1866, provided the holder thereof shall conform to the requirements of said Act, and of such other Act or Acts as are now or may hereafter be in this behalf enacted.

Given under my hand and seal, at Charleston, this Second day of April, A. D. 1866

Jos. H. Sawyer

Dy., Collector of the 2d Collection District, State of S. Ca.

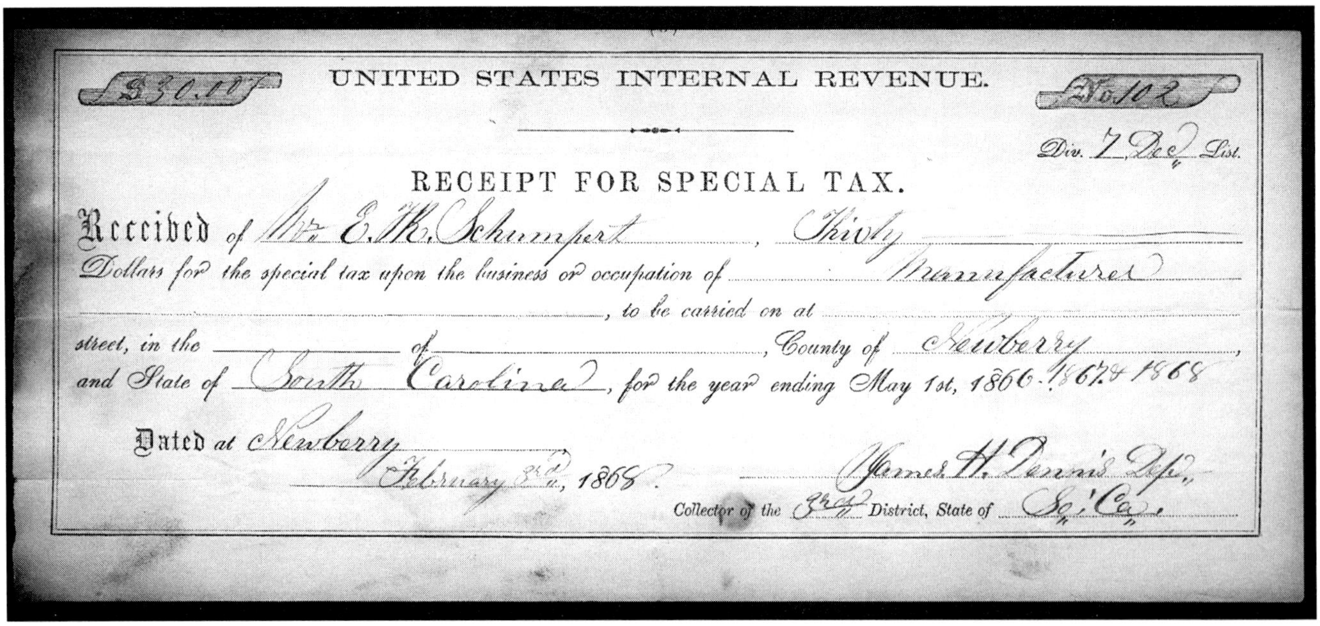

$30.00

UNITED STATES INTERNAL REVENUE.

No 102

Div. 7 Dec. List.

RECEIPT FOR SPECIAL TAX.

Received of Mr. E. H. Schumpert, Thirty Dollars for the special tax upon the business or occupation of Manufacturer, to be carried on at street, in the of, County of Newberry, and State of South Carolina, for the year ending May 1st, 1866, 1867 & 1868

Dated at Newberry February 3rd, 1868.

James H. Dennis Dep.

Collector of the 3rd District, State of So. Ca.

Top: **Figure 77. Receipt by Real Estate License, Collector. Charleston, April 2, 1866.** ***Bottom:*** **Figure 78. Receipt for "Special Tax" Paid to Manufacturer for 1866, 1867, and 1868, Collector. Newberry, South Carolina, February 3, 1868.**

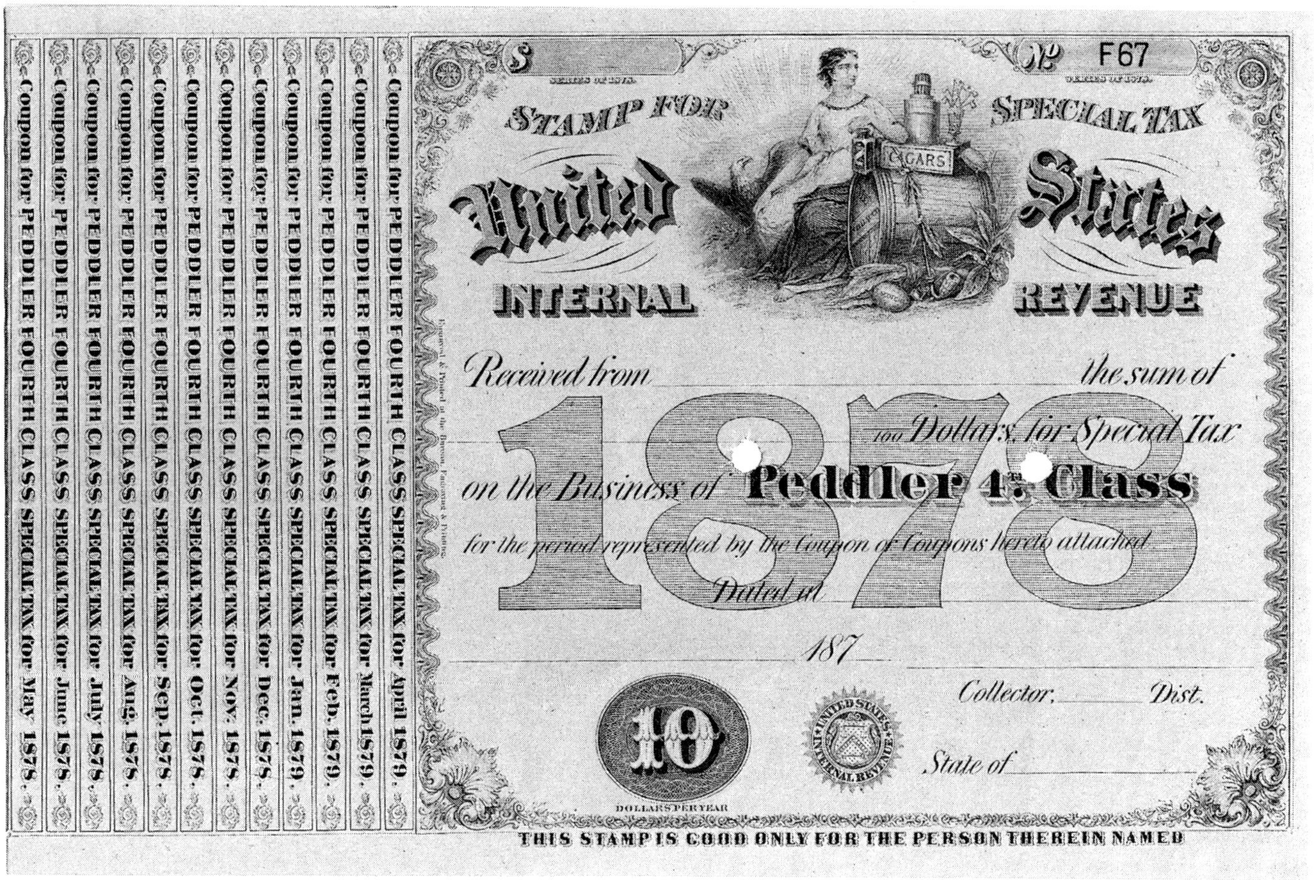
Series of 1878.
No. F67
Stamp for Special Tax
United States
Internal Revenue
CIGARS
Received from the sum of
100 Dollars, for Special Tax
on the Business of Peddler 4th Class
for the period represented by the Coupon or Coupons hereto attached.
Dated at
187
Collector, Dist.
State of
10
DOLLARS PER YEAR
UNITED STATES INTERNAL REVENUE
1878
THIS STAMP IS GOOD ONLY FOR THE PERSON THEREIN NAMED
Coupon for PEDDLER FOURTH CLASS SPECIAL TAX for April 1879.
Coupon for PEDDLER FOURTH CLASS SPECIAL TAX for March 1879.
Coupon for PEDDLER FOURTH CLASS SPECIAL TAX for Feb. 1879.
Coupon for PEDDLER FOURTH CLASS SPECIAL TAX for Jan. 1879.
Coupon for PEDDLER FOURTH CLASS SPECIAL TAX for Dec. 1878.
Coupon for PEDDLER FOURTH CLASS SPECIAL TAX for Nov. 1878.
Coupon for PEDDLER FOURTH CLASS SPECIAL TAX for Oct. 1878.
Coupon for PEDDLER FOURTH CLASS SPECIAL TAX for Sep. 1878.
Coupon for PEDDLER FOURTH CLASS SPECIAL TAX for Aug. 1878.
Coupon for PEDDLER FOURTH CLASS SPECIAL TAX for July 1878.
Coupon for PEDDLER FOURTH CLASS SPECIAL TAX for June 1878.
Coupon for PEDDLER FOURTH CLASS SPECIAL TAX for May 1878.

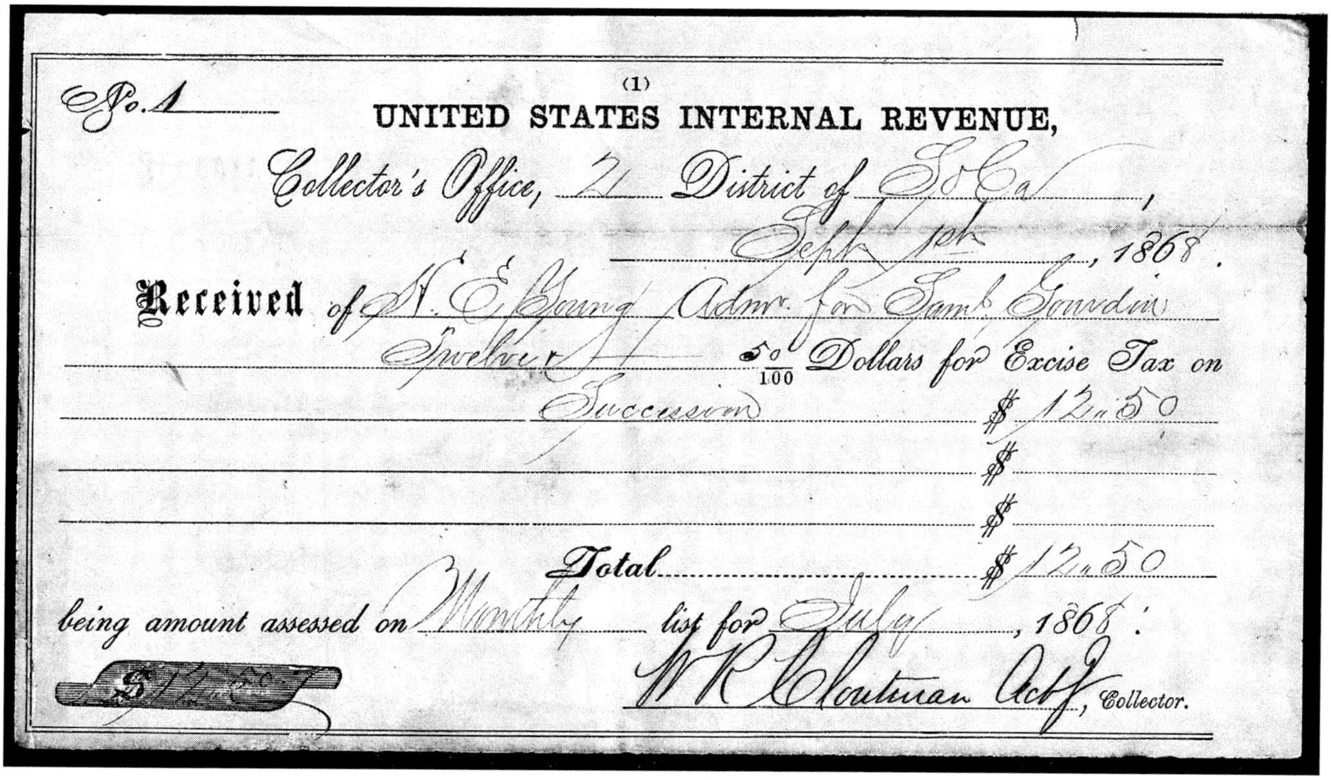
No. 1 (1)
UNITED STATES INTERNAL REVENUE,
Collector's Office, 2 District of So Ca,
Sept 1st, 1868.
Received of H. E. Young Admr. for Saml. Gourdin
Twelve 50/100 Dollars for Excise Tax on
Succession $12.50
$
$
Total $12.50
being amount assessed on Monthly list for July, 1868.
W R Clarkson Actg, Collector.

Top: Figure 79. $10.00 "Special Stamp" for April Tax Receipt for 4th Class Peddler. [Blank], 1878. *Bottom:* Figure 80. Tax Receipt for Succession Tax, Collector. South Carolina, September 1, 1868.

TAX IN KIND.

FORM NO. 1. ESTIMATE NO. 247

Estimate and Assessment of AGRICULTURAL PRODUCTS which are taxed in kind, agreed upon by the Assessor and Tax Payer, and the value of the portion thereof to which the Government is entitled, in accordance with the provisions of "An Act to lay taxes for the common defence, and carry on the Government of the Confederate States," and an "Act to amend said Act, approved 17th of February, 1864;" said Estimate and Assessment to be returned to the District Quartermaster on or before the 1st day of September of each year.

AGRICULTURAL PRODUCTS	QUANTITY OF GROSS CROPS	QUALITY	TITHE	VALUE OF TITHE
Wheat	55 Bu		5½ 8	44
Oats	50 "		5 4.50	22.50
Sheaf Oats				
Rye				
Cured Hay				
Wool	10 "		1	4
			Total Value, $	

I S E Shealy of the Dist of Lexington and State of South Carolina do swear that the above is a true statement and estimate of all the Agricultural Products above named produced by me during the year 186 which are taxable by the provisions of the above stated Acts, including what may have been sold or consumed by me, to the best of my knowledge and belief.

J W Ballentine Aty TAX PAYER.

Sworn to and subscribed before me, the 24 *day of* Sept 1864 *and I further certify that the above Estimate and Assessment has been agreed upon by said* S E Shealy *and myself, as a correct and true statement of the amount of his crops, and that the value of the portion to which the Government is entitled is correctly stated.*

W A Merritt ASSESSOR.

20 *Tax District, State of* S C

RECEIVED at Depot No. , Congressional District, State of

of , Bushels Pounds of Wheat,

Bushels Pounds of Oats, Bushels Pounds of

Rye, Pounds of Cured Hay, Pounds Ounces of Wool,

of the above estimate.

AGENT.

day of 186

Figure 81. "Tax In Kind." Estimate and Assessment of Agricultural Products [Form 1] assessed. Lexington, South Carolina, September 24, 1864.

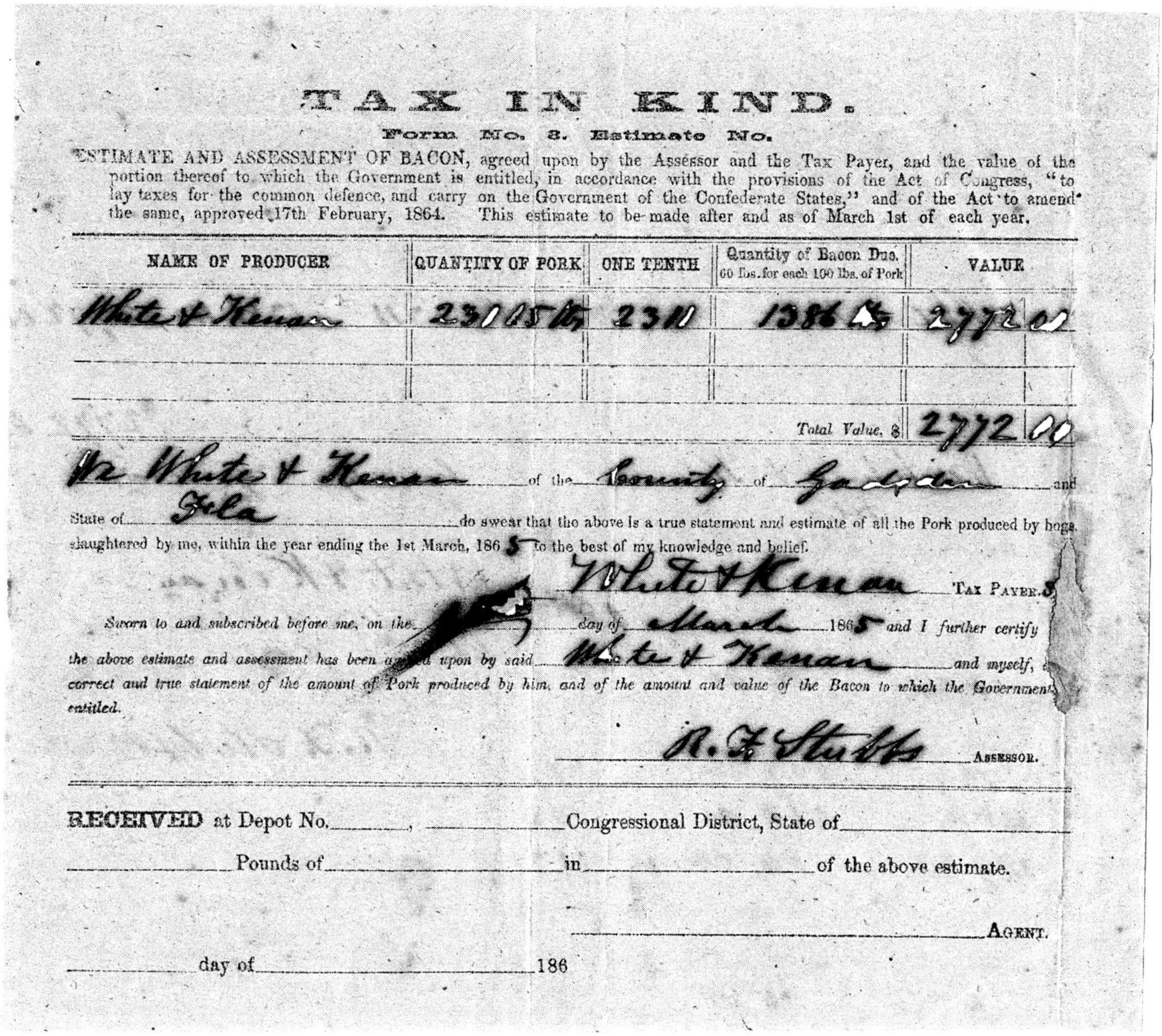

TAX IN KIND.

Form No. 8. Estimate No.

ESTIMATE AND ASSESSMENT OF BACON, agreed upon by the Assessor and the Tax Payer, and the value of the portion thereof to which the Government is entitled, in accordance with the provisions of the Act of Congress, "to lay taxes for the common defence, and carry on the Government of the Confederate States," and of the Act to amend the same, approved 17th February, 1864. This estimate to be made after and as of March 1st of each year.

NAME OF PRODUCER	QUANTITY OF PORK	ONE TENTH	Quantity of Bacon Due. 60 lbs. for each 100 lbs. of Pork	VALUE
White & Kenan	23105 lbs	2310	1386 lbs	2772 00
			Total Value, $	2772 00

We White & Kenan of the County of Gadsden and State of Fla do swear that the above is a true statement and estimate of all the Pork produced by hogs slaughtered by me, within the year ending the 1st March, 1865 to the best of my knowledge and belief.

White & Kenan Tax Payer.

Sworn to and subscribed before me, on the ______ *day of* March 1865 *and I further certify the above estimate and assessment has been agreed upon by said* White & Kenan *and myself, a correct and true statement of the amount of Pork produced by him, and of the amount and value of the Bacon to which the Government is entitled.*

R. F. Stubbs Assessor.

RECEIVED at Depot No.______, ______Congressional District, State of______

______Pounds of______in______of the above estimate.

______Agent.

______day of______186

Figure 82. "Tax In Kind" Estimate and Assessment of Agricultural Products [Form 2]. District Quartermaster [1864].

NOTICE TO
PAYERS OF TAX IN KIND.

COUNTY AGENT'S OFFICE,
Reidsville N. C. 1864.

Notice is hereby given to all persons holding Assessors' estimates of the tax in kind due by them to the Confederate States that I will be ready to receive said tax at Reidsville on Monday the 19th September 1864

All tax payers are earnestly requested to bring forward their Wheat or ~~quota~~ Oats of produce immediately as the Government needs it.

~~Any persons hauling their quota over 8 miles will be paid for the excess cents per mile per 100 pounds.~~

In case of the failure of any one, to deliver the whole or any portion of the tax due by them, within two months from the date hereof, the Quartermaster is instructed to turn over the estimate of the amount in default, to the District collector, who will at once proceed to collect the same with five hundred 500per cent. and costs additional, by warrant of distress, to be levied on any property belonging to the party in default.

The tax payer will be required to deliver his produce in such form and ordinary marketable condition, as may be usual in the section in which it is to be delivered---tobacco stripped and packed in boxes, cotton ginned and packed in some secure manner.

Grain will be received by the standard weight. Bags will be furnished, for the delivery of grain, at this office. Oats must be shelled before delivery

Wm Lindsey Agent,
for Rockingham County.

Figure 83. "Notice to Payers of Tax In Kind," County Agent. Reidsville, North Carolina, September 19, 1864.

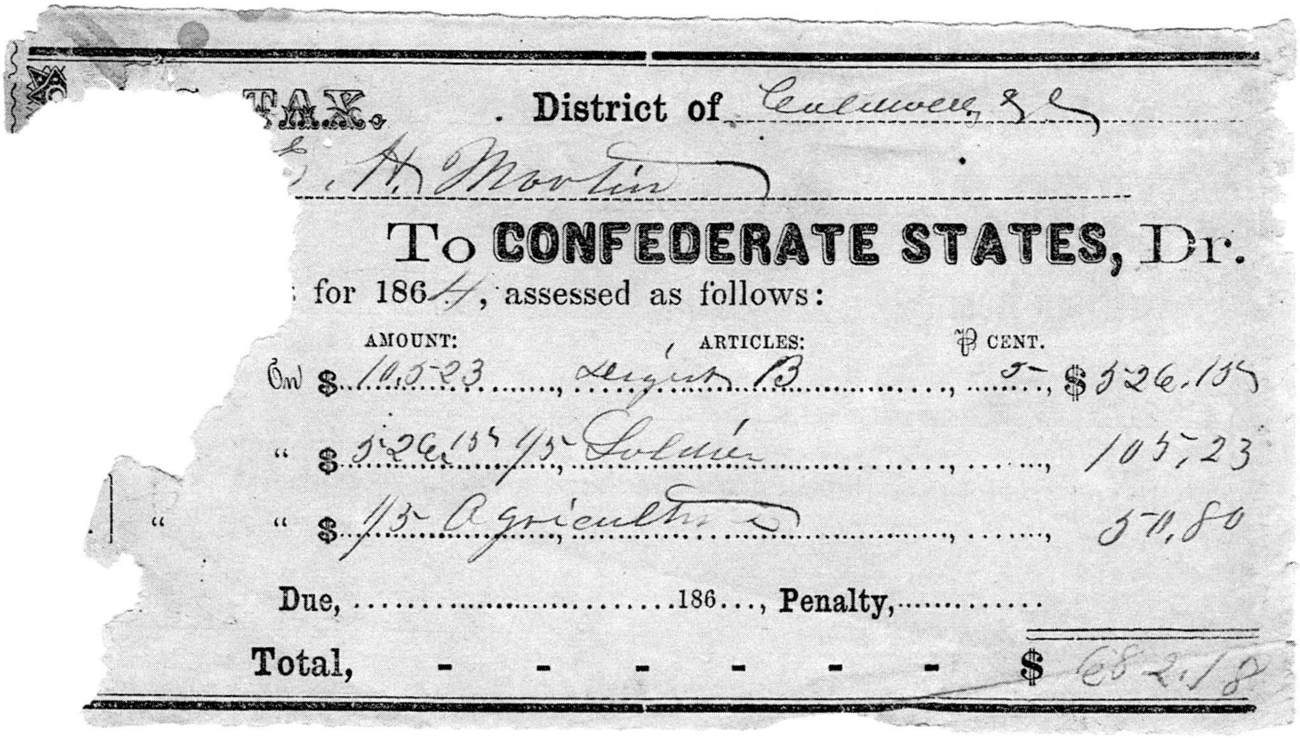

TAX. District of Caldwell P. L.

E. H. Morton

To CONFEDERATE STATES, Dr.

for 1864, assessed as follows:

AMOUNT:	ARTICLES:	℔ CENT.	
On $ 10.523	Legist B	5	$ 526.15
" $ 526.15	1/5 Soldier		105.23
" $	1/5 Agriculture		50.80

Due, ...186..., Penalty,..........

Total, - - - - - - $ 682.18

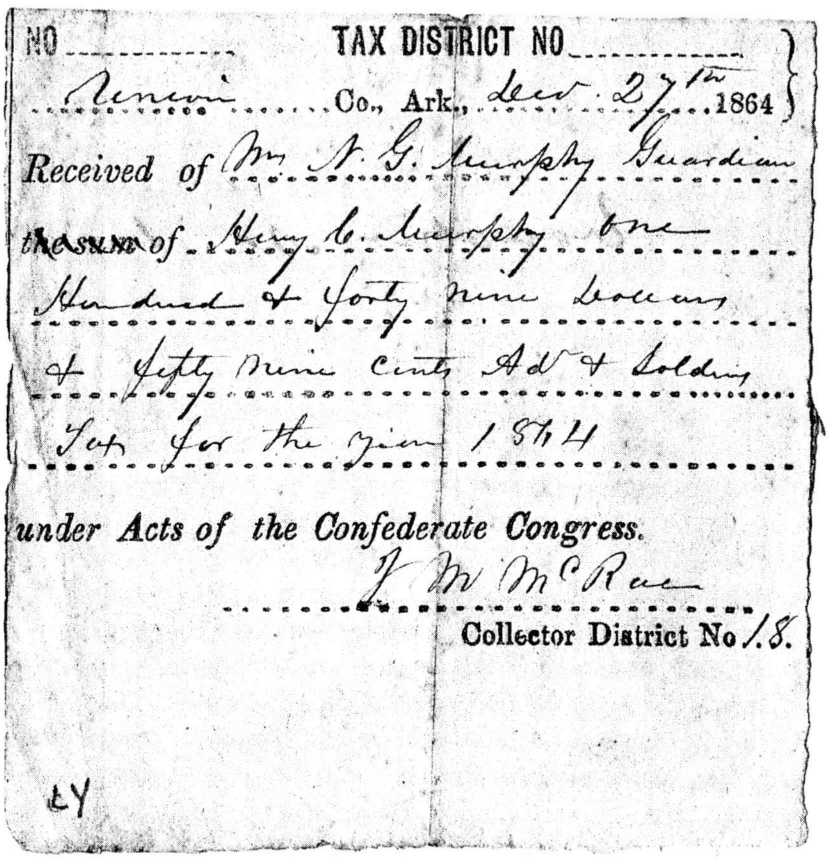

NO........ TAX DISTRICT NO........

Union Co., Ark., Dec 27th 1864

Received of Mr N. G. Murphy Guardian

the sum of Henry C. Murphy One

Hundred & Forty nine Dollars

& fifty nine cents Ad & Soldiers

Tax for the year 1864

under Acts of the Confederate Congress.

J M McRae

Collector District No 18.

Top: **Figure 84. Assessment of Land, Agriculture and Soldiers Tax, Collector. Caldwell Parish, Columbia, Louisiana [1864].** ***Bottom:*** **Figure 85. Receipt of Soldier's Tax, Collector. Union County, Arkansas, December 27, 1864.**

CERTIFICATE OF DEPOSIT.

No

$

Confederate States Depy.

April 2nd 1864.

The holder of this Certificate, is entitled to

Dollars,

in Treasury Notes, issued by Authority of the Act of Congress of February 17th 1864, on its presentation at this Office, in Exchange for Notes of Old Issues, this day deposited.

Depositary.

Archer, Lithog. Richmond, Va.

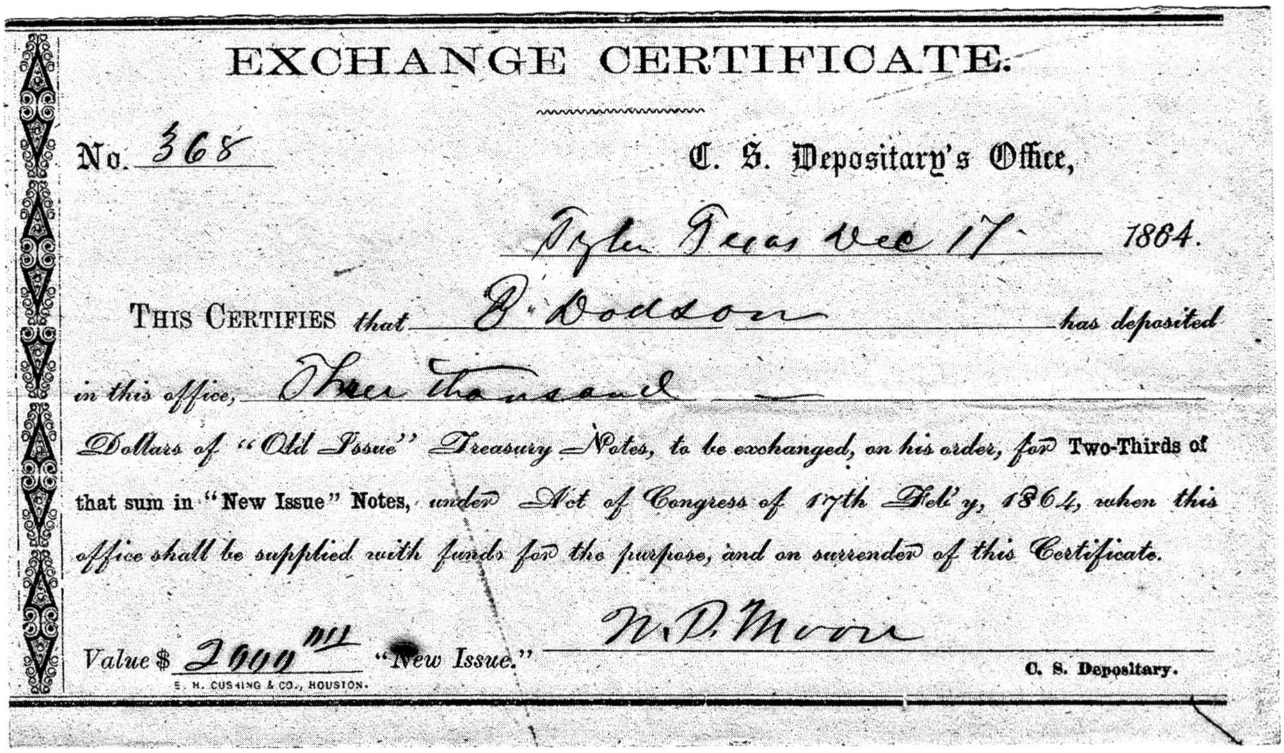

EXCHANGE CERTIFICATE.

No. 368

C. S. Depositary's Office,

Tyler Texas Dec 17 1864.

THIS CERTIFIES that J. Dodson has deposited in this office, Three thousand — Dollars of "Old Issue" Treasury Notes, to be exchanged, on his order, for Two-Thirds of that sum in "New Issue" Notes, under Act of Congress of 17th Feb'y, 1864, when this office shall be supplied with funds for the purpose, and on surrender of this Certificate.

Value $ 2000 "New Issue."

W. D. Moore

C. S. Depositary.

E. H. CUSHING & CO., HOUSTON.

Top: **Figure 86. "Certificate of Deposit" Exchange of Old Issue Notes for New, Depositary. April 2, 1864 [Blank]** *Bottom:* **Figure 87. "Exchange Certificate" Old Issue Notes for New, Depository. Tyler, Texas, December 17, 1864.**

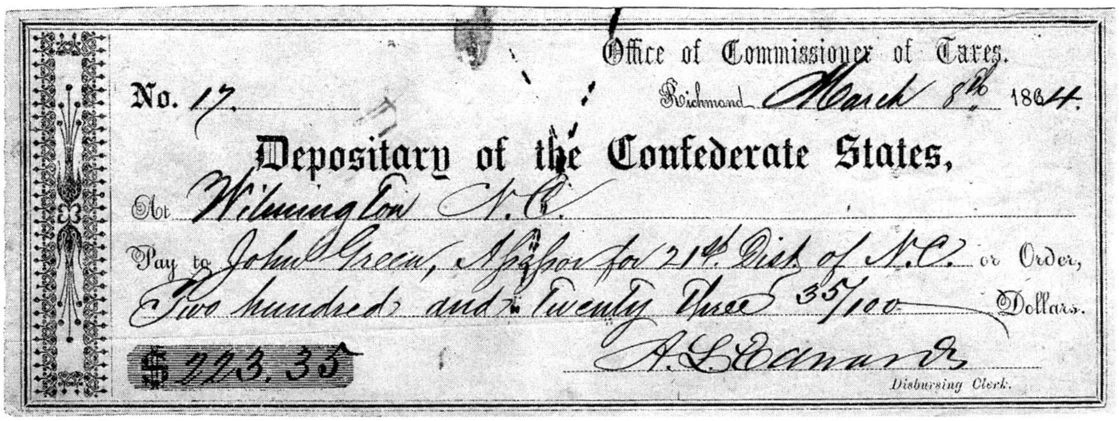
Office of Commissioner of Taxes.
No. 17. Richmond March 8th 1864.
Depositary of the Confederate States,
At Wilmington N.C.
Pay to John Green, Assessor for 21st Dist of N.C. or Order,
Two hundred and twenty three 35/100 Dollars.
$223.35 A.L. Edwards
Disbursing Clerk.

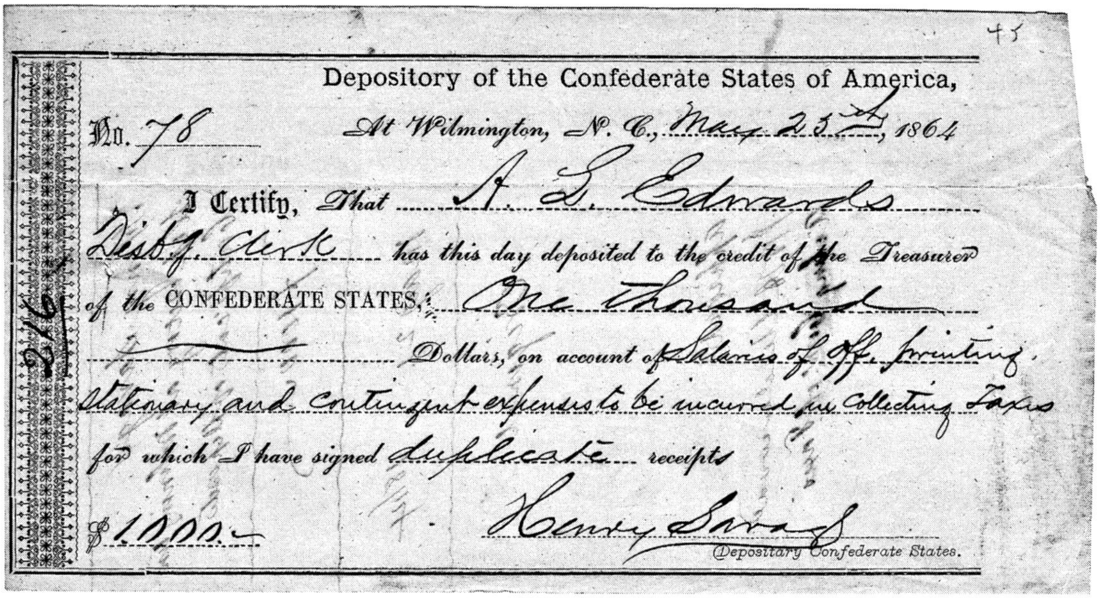
Depository of the Confederate States of America,
No. 78 At Wilmington, N. C., May 25th, 1864
I Certify, That A. L. Edwards
Disb'g Clerk has this day deposited to the credit of the Treasurer
of the CONFEDERATE STATES, One thousand
Dollars, on account of Salaries of Off. printing, stationary and contingent expenses to be incurred in collecting Taxes
for which I have signed duplicate receipts
$1000 Henry Savage
Depositary Confederate States.

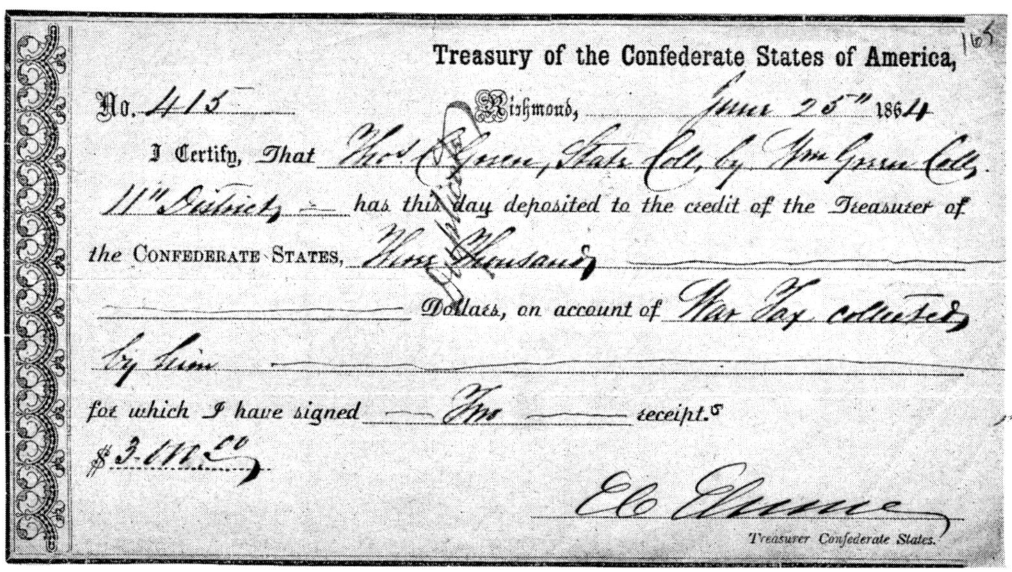
Treasury of the Confederate States of America,
No. 415 Richmond, June 25th 1864
I Certify, That Thos S Green, State Coll, by Wm Green Coll,
11th District has this day deposited to the credit of the Treasurer of
the CONFEDERATE STATES, Three Thousand
Dollars, on account of War Tax collected
by him
for which I have signed Two receipts
$3.000
E C Elmore
Treasurer Confederate States.

Top: **Figure 88. Depositary Draft Tax Assessor Salary. Commissioner of Taxes, Disbursing Clerk, Wilmington, North Carolina, March 8, 1864.** ***Middle:*** **Figure 89. Deposit to Credit of Treasurer for Salaries, etc. Depository at Wilmington, North Carolina. May 25, 1864.** ***Bottom:*** **Figure 90. Deposit to Credit of Treasurer for War Tax, Treasurer of Richmond County, South Carolina, June 25, 1864.**

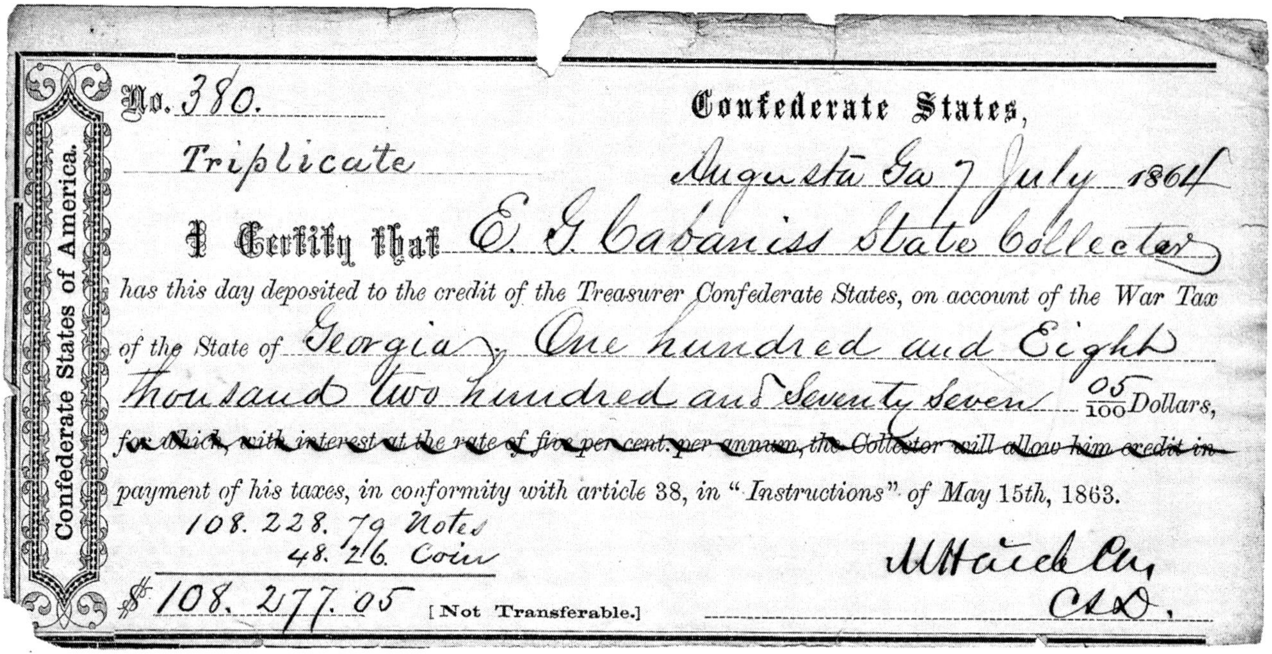

No. 380. Confederate States,
Triplicate Augusta Ga 7 July 1864
I Certify that E. G. Cabaniss State Collector
has this day deposited to the credit of the Treasurer Confederate States, on account of the War Tax of the State of Georgia One hundred and Eight thousand two hundred and Seventy Seven 05/100 Dollars,
~~for which, with interest at the rate of five per cent. per annum, the Collector will allow him credit in~~
payment of his taxes, in conformity with article 38, in "Instructions" of May 15th, 1863.
108.228.79 Notes
48.26 Coin
$108.277.05 [Not Transferable.] M Hack Ca. C.S.D.

Confederate States of America.

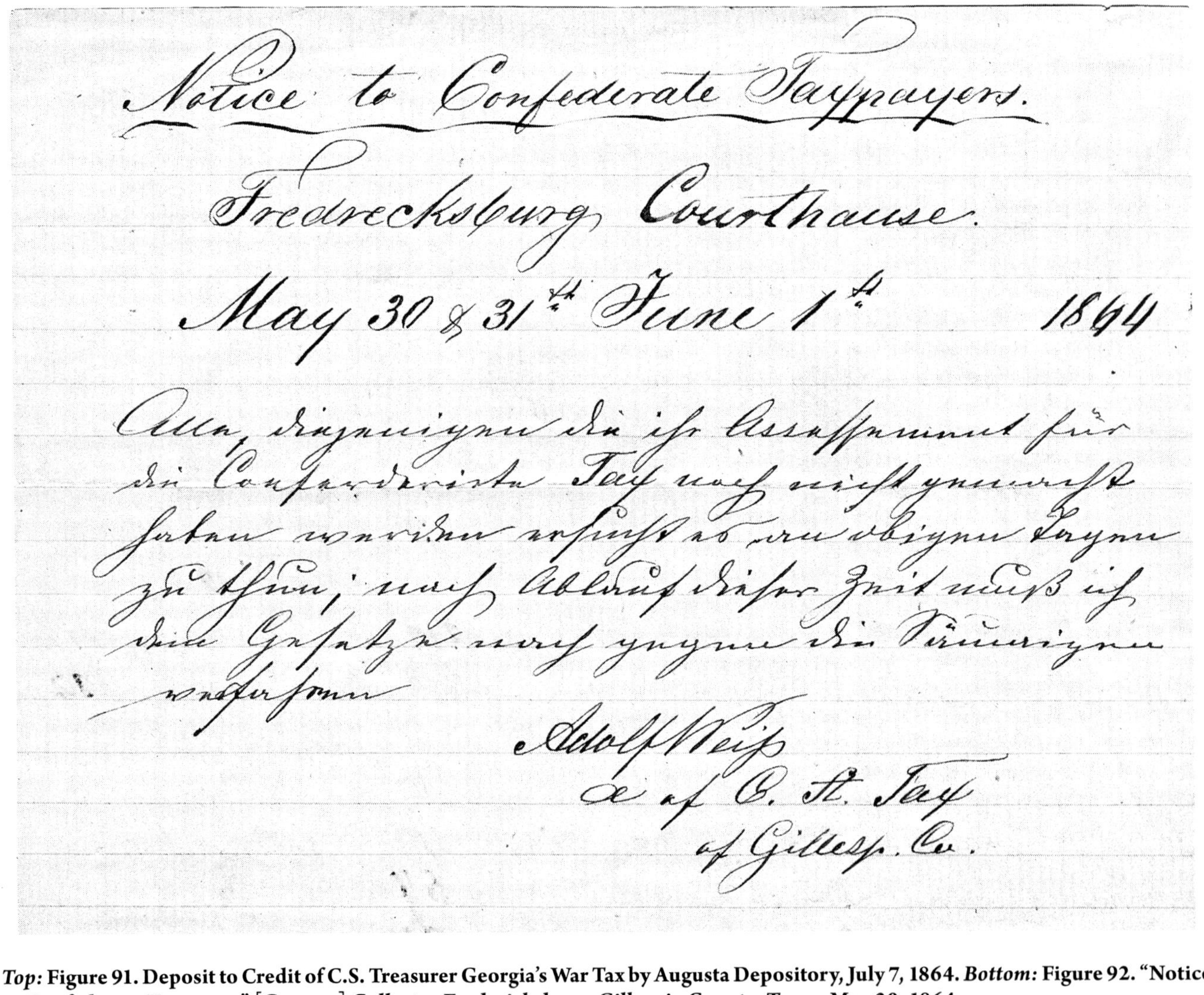

Notice to Confederate Taxpayers.

Fredrecksburg Courthause.

May 30 & 31st June 1st 1864

Alle diejenigen die ihr Assessment für die Confoederirte Tax noch nicht gemacht haben werden ersucht es an obigen Tagen zu thun; nach Ablauf dieser Zeit muß ich die Gesetze nach gegen die Säumigen verfahren

Adolf Weiß
a of C. S. Tax
of Gillesp. Co.

Top: **Figure 91. Deposit to Credit of C.S. Treasurer Georgia's War Tax by Augusta Depository, July 7, 1864.** ***Bottom:*** **Figure 92. "Notice to Confederate Taxpayers" [German] Collector Fredericksburg, Gillespie County, Texas. May 30, 1864.**

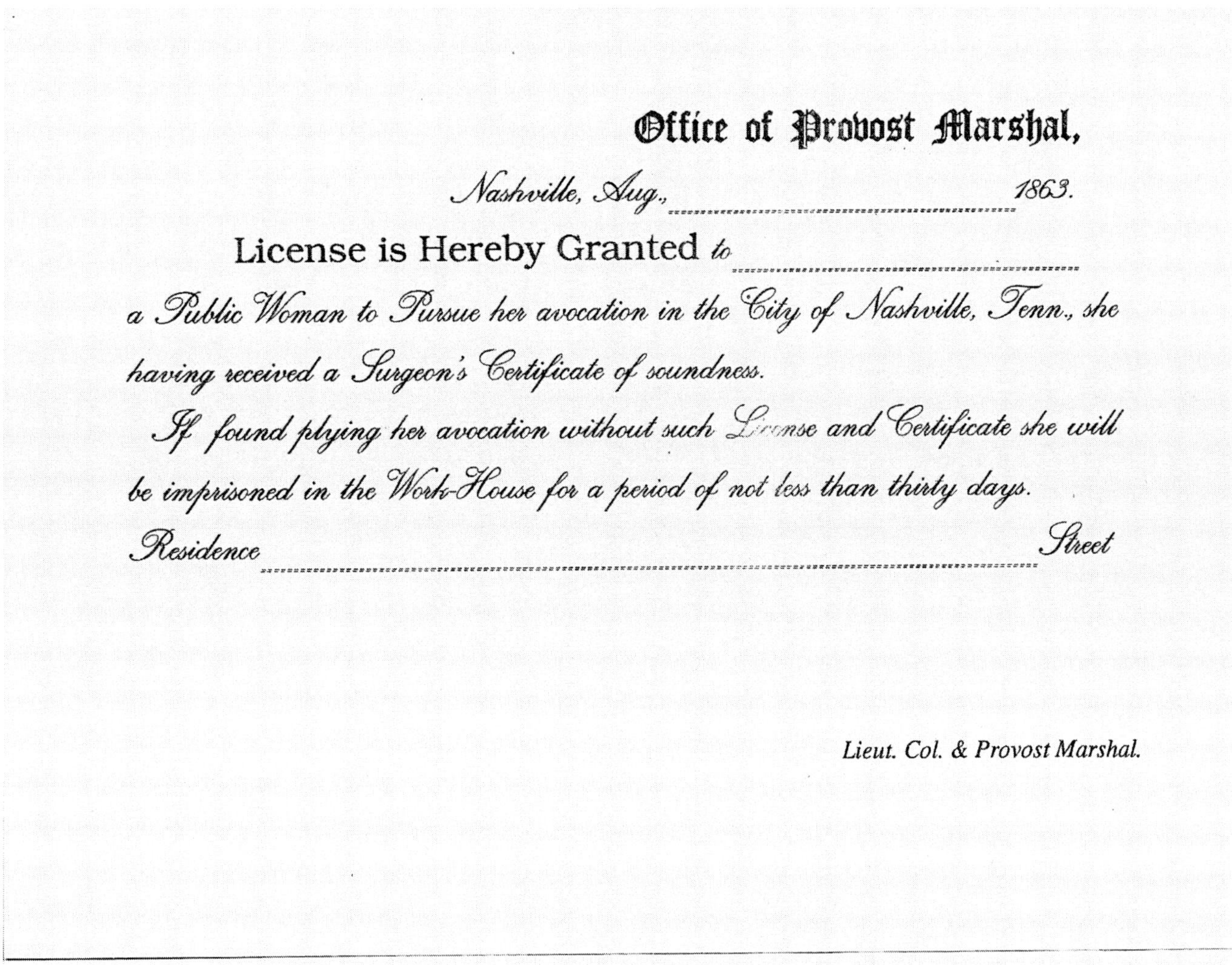

Office of Provost Marshal,

Nashville, Aug., ... *1863.*

License is Hereby Granted *to* ....

a Public Woman to Pursue her avocation in the City of Nashville, Tenn., she having received a Surgeon's Certificate of soundness.

If found plying her avocation without such License and Certificate she will be imprisoned in the Work-House for a period of not less than thirty days.

Residence .... *Street*

Lieut. Col. & Provost Marshal.

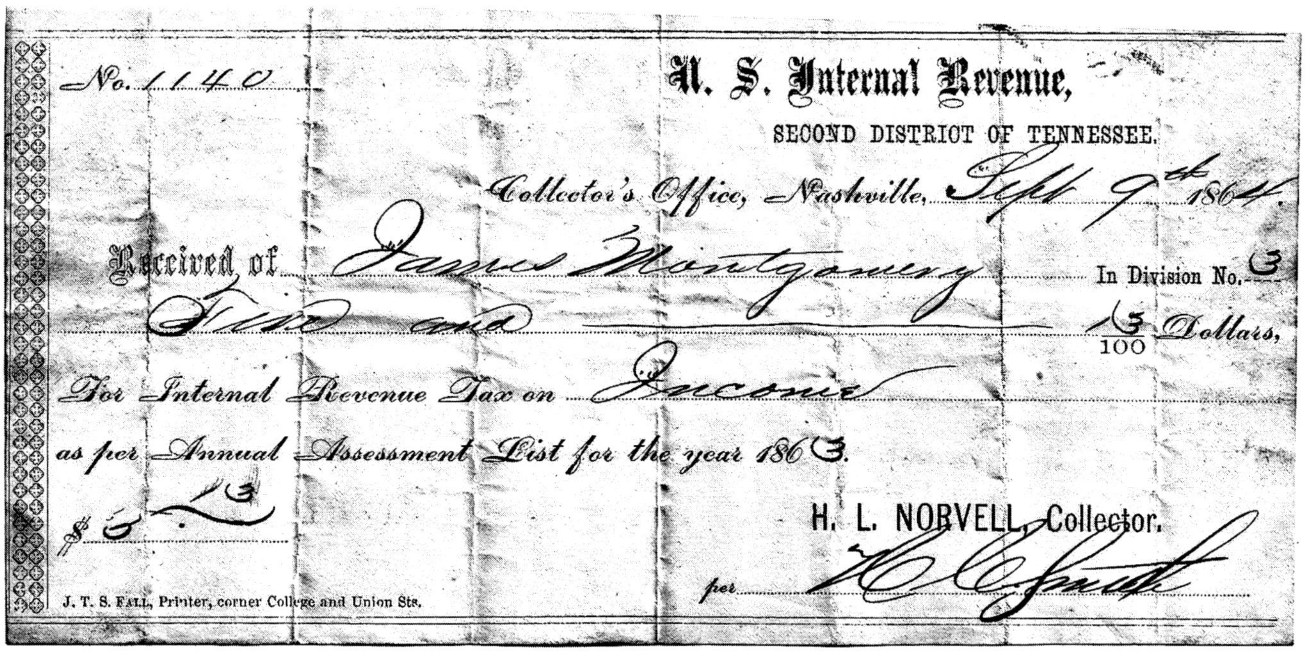

No. 1140

U. S. Internal Revenue,

SECOND DISTRICT OF TENNESSEE.

Collector's Office, Nashville, Sept 9th 1864.

Received of James Montgomery In Division No. 3

Five and 13/100 *Dollars,*

For Internal Revenue Tax on Income

*as per Annual Assessment List for the year 186*3.

$5.13

H. L. NORVELL, Collector.

per [illegible]

J. T. S. FALL, Printer, corner College and Union Sts.

Top: **Figure 93. License to "Public Woman to Pursue Her Vocation," Provost Marshal. [Facsimile] Nashville, Tennessee [August ___, 1863]. *Bottom:* Figure 94. Receipt for 1863 Income Tax, Collector. Nashville, Tennessee, September 9, 1864.**

1115

(19.)

Collector's Office,

1 District, State of Georgia

Div. No. 4 November 15th, 1867.

Mr Robit Raines Ex Est
L H Raines
Thomasville

To **The United States,** Dr.

(FOR INTERNAL REVENUE.)

	RATE.	AMOUNT TAX.
Tax on Income for the year 1866 Amount, $ 2030.	5 PER CENT.	101 50
Tax on the following articles, for the year ending March 1, 1867:		
Billiard Tables, kept for private use		
Carriages		
Plate, oz.		
Gold Watches		3 00

Amount of Tax . . . . $ 104. 50

Penalty . . . . . 5 per cent. . . . .

Total . . . . . $

Received Payment, H. F. Mabbett

Collector

Figure 95. Receipt for 1866 Income and Watch Tax, Collector. Thomasville, Georgia, November 15, 1867.

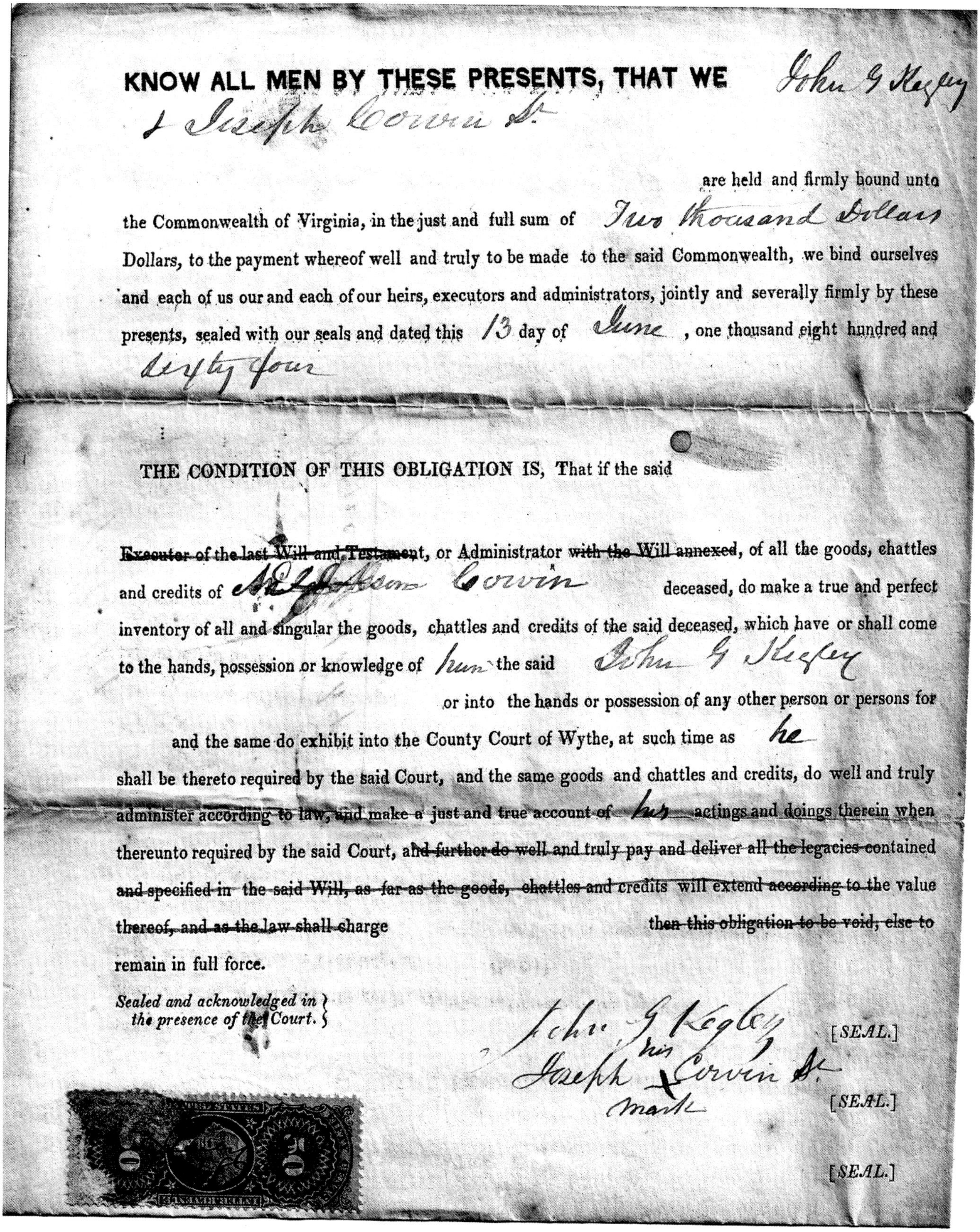

KNOW ALL MEN BY THESE PRESENTS, THAT WE John G Kegley & Joseph Corwin Sr.

are held and firmly bound unto the Commonwealth of Virginia, in the just and full sum of Two thousand Dollars Dollars, to the payment whereof well and truly to be made to the said Commonwealth, we bind ourselves and each of us our and each of our heirs, executors and administrators, jointly and severally firmly by these presents, sealed with our seals and dated this 13 day of June, one thousand eight hundred and sixty four

THE CONDITION OF THIS OBLIGATION IS, That if the said

~~Executor of the last Will and Testament~~, or Administrator ~~with the Will annexed~~, of all the goods, chattles and credits of N. Jefferson Corwin deceased, do make a true and perfect inventory of all and singular the goods, chattles and credits of the said deceased, which have or shall come to the hands, possession or knowledge of him the said John G Kegley or into the hands or possession of any other person or persons for and the same do exhibit into the County Court of Wythe, at such time as he shall be thereto required by the said Court, and the same goods and chattles and credits, do well and truly administer according to law, and make a just and true account of his actings and doings therein when thereunto required by the said Court, a~~nd further do well and truly pay and deliver all the legacies contained and specified in the said Will, as far as the goods, chattles and credits will extend according to the value thereof, and as the law shall charge~~ ~~then this obligation to be void, else to~~ remain in full force.

Sealed and acknowledged in the presence of the Court.

John G Kegley [SEAL.]

Joseph his X mark Corwin Sr. [SEAL.]

[SEAL.]

Figure 96. $12,000 Executor Bond with 50¢ U.S. Revenue Stamp affixed, County Clerk Wythe County, Virginia, July 10, 1867.

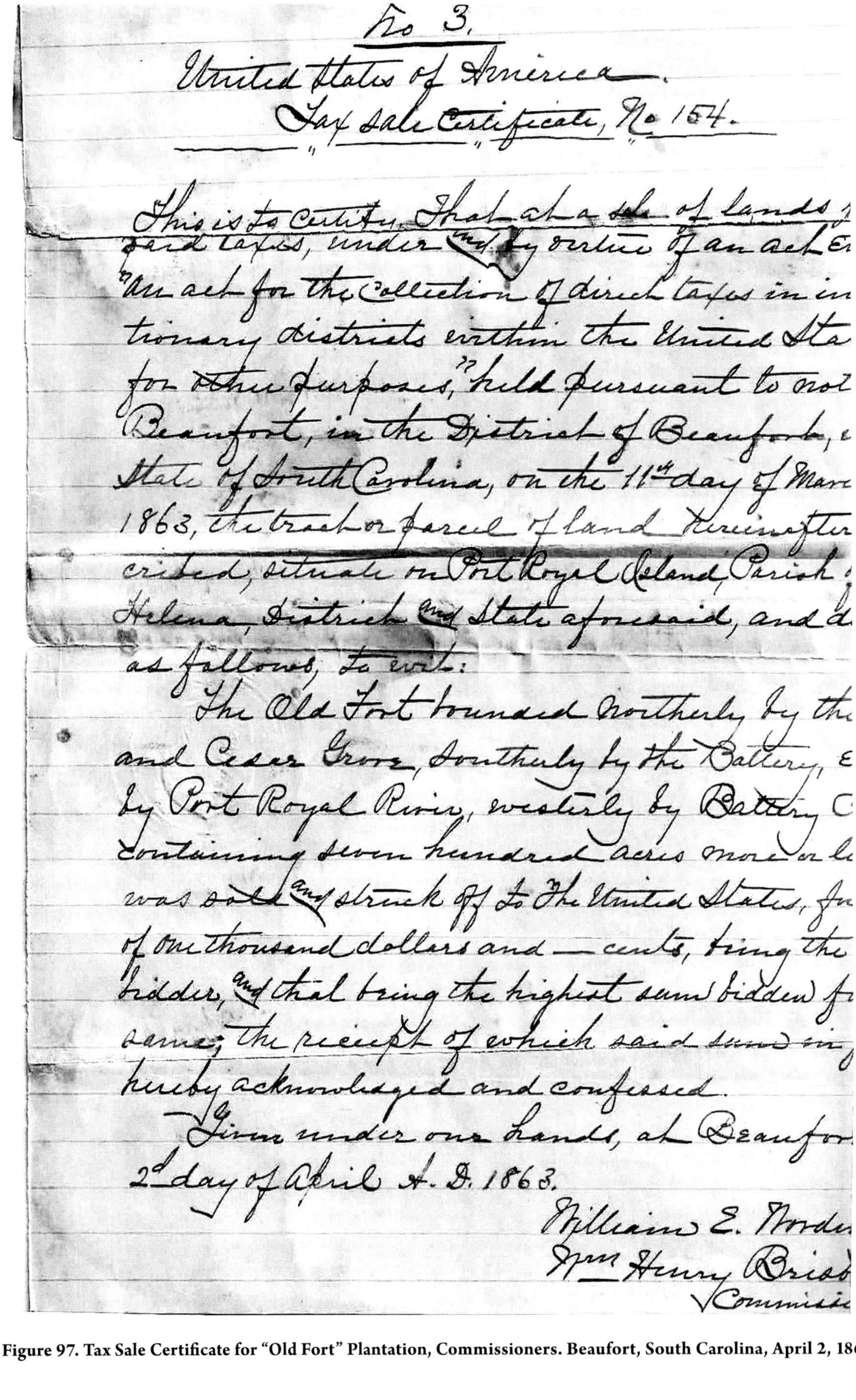

No 3.

United States of America.

Tax Sale Certificate, No 154.

This is to certify, That at a sale of lands
said taxes, under and by virtue of an act en
"An act for the Collection of direct taxes in in
tionary districts within the United Sta
for other purposes," held pursuant to not
Beaufort, in the District of Beaufort, a
State of South Carolina, on the 11th day of Marc
1863, the tract or parcel of land hereinafter
cribed, situate on Port Royal Island, Parish
Helena, District and State aforesaid, and d
as follows, to wit:

The Old Fort bounded Northerly by the
and Cedar Grove, Southerly by the Battery, E
by Port Royal River, westerly by Battery C
containing seven hundred acres more or le
was sold and struck off to The United States, fo
of one thousand dollars and — cents, being the
bidder, and that being the highest sum bidden f
same; the receipt of which said sum is
hereby acknowledged and confessed.

Given under our hands, at Beaufor
2d day of April A. D. 1863.

William E. Worde
Wm Henry Brisb
Commissi

Figure 97. Tax Sale Certificate for "Old Fort" Plantation, Commissioners. Beaufort, South Carolina, April 2, 1863.

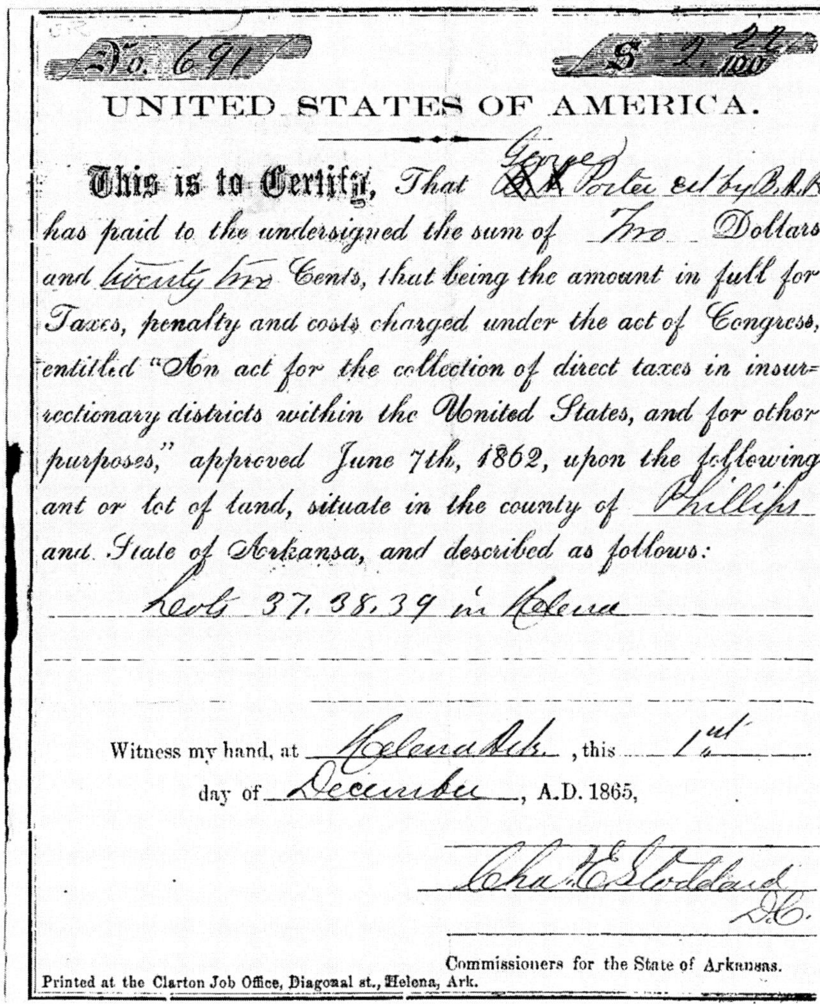

No. 691 $ 2.22/100

UNITED STATES OF AMERICA.

This is to Certify, That George Porter [illegible] by B. A. Porter has paid to the undersigned the sum of Two Dollars and twenty two Cents, that being the amount in full for Taxes, penalty and costs charged under the act of Congress, entitled "An act for the collection of direct taxes in insurrectionary districts within the United States, and for other purposes," approved June 7th, 1862, upon the following ant or lot of land, situate in the county of Phillips and State of Arkansa, and described as follows:

Lots 37, 38, 39 in Helena

Witness my hand, at Helena Ark, this 1st day of December, A.D. 1865,

Chas. E. Stoddard
D.C.

Commissioners for the State of Arkansas.

Printed at the Clarton Job Office, Diagonal st., Helena, Ark.

Figure 98. Receipt for Direct Taxes Paid, Commissioners. Charleston, South Carolina, May 5, 1865.

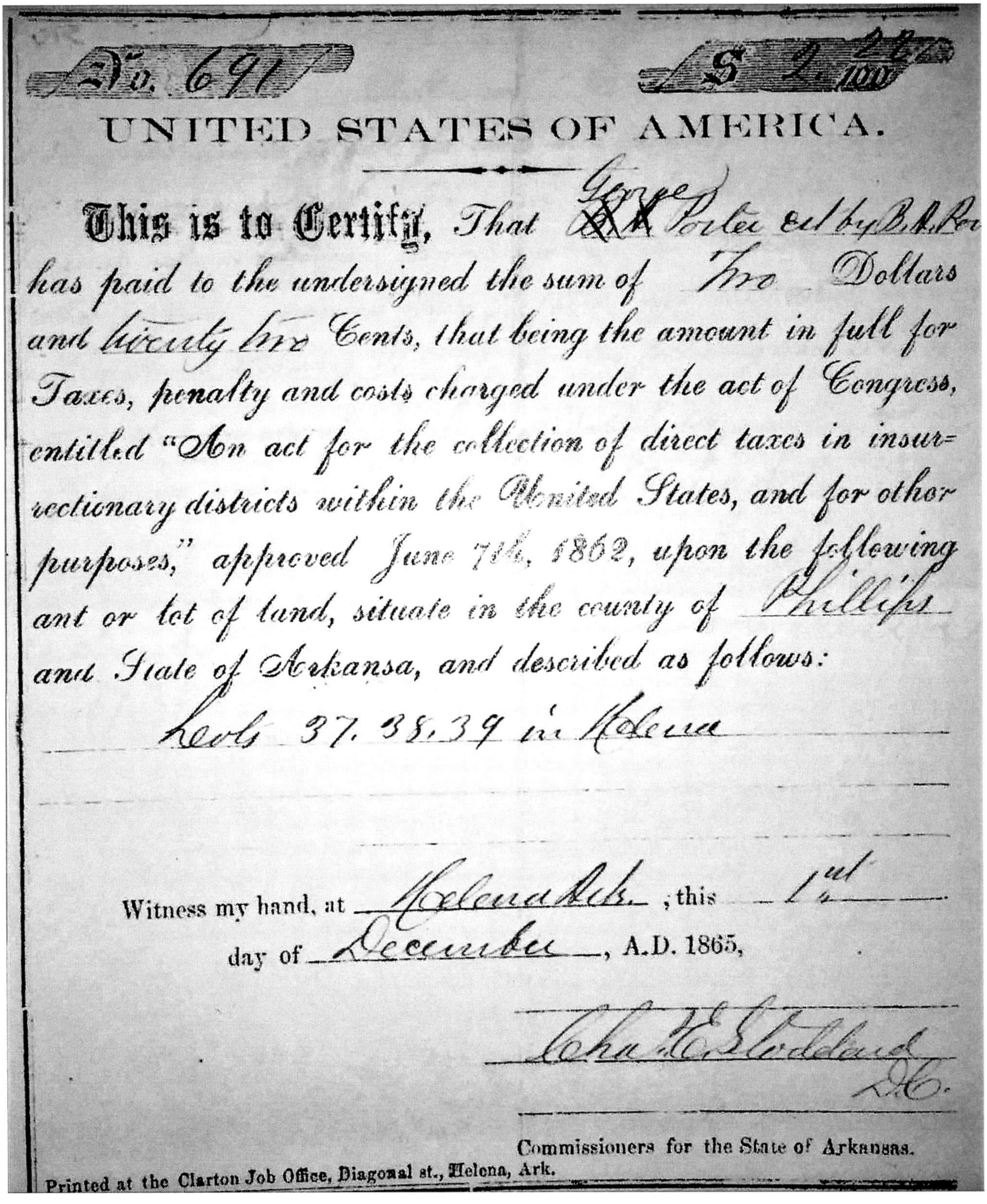

No. 691 $ 2 22/100

UNITED STATES OF AMERICA.

This is to Certify, That George Porter ex'd by B. A. Por has paid to the undersigned the sum of Two Dollars and twenty two Cents, that being the amount in full for Taxes, penalty and costs charged under the act of Congress, entitled "An act for the collection of direct taxes in insurrectionary districts within the United States, and for other purposes," approved June 7th, 1862, upon the following ant or lot of land, situate in the county of Phillips and State of Arkansa, and described as follows:

Lots 37. 38. 39 in Helena

Witness my hand, at Helena Ark., this 1st day of December, A.D. 1865,

Chas E. Stoddard
D.C.

Commissioners for the State of Arkansas.

Printed at the Clarton Job Office, Diagonal st., Helena, Ark.

Figure 99. Receipt for Direct Taxes, Commissioners. Helena, Arkansas, December 1, 1865.

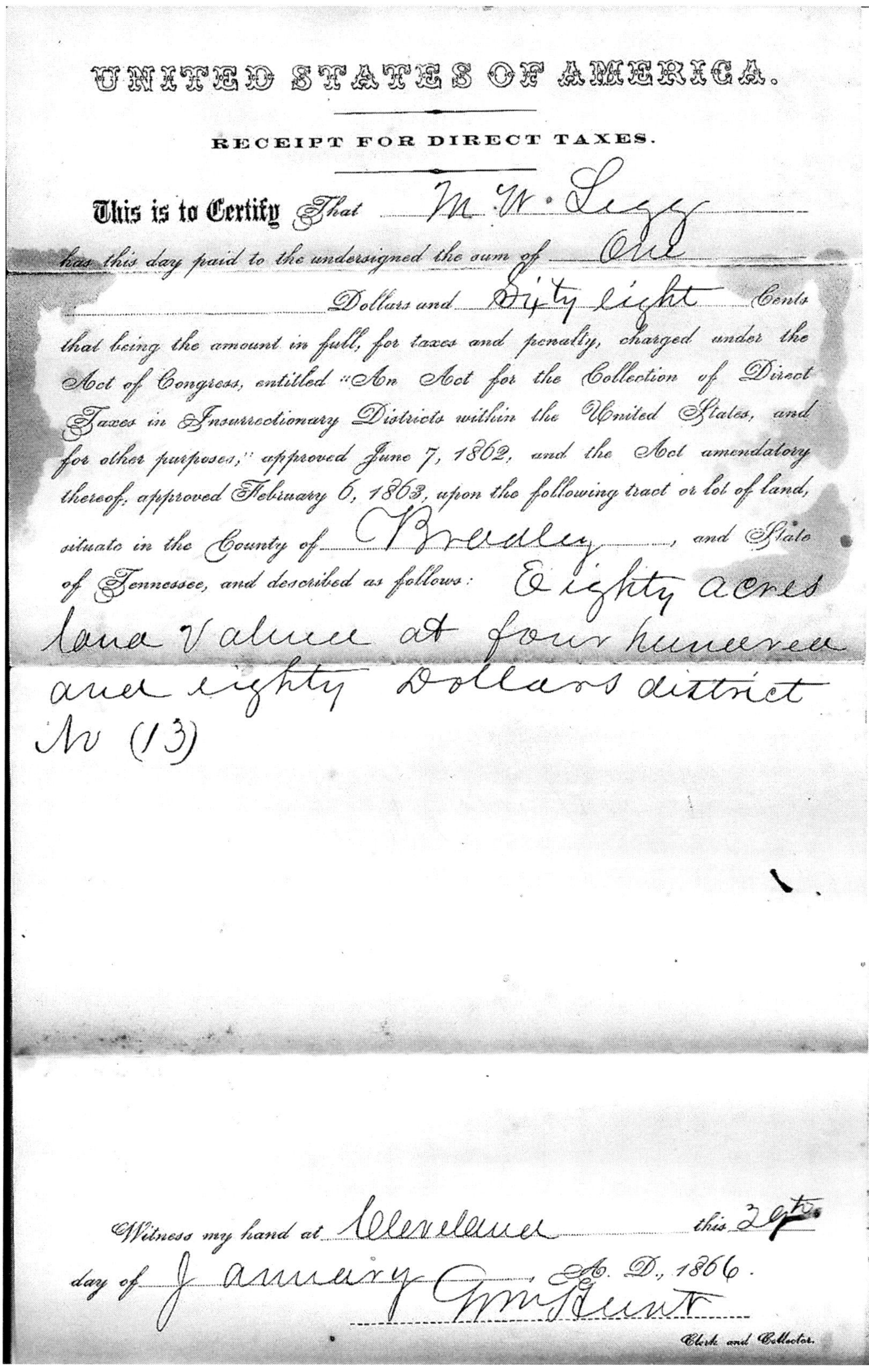

UNITED STATES OF AMERICA.

RECEIPT FOR DIRECT TAXES.

This is to Certify That M. W. Legg has this day paid to the undersigned the sum of One Dollars and Sixty eight Cents that being the amount in full, for taxes and penalty, charged under the Act of Congress, entitled "An Act for the Collection of Direct Taxes in Insurrectionary Districts within the United States, and for other purposes," approved June 7, 1862, and the Act amendatory thereof, approved February 6, 1863, upon the following tract or lot of land, situate in the County of Bradley, and State of Tennessee, and described as follows: Eighty acres land valued at four hundred and eighty Dollars district No (13)

Witness my hand at Cleveland this 21st day of January A. D., 1866.

Wm Hunt

Clerk and Collector.

Figure 100. Receipt for Direct Taxes, Collector. Cleveland, Bradley County, Tennessee, January 21, 1866.

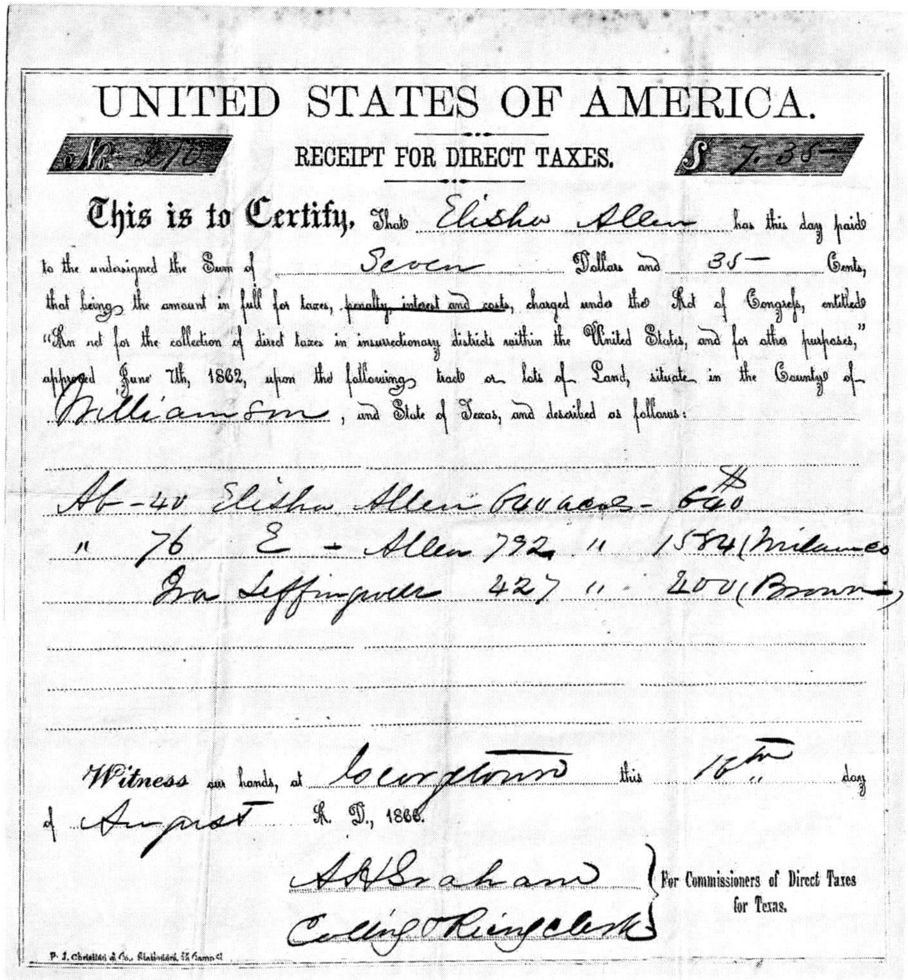

UNITED STATES OF AMERICA.

No. 210 RECEIPT FOR DIRECT TAXES. $7.35

This is to Certify, That Elisha Allen has this day paid to the undersigned the Sum of Seven Dollars and 35 Cents, that being the amount in full for taxes, penalty interest and costs, charged under the Act of Congress, entitled "An act for the collection of direct taxes in insurrectionary districts within the United States, and for other purposes," approved June 7th, 1862, upon the following tract or lots of Land, situate in the County of Williamson, and State of Texas, and described as follows:

Ab-40 Elisha Allen 640 acres - 640
" 76 E. Allen 792 " 1584 (Milam Co)
Ira Leffingwell 427 " 200 (Brown)

Witness our hands, at Georgetown this 16th day of August A. D., 1866.

A. H. Graham } For Commissioners of Direct Taxes for Texas.
Collins O King clerk

P. J. Christian & Co. Stationers, 55 Camp St.

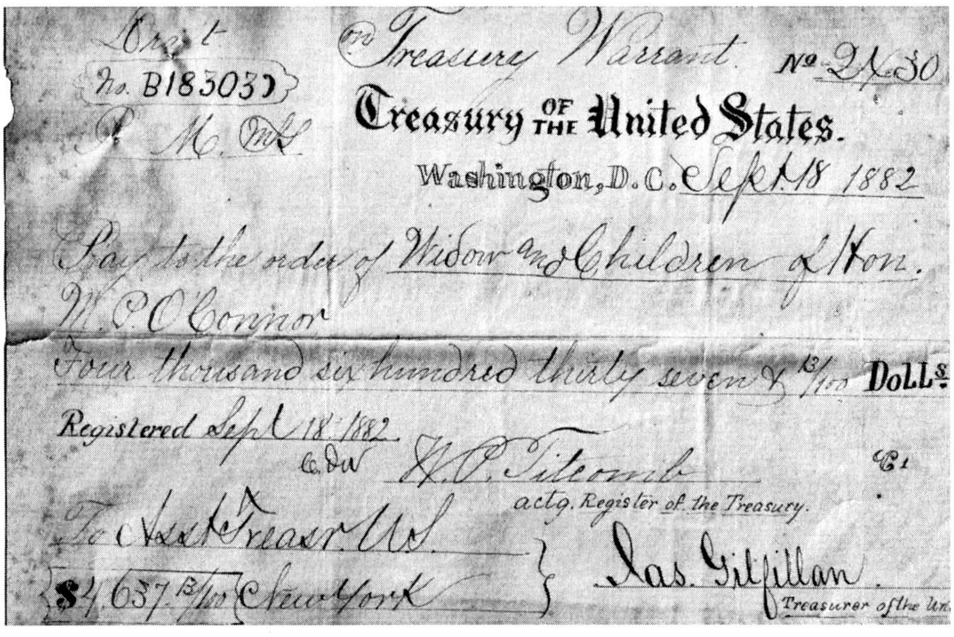

Treasury Warrant No. 2430

No. B183037

Treasury of the United States.

Washington, D.C. Sept 18 1882

Pay to the order of Widow and Children of Hon. M. P. O'Connor

Four thousand six hundred thirty seven & 13/100 Dolls.

Registered Sept 18 1882

H. C. Titcomb
actg. Register of the Treasury.

To Asst Treasr U.S.
$4,637 13/100 New York } Jas. Gilfillan
Treasurer of the Un[ited States]

Figure 101. Receipt for Direct Tax, Commissioner. Georgetown, Texas, April 16, 1866.
Figure 102. Treasury Warrant For Property Sold for Unpaid Direct Tax, Treasurer. Beaufort, South Carolina, Washington, [Manuscript], September 18, 1882.

EXECUTIVE DEPARTMENT,

MILLEDGEVILLE, GA., JAN. 18TH, 1866.

TO THE JUSTICES OF THE INFERIOR COURT:

GENTLEMEN:—By an Act, approved March 17, 1864, it is provided that all Bonds hereafter taken from Receivers of Tax Returns, shall be taken for one-half of the amount of the State Tax, supposed to be due from the county for the year in which said officers shall give Bond; and Tax Collectors are to give Bond for thirty-three and one-third per cent. more than the supposed tax; "the amount of said Bonds to be filled up by the Comptroller General before being sent out to the several counties from the Executive office."

As the Legislature has not yet passed a Tax Act, and the Comptroller General cannot fill up the Bonds until said Act is passed, they are withheld for the present. As soon as the Comptroller General fills up the Bonds they will be forwarded.

Very respectfully,

H. J. G. Williams

SECRETARY EXECUTIVE DEPARTMENT.

Joseph Walker, Agt., Printer, 129 Meeting-street

No. 2852 CHARLESTON, May 26 1866.

Received from Miss Abbey S. Legare
Six
Dollars, — Cents, the amount of her General Tax, for the year one thousand eight hundred and sixty-five, for the Parishes of St. Philip's and St. Michael's, as per Return.

[signature]
Tax Collector for St. Philip's and St. Michael's.

6.00	St. Philip's and St Michael's.
60	Road Tax.
—	Cross-Road Tax.
60	Pub. Build. Tax.
7.20	Fee for late Return $1.00

Top: **Figure 103. Notice of Surety Bond Reduction for Tax Receivers, Executive Department. Milledgeville, Georgia, June 18, 1866.**
Bottom: **Figure 104. Receipt of General Taxes for St. Philip's and St. Michael's Parishes, Tax Collector. Charleston, May 26, 1866.**

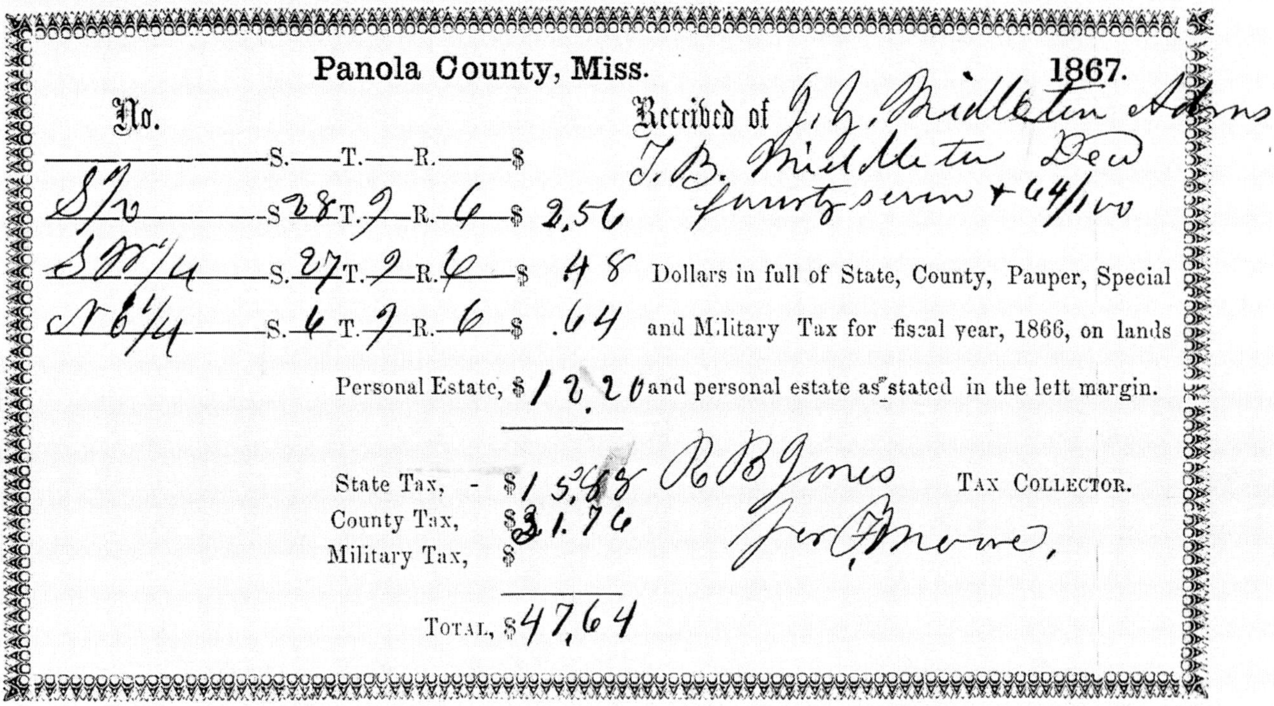

Panola County, Miss. 1867.

No. Received of J. J. Middleton Adms T. B. Middleton Decd

———S.——T.——R.——$

S ½ ——S. 28 T. 9 R. 6 $ 2.56 forty seven + 64/100

S W ¼ ——S. 27 T. 9 R. 6 $ 48 Dollars in full of State, County, Pauper, Special

N E ¼ ——S. 4 T. 9 R. 6 $ .64 and Military Tax for fiscal year, 1866, on lands

Personal Estate, $ 12.20 and personal estate as stated in the left margin.

State Tax, - $ 15.88 R B Jones TAX COLLECTOR.

County Tax, $ 31.76

Military Tax, $

TOTAL, $ 47.64

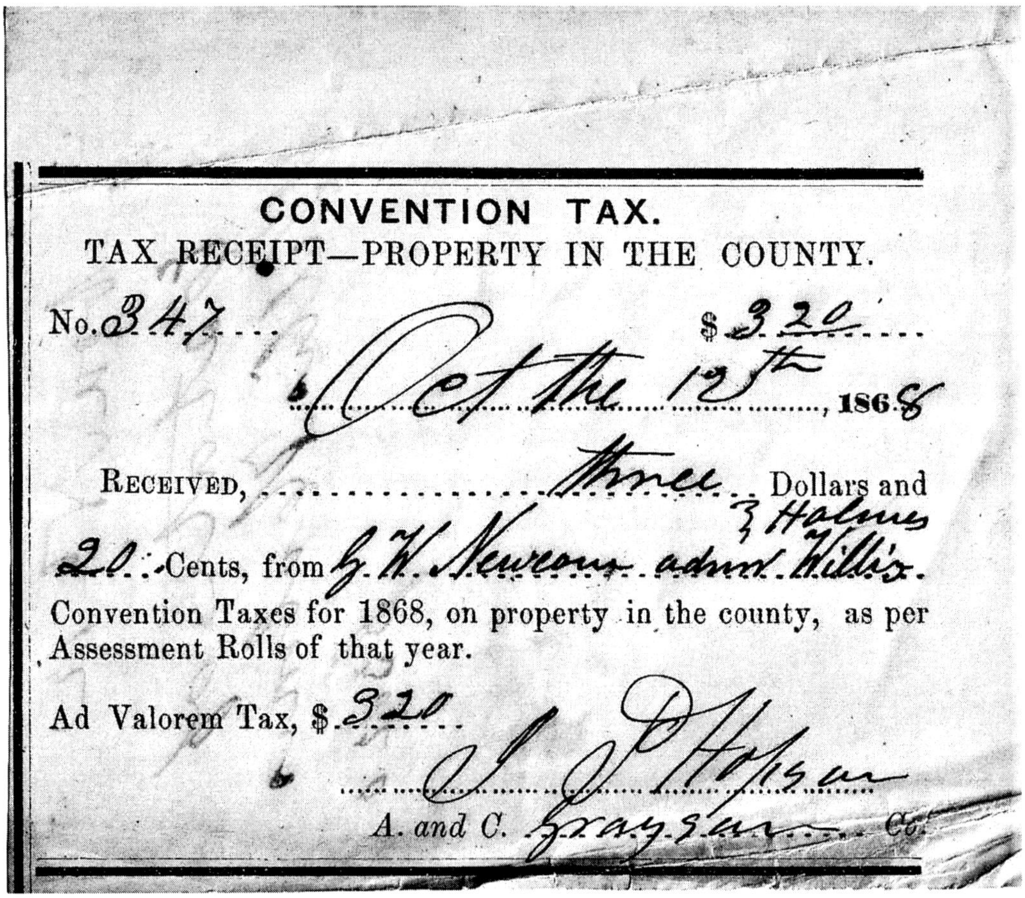

CONVENTION TAX.

TAX RECEIPT—PROPERTY IN THE COUNTY.

No. 347 $ 3.20

Oct the 12th, 1868

RECEIVED, three Dollars and

20 Cents, from G. W. Newsom adm. Willis Holmes

Convention Taxes for 1868, on property in the county, as per Assessment Rolls of that year.

Ad Valorem Tax, $ 3.20

A. and C. Grayson Co.

Top: **Figure 105. Receipt for State, Pauper, Special and Military Tax, Tax Collector. Panola County, Mississippi, 1867.** ***Bottom:*** **Figure 106. "Convention Tax" Receipt, Collector. Grayson County, Texas, October 12, 1868.**

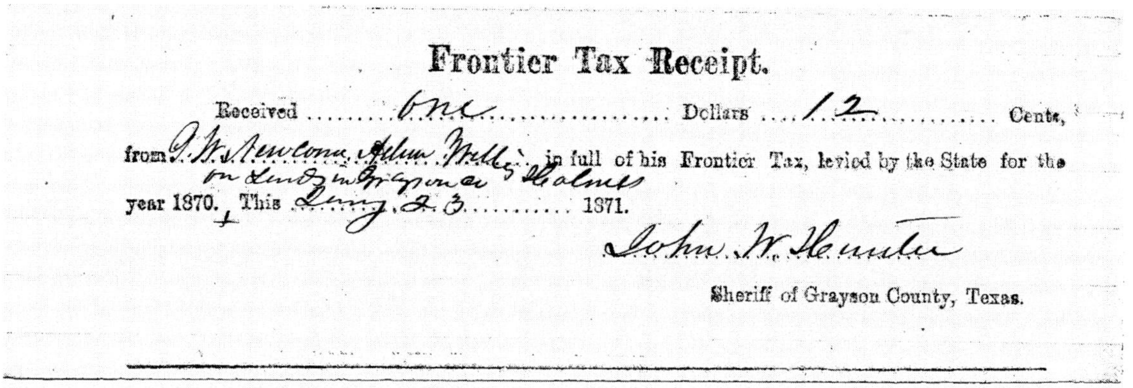

Frontier Tax Receipt.

Received .... one .... Dollars .... 12 .... Cents,

from [illegible] in full of his Frontier Tax, levied by the State for the year 1870. This Jany. 23 .... 1871.

John W. Hunter

Sheriff of Grayson County, Texas.

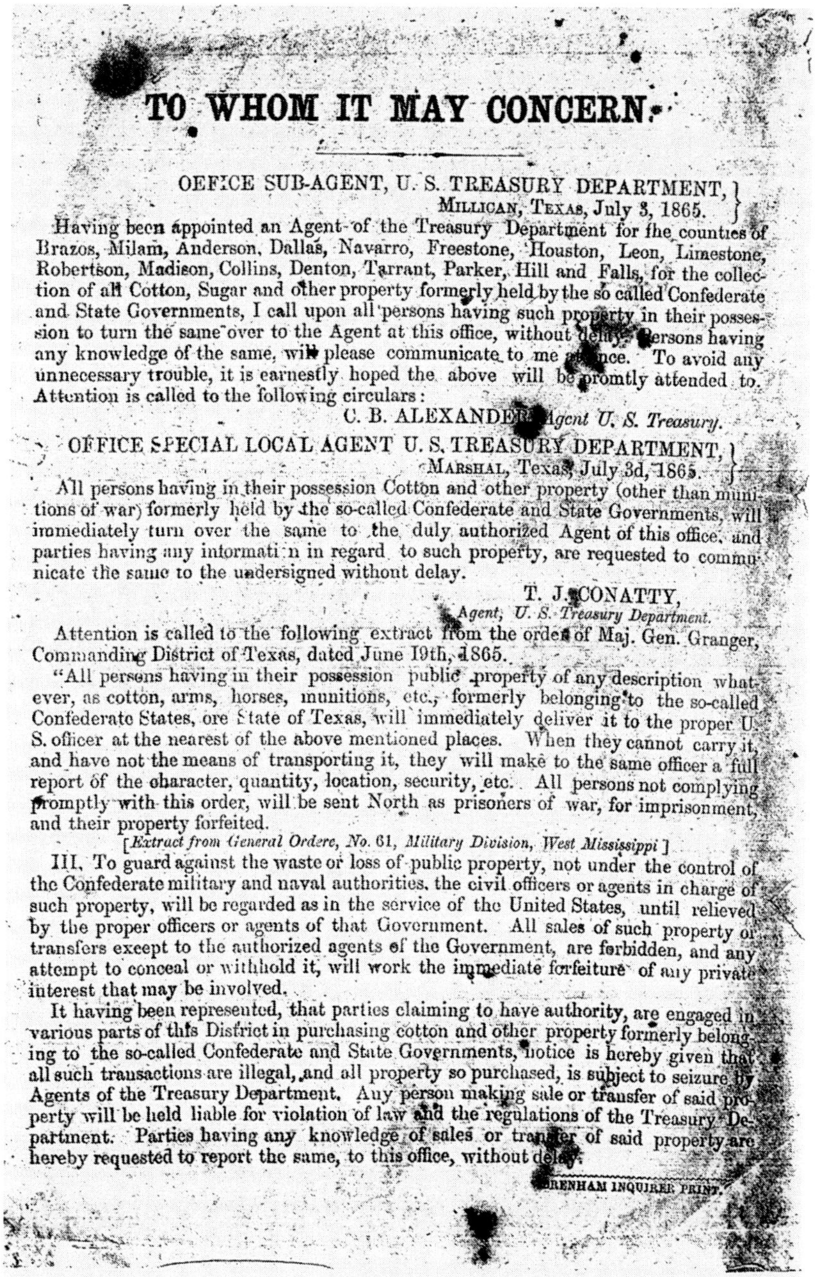

TO WHOM IT MAY CONCERN.

OFFICE SUB-AGENT, U. S. TREASURY DEPARTMENT,
MILLICAN, TEXAS, July 3, 1865.

Having been appointed an Agent of the Treasury Department for the counties of Brazos, Milam, Anderson, Dallas, Navarro, Freestone, Houston, Leon, Limestone, Robertson, Madison, Collins, Denton, Tarrant, Parker, Hill and Falls, for the collection of all Cotton, Sugar and other property formerly held by the so called Confederate and State Governments, I call upon all persons having such property in their possession to turn the same over to the Agent at this office, without delay. Persons having any knowledge of the same, will please communicate to me at once. To avoid any unnecessary trouble, it is earnestly hoped the above will be promtly attended to. Attention is called to the following circulars:

C. B. ALEXANDER, *Agent U. S. Treasury.*

OFFICE SPECIAL LOCAL AGENT U. S. TREASURY DEPARTMENT,
MARSHAL, Texas, July 3d, 1865.

All persons having in their possession Cotton and other property (other than munitions of war) formerly held by the so-called Confederate and State Governments, will immediately turn over the same to the duly authorized Agent of this office, and parties having any information in regard to such property, are requested to communicate the same to the undersigned without delay.

T. J. CONATTY,
Agent, U. S. Treasury Department.

Attention is called to the following extract from the order of Maj. Gen. Granger, Commanding District of Texas, dated June 19th, 1865.

"All persons having in their possession public property of any description whatever, as cotton, arms, horses, munitions, etc., formerly belonging to the so-called Confederate States, ore State of Texas, will immediately deliver it to the proper U. S. officer at the nearest of the above mentioned places. When they cannot carry it, and have not the means of transporting it, they will make to the same officer a full report of the character, quantity, location, security, etc. All persons not complying promptly with this order, will be sent North as prisoners of war, for imprisonment, and their property forfeited.

[*Extract from General Ordere, No. 61, Military Division, West Mississippi*]

III. To guard against the waste or loss of public property, not under the control of the Confederate military and naval authorities, the civil officers or agents in charge of such property, will be regarded as in the service of the United States, until relieved by the proper officers or agents of that Government. All sales of such property or transfers except to the authorized agents of the Government, are forbidden, and any attempt to conceal or withhold it, will work the immediate forfeiture of any private interest that may be involved.

It having been represented, that parties claiming to have authority, are engaged in various parts of this District in purchasing cotton and other property formerly belonging to the so-called Confederate and State Governments, notice is hereby given that all such transactions are illegal, and all property so purchased, is subject to seizure by Agents of the Treasury Department. Any person making sale or transfer of said property will be held liable for violation of law and the regulations of the Treasury Department. Parties having any knowledge of sales or transfer of said property are hereby requested to report the same, to this office, without delay.

BRENHAM INQUIRER PRINT.

Top: Figure 107. "Frontier Tax" Receipt, Sheriff. Grayson County, Texas, January 23, 1871. *Bottom:* Figure 108. Notice "To Whom It May Concern" To Turn Over Cotton, etc., Agent. Millican and Marshall, Texas, July 3, 1865.

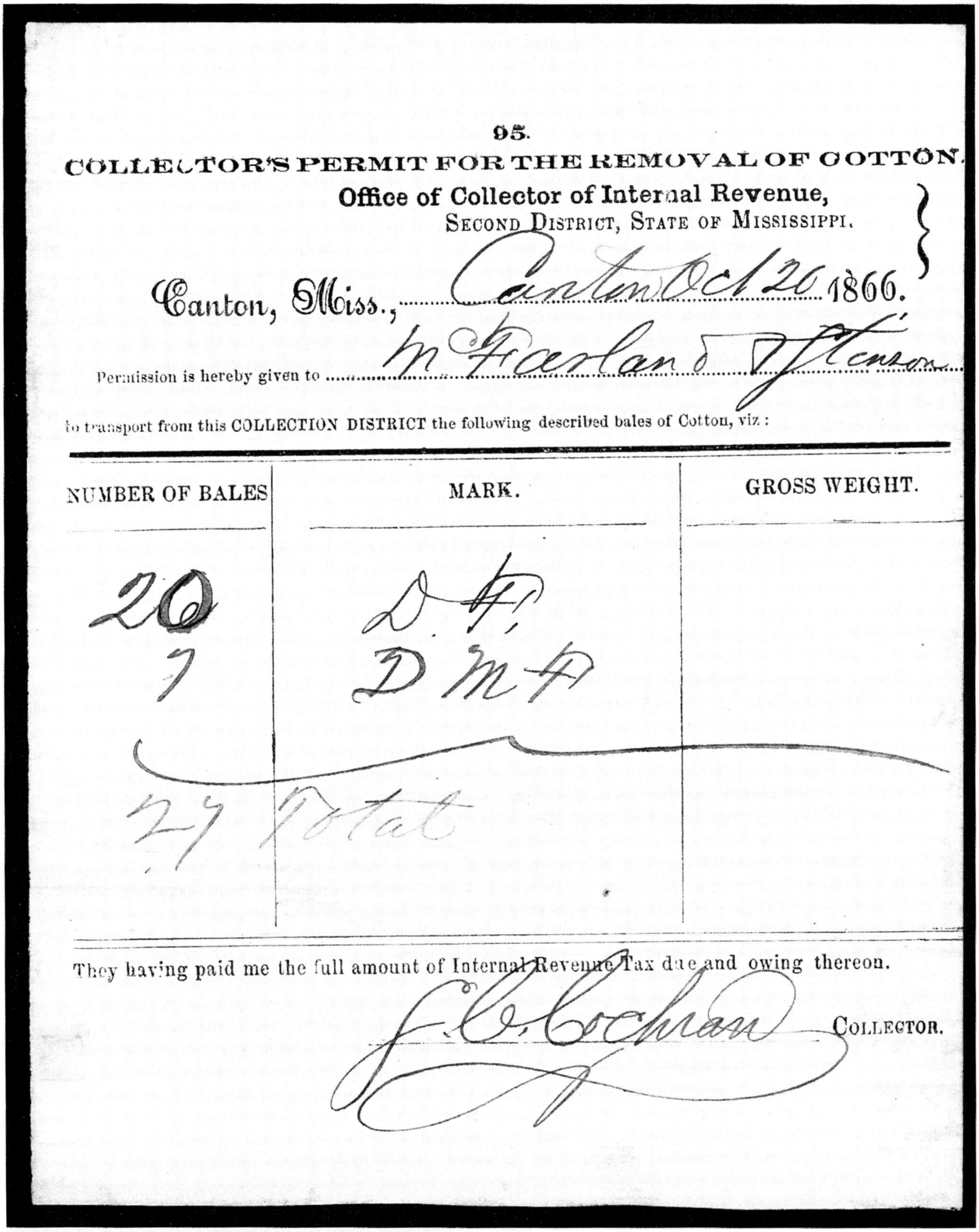

95.

COLLECTOR'S PERMIT FOR THE REMOVAL OF COTTON.

Office of Collector of Internal Revenue,
SECOND DISTRICT, STATE OF MISSISSIPPI.

Canton, Miss., Canton Oct 20 1866.

Permission is hereby given to McFarland & Stenson

to transport from this COLLECTION DISTRICT the following described bales of Cotton, viz:

NUMBER OF BALES	MARK.	GROSS WEIGHT.
20	D F	
7	D M F	
27	Total	

They having paid me the full amount of Internal Revenue Tax due and owing thereon.

J. C. Cochran COLLECTOR.

Figure 109. Permit Removal of Cotton, Collector. Canton, Mississippi, October 26, 1866.

State of Indiana, } SS.:
Cass County, }

Auditor's Office, Jany 20 A. D., 1866

On this 20" day of January, A. D., 1866, personally appeared before W. G. Nash Auditor of said County Matthias Bechdol who being duly sworn upon his oath declares that Daniel S. Bechdol

was a soldier in the service of the United States, in the war for the suppression of the Southern Rebellion; that he was in such service for more than one year; that he was not a substitute, and has not received bounty from any county to the amount of three hundred dollars, or over.

Subscribed and sworn to this 20 day of Jany 1864

Witness W. G. Nash

Auditor of said County, this 20th

... A. D. 1866

Figure 110. Application for Soldier Exemption from Military Poll Tax, Auditor. Cass County, Indiana, January 20, 1866.

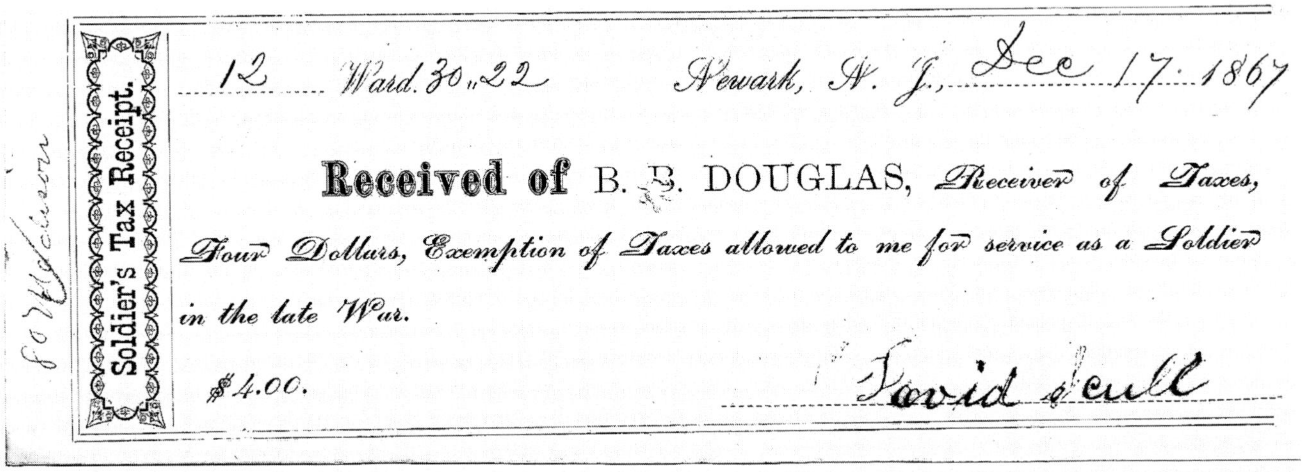

Soldier's Tax Receipt.

12 Ward. 30 " 22 Newark, N. J., Dec 17 1867

Received of B. B. DOUGLAS, Receiver of Taxes,

Four Dollars, Exemption of Taxes allowed to me for service as a Soldier in the late War.

$4.00. David Scull

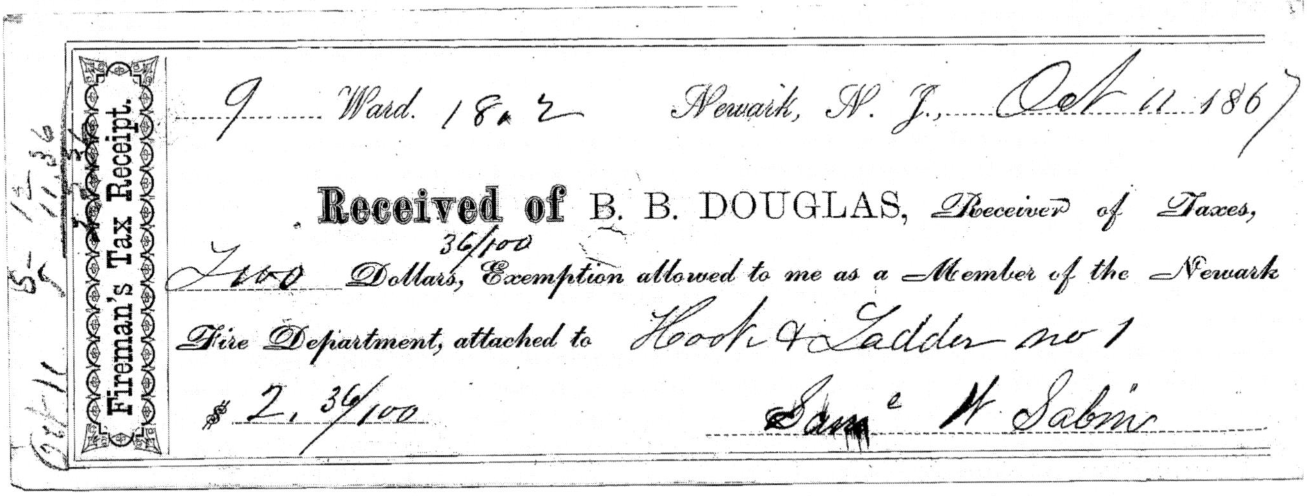

Fireman's Tax Receipt.

9 Ward. 18 " 2 Newark, N. J., Oct 11 1867

Received of B. B. DOUGLAS, Receiver of Taxes,

Two 36/100 Dollars, Exemption allowed to me as a Member of the Newark Fire Department, attached to Hook & Ladder no 1

$ 2, 36/100 Saml W. Sabin

Top: **Figure 111. Receipt of $4.00 for Tax Credit for Soldier Poll Tax Exemption, Receiver. Newark, New Jersey, December 17, 1867.**
Bottom: **Figure 112. Receipt of 10 percent Tax Credit for Fireman, Receiver. Newark, New Jersey, October 11, 1867.**

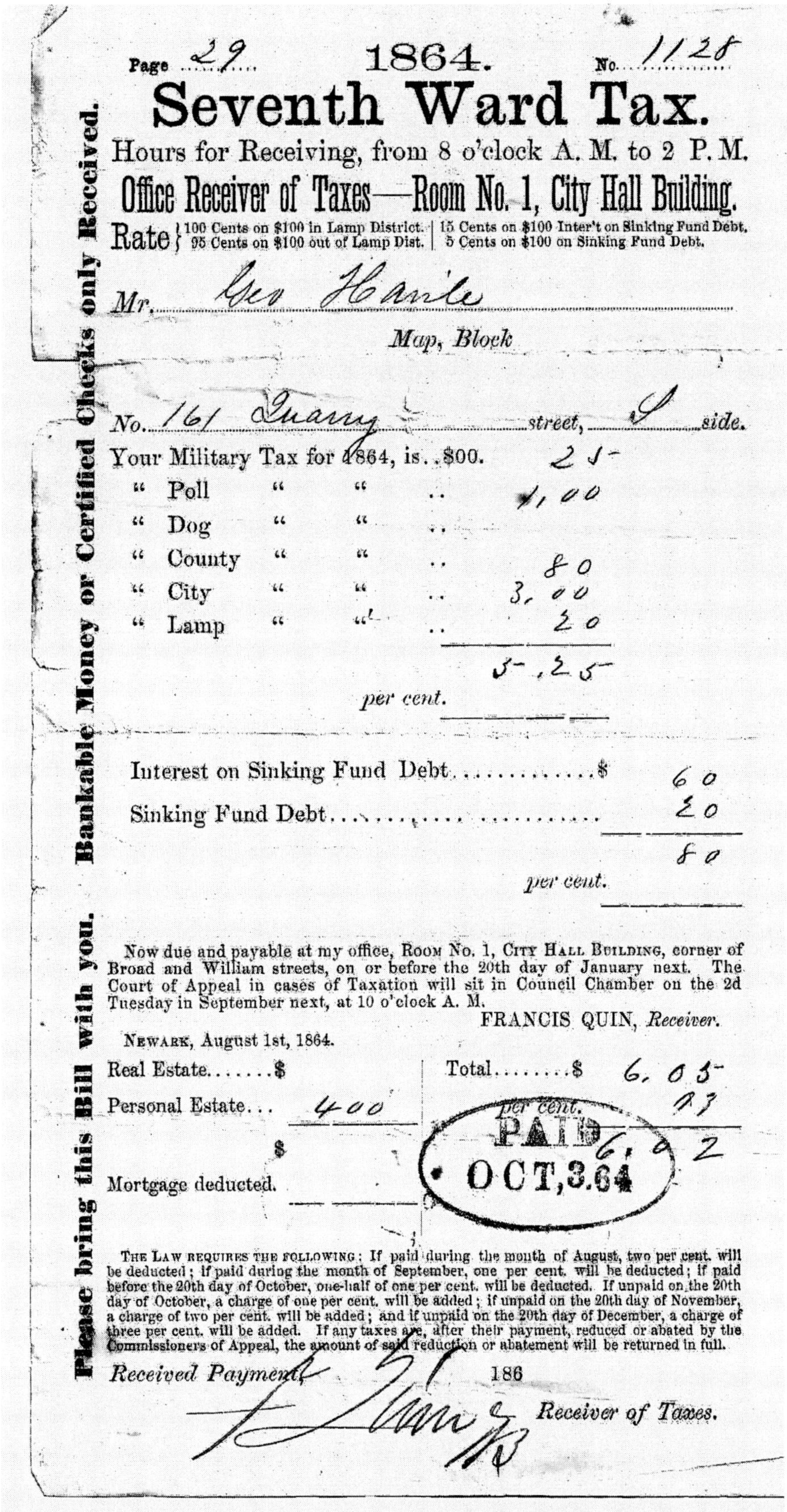

Page 29 1864. No. 1128

Seventh Ward Tax.

Hours for Receiving, from 8 o'clock A. M. to 2 P. M.

Office Receiver of Taxes—Room No. 1, City Hall Building.

Rate { 100 Cents on $100 in Lamp District. / 95 Cents on $100 out of Lamp Dist. | 15 Cents on $100 Inter't on Sinking Fund Debt. / 5 Cents on $100 on Sinking Fund Debt.

Mr. Geo Haile

Map, Block

No. 161 Quarry *street,* S *side.*

Your Military Tax for 1864, is..$00.	25
" Poll " " ..	1,00
" Dog " " ..	
" County " " ..	80
" City " " ..	3,00
" Lamp " " ..	20
	5,25
per cent.	

Interest on Sinking Fund Debt............$	60
Sinking Fund Debt........................	20
	80
per cent.	

Now due and payable at my office, Room No. 1, City Hall Building, corner of Broad and William streets, on or before the 20th day of January next. The Court of Appeal in cases of Taxation will sit in Council Chamber on the 2d Tuesday in September next, at 10 o'clock A. M.

FRANCIS QUIN, *Receiver.*

Newark, August 1st, 1864.

Real Estate.......$		Total........$	6,05
Personal Estate...	400	*per cent.*	03
$			6,02
Mortgage deducted.			

PAID OCT,3.64

The Law requires the following: If paid during the month of August, two per cent. will be deducted; if paid during the month of September, one per cent. will be deducted; if paid before the 20th day of October, one-half of one per cent. will be deducted. If unpaid on the 20th day of October, a charge of one per cent. will be added; if unpaid on the 20th day of November, a charge of two per cent. will be added; and if unpaid on the 20th day of December, a charge of three per cent. will be added. If any taxes are, after their payment, reduced or abated by the Commissioners of Appeal, the amount of said reduction or abatement will be returned in full.

Received Payment 186

Receiver of Taxes.

Please bring this Bill with you. Bankable Money or Certified Checks only Received.

Figure 113. Receipt for 1864 Military, Poll, etc., tax, Receiver. Newark, New Jersey, October 3, 1864.

(24.)

UNITED STATES INTERNAL REVENUE.

ANNUAL TAXES, 1869.

By the act of June 30, 1864, as amended by the first section of the act of March 2, 1867, it is made the duty of any person liable to annual tax, on or before the first day of March in each year, to make a return to the assistant assessor of the district wherein he resides, of his income, and of the articles in Schedule A owned or kept by him on the first day of March.

Every person failing to make such return by the day specified will be liable to be assessed by the assistant assessor according to the best information which he can obtain; and in such case the assistant assessor will add fifty per cent. to the amount of the tax, and from the valuation and enumeration so made there can be no appeal.

In case any person shall deliver to an assessor any false or fraudulent list or statement, with intent to defeat or evade the valuation or enumeration required by law, the assistant assessor will add one hundred per cent. to the tax.

The assessment list, when completed, will be returned to the collector, who will "give notice by advertisement in one newspaper published in each county in his collection district, if any there be, and if not, then in a newspaper printed in an adjoining county, and by notification, to be posted in at least four public places in each county in his collection district, that the said duties have become due and payable, and state the time and place within said county at which he or his deputy will attend to receive the same;" and to any sum unpaid after the thirtieth day of April, and for ten days after demand, there will be an addition of five per cent. as a penalty for such neglect, and of interest at one per cent. per month.

Guardians, trustees, executors and administrators, and persons acting in any other fiduciary capacity, are required to make returns of the income belonging to minors, or other persons for whom they act, and the income tax will be assessed upon the amount returned, after deducting such sums as are exempted by law; *provided* that the exemption of one thousand dollars shall not be allowed on account of any minor or other beneficiary of a trust except upon the statement of the guardian or trustee, made under oath, that the minor or beneficiary has no other income from which the said amount may be exempted and deducted.

When coupons of United States bonds, or gold received as interest on bonds, are sold within the year, the amount of legal tender currency received therefor should be returned as income under paragraph 9.

When any person has gold, or coupons payable in gold, on hand at the close of the year, its value should be returned at the value of gold at the close of the year. This value in New York was 135.

Articles embraced in Schedule A must be returned in the list printed on this sheet.

The following table may be used for converting Avoirdupois into Troy ounces:

10 ounces Avoirdupois equal	9 ounces Troy.	80 ounces Avoirdupois equal	73 ounces Troy.
20 " " "	19 " "	90 " " "	82 " "
40 " " "	37 " "	100 " " "	91 " "
50 " " "	46 " "	200 " " "	182 " "
60 " " "	55 " "	500 " " "	456 " "
70 " " "	64 " "	1000 " " "	912 " "

Where any articles named in Schedule A are owned, possessed, or kept by a partnership, firm, association, or corporation, they must be returned to the assistant assessor of the district in which such partnership, firm, association, or corporation has its office or principal place of business.

When such articles are held by an individual, the return will be made in the district in which he or she resides

Figure 114 (this page and 2 pages following). Internal Revenue Annual Tax Return, Assistant Treasurer. Logan County, Ohio, June 9, 1869.

CARRIAGES, GOLD WATCHES, BILLIARD TABLES, GOLD AND SILVER PLATE.

SCHEDULE A—SECTION 100, ACT JUNE 30, 1864, AS AMENDED JULY 13, 1866.

No.	TAXABLE ARTICLES.	RATE.	AMOUNT OF TAX.	
	Carriage, phæton, carryall, rockaway, or other like carriage, and any coach, hackney coach, omnibus, or four-wheeled carriage, the body of which rests upon springs of any description, which is kept for use, for hire, or for passengers, and which is not used exclusively in husbandry or in the transportation of merchandise, valued at exceeding three hundred dollars and not exceeding five hundred dollars, including harness used therewith........	$6 00		
	Carriages of like description valued at above five hundred dollars........................	10 00		
	Gold watches, composed wholly or in part of gold or gilt, kept for use, valued at one hundred dollars or less..................	1 00		
	Gold watches, composed wholly or in part of gold or gilt, kept for use, valued at above one hundred dollars..................	2 00		
	Billiard tables kept for use, and not subject to special tax.....	10 00		
	Oz. plate of gold, kept for use, per ounce troy..................	50		
	Oz. plate of silver, kept for use, per ounce troy, exceeding 40 ounces, used by one family.....	05		

STATE OF .... }
COUNTY OF .... } ss.

...., being sworn according to law, deposes and says that the within statement contains a full, true, particular, and correct account of his income for the year A. D. 1868, which he has received, whether derived from any kind of property, rents, interest, dividends, or salary, or from any profession, trade, employment, or vocation, or from any other source whatever, from the first day of January to the thirty-first day of December, A. D. 1868, both days inclusive, and subject to an income tax under the excise laws of the United States; and that he has not received, and is not entitled to receive, from any or all sources of income together, any other sum for the said year besides what is herein set forth in detail, except such amounts as, though justly due to the affiant, are not good and collectible; and that he is honestly and truly entitled to make the deductions from his income for said year as specifically stated in detail, in accordance with the true intent of the excise laws of the United States; that the statement of the number or weight and value of the articles enumerated in schedule A, owned, possessed, or kept by him, or of which he had the care or management, on the first day of March, A. D. 1869, is also just and true; and that the several rates and amounts therein contained are stated in legal tender currency.

....

Sworn and subscribed, this ....day of ...., A. D. 1869, before me.

....

Assistant Assessor .... *Division* .... *District, State of* ....

Assessors should ask the following Questions:

Had your wife any income last year?
Did any minor child of yours receive any salary last year?
Have you included in this return the income of your wife, and salary received by minor children?
Have you any stocks, and what are they?
Have you bought or sold stocks or other property?
Have you any United States securities?
Have you kept any book account?
Is your income estimated, or taken from your books?
Have any of the deductions claimed in your return already been taken out of the amount reported as profits?
Did you estimate any portion of your profits in making your return for previous years?
Was any portion treated as worthless, and, if since paid, have you included it in this return?

Detailed Statement *of Income, Gains, and Profits of* ....

of ...., *County of* ...., *and State of* ...., *during the year* 1868, *and of Carriages, &c., &c., owned or kept by him, March* 1, 1869.

1. From profits in any trade, business, or vocation, from which income is actually derived, or any interest therein wherever carried on	2800	00
2. From the payment of debts in a former year considered lost, and which have not paid a previous income tax		
3. From rents	200	00
4. From farming operations—Amount of live-stock sold		
Amount of agricultural products sold		
5. From profits realized by sales of real estate purchased since December 31, 1865		
6. From interest on any bonds or other evidences of indebtedness of any railroad, canal, turnpike, canal navigation, or slack-water company; or interest or dividends on stock, capital, or deposits in any bank, trust company, savings institution, insurance, railroad, canal, turnpike, canal navigation, or slackwater company		
7. From dividends of any incorporated company other than those above mentioned		
8. From gains and profits of any incorporated company not divided		
9. From interest on notes, bonds, or other securities of the United States		
10. From interest on notes, bonds, mortgages, or securities other than those enumerated above	240	00
11. From salary other than as an officer or employee of the United States		
12. From salary or pay as an officer or employee of the United States		
13. From profits on sales of gold or stocks, whenever purchased		
14. From all sources not above enumerated		
Gross income	3240	00

DEDUCTIONS.

1. Exempt by law	$1,000	00		
2. National, State, county, and municipal taxes paid within the year	229	00		
3. Losses actually sustained during the year from fire, shipwreck, or incurred in trade, and not already deducted in ascertaining profits				
4. Losses on sales of real estate purchased since December 31, 1865				
5. Amount paid for hired labor to cultivate land from which income is derived				
6. Amount paid for the live stock which was sold within the year				
7. Amount actually paid for rent of homestead				
8. Amount paid for usual or ordinary repairs, excluding payments for new buildings, permanent improvements or betterments				
9. Interest paid out or falling due within the year	240	00		
10. Salary or pay as an officer or employee of the United States from which a tax has been withheld				
11. Interest or dividends from corporations enumerated above in paragraph 6			1469	00
Taxable income			1771	00
Amount of tax at 5 per cent			88	55

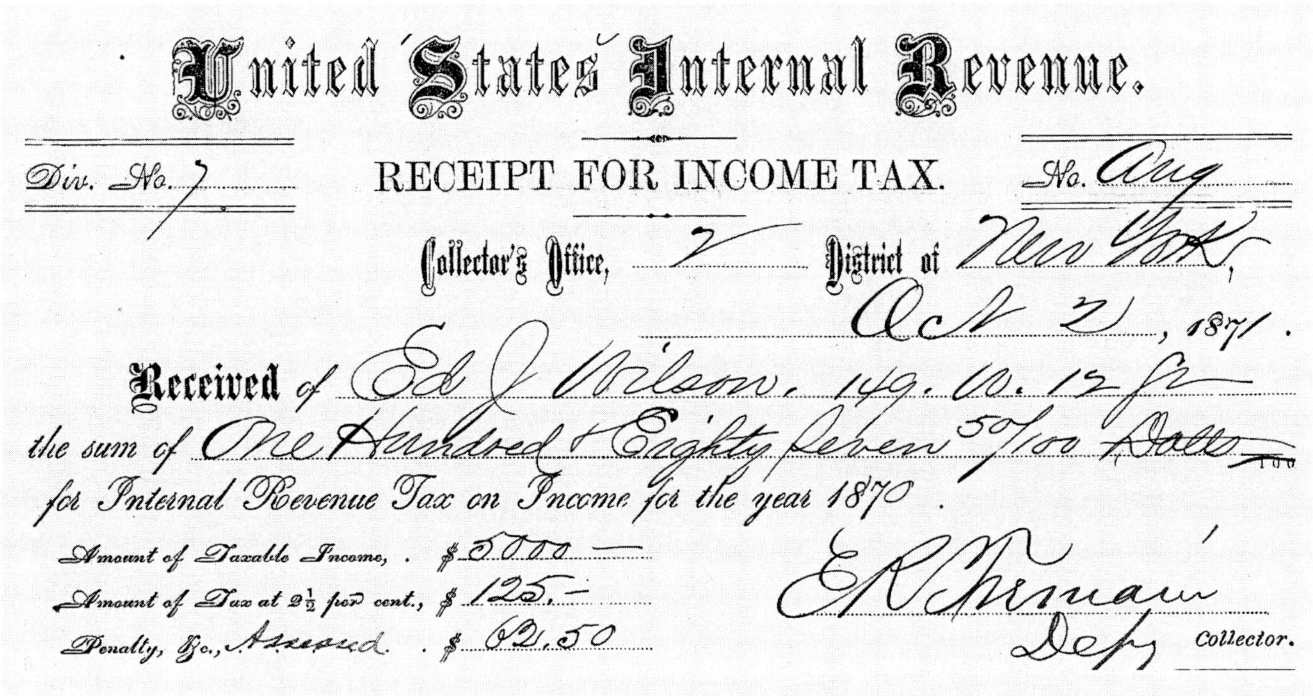

United States Internal Revenue.

Div. No. 7 RECEIPT FOR INCOME TAX. No. Aug

Collector's Office, 2 District of New York,

Oct 2, 1871.

Received of Ed J Wilson, 149. W. 12 St

the sum of One Hundred & Eighty Seven 50/100 Dolls

for Internal Revenue Tax on Income for the year 1870.

Amount of Taxable Income, . $5000 —

Amount of Tax at 2½ per cent., $125. —

Penalty, &c., Assessed . $62.50

E R Chinnan

Dep Collector.

Figure 115. Receipt for Income Tax and Penalty, Collector. New York, October 2, 1871.

Fill work sheet first

DELIVER OR SEND THIS RETURN WITH PAYMENT TO COLLECTOR OF INTERNAL REVENUE ON OR BEFORE MARCH 15, 1919

DETACH AND KEEP WORK SHEET AND INSTRUCTION SHEET

Page 1 of Return

Form 1040A.—UNITED STATES INTERNAL REVENUE SERVICE

INDIVIDUAL INCOME TAX RETURN

FOR NET INCOMES OF NOT MORE THAN $5,000

For Calendar Year 1918

IF NAME AND ADDRESS PRINTED BELOW ARE INCORRECT PLEASE MAKE CORRECTIONS

58010336 MARY AMANDA
HARVIN
116 WENTWORTH ST
CHARLESTON S C

Do not write in this space

FIRST PAYMENT

$

(Cashier's Stamp.)

CASH CHECK M. O.

Examined by

DETACH RETURN HERE AND SEND IT TO COLLECTOR OF INTERNAL REVENUE AT COLUMBIA, S. C.

1. Did you make a return for 1917? ....
2. If so, what address did you give on that return? ....
3. To what collector's office was it sent? .... (Give district or city and State.)
4. Give number, if any, assigned to you for 1917 if it does not appear in address at head of return ....
5. Were you in 1918 married and living with wife (or husband)? ....
6. If not, were you the head of a family as defined in instructions under "Personal Exemption?" ....
7. How many dependent persons under 18 (or mentally or physically defective) received their chief support from you during 1918? ....
8. If you claim any additional exemption on account of dependent persons other than your children, what was their relationship to you? ....
9. Write "R" if this return shows income received, or "A" if it shows income accrued ....
10. Did your wife (or husband) or minor child make a separate return? .... (If so, give name and address thereon.)
11. Did you or your wife (or husband) or dependent minor children receive any interest on U. S. Liberty Bonds, or any salary not reported elsewhere in this return or in a separate return? .... (If so, give sources and amounts.)
12. Enter name and address of each organization to which you made contributions claimed as deductions, and amount paid to each.
13. Enter in this table details concerning repairs, wear and tear, and property losses, claimed as deductions in Schedules A, E, and I on page 2 of return (see instructions):

1. Refer to "A," "E," or "I."	2. Kind of property. (If buildings, state also material of which constructed.)	3. Year acquired.	4. Cost of property (or market value March 1, 1913).	5. Repairs not offset by claims for wear and tear or losses.	Wear and tear (depreciation) and depletion charged off— 6. Rate.	7. Amount previous years.	8. Amount this year.	Losses not compensated for by insurance. 9. Cause of loss.	10. Amount of loss.
			$	$		$	$		$

CALCULATION OF TAX

Do not write here.			Do not write here.		
	M. Net income shown on page 2, Item J	$		P. Tax due (6% on amount of Item O)	$
	N. Less personal exemption (see Instruction VI)			Q. Less normal tax of 2% on Item F	
	O. Balance (income taxable at 6%)	$		R. Balance of tax due	$
				S. Amount of tax paid on submission of return	$

NOTE.—If the amount on line O exceeds $4,000, the excess is taxable at 12%, and your return should be made on Form 1040.

AFFIDAVIT

I swear (or affirm) that this return, to the best of my knowledge and belief, is a true and complete statement of all taxable gains, profits, and income received by or accrued to me (or the person for whom this return is made) during the year 1918, and that all deductions entered or claimed herein are allowable under the law.

(If return is made by agent, the reason therefor must be stated on this line.)

Sworn to and subscribed before me this .... day of ...., 1919. .... (Signature of individual or agent.)

(Signature of officer administering oath.) (Title.) (Address of individual or agent.)

Figure 116. Individual Income Tax Return (Form 1040A) [Blank]. Charleston, 1918.

Form 1042. [redacted]

UNITED STATES INTERNAL REVENUE.

ANNUAL LIST RETURN OF AMOUNT OF NORMAL INCOME TAX WITHHELD AT THE SOURCE

ON SALARIES, WAGES, RENT, INTEREST, OR OTHER FIXED AND DETERMINABLE ANNUAL GAINS, PROFITS, AND INCOME EXCEEDING $3,000 FOR THE TAXABLE YEAR.

The income to be made the subject of this return does not include dividends on capital stock or net earnings of corporations, joint-stock companies, etc., subject to like tax or income derived from interest upon bonds or mortgages, or deeds of trusts, or other similar obligations of corporations, joint-stock companies, etc., or from interest upon bonds, mortgages, or dividends of foreign corporations.

Filed by ______________________________ (Name of debtor or withholding agent.), *for the year 191*

To be made in duplicate to the Collector of Internal Revenue for the District in which the debtor or his duly appointed withholding agent, as the case may be, is located, on or before the first day of March, showing the names and addresses of persons who have received salaries, wages, rent, etc., as above described, in excess of $3,000, on which the normal tax of 1 per cent has been deducted and withheld during the preceding calendar year.

I (we), ______________ (Name.), of ______________ (Address in full.)

the ______________ (State official title.) of ______________ (Debtor or withholding agent.), located at ______________ (Address in full.)

do solemnly swear (or affirm) that the following is a true and complete return of all salaries, wages, rent, and other fixed and determinable annual gains, profits, and income in excess of $3,000 as above described, which were paid (or were payable) to each of the persons listed herein, and on which the normal tax of 1 per cent was deducted and withheld during the year stated, and there are herewith inclosed all certificates claiming exemptions and deductions with respect to said income.

Name.	Address in Full.	Character of Income. (State whether Rent, Wages, etc.)	Amount of Income.	Amount of Exemption Claimed.	Amount of Income on which Withholding Agent is Liable for Tax.	Amount of Tax Withheld.
			$	$	$	$
Totals for calendar year			$	$	$	$
Amount of tax remitted herewith (if any) to Collector						$

To ______________ Collector.

______________ District of ______________

______________ (Address.)

Sworn to and subscribed before me this ______ day of ______, 191

Signed: ______________

______________ (Capacity in which acting.)

Figure 117. Annual Return of Income Tax Withheld at Source (Form 1042) [Blank].

Chapter Notes

Chapter I

1. Adams, Henry Carter. *Taxation in the United States: 1789–1816.* New York: Burt Franklin (1884/1970). 45–50; Schmeckebier, Laurence F. and Francis X. A. Eble. *The Bureau of Internal Revenue: Its History, Activities and Organization.* Baltimore: The John Hopkins Press (1923). 2–4.

2. Taussig, Frank N. *The Tariff History of the United States.* New York: G. P. Putnam's Sons (1931). 67; 118–119.

3. Schmeckebier, Laurence F. *The Customs Service: Its History, Activities and Organizations.* Baltimore: The John Hopkins Press (1923). 3–8; 58–60.

4. *Ibid.*

5. *Ibid.*, 6–11.

6. Adams, *Taxation in the U.S.*, 53–57; Schmeckebier, *Bureau of Internal Revenue*, 4.

7. Adams, *Taxation in the U.S.*, 57–61; Schmeckebier, *Bureau of Internal Revenue*, 5–6.

8. Adams, *Taxation in the U.S.*, 35–39.

9. "Report of the Secretary of the Treasury on the State of the Finances for the Year Ended June, 30, 1856" 34th Congress. 3d Sess. H. Rep Doc. No. 2, Washington, DC: GPO (1856).

10. Gouge, William H. *The Fiscal History of Texas.* Philadelphia: Lippincott, Grambo and Co. (1852) 270–272.

Chapter II

11. Laws of the United States Relating to Loans, Paper Money, Banking and Coinage, 1790–1895. Washington, D.C.: GPO (1896), 53rd Cong-3rd Sen, No. 831, S Rep. 3–157.

12. *Appleton's Annual Cyclopedia and Register of Important Events.* New York: D. Appleton's & Co. (1888). Vol. I (1861) 295–296.

13. Curry, Leonard P. *Blueprint for Modern America: Nonmilitary Legislation of the First Civil War Congress.* Nashville: Vanderbilt University Press (1968). 154–155. Victor, Orville J. *History, Civil Political and Military of the Southern Rebellion.* New York: James D. Torrey, Publisher (1865). Vol. II, 243–247.

14. Frediel, Frank, Editor. *Union Pamphlets of the Civil War, 1861–1865.* Cambridge: Harvard University Press (1967). Vol. I, 445.

15. Beaman, F. C. "Confiscation of Rebel Property." Washington, DC: Scammell & Co. Printers (1862). 2–3; 6.

16. "Letter of Secretary of the Treasury ... List of Special Agents, March 28, 1864." Washington, DC: GPO (1864) Sen. Ex. Doc. No. 31.

17. Curry, *Blueprint*, 81; 98–99.

18. *Official Records of the War of the Rebellion.* (ORR) Washington, DC: GPO (1900), Series III, Vol. 2, 765–766; Vol. 4, 408–409.

19. *Appleton's Cyclopedia.* Vol. I (1861), 645–646; 755; Rose, Willie Lee. *Rehearsal for Reconstruction: The Port Royal Experiment.* London: Oxford University Press (1964), 26–31; 33–34; 49; 62; 128; 142.

20. *Appleton's Cyclopedia*, Vol. II (1862), 756; *Harper's Weekly*, January 4; 25, 1862.

21. "Message for the President ... in Answer to Information Relative to Captured and Forfeited Cotton." Washington, DC: GPO (1867). 39th Cong. 2d. Sess H. Rep. Ex. Doc. No. 97. February 19, 1867.

22. *ORR*, Series III, Vol. 2, 274; 141; Vol. 25. 592–595; 643–644; Vol. 3, 115.

23. *Official Records of the War of Rebellion, Union and Confederate Navies.* (OR Navy), Washington, DC: GPO (1908), Vol 22, 614–615; *ORR*, Series III, Vol. 2, 25–26; 152–153; OR Navy, Washington, DC: GPO (1908), Vol 22, 614–615; ORR, Series III, Vol. 2, 25–26; 152–153; *Appleton's Cyclopedia*, Vol. III (1863), 219–220.

24. *Appleton's Cyclopedia*, Vol I (1861), 585; 592; Vol. III (1863), 765–766; OR Navy, Series I, Vol. 16, 211–212; 426.

25. *Appleton's Cyclopedia*, Vol. III (1863) 765–776; OR Navy, Series I, Vol. 19, 349; 608; 512.

26. OR Navy, Series I, Vol. 25, 401–502.

27. *Appleton's Cyclopedia*, Vol. I (1861), 295–301; Smith, Harry Edwin. *The United States Federal Income Tax History from 1861 to 1871.* Boston: Houghton Mifflin Company (1914), 17–31.

Chapter III

28. Russell, Robert Royal. "Economic Aspects of Southern Sectionalism, 1840–1861." *University of Illinois Studies in Social Sciences.* Vol. II, Nos. 1–2, 293–294.

29. Hawk, Emory Q. *Economic History of the South.* New York; Prentice Hall (1934). 369–379; Moneyhon, Carl H. *The Impact of the Civil War and Reconstruction in Arkansas.* Baton Rouge: LSU Press (1994). 84–85.

30. *Appleton's Cyclopedia*, Vol. I (1861), 43; 157; Russell, *Economic Aspects (1840–1861)*, 260–263; Robinson, William M. Jr. *Justice in Gray: A History of the Judicial System of the Confederate States of America.* Cambridge: Harvard University Press (1941). 9.

31. Todd, Richard Cecil. *Confederate Finance.* Athens: University of Georgia Press (1954). 123.

32. *Ibid.*, 125–127; 156.

33. "Confederate States Treasury Regulations," No. 4, March 22, 1861; April 10, 1861; "Treasury Circular" No. I, March 1, 1861, Richmond (1861).

34. Todd, *Confederate Finance*, 123;Confederate Treasury "Circular" No. 9, May 14, 1861.

35. Owsley, Frank L. *King Cotton Diplomacy.* Chicago, University of Chicago Press (1931), 19–20; Bell, Douglas B. *Financial Failure and Confederate Defeat.* Urbana, University of Illinois Press (1991). 62–69.

36. *New York Times*, March 2, 1861; Confederate Treasury "Instruction" No. 12, April 10, 1861; "Instruction" No. 14, September 12, 1861.

37. Confederate Sequestration Acts of May 21, 1861; August 21, 1861; August 30, 1861; and May 14, 1863.

38. Confederate Department of the Trans-Mississippi "Circular to Receivers Under the Sequestration Act," February 12, 1862.

39. Confederate Secretary of the Treasury "Report to the Speaker of the House of Representatives," December 7, 1863.

40. Robinson, *Justice in Gray*, 496–497; 506–507; ORR, Series IV, Vol. 1, 932–939; Series IV, Vol. 1, 809.

41. Robinson, *Justice in Gray*, 261; 626.

42. Victor, *History of the Southern Rebellion*, 88–89; 302–304; 366–367.

43. OR Navy, Series II, Vol. 2, 225–342; Series IV, Vol. 1, 528–529; *Appleton's Cyclopedia*, Vol. I (1861), 161; 585–587.

44. Todd, *Confederate Finance*, 130–133.

45. Schwab, John Christopher. *The Confederate States of America 1861–1865: A Financial and Industrial History*. New York: C. Scribner's Sons (1901), 7–8.

46. Todd, *Confederate Finance*, 25–34.

Chapter IV

47. *Appleton's Cyclopedia*, Vol. III (1863), 396–398; Smith, *Federal Income Tax History*, 45–56.

48. Appleton's *Cyclopedia*, Vol. I (1861), 301; Schmeckebier, *The Bureau of Interest Revenue*, 61; 71.

49. *Appleton's Cyclopedia*, Vol. III (1863), 329; 533; 561; 563; 763. *ORR*, Series III, Vol. 2, 282.

50. *Appleton's Cyclopedia*, Vol. II (1862), 460–461.

51. *Ibid.*

52. *Ibid.*; Smith, *Federal Income Tax History*, 253–256.

53. *Appleton's Cyclopedia*, Vol. II (1862), 460; Redfield, Amasa A. *A Hand Book of the U.S. Tax Laws, Approved July 1, 1862 with all the Amendments to March 4, 1863*. New York: Baker & Goodwin (1863), 180–189. Smith, *Federal Income Tax History*, 145–165. ORR, Series III, Vol. 4, 674–675.

54. West, *Revenue Stamps of the United States*, 6–11.

55. Smith, *Federal Income Tax History*, 166–168; 174; 183. Hicks, John Alan. *Civil War Era Occupational Licenses, 1863–1873*. Morristown, NJ: Self-published (2004), 15.

56. Smith, *Federal Income Tax History*, 213; 221–222. Letter from Collector of 1st District, Cecil County, Maryland, to Deputy Commissioner of the Office to Internal Revenue, Washington, DC, October 18, 1864, in author's collection.

57. Redfield, *A Hand Book of U.S. Tax Laws*, 61–62; 174–176.

58. Smith, *Federal Income Tax History*, 112; 259–261.

59. *Ibid.*, 98–101

60. *Appleton's Cyclopedia*, Vol. III (1863), 406.

Chapter V

61. *Appleton's Cyclopedia*, Vol. I (1861), 692.

62. Miller, Edmund Thompson. *A Financial History of Texas*. Austin: University of Texas Bulletin No. 37 (1918), 7–16. Grammel, Hans Peter Nielson. *The Laws of Texas 1822–1899*. Austin: The Grammel Book Company (1898). Vol. V, 376. Day, "House Journal of the 9th [Texas] Legislature, Reg. Sess. (1862)," 30; 59; 95.

63. "Instructions for Collectors of Texas ... War Taxes" September 28, 1861; "Instructions (Supplemental) for Collection of the War Tax" December 21, 1861.

64. Day, "House Journal 9th Leg. Rep. Sess," 30–31; 14–16. ORR, Series IV, Vol. 1, 697–711;Todd, *Confederate Finance* (Note 48), 132.

65. ORR, Series IV, Vol. 2, 115; 118. ORR, Series IIV, Vol. 1, 1078. Todd, *Confederate Finance* (Note 83), 1440.

66. ORR, Series IV, Vol. 1, 567–574. ORR, Series IIV, Col. 1, 803–804.

67. Robinson, *Justice in Gray*, 576.

68. ORR, Series IV, Vol. 1, 1041–1042.

69. "Report to C.S. Secretary of the Treasury from Clerk of War Tax Office," February 28, 1862.

70. ORR, Series IV, Vol. 2, 309–323; 332. *Appleton's Cyclopedia*, Vol. II (1862), 250–252.

71. ORR, Series IV, Vol. 2, 314–315. Seligman, Edwin R. A. *The Income Tax: A Story of the History, Theory and Practice of Income Taxation at Home and Abroad*. New York: Macmillan (1911), 483–488. ORR, Series IV, Vol. 2, 794–796.

72. "Instructions to [Texas] District Collectors Relations to the Collection ... and Redemption of Property Sold for Tax." Austin: 1863.

Chapter VI

73. ORR, Series III, Vol. 4, 721–723; *Appleton's Cyclopedia*, Vol. III (1863), 199.

74. Berlin, Ira, Reidy, Joseph P., Miller, Steven F., and Rowland, Leslie S.; *Freedman: A Documentary History of Emancipation*, Doc. No. 1. New York: Cambridge University Press, 1993.

75. "Letter for Secretary Treasury" Ex. Doc. No. 3, 38th Cong. 1st Sess., *Free South*, December 12, 1863.

76. *Appleton's Cyclopedia*, Vol. III (1863), 199; Vol. IV (1864), 190.

77. "Letter of Secretary of Treasury ... List of Special Agents," march 28. 1863. 38th Cong. 1st Sess. Ex. Doc. No. 31.

78. *Appleton's Cyclopedia*, Vol. III (1863), 196–198. ORR, Series III, Vol. 3, 98–99.

79. ORR, Series III, Vol. 3, 872. ORR, Series IV, Vol. 4, 721–723. General Order No. 257, War Department, AGO, Washington, DC: September 15, 1864; General Order No. 331, War Department, AGO, October 31, 1863.

80. "Message for the President ... Captured and Forfeited Cotton." 39th Cong. 2nd Sess., H. Rep. Ex. Doc. No 97, February 19, 1867.

81. *Appleton's Cyclopedia*, Vol. VI (1865), 342–343; Johnson, Ludwell H. "Northern Profits and Profiteers: Those Cotton Kings of 1864–1865." *Civil War History*. Kent, OH: Kent State University Press, Vol. 12, No. 2, 101–115.

82. "Message for the President ... Captured and Forfeited Cotton."

83. *Ibid.*

84. Niven, John. *Salmon P. Chase*. 316–320; *Harper's Weekly*, May 12, 1864; Buggett, James Alex. "The Scalawags: Southern Dissenters in Baton Rouge," *The Civil War and Reconstruction*. Baton Rouge: LSU Press (2004), 111.

85. Doyle, Elizabeth Joan. "Rattlesnakes in Every Direction." *Civil War History*, Vol 18, No. 1, 22–41.

86. *New York Times*, January 15, 16, 18, 1864; *New York Times*, February 11, 1864; *New York Times* November 5, 11, 1864.

87. Johnson, "Northern Profits," 101–103.

88. Laws of the U.S. Relative to Loans ... 1790–1895."

89. Oberholtzer, Ellis Parson. *Jay Cooke: Financer of the Civil War*. New York: Augustus M. Kelley Publisher (1907/1968), Vol. 1, 326–327; 339.

90. Oberholtzer, *Jay Cooke*, Vol. 1, 320–334.

91. *Appleton's Cyclopedia*, Vol. II (1862), 452–455.

92. Sherman, John, "Taxation of Bonds, Bills Documents ... January 8, 1863." Washington, DC: Congressional Globe Office (1863).

93. *Ibid.*

94. Smith, *U.S. Income Tax*, 24–29; *Appleton's Cyclopedia*, Vol III (1863), 296–304; 411.

95. Redfield, *Handbook of U.S. Tax Laws*, 315–316.

96. *Appleton's Cyclopedia*, Vol. III (1863), 777–778; Fite, Emerson David. *Social and Industrial Conditions in the North During the Civil War*. New York: The Macmillan Company (1910), 117–118.

97. Robertson, Ross M. *The Comptroller and Bank Supervision: A Historical Appraisal*. Washington, DC: The Office of the Comptroller of Currency (1968/1998), 34; 43–53.

98. *Appleton's Cyclopedia*, Vol IV (1864), 493; Vol V (1865), 110.

99. Fite, *Social and Industrial Conditions in the North During the Civil War*, 119–120; "Report of Comptroller of Currency, December 3, 1917," Washington, DC: GPO (1918), Vol. I, 82; Hammond, Bray. *Sovereignty and a Empty Peace: Banks and Politics in the Civil War*. Princeton, NJ: Princeton University Press (1978), 347; 361–362; *Veazie, Bank v. Fenno*, 43; 533 (1869).

100. "Report of Comptroller of Currency," Vol. I, 9–10. Bank, Steven A., Kirk J. Stark and Joseph J. Thorndike. *War and Taxes*. Washington, DC: The Urban Institute Press (2008), 34.

101. Knox, John Jay. *A History of Banking in the United States*, New York: Augustus M. Kellye Publisher (1903/1969), 132–134; 149; 298.

Chapter VII

102. ORR, Series IV, Vol. 2. 17–18; 128; General Order No. 7, District of Texas, Houston, June 14, 1862.

103. ORR, Series IV, Vol. 2, 124–125.

104. ORR, Series IV, Vol, 2, 469–472; 534; 897–898.

105. ORR, Series IV, Vol. 2, 853; 943–944.

106. ORR, Series IV, Vol. 2, 1049–1051; ORR, Series IV, Vol. 3, 249–250; 1169–1173.

107. *Appleton's Cyclopedia*, Vol. III (1863), 205.

108. Christ, Lynde Lasswell, editor. *The Papers of Jefferson Davis*, Vol. 9. Baton Rouge: LSU Press (1997), viii; 184; 222.

109. ORR, Series IV, Vol. 2, 513–514; Todd, *Confederate Finance*, 140–146.

110. ORR, Series IV, Vol. 2, 786–787; 990–1018; ORR, Series IV, Col. 3, 63–64. Todd, *Confederate Finance* (Note 93), 146; Christ, *The Papers of Jefferson Davis*, Vol. 10, 89; 373.

111. "Instructions to Confederate Tax Officers …," July 24, 1863; October 9, 1863; December 23, 1867.

112. ORR, Series I, Vol. 53. 992–998; 1023; 1033–1034.

Chapter VIII

113. Smith, *U.S. Federal Internal Tax*, 262; 272.

114. Smith, *U.S. Federal Internal Tax*, 280.

115. Schmeckebier, *The Bureau of Internal Revenue*, 9–13.

116. Smith, *U.S. Federal Internal Tax*, 212–219.

117. Smith, *U.S. Federal Internal Tax*, 61; 66–67.

118. Arthur, Timothy Shay. "Growlers Income Tax." Loyal Publication Society, No. 57, New York (1864).

119. Smith, *U.S. Federal Internal Tax*, 64.

120. Smith, *U.S. Federal Internal Tax*, 66–68.

121. Davis, Lillian, *The American Way in Taxation: Internal Revenue 1862–1863*, Englewood Cliffs, NJ: Prentice-Hall (1863), 21; 283–285.

122. Seligman, *The Income Tax* (Table I), 480.

123. *Appleton's Cyclopedia*, Vol. IV (1864), 371–372.

124. Smith, *U.S. Federal Internal Tax* (Table I) 293; (Table XII) 303; 183.

125. Smith, *U.S. Federal Internal Tax*, 98–107.

126. Smith, *U.S. Federal Internal Tax* (Tables VI and VII), 297–298.

Chapter IX

127. *Southern History*, Vol. 50, 211; 383–384.

128. Todd, *Confederate Finance*, 147–148.

129. ORR, Series IV, Vol. 2, 1068.

130. Todd, *Confederate Finance*, 156; Andreano, Rolf Louis, "A Theory of Confederate Finances," *Civil War History*. Kent, OH: Kent State University Press, Vol. 2, No. 4, 25.

131. ORR, Series IV, Vol. 3, 140–152.

132. "An Act to Authorize the Appointment of an Agent of the Treasury Department West of the Mississippi" as authorized February 17, 1864. Houston's Treasury Agency, TMD, May 29, 1864.

133. "Instructions for Carrying into Effect the Act of February 17, 1864." Treasury Agency, TMD. Houston, April 7, 1864; *Shreveport News*, April 7, 1864.

134. See Tremmel, Fricke and Davis, *Confederate Treasury Certificates: A Collectors Guide to Interim Depository Receipts*, 462–478.

135. "Circulars to Department Deputies." Treasury Agency, TMD, May 20, 1864; May 26, 1864, *Galveston News*, May 3, 1865.

136. "Circular to Deputy Depositaries." Treasury Agency, TMD, September 20, 1864.

137. "Statement" of "An Act Permitting States to Fund Their Treasury Notes by One of Two Alternative Methods." Richmond: CS Treasury, June 14, 1864.

138. Tremmel, Fricke and Davis (Fig.TX-66), 377.

139. "Report of Treasury Agency, TMD." Marshall, October 1, 1864.

140. "Report of Quartermaster General Including Tax In Kind for Texas." C.S. Commissioner of Taxes. Richmond, November 7, 1864.

141. *Ibid.*

142. "Communication of the Treasury Agent," TMD, Marshall, Texas of December 26, 1864; Secretary of the Treasury, Richmond, February 20, 1865.

143. *Appleton's Cyclopedia*, Vol. IV (1864), 193–194.

144. Todd, *Confederate Finance*, 152; *Appleton's Cyclopedia*, Vol. V (1865), 195; Schwab, John Christopher. *The Confederate States of America, 1861–1865: A Financial and Industrial History of The South During the War*. New York: C. Scribner's Sons (1901), 300–302.

145. "Henry Sampson Papers." Manuscript Collection, Rosenburg Library, Galveston (MS No. 72–1239); Todd, *Confederate Finance*, 188–194.

146. Hutchins, W. J. "To the Senators and Representatives in Congress from the State of Texas." Houston: News Print, 1864.

147. ORR, Series VI, Vol. 3, 841–845.

148. Schwab, *Confederate States of America*, 302–310. Todd, *Confederate Finance*, 153.

149. Todd, *Confederate Finance*, 156.

Chapter X

150. *Appleton's Cyclopedia*, Vol IV (1864), 375.

151. *Appleton's Cyclopedia*, Vol. V (1865), 339.

152. Smith, *U.S. Federal Income Tax*, 256–257.

153. *Appleton's Cyclopedia*, Vol. IV (1864), 164; 769–771.

154. Smith, *U.S. Federal Income Tax*, 34; 44, (Tables I and II); Redfield, *Handbook of U.S. Tax*, 30–31.

155. Redfield, *Handbook of U.S. Tax*, 23–25; 30–31; *Appleton's Cyclopedia*, Vol II (1862), 795.

156. ORR, Series III, Vol. 2, 185; Smith *U.S. Federal Income Tax*, 28–31.

157. "Report of the Commission Appointed for the District of South Carolina … Taxes in Insurrecting Districts."

158. *Ibid.*

159. "Letter … Reports … the Sale of Plantations in South Carolina."

160. Peason, "Letters from Port Royal," 15; Rose, *Rehearsal for Reconstruction*, 272–278; "Letter … South Carolina Plantations."

161. "Instructions to the Tax Commission of South Carolina," (1868); H. Doc. No. 146, 40th Cong. 2nd Sess; Hendricks, *Union Occupation of the Southern Seaboard*, 116–151; ORR, Series III, Vol. 4, 1022–1031.

162. *New York Times*, June 24, 1864; Rose, *Rehearsal for Reconstruction*, 278–296.

163. "Report on Sea Islands, Beaufort, South Carolina"; Powell, "The American Land Company and Agency," 293–308.

164. *The New South*, April 22, 1865; "Report on Sea Islands, Beaufort, South Carolina."

165. "Report … Tax Commissions for the District of Florida."

166. Davis, *Reconstruction in Florida*, 249–250; 341–352.

167. "Report … Tax Commissioners for the District of Florida."

168. *New South*, April 22; May 13, 1865; "Letter … Direct Tax Officials," (April 12, 1864); *Bennett v Hunter*, 76 U.S.326 (1869); Smith, *U.S. Federal Income Tax*, 29–33.

169. Smith, *U.S, Federal Income Tax*, 31–34.

Chapter XI

170. Davis, John Martin, Jr., and Tremmel, George, *Paroles, Pardons, Passes and Amnesties*, 92–109.

171. Fleming, Walter L., *Documentary History of Reconstruction: Political, Military, Social, Religious, Education and Industrial, 1863 to the Present Time*, Cleveland: The Arthur H. Clark Company (1906), 150–153.

172. *Ibid.*

173. ORR, Series III, Vol. 5, 19–20; 51.

174. *Appleton's Cyclopedia*, Vol. V (1865), 184–186.

175. Powell, *The American Land Company and Agency*, 293–308; Letter in author's collection.

176. *Appleton's Cyclopedia*, Vol. V (1865), 16; 29; 363; 761.

177. Garner, *Reconstruction in Mississippi*, 127–133; Henry, Robert Selph, *The Story of*

Reconstruction. New York: Bobbs Merrill Company (1938), 298–299; "Captured Cotton," S. Ex. Doc, No. 97, 39th Cong., 2d Sess.

178. Fleming, *Documents of Reconstruction*, 34–35; Garner, *Reconstruction in Mississippi*, 127–129.

179. Letter from Author's Collection; "Captured and Forfeited Cotton."

180. Reynolds, John S., *Reconstruction in South Carolina*, Columbia: The State Company Publisher (1905), 250–265.

181. Letter from Author's Collection; *Houston Daily Post*, June 22, 1908.

182. Smith, *U.S. Federal Income Tax*, 250; Hicks, *Civil War Occupational Licenses*, 21–23.

183. Wright, Chester Whitney, *Economic History of the United States*. New York: McGraw Hill (1941/1949), 440; *Appleton's Cyclopedia*, Vol. VII (1882), 299; *Appleton's Cyclopedia*, Vol. V (1880), 257–258.

184. *Appleton's Cyclopedia*, Vol. V (1880), 259.

185. Davis, John Martin, Jr., "Bankless in Beaufort," *South Carolina Historical Quarterly*, June 2003, Vol. 104, No. 1, 25–55.

186. *Appleton's Cyclopedia*, Vol X (1885), 770.

Bibliography

Adams, Henry Carter. *Taxation in the United States, 1789–1816*. New York: Burt Franklin, 1884/1970.

Andreano, Ralph Louis. "A Theory of Confederate Finance." *Civil War History*. December 3, 1917. 2 Vols. Washington, D.C.: Government Printing Office, 1918.

Appleton's American Annual Cyclopedia and Register of Important Events, 1861–1875. New York: D. Appleton & Co., 1862–1876.

Appleton's Annual Cyclopedia and Register of Important Events, 1876–1887. New York: D. Appleton & Co., 1888.

Arthur, Timothy Shay. "Grumbler's Income Tax." *Loyal Publication Society*, No. 57. New York: 1864.

Ball, Douglas B. *Financial Failure and Confederate Defeat*. Urbana: University of Illinois Press, 1991.

Bank, Steven A., Kirk J. Stark, and Joseph J. Thorndike. *War and Taxes*. Washington, D.C.: The Urbana Institute Press, 2008.

Ben, Perley Poor. *Congressional Directory*. Washington, D.C.: Government Printing Office, 1872.

Berlin, Ira, Thanolia Gymph, and Joseph P. Reidy. *Freedom: A Documentary History of Emancipation 1861–1867*. Cambridge: Cambridge University Press, 1953.

Boutwell, George S. *A Manual of the Direct and Excise Tax System of the United States*. Boston: Little Brown & Co., 1863/1866.

Breudel, Fernand. *The Wheels of Commerce: Civilization and Capitalism 15th–18th Century*, Vol. 2. New York: Harper & Row, 1979/1982.

Brown, Roger H. *Redeeming the Republic: Federalists Taxation and the Origins of the Constitution*, Baltimore: John Hopkins University Press, 1993.

Brownlee, W. Elliot. *Federal Taxation in America: A Short History*, Cambridge: Cambridge University Press, 1996.

Capers, Henry Dickson. *The Life and Times of C.G. Memminger*. Richmond, VA: Everett Waddey Company, 1893.

"Captured and Forfeited Cotton." Message for the President of the United States. H. of Rep Ex. Doc No. 97. 39th Cong. 2nd Sess. Feb. 20, 1867.

Christ, Lynda Laswell, ed. *The Papers of Jefferson Davis*. Vol. 9, Jan-Sept 1863. Baton Rouge: LSU Press, 1997.

Circular, "Taxes in Kind." Commissioner of Taxes, Trans-Mississippi Department, April 10, 1863.

Citizens Edition of the New National Tax Law. New York: Beadle and Company, 1862.

The Comptroller and Bank Supervision: A Historical Appraisal. Washington, D.C.: The Office of the Comptroller of Currency, 1968/1995.

"Confiscation of Rebel Property." Speech of Hon. F. C. Beaman of Michigan in H. of Rep., May 234, 1862. Washington, D.C.: Scammell & Co. Printers, 1862.

Cooke, Jacob C. *The Federalist*. Middleton, CT: Wesleyan University Press, 1961.

Cooper, Thomas V., and Hector T. Fenton. *American Politics, From the Beginning to Date, "Federal Blue Book."* Philadelphia: Fireside Publishing Co., 1882.

Cox, Samuel S. *Disunion-Reunion: The Decades of Federal Legislation, 1855 to 1885*. Providence: J. A. & R. A. Reid Pub., 1885.

Current, Richard N., ed. *Encyclopedia of the Confederacy*. New York: Simon & Shuster, 1993.

Curry, Leonard P. *Blueprint for Modern America: Nonmilitary Legislation of the First Civil War Congress*. Nashville: Vanderbilt University Press, 1968.

Davis, John Martin Jr., and George B. Tremmel. *Paroles, Pardons, Passes and Amnesty Documents of the Civil War: An Illustrated History*. Jefferson, NC: McFarland, 2013.

Davis, William Watson. *The Civil War and Reconstruction in Florida*. New York: Columbia University Press, 1913.

Day, James M. *House and Senate Journals of the State of Texas* [1861–1864]. Waco: Texas Library and Historical Commission, 1966.

Dewey, Davis R. *Financial History of the United States*. New York: Longmans, Green & Company, 1939.

Doris, Lillian. *The American Way of Taxation: Internal Revenue, 1862–1863*. Englewood Cliffs, NJ: Prentice-Hall, 1963.

Doyle, Elizabeth Jean. "Rattlesnakes in Every Direction: The Stokes Investigation in Civil War New Orleans." *Civil War History*, Vol. XVIII, No. 1, 22–41.

Evans, Stephen H. *The United States Coast Guard, 1790–1915, A Definitive History*. Annapolis, MD: U.S. Naval Institute, 1949.

Ferguson, E. James. *The Power of the Purse: A History of American Public Finance, 1776–1790*. Chapel Hill: University of North Carolina Press, 1961.

Fessenden, Francis. *William Pitt Fessenden*. Boston: Houghton, Mifflin and Co., 1902.

Fite, Emerson David. *Social and Industrial Conditions in the North During the Civil War*. New York: Macmillan, 1910.

Fleming, Walter L. *Civil War and Reconstruction in Alabama*. New York: The Columbia University Press, 1905.

______. *Documentary History of Reconstruction: Political, Military, Social, Religious, Education and Industrial, 1865 to the Present Time*. Cleveland: The Arthur H. Clark Company, 1906.

Forysthe, Doll W. *Taxation and Political Change in the Young Nation, 1781–1873*. New York: Columbia University Press, 1977.

Friedel, Frank, ed. *Union Pamphlets of the Civil War, 1861–1865*. Cambridge: Harvard University Press, 1967.

Gammel, Hans Peter, Compiler. *The Laws of Texas 1822–1897*. Austin: The Gammel Book Company, 1898.

Garner, James W. *Reconstruction in Mississippi*. Baton Rouge: LSU Press, 1901/1968.

"General Regulations Regarding the Administration of the Tax In Kind." Inspector in Charge of Taxes in Kind, TMD, 1864.

Goff, Richard. *Confederate Supply*. Durham, NC: Duke University Press, 1969.

Gouge, William M. *The Fiscal History of Texas*. Philadelphia: Lippincott, Grambo and Co., 1852.

Gresham, Otto. *The Greenbacks: Or, the Money That Won the Civil War and the World War*. Chicago: The Book Press, 1927.

Hammond, Bray. *Sovereignty and an Empty Purse: Banks and Politics in the Civil War*. Princeton: Princeton University Press, 1970.

Hawk, Emory Q. *Economic History of the South*. New York: Prentice-Hall, 1934.

Henry, Robert Selph. *The Story of Reconstruction*. Gloucester: Peter Smith, 1938/1963.

Hertwig, J.G. *A National Income Tax*. Indianapolis: The Ironclad Age, 1893.
Hicks, John Alan. *Civil War Era Occupational Licenses, 1863–1873*. Morristown, NJ: John Alan Hicks, 2004.
Hicks, J. R. *A Contribution to the Theory of the Trade Cycle*. New York: Oxford University Press, 1950.
Howe, Frederic Clemson. *Taxation and Taxes in the United States Under the Internal Revenue System, 1791–1895*. New York: T. W. Crowell and Company, 1896.
"Instructions for Act of February 17, 1864." Notice of Treasury Agency. April 7, 1864. Houston: C.S. Treasury, TMD.
"Instructions to Assessors ... Taxes In Kind." November 25, 1863. C.S. Treasury.
"Instructions to Assessors and Collectors and Schedule of Blank Forms." January 1, 1866, Series 2, No. 1. Washington, D.C.: GPO, 1866.
"Instructions (Supplementary) for the Collection of the War Tax." December 28, 1861. C.S. Treasury, TMD.
"Instructions for Collectors. .. War Tax." September 28, 1861. C.S. Treasury, TMD.
"Instructions to Confederate Tax Officers." October 9, 1863: December 23, 1863: July 24, 1863. C.S. Commissioner of Taxes. C.S. Treasury.
"Instructions to District Collectors Relative to the Collection. .. and Redemption of Property Sold for Tax." Austin: Treasury, TMD, 1863.
"Instructions to the Tax Commission of South Carolina." U.S. Treasury, 1868. H. Doc. No 146, 4th Congress, 2nd Sess.
"Instructions to United States Assessors." April 26, 1866. Series 2, No. 4. Washington, D.C.: GPO, 1866.
Johnson, Ludwell H. "Northern Profit and Profiteers: The Cotton Rings of 1864–1865." *Civil War History*. Kent State University Press, Vol. 12, No. 2 (1973), 101–115.
______. "The Butler Expedition of 1861–1862: The Profitable Side of the War." *Civil War History*. Kent State University Press, Vol. 11 (1973), No. 2, 229–236.
Kleinbard, Edward D. "An American Dual Income Tax: Nordic Precedents." *Northwestern Journal of Law & Social Policy* Vol. 5, No. 1, Spring 2010.
Knox, John Jay. *A History of Banking in the United States*. New York: Augustus M. Kelley, 1903/1969.
Laws of the United States Relative to Loans, Paper Money, Banking and Coinage, 1790–1895. Washington, D.C.: GPO, 1896.
Lee, Charles Robert. *The Confederate Constitutions*. Chapel Hill: University of North Carolina Press, 1963.
"Letter for the Secretary of the Treasury." April 12, 1864. 38th Cong., 1st Sess. Ex. Doc. No. 3.
"Letter for the Secretary of the Treasury in Regards to the Sale of Plantations in South Carolina." 47th Cong., 1st Sess. Ex. Doc., No. 82.
"Letter from the President ... Transmitting A Communication of the Secretary of War ... Operations of the Bureau of Refugees, Freedmen and Abandoned Lands." May 30, 1866. 39th Cong., 1st Sess. Ex. Doc. No. 123.
"Letter from the Secretary of the Treasury ... Report of Austin Smith on the Conduct of the Tax Commissioner for the District of Florida." January 4, 1865, 38th Cong., 2nd Sess, H. Rep. Ex. Doc. No. 18.
"Letter from the Secretary of War Communicating ... An Act to Authorize the Sale of Certain Public Property Approved June 30, 1872." December 9, 1872. 42nd Cong., 3rd Sess. Ex. Doc. No. 11.
"Letter of the Secretary of the Treasury ... List of Special Agents." March 28, 1864, Washington, D.C.: GPO. 38th Cong., 1st Sess., Ex. Doc. No. 31.
"Letter of the Secretary of the Treasury Communicating ... Report of the Commission Appointed for the District of South Carolina Under the Act for the Collection of Taxes in Insurrectionary Districts." January 25, 1863, 37th Cong., 3rd Sess, Sen. Ex. Doc. No. 26.
Lowry, Thomas P. *The Story Soldiers Wouldn't Tell: Sex in the Civil War*. Mechanicsville, PA: Stackpole Books, 1994.
Lucie, Patricia M. L. "Confiscation: Constitutional Crossroads." *Civil War History*. Kent, OH: Kent State University Press, Vol. 23, No. 4, 307–321.
Matthews, James M., ed. *The Statutes at Large of the Confederate States of America*. Richmond: R. M. Smith, 1862–1864.
McGrane, Reginald Charles. *The Panic of 1837: Some Financial Problems of the Jackson Era*. Chicago: The University of Chicago Press, 1924/1965.
"Message from the President ... Relative to Refugees, Freedmen and Abandoned Lands." May 26, 1966. 39th Cong. 1st Sess. Ex. Doc. 120.
"Message from the President of the United States in Answer to Information Relative to Capture and Forfeited Cotton." February 19, 1867. 39th Cong., 2nd Sess., H. Rep. Ex. Doc. No. 97.
"Message of His Excellency Franklin J. Moses, Governor of South Carolina ... ." October 1, 1873. Columbia's Republican Printing Company, 1873.
Miller, Edmund Thorton. *A Financial History of Texas*. Austin: University of Texas Bulletin No. 37 (1916).
Moneyhon, Carl H. *The Impact of the Civil War and Reconstruction in Arkansas*. Baton Rouge: LSU Press, 1994.
Montesquieu, Baron, M. de Secondat. *The Spirit Laws*. (First American Edition), Worcester: Isiah Thomas, Jun., 1748/1802.
National Tax Law as Approved June 30, 1864 ... Articles Taxed, Rates Imposed, & c. New York: Beadle and Company, Publishers, 1864.
Niven, John. *Salmon P. Chase, A Biography*. Oxford: Oxford University Press, 1995.
Oberholtzer, Ellis Parson. *Jay Cooke: Financier of the Civil War*. New York: Augustus M. Kelley Publishers, 1907/1968.
O'Connor, Thomas H. "Lincoln and the Cotton Trade." *Civil War History*. Kent State University Press: Vol. 7, No. 1, 20–35.
Official Records of the War of the Rebellion, Union and Confederate. Washington, D.C.: GPO, 1908.
Owsley, Franklin L. *King Cotton Diplomacy*. Chicago: University of Chicago Press, 1931.
Pearson, Elizabeth Ware. *Letters from Port Royal, 1862–1868*. New York: Arno Press, 1969.
Powell, Lawrence N. "The American Land Company and Agency: John A. Andrews and the Northernization of the South." *Civil War History*. Kent, OH: Kent State University Press, Vol.21, No. 4, 293–308.
"Proceedings of the Confederate Congress." *Southern Historical Papers*. New York: Korus Reprint Co., Vols. 44–52.
"Proceedings of the Taxpayer Convention of South Carolina Held at Columbia, Beginning May 9th and Ending May 12th, 1871." Charleston: Edward Penny Printer, 1871.
Ramsdell, Charles W. *Behind the Lines in the Southern Confederacy*. Baton Rouge: LSU Press, 1944.
______, ed. *Laws and Joint Resolutions after the Last Session of the Confederate Congress, November 7, 1864 to March 18, 1865*. Durham, NC: Duke University Press, 1941.
Randall, J. G. "Captured and Abandoned Property During the Civil War." *American Historical Review*. Vol. 19: 66–69.
______. *The Civil War and Reconstruction*. Boston: D. C. Heath and Co., 1937.
Redfield, Amasa. *A Handbook of the U.S. Tax Laws, Approved July 1, 1862 with All the Amendments to March 4, 1863*. New York: Baker and Goodwin, 1863.
"Report of the Commission of Internal Revenue on the Operations of the Internal Revenue System for the Year Ending June 30, 1863." Treasury Department. Washington, D.C.: GPO, 1864.
"Report of the Secretary of the Treasury ... State of the Finances ... June 30, 1856." Washington, D.C.: GPO. 34th Cong., 3rd Sess., H. Ex. Doc. No. 2, 1856.
"Report on Sea Islands, Beaufort, South Carolina." Committee on Reconstruction, 41st Cong., 2nd Sess. HR No. 108.
"Report to [C.S.] Secretary of Treasury. .. T. Allan, Chief Clerk of War Tax." February 28, 1862, C.S. Treasury.
"Reports of James B. Fry, Provost Marshal General." Washington, D.C.: GPO 39th Cong., 1st Sess, H. Ex. Doc. No. 1, 1866.
Reynolds, John S. *Reconstruction in South Carolina*. Columbia: The State Company Publishers, 1905.
Ricardo, David. *On the Principles of Political Economy and Taxation*. London: John Murray, 1817.

Robertson, Craig. *The Passport in America: The History of A Document*. New York: Oxford University Press, 2010.
Robinson, William M. Jr. *Justice in Gray: A History of the Judicial System of the Confederate States of America*. Cambridge: Harvard University Press, 1941.
Rose, Willie Lee. *Rehearsal for Reconstruction: The Port Royal Experiment*. London: Oxford University Press, 1964.
Russell, Robert Royal. "Economic Aspects of Southern Sectionalism, 1840–1861." *University of Illinois Studies*. Vol. 11, Nos. 1–2.
Schmeckebier, Lawrence F. *The Customs Service: Its History, Activities and Organizations* (No. 33). Baltimore: The John Hopkins Press, 1924.
Schmeckebier, Lawrence F. and Francis X. A. Eble. *The Bureau of Internal Revenue: Its History, Activities and Organizations* (No. 25). Baltimore: The John Hopkins Press, 1923.
Schmeckebier, Lawrence F. *The Bureau of Prohibition: Its History, Activities and Organizations*. Washington, D.C.: The Brookings Institute, 1929.
Schwab, John Christopher. *The Confederate States of America, 1861–1865: A Financial and Industrial History of the South During the War*. New York: C. Scribner's Sons, 1901.
Seligman, Edwin R. A. *The Income Tax: A Study of the History, Theory and Practice of Income Taxation at Home and Abroad*. New York: Macmillan Co., 1911.
Shepard, Christopher. *The Civil War Income Tax and the Republican Party*. New York: Algora Publishing, 2010.
Sherman, John. *Selected Speeches and Reports on Finance and Taxation from 1859 to 1878*. New York: D. Appleton and Company, 1879.
Sherman, John. "Taxation of Bank Bills ... January 8, 1863." Washington, D.C.: Congressional Clerk Office, 1863.
Simkins, Francis Butler, and Robert Henley Woody. *South Carolina During Reconstruction*. Chapel Hill: University of North Carolina Press, 1932.
Smith, Harry Edwin. *The United States Federal Income Tax History From 1861 to 1871*. Boston: Houghton Mifflin Company, 1914.
Sprague, O. M. W., ed. *Charles Franklin Dunbar, Economic Essays*. New York: Nabu Press, 1904/2013.
Stanley, Robert. *Dimension of Laws in the Service of Order: Origins of the Federal Income Tax, 1861–1913*. New York: Oxford University Press, 1993.
Storing, Herbert J., ed. *The Complete Anti-Federalist*. 7 Vols. Chicago: University of Chicago Press, 1981.
Taussig, Frank N. *The Tariff History of the United States*. New York: G. P. Putnam's Sons, 1931.
"The Disabilities of Charleston for Complete and Equal Taxation and the Influence of State Taxation on Her Property." Reports of the Committee on Ways and Means made to the Council of Charleston, April 1, 1857. Charleston: Walker, Evans & Co., Stationers and Printers, 1857.
The National Bank Act, June 3, 1864 with the Amendments of 1865–1870. New York: Bankers Magazine, 1870.
The Tax-payer's Manual: Containing the Acts of Congress imposing direct and excise Taxes. New York: D. Appleton & Company, 1862.
The Tribune Almanac, 1861–1865. New York: The Tribune Association, 1861–1865.
Thompson, C. Mildred. *Reconstruction in Georgia: Economic, Social, Political, 1865–1872*. Gloucester: Peter Smith, 1915/1964.
Todd, Richard Cecil. *Confederate Finance*. Athens: University of Georgia Press, 1954.
Trelousse, Hans L. *Thaddeus Stevens: Nineteenth Century Egalitarian*. Chapel Hill: University of North Carolina Press, 1997.
Tremmel, George B, John Martin Davis, Jr. and Pierre Fricke. *Confederate Treasury Certificates: A Collector's Guide to IDRs*. Stanton Books. Cross Blue Overseas Printing, 2010.
Unger, Irwin. *The Greenback Era: A Social and Political History of American Finances, 1865–1879*. Princeton University Press, 1964.
Victor, Orville J. *History, Civil, Political and Military of the Southern Rebellion*. New York: James D. Torrey Publisher, 1865.
Willis, Anson. *Our Rulers and Our Rights: Outlines of the United States Government*. New York: C. L. Van Allen, 1870.
Winthrop, W., edr.
Digest of Opinions of the Judge Advocate General of the Army, 3rd Edition, Washington, D.C.: GPO, 1868.
Wise, Stephen R., and Lawrence S. Rowland. *The History of Beaufort County, South Carolina, Rebellion, Reconstruction and Redemption*. Vol. 2. Columbia: University of South Carolina Press, 2015.
Wright, Chester Whitney. *Economic History of the United States*, 2nd Edition. New York: McGraw-Hill, 1941/1949.

Index

Numbers in ***bold italics*** indicate pages with illustrations